An Introduction to Feminist Epistemologies

Introducing Philosophy

Introducing Philosophy is a series of textbooks designed to introduce the basic topics of philosophy for any student approaching the subject for the first time. Each volume presents a central subject of philosophy by considering the key issues and outlooks associated with the area. With the emphasis firmly on the arguments for and against a philosophical position, the reader is encouraged to think philosophically about the subject.

1 An Introduction to the Philosophy of Religion   *B. R. Tilghman*
2 Ethics and Human Well-being   *E. J. Bond*
3 An Introduction to Business Ethics   *Jennifer Jackson*
4 An Introduction to Epistemology   *Charles Landesman*
5 An Introduction to Aesthetics   *Dabney Townsend*
6 Philosophy of Mind: An Introduction (Second Edition)   *George Graham*
7 An Introduction to Feminist Epistemologies   *Alessandra Tanesini*

An Introduction to Feminist Epistemologies

Alessandra Tanesini

BLACKWELL
Publishers

First published 1999

2 4 6 8 10 9 7 5 3 1

Blackwell Publishers Inc.
350 Main Street
Malden, Massachusetts 02148
USA

Blackwell Publishers Ltd
108 Cowley Road
Oxford OX4 1JF
UK

Library of Congress Cataloging-in-Publication Data

Tanesini, Alessandra.
　　An introduction to feminist epistemologies / Alessandra Tanesini.
　　　　p.　cm. — (Introducing philosophy ; 7)
　　Includes bibliographical references and index.
　　ISBN 0–631–20012–6 (alk. paper). — ISBN 0–631–20013–4 (pbk. :
alk. paper).
　　　1. Feminist theory.　2. Knowledge, Theory of.　I. Title
II. Series.
　　305.42′01 — dc21　　　　　　　　　　　　　　　　　98–8784
　　　　　　　　　　　　　　　　　　　　　　　　　　　　CIP

British Library Cataloguing in Publication Data

A CIP catalogue record for this book is available
from the British Library.

Typeset in 10.5 on 12 pt Monotype Garamond
by SetSystem Ltd, Saffron Walden, Essex

This book is printed on acid-free paper

Contents

Acknowledgments   vii

Introduction   1

1 Varieties of Epistemology   3

Epistemology   4

The Study of Scientific Knowledge   22

2 Feminism and 'Malestream' Epistemology   38

Feminist Criticisms of Individualism in Epistemology   39

Feminist Objections to the Traditional Epistemic Subject   53

3 Feminism and Science   66

Sexist Science   69

Science and Values   82

4 Feminist Empiricism   95

Contextual Empiricism   98

Naturalized Empiricism   101

The Limits of Empiricism   109

5 Naturalized Feminist Epistemology   114

Feminism and Naturalized Epistemology   116

Sociology and Naturalized Epistemology   129

6 The Importance of Standpoint in Feminism 138

What is a Standpoint?: Beginning from Women's Experience 138

Starting from Marginal Lives 150

7 Objectivity and Feminism 160

What is Objectivity? 161

Objectivity and Objectification 166

Objectivity, Values, and Responsibility 171

8 Knowledge and Power 186

Power, Knowledge, and Human Interests 190

Disciplinary Power, Bio-Power, and Science 196

9 Reason and Unreason in Feminism 212

Reason and Masculinity 215

Reason and the Philosophical Imaginary 232

10 Feminism and Postmodernism 237

Epistemology: Rejection or Transformation? 239

Knowledge and the Subject 255

References 270

Index 281

Acknowledgments

Books owe their existence to the collaboration of many individuals, and the support of several institutions. This one is no exception. I have written and revised the manuscript on three different continents, and thus I have incurred more debts than I can explicitly acknowledge here.

My colleagues and friends in Philosophy, Critical Theory, and Cultural Criticism at the University of Wales, Cardiff, have stimulated and challenged me. Conversations with them have led me to modify my position and strengthen my arguments. I am especially indebted to Michael Durrant for his unfailing support and probing questions, to Chris Norris for our fierce – but friendly – disagreements, and to Peter Sedgwick for his insights into French and German post-Kantian philosophy. I have shared several good meals and excellent wines with Diane Elam. Her views on postmodernism have forced me to take this position much more seriously than I ever had before. I am also grateful for her help and support during these last few years which have been enormously difficult for me.

The University of Sydney has provided a challenging environment in which to discuss the ideas contained in this book. I have particularly enjoyed conversations with Moira Gatens, Huw Price, Steve Buckle, and Lloyd Reinhardt. I am also grateful to John Bigelow for sharpening my ideas on objectivity and for his hospitality in Melbourne.

The final version of the manuscript was prepared while I was visiting Georgetown University in Washington DC. The Philosophy Department at Georgetown provided me with a friendly and supportive institutional home for one year. I am thankful to Wayne Davis for making this visit possible. I am also particularly indebted to Maggie Little and Linda Wetzel, who read parts of the manuscript. I have greatly benefited from their comments.

The ideas I present in this book were first developed in my classes at the University of Wales, Cardiff, and at the University of Sydney. I am grateful to my students, whose questions, comments, and papers have greatly helped to clarify and focus what I have to say.

I owe a great debt to the members of the Society of Women in Philosophy (UK), who, over the years, have fostered my work, and provided a truly supportive environment. I am especially grateful to Christine Battersby for her unfaltering encouragement, and her insightful comments.

My greatest debt is to Linda Martín Alcoff, Kathleen Lennon, and Mark Lance, who introduced me to feminist epistemology. Their views have deeply influenced my thinking. I have no doubt that without their support, their comments, and their friendship this book would not have been written.

Steve Smith and Mary Riso at Blackwell have been very helpful and encouraging. It has been a pleasure to work with them.

For many years I shared my life and my thinking with Helen Gilroy. She was my staunchest critic, my editor, and my greatest friend. Although Helen died before this manuscript was written, her influence on my ideas is everlasting. A few months before the completion of this work my life was saddened by the death of my sister Maria Ramadhani Mussa Tanesini, whose humor and sharp wit I greatly miss. This book is dedicated to their memory.

Introduction

This book is conceived as an introduction to feminist epistemology. It is written so as to be accessible to readers who have little or no previous knowledge of the field. Its style is philosophical, but it aims to provide extensive discussions of many feminist accounts of knowledge, some of which have not been elaborated from within the discipline of philosophy. Since epistemology has been a concern primarily for feminists working in the English-speaking world, many of the theorists discussed in this book are either British, American, or Australian. I have, however, presented some of the views held by French feminists which are pertinent to epistemic questions.

Although the book aims to be an introduction, I hope it will be of interest also to specialists in the field since it presents a novel theory of knowledge. This new approach develops some recurrent feminist themes in a new direction. It encourages us to think of knowledge in terms of practices, and provides a new understanding of the socially constituted character of knowledge. I use this new approach, which I explain in the first chapter, to clarify some of the issues that have been debated among feminists.

In chapter 1 I provide a survey of epistemology, philosophy of science, the sociology of knowledge, and the cultural studies of science. The chapter presents an overview of the similarities and differences between feminist theories of knowledge and more traditional approaches. In chapter 2 I discuss feminist criticisms of mainstream epistemology. In particular, I present philosophical critiques of the individualism of traditional theories of knowledge, and psychoanalytic elucidations of the notion of the subject which is implicit in these theories. Chapter 3 focuses on feminist critiques of science. I present several examples of feminist accounts of sexist bias in science. In the second section of the chapter I discuss some feminist theories about the role of values in science.

Chapters 4, 5, and 6 deal with three different types of feminist epistemologies. In chapter 4 I discuss feminist empiricism, a position which has been held by Helen Longino and Lynn Nelson. In chapter 5 I present naturalized epistemology and analyze the different ways in which this approach has been appropriated by feminists. In chapter 6 I discuss the most popular form of feminist epistemology, namely standpoint theory.

Chapters 7, 8, and 9 concern three topics that have been extensively discussed by feminist epistemologists. In chapter 7 I present traditional conceptions of objectivity, and its feminist alternatives. My discussion is focused on the alleged connection between objectivity and objectification. In chapter 8 I consider the relations between power and knowledge. I present Michel Foucault's views on this issue, and argue with Joseph Rouse that power relations are, sometimes, constitutive of knowledge. In chapter 9 I consider the debate about reason internal to feminism. I present some arguments for the claim that philosophical reason has been symbolized as male. I discuss psychoanalytic challenges to the notion of reason, and consider whether metaphors of sexual difference are inevitably part of the symbolic connotation of this notion. Finally, I present some arguments about the role of 'woman' as a symbol in philosophy.

Finally, in chapter 10 I discuss the relations between postmodernism and feminist epistemology. I consider postmodernists' arguments about the evaluative character of epistemology, and argue that some of their more radical claims are unwarranted. I also discuss postmodernists' rejections of a philosophy of the subject. I argue in favor of this rejection, but show that the majority of the claims made by feminist epistemologists could nevertheless be accepted.

1

Varieties of Epistemology

We hear from some quarters that we have come to the end of epistemology. The theory of knowledge, which was once at the center of philosophy, has now been put aside, and rejected. This phenomenon is particularly in evidence among French philosophers, but even the Anglo-American world is not immune from it. It would seem all the more surprising, therefore, that epistemology is so prominent in feminist philosophy.

Feminists, I believe, are correct in continuing to pursue epistemology. The philosophical study of knowledge, I shall argue in this book, is of fundamental importance to understand our position in the world. We need, for example, accounts of the relations between knowledge and politics. These accounts must contain an evaluative dimension, and therefore give us the means to distinguish between what we merely take to be knowledge and real knowledge. Epistemology provides the context within which to pursue this evaluative task. Of course, some old philosophical views about knowledge need to be opposed, but their place should be taken by new accounts rather than be left vacant. Feminist epistemology provides a critique of old models, and develops new alternatives to them. It is not alone in pursuing these goals. Although there are similarities between feminist theories of knowledge and other critiques of traditional accounts, there are also innovations which are specific to feminist theory.[1]

This book is conceived primarily as a guide to the ways in which knowledge has been understood by scholars and scientists whose work is informed by feminist concerns. Their feminism has enabled them to start their thinking about knowledge from unusual places. They have asked questions about knowledge that rarely had been posed before, and they have given prominence to cognitive issues that previously had been marginalized. The second aim of this book is to outline a new account of knowledge which builds on the work feminists have produced so far.

The novelty of feminist approaches to the theory of knowledge is exemplified by the sense of surprise which we may feel when we read the geneticist Barbara McClintock treating the plants she studies as friends. It is in part due to this novelty that feminist epistemology has been too easily dismissed by traditional thinkers. An epistemology which values emotions, which is informed by social and political concerns, has seemed to many an oxymoron – that is, a contradiction in terms (Alcoff and Potter, 1993: 1).

It would be a mistake, however, to believe that there is a unique and agreed-upon feminist epistemology. Rather it is more accurate to say that there are many partly overlapping accounts of knowledge which rightly could be called 'feminist.' These accounts often present similar concerns and basic assumptions, but differ from each other not just in matters of detail. One of my goals in this chapter is to illustrate some of the characteristics and aims that feminist epistemologists appear to share. Another is to clarify both the similarities and differences between traditional philosophical accounts of knowledge and science and their feminist alternatives.

Epistemology

There are at least two quite distinct traditions in philosophy, which have, since Kant, lived separate lives. Analytical philosophy, which is usually practiced in philosophy departments in the English-speaking world, has developed out of the logical positivist movement based in Vienna at the beginning of this century.[2] The other tradition, which is labeled 'Continental Philosophy,' is mainly pursued in philosophy departments in continental Europe. Continental philosophy is not, however, a monolithic tradition.[3] For example, there are radical differences between German philosophers working within the Frankfurt School of critical theory, and French post-structuralist and postmodernist thinkers. Both analytic and continental are, albeit in different contexts, mainstream philosophy.

These traditions have developed different ways to think philosophically about knowledge. They are each equipped with their paradigmatic methodologies, questions, and unargued assumptions. None of them has succeeded in defeating or assimilating its rivals. Rather, they have survived mainly in splendid isolation from each other in the contemporary philosophical theater. There are, however, 'bridge builders,' and feminist philosophers are prominent among them. These feminists attempt to build on the insights offered by all traditions. In particular, even feminists trained within the context of analytic philosophy have found some aspects of the continental tradition more hospitable to their views.[4] This is the approach adopted in this book.

The shape of current philosophical reflection about knowledge is further complicated by the recent prominence of 'negative' epistemologies: that is, theories that deny that knowledge is an appropriate object of philosophical inquiry. Such tendencies are instantiated by philosophers like Richard Rorty (1979)[5] and by some feminist thinkers influenced by postmodernism, notably Jane Flax (1993). They encourage us to abandon every epistemological project.

In this chapter I describe and evaluate some of the traditions in epistemology. It is, I believe, important to provide a geography of epistemology, an account of its different formations, and of its geological history. Showing the variety of forms that legitimate (even if, perhaps, mistaken) epistemology has assumed helps, for example, to undermine one of the most commonly heard dismissals of feminist epistemology. The dismissal goes like this: 'Whatever you do might be interesting – says the mainstream philosopher – but it isn't what I do, I do epistemology; therefore, what you do, which you call "feminist epistemology," isn't epistemology at all.' This sort of dismissal *mutatis mutandis* is one that feminist philosophers often have to endure whenever they claim that what they do is philosophy, however different it may be from what so-called 'mainstream' philosophers do.

Discussing the variety of forms that the theory of knowledge has taken does not just help to establish the legitimacy of feminist epistemology as a new species of an old genus, it also sheds light on the continuity between some traditions in epistemology and a theory of knowledge informed by feminist concerns. Feminist epistemology, I believe, is a rebellious child of epistemology. It bears the sign of its parentage, but it is also a daughter of different times and, therefore, it is different from the tradition that generated it. This is a phenomenon that has not gone unrecognized by feminists who, while they distance themselves from a narrow understanding of mainstream epistemology, also claim that their work ought to be recognized as being concerned with 'many of the problems that have vexed traditional epistemology' (Alcoff and Potter, 1993: 1).

There are, however, three tenets present in traditional philosophical accounts of knowledge which, in my opinion, feminists ought to reject.

The first tenet is the belief that epistemology is first philosophy. The second is the belief that knowledge depends on foundations. The third is the belief that knowledge is best understood in terms of how subjects represent their environment. The first two of these tenets have already fallen in disrepute, while the third still has a grip on much current work in epistemology. In this chapter I do not provide arguments why I believe these tenets should be rejected. Instead, I want to explain what they are, and justify my claim that they are present in most traditional work in epistemology. I shall then present an outline of an approach that rejects all of these tenets, and show how many feminist claims can be supported from within this framework.

The claim that epistemology is first philosophy is open to more than one interpretation. These must be teased out in order to understand this tenet. The theory of knowledge, I have said, is concerned with the distinction between knowledge and what we merely take to be knowledge. Those who believe epistemology to be first philosophy also believe that this distinction can be drawn from the armchair. They hold that all cases of knowledge have some common features, and that we can find out by philosophical reflection alone what these features are. Of course, they do not hold that we find out in this manner *which* claims have the required features. For example, an epistemologist might hold that a claim counts as knowledge only if it is true, and there is a justification for it. She does not tell us which claims are true. And, although the epistemologist will tell us something about justification, she will not tell us which claims are justified. So understood the theory of knowledge does not confer epistemic authority to claims, it merely provides a way of finding out whether some claims have this legitimacy.

There is, however, another reading of epistemology as first philosophy. Like the first, it attempts to separate knowledge from presumed knowledge solely by means of armchair reflection. It also assumes that all cases of knowledge have something in common. However, according to this second interpretation, epistemology itself constitutes at least in part the legitimacy of claims to knowledge. Hence, according to this view we cannot have knowledge until we have worked out our theory of knowledge. These two interpretations are different. According to the first we can have scientific knowledge, for example, even if we have not developed a theory of knowledge. In such a case, we would know about science without knowing whether we know about science. This possibility is ruled out by the second interpretation which takes it to be impossible for us to know something without also knowing that we know it. It holds this view because it takes epistemology to confer validity upon claims, rather than simply find out whether they have it.

There have been many philosophers who have taken epistemology to be first philosophy in either or both of the interpretations I have given above. The best example is provided by the German philosopher Immanuel Kant. In the *Critique of Pure Reason* Kant investigated the limits of human reason. He believed that there are questions for which humans with their limited capacities cannot ever hope to find an answer. He gave knowledge of God's existence and of the finitude of the cosmos as examples. He endeavored, therefore, to find out the limits of human knowledge, and at the same time to establish that, within those limits, we do indeed have knowledge. Epistemology delineates the necessary conditions under which knowledge is possible. In this way it helps us to establish the validity of some claims to knowledge and to disqualify others. For Kant armchair reflection on the power of human reason gives us what we need to make the distinction between real and presumed knowledge.

I have said that there are two ways in which one can understand epistemology as first philosophy. I do not know whether Kant adopted the second reading, or whether he subscribed only to the first one. However, in more recent times the first interpretation has been more common among analytic philosophers, and the second among some continentals. For example, the American philosopher W. V. O. Quine has rejected epistemology as first philosophy, and has argued instead that we cannot distinguish real from presumed knowledge by means of armchair reflection alone (1969: 83). He has held that we must use science to make this distinction, even when we are applying the distinction to science itself. On the other side of the divide, the French philosopher Jean-François Lyotard has argued that what is most distinctive about the postmodern condition is that what is taken to give legitimacy to science must be immanent to it (1984: 54). What we have lost, presumably, is epistemology as first philosophy in the second of the two senses I have distinguished. That is, a discipline that, while being external to science, confers epistemic authority to scientific claims.[6] Lyotard seems to believe that epistemology must be first philosophy in this second sense. This is not so. One may argue with Quine that epistemology can be pursued in a scientific setting. Alternatively, one may argue that epistemology is not concerned with finding out the features that all cases of knowledge have in common.

It is now time turn to the second tenet of much traditional epistemology: foundationalism. According to this view, we have no knowledge unless there are foundations or grounds on which all the remaining knowledge can be based. Descartes, for example, enjoined us to distrust even the authority of sense perception unless we could find some secure foundation for all knowledge. According to him, the cogito 'I think, therefore I am' provided such a foundation. In general, however, foundationalism is characterized by the belief that there are self-legitimating states. These states could be, for example, experiences. They would constitute foundations if and only if they were the sources of their own legitimacy. So understood foundations are examples of knowledge one can acquire without presupposing in any sense any other knowledge. If experiences were foundational in this way, they could never be challenged. Experiential reports would always be justified. Our experiences might not match reality, but it would be impossible for any of us to be wrong about how we experience reality to be. Despite its initial plausibility, this view, as many feminists have pointed out, must be rejected. Feminists are not alone in holding this position. Among continental philosophers, foundationalism has been abandoned at least since Hegel; and foundationalism does not have nowadays many friends even in analytic philosophy.

There are no foundations, and even experiential knowledge depends on other knowledge. It is important, however, to be clear about the nature of this dependency. We do not have to say that knowledge is always inferred from other knowledge. There is knowledge which we acquire without making inferences, even tacitly, from other bits of knowledge we already possess. This is not to say, however, that this knowledge is self-authenticating, since it would not count as knowledge unless we also had other knowledge.[7] For example, suppose I see a thermometer in a room, and observe that the temperature is 20 degrees centigrade. I know what the temperature is, and I can not have this knowledge unless I also have other knowledge in the background. I need to know how to recognize thermometers, and to know what they are for. I also need to be able to read. If a baby looked at the thermometer, she would not come to know the temperature. And yet, in my case I do not acquire knowledge of the temperature by making inferences even implicitly from my knowledge of thermometers and what their purpose is. I know the temperature by means of observation without inferring it from other knowledge I already possess. Nevertheless, my observation would not even count as an observation of the temperature unless I had other knowledge in the background.

This is no argument that foundationalism must be false. However, the example illustrates an alternative conception of the structure of justification. There would be no foundations because all knowledge is dependent on other knowledge; nevertheless, knowledge is not always a matter of inference.[8] My example also suggests that we have non-inferential knowledge about external reality. There is no need to assume, as foundationalists have often done, that, without making inferences, we can only know the contents of our minds. Instead, we can have direct knowledge of the world, although this knowledge can only emerge in the context of other knowledge.

Of course, I have not established that beliefs can gain legitimacy in the way suggested by my example, but I have given some reason to think that it is possible to do epistemology without foundationalism. This is a possibility which has already been explored by several philosophers.[9] *Pace* Rorty (1979: 132), foundationalism has never commanded universal approval among epistemologists. It might be possible that some of our claims have epistemic authority even if none of them is self-authorizing.

The third tenet of epistemology is the view that knowledge is best understood in terms of how individuals represent their environment. I call this tenet 'representationalism.' Its presence is still deeply felt in contemporary epistemology, since the conviction that knowledge must be some special kind of relation between subjects and objects is hard to shake. The representationalist view seems 'natural' because it is difficult to see any alternatives to it. According to this view, when we think about knowledge we must think of a world composed of objects with causal properties which individuals attempt to know. Thus, we have individuals on one side, and things on the other. Knowledge must be some sort of relation between the two. How do individuals get to know external reality? It is assumed that our ability to represent the environment must constitute the starting point. So, when by means of perception I know that there is a table in front of me, I have this knowledge because I have a mental representation of this table being in front of me, and my representation meets some other criteria to be specified. Philosophers of mind will study the notion of mental representation; they will try to explain how something can be both 'in' us and about external reality. Epistemologists will, instead, find out which conditions must be met by representations to count as knowledge. Broadly speaking, there seem to be two such conditions. The representations must be accurate or true; and they cannot be merely lucky guesses.

This is the picture that has dominated the recent history of Western epistemology. Since the early modern period philosophers have understood knowledge in terms of representations. Their accounts of representations, however, have changed. In particular, as the French historian and philosopher Michel Foucault has pointed out in *The Order of Things* (1970), the representational capacities of the human mind come to be seen as problematic only at the end of the eighteenth century. In the early modern period, instead, representation is not taken to be a problem. It is merely assumed that there are states of the mind which are about external objects. This is an assumption which, in the seventeenth century, is shared by rationalists and empiricists alike. According to Foucault, this presupposition characterizes the epistemology of the period which he calls the 'classical episteme.'

Thus, Descartes, a rationalist, draws a sharp boundary between an inner private space of the mind, where representations occur, and an external space of material things, what he calls 'bodies.' The mind, for him, is transparent to the subject, there is nothing in it but representations. Thought, which is conducted through the medium of representation, comprises the whole of human cognitive faculties.[10] Representations can be, according to Descartes, about external reality. Nevertheless, he does not ask how this is possible; for him, representations are not a problem. Instead, he tries to discover which representations we should trust. He wants to find out which representations constitute knowledge. Descartes's solution to this problem consists in finding some special representations on which to base all others. He adopts foundationalism. Thus, he believes that there is some knowledge which is independent of all other knowledge. These representations would be the source of their own legitimacy.

The English empiricist John Locke also takes knowledge to be a matter of representations. This view is exemplified by his theory of perception, which is commonly known as 'indirect realism.' When we perceive, according to Locke, we have direct access only to representations in our minds. We can be said to perceive external reality because this reality is the cause of the representations we are in direct contact with. It is as if a picture of what goes on around us was constantly projected on a mental screen, we know what is outside because we are spectators of the mental movie. Locke's theory of perception gives rise to the doctrine of the 'veil of perception.' Between us and reality there is always an interface of representations; we cannot ever step outside and check directly whether these representations correspond to reality. It is this doctrine which gives rise to Hume's scepticism about the extent of human knowledge, to which Kant responds by attempting to find a new account of representations.

Kant does not simply presume that something 'in' us can be about what is outside. Instead, he takes representations to be a problem. He attempts to spell out the conditions for their possibility. According to Foucault, Kant's recognition for the need to explain how mental states can be about something outside constitutes the beginning of a new episteme, which

Foucault calls the 'modern episteme.' Foucault takes Kant to be concerned both with the conditions of intentionality (the 'aboutness' of representations), and with the conditions under which representations have epistemic authority. These conditions are to be found in the subject who is capable of knowledge: they constitute the non-representational ground of representations. In other words, the subject can have adequate representations only if she has other non-representational capacities. The presence of their grounds is what confers legitimacy to any representations. Epistemology aims to find out what the grounds are and whether they are present.

The view that thought and knowledge essentially involve representations is still very common in both analytic and continental traditions. For example, the representational theory of mind is the dominant position about human cognition in analytic philosophy. It claims that thought is a matter of processing mental representations.[11] Some French philosophers also assume that knowledge must be a matter of representations. For example, Jean-François Lyotard has argued that, since nothing outside science can give it legitimacy, questions of validity must be replaced by an analysis of power. He holds that only epistemology as first philosophy, in the second of the two senses I have mentioned, could confer legitimacy to our representations. This position finds its origin in Nietzsche's belief that we cannot have adequate representations. Nietzsche denies the existence of things in themselves beyond the veil of appearance, but what he is left with is a reality that has all the features of appearances. For Nietzsche, knowledge has evolved to enhance our power, to increase our ability to have an effect on our surroundings. It involves developing a conception of reality that includes enough stability to base patterns of behavior on it.[12] Nietzsche's position, and consequently Lyotard's, has not gone beyond the theory of knowledge as representation. Knowledge is that sort of misrepresentation which enhances our power.

There is an alternative to this representationalist approach, which has dominated the history of Western philosophy since the early modern period. It is an alternative that does not deny that we have representations of the external environment. However, this alternative suggests that we do not start our thinking about knowledge from representations. They come last, rather than first, in the account. This alternative has been, at least in part, formulated at the beginning of this century by the German philosopher Martin Heidegger in his book *Being and Time* (1962).[13] I believe that such an alternative offers a useful framework for an epistemology informed by feminist concerns.

First, this alternative approach provides an account of practical knowledge. Further, it takes theoretical knowledge to be a kind of practical knowledge. Women's knowledge has traditionally been practical, and epistemologists have often considered knowledge of this kind to be second rate. The alternative I present reverses this value judgment.[14] Second, this account of knowledge takes all knowledge to be essentially social. This is a claim that has already been made by feminists; this account offers a way of explaining how this is so. Third, this approach rejects the view that knowledge requires value-neutrality. Instead, it holds that values are constitutive of knowledge. In what follows I provide only a sketch of this alternative, and attempt to show how it can support some of the claims that have already been made by feminist philosophers.

Practical, rather than theoretical, knowledge provides the starting point of this approach. We are thus concerned with the kind of knowledge we manifest in our everyday dealings with the world. This knowledge is practical mastery. It involves the ability to use, respond to, and produce things. It is the sort of knowledge we manifest when we drive, build a table, or prepare a meal. These things which we use and produce are already invested with human values. They are socially constituted. Heidegger's favorite example of a socially constituted thing is the hammer. How do we distinguish a hammer from something else? Hammers have different colors, weight, dimensions. They are made of different materials. What all hammers have in common is what they are for.

Hammers are the sort of thing whose purpose is to hammer nails in wood, in walls, and so on. Thus, hammers are defined in terms of their significance for human beings. It would be a mistake to think of hammers as something that can be defined in terms of their physical features, and to which human values are added on. The significance it has for us is what makes it possible to classify something as a hammer. In other words, hammers are socially constituted. We manifest our practical knowledge of hammers when we use them appropriately, when we use them to do what they are for. In our everyday life we deal with a variety of tools, we manifest our practical knowledge by responding to them in appropriate ways. Nails, tables, and cars are tools. The things found in a scientific laboratory are also pieces of equipment. They are all socially constituted. For example, what makes a thing a thermometer is its significance for us. We have practical mastery of a thermometer when we use and respond to it appropriately.

Tools are socially constituted because their existence depends on socially instituted practices. In a society where the sport of football had not been invented, there could be an inflated spherical object made of leather.

This object could have all the physical properties of a typical football. And yet, it would not be a football. The existence of footballs depends on the existence of a complex social practice; that is, the sport of football.[15] A football, like a hammer, is partly constituted by its significance for us. These tools acquire their significance from our uses of them. But, not any use will do. I can successfully use a football to break a window. Nevertheless, this is not what footballs are for. Equipment is what it is because of its purpose, and its purpose is something it acquires because we take it to be appropriate to use it in some ways rather than others. Equipment inherits its significance from the significance of human performances that involve it.

Human performances or actions are also, like tools, socially constituted. An immersion in water is a performance. It can be an instance of a baptism only in the context of a society that has instituted religious social practices of a given sort. Outside the context of these practices an action which is physically identical to something that in a christian society counts as a baptism could at most be a bath. A social practice like the sport of football, or religion, or even carpentry is a nexus of many interrelated performances. They include many actions which are classified in terms of their significance or purpose.

Societies institute practices. Their institution may occur in many ways. However, we have a practice when performances get sorted out in terms of their significance. People learn what is appropriate to do, in accordance with the practice, in given circumstances. For example, children get inducted into the practice of football when they learn to score a goal, and also learn that scoring a goal is appropriate in football. They, thus, acquire some mastery of the game of football. The ball employed in football acquires its significance from being used in ways deemed to be appropriate in the practice.

Practical knowledge, therefore, is a matter of getting inducted in socially instituted practices. We acquire a mastery of cooking when we learn how to respond appropriately to kitchen utensils and to the raw materials. We manifest our knowledge of knives and saucepans by using them appropriately. Of course, we can have this kind of knowledge without knowing that tools and actions are socially constituted. Practical knowledge of cookery only requires that we respond to tools and actions in accordance with our practices, it does not require that we also know that practical competence is a matter of responding appropriately to equipment and human performances.

Theoretical knowledge is a special case of practical knowledge. It involves producing and evaluating theories. But, theorizing must be understood as something we do. It is a matter of performances which crucially involve knowing how to make assertions. Thus, theorizing is a kind of practical competence. It involves using and responding to equipment in accordance with our practices. The tool used in theorizing is linguistic assertion. The actions we perform using this piece of equipment are called 'assertings.' The practice which invests these actions with significance is the practice of giving and asking for reasons. When we speak we utter noise, it is only in the context of our practices that a bit of behaviour can count as an act of asserting, and the noise made can count as language.

The practice of giving and asking for reasons invests some actions with significance, they become performances of assertions. Asserting plays a special role in communication. We respond to actions which we take as instances of having appropriately made an assertion by taking them to be authoritative. We treat these actions as licensing us to repeat the assertion, and to draw conclusions from it. For example, suppose somebody claims that water molecules are composed of two atoms of hydrogen and one of oxygen. We take in practice that assertion to be appropriate if we treat it as giving us the license to assert the same, or to conclude that oxygen is one of the constituents of water. To recognise a performance as an appropriate act of asserting is to recognise that act as having authority. With authority, however, comes responsibility. While the appropriate response to taking someone to have appropriately made an assertion is to treat it as authoritative, the appropriate production of an assertion requires that one undertakes the responsibility to justify one's claim. Asserting is appropriately made only if one can fulfill the responsibility to justify the claim. If one has relied on the authority of a previous assertor, one discharges one's responsibility by deferring to the original speaker. The latter, if challenged, will fulfill her responsibility by making other assertions that support the claim that has been challenged.

This structure of authority and responsibility is instituted by the practice of giving and asking for reasons. This is the practice which determines the significance of our acts of asserting. We know how to make assertions when we engage in this practice, when we recognise in practice that it is appropriate to make a claim only if, when challenged, we can fulfill the responsibility to justify it either by deferring authority or by supporting it. We must also know how to respond to claims; in this case we treat them as authoritative if we take them to have been appropriately produced. In the same way in which an action counts as a baptism only in the context of instituted religious practices, an action can count as an assertion only in the context of the practice of giving and asking for reasons. Justifying a claim is a kind of assertion; hence, nothing counts as a justification outside the context of this socially instituted practice.

The picture I have sketched so far points toward a conception of knowledge that is radically different from the picture offered by much traditional epistemology. Several features of this picture make it an appealing framework for feminist epistemology. I have already mentioned three of these features: the centrality given to practical knowledge, the conception of knowledge as essentially social, and the rejection of value-neutrality. The last two points need further explanation because of the many different ways in which they have been understood.

Value-neutrality can seem appealing only if we conceive of knowledge as a relation between things devoid of meaning and human representations of them. This ideal loses all its appeal if we take knowledge to be a matter of engaging with things. The things we engage with are, according to the Heideggerian account I have outlined above, already invested with human values. They are so invested because they do not exist independently of our dealings with them. It would be a mistake, however, to interpret this claim in a subjectivist manner. Things do not have their significance because individuals in isolation bestow values to them by means of their mental activity. Rather, equipment and human performances involving it have their significance against a background of socially instituted practices.

This does not mean, of course, that we cannot treat things as existing independently of us. But we must be clear that when we do it, we are just adopting a different way of dealing with them. We are attributing to them a new significance, they assume a new value for us. They become the sort of thing we can have theories about. That is, we take it to be appropriate to respond to them by making assertions. When we produce theories, we engage with things in new ways. By means of assertion, we can represent how things are independently of us. This ability, however, depends on our engagement with linguistic equipment.

Value-neutrality is neither possible nor desirable. The equipment we master is constituted by the significance we attribute to it in practice. Human performances involving equipment are also constituted by the values attributed to them by social practices. Hence, practical knowledge is constituted by values. For example, practical mastery of thermometers is manifested in our engagement with this kind of equipment. An observation can be an instance of reading the temperature only against the background of practices that invest it with values. Because theoretical knowledge involves practical mastery of assertions, it is also constituted by values. Our practice of giving and asking for reasons invests some performances with the significance that pertains to justifications. Once I have mastered thermometers, I can have non-inferential knowledge of temperature. This context of significance gives legitimacy to my assertions about the temperature. In turn, in the context of our inferential practices, making these assertions can constitute providing a justification for other claims.

This Heideggerian framework, therefore, provides an account of the essentially social character of all knowledge. It is only against the background of social practices that a performance can count as a justification for a claim. Outside this context nothing could have the special kind of authority that pertains to justifications. This is not to say, however, that society is the final arbiter of what counts as knowledge. Even if all members of a society take the production of a justifying claim to be in accordance with their practices, they might be wrong about it. Furthermore, the practices of a society are also subject to evaluation. This is, I believe, the main purpose of epistemology. Thus conceived, epistemology is the study of all those practices whose purposes are centered on knowledge. For example, experimenting and theorizing whose purpose is to increase knowledge, but also teaching whose purposes include the transmission of knowledge. Epistemology is not primarily concerned with describing these practices but with their evaluation. It considers how practices can be improved upon, and whether they should be sustained or abandoned. On a more general level, it attempts to understand what it means to say that knowledge can only be understood in the context of specific practices.

Feminist epistemologists hold that knowledge has a social character. They explain the many ways in which social and political factors are relevant to knowledge. However, feminist accounts of these factors are varied.[16] Some, but not all, mention the notion of practice; fewer employ it along the lines I have suggested above. Nevertheless, because they take knowledge to be social, feminists reject at least some aspects of traditional analytic epistemology which focuses on the individual while abstracting from any social constraints.

These differences in approach between mainstream analytic and feminist theories of knowledge have noteworthy consequences. For example, Lorraine Code holds that the effect of feminists' attention to epistemic practices has been 'to move the question "Whose knowledge are we talking about?" to a central analytical position' (1992: 138). She argues that when we consider knowledge as the product of social cognitive practices, knowledge emerges as a socially located phenomenon. This is not to say that knowledge should be seen as 'a purely social product', unconstrained by any epistemic criteria of adequacy (Code, 1991: 43). Rather, it is to say that the social location of the knower is relevant to epistemic evaluation.[17]

There are several, not necessarily incompatible, ways in which this claim can be understood. For example, one could argue that practices involve agents who are partly defined by their roles in these practices. For instance, being a teacher is part of who I am; and I could not be a teacher unless I engaged at least sometimes in the practice of teaching. However, I could not take up my role in this practice, at least in the formal setting of academia, if I had not been trained. That is, I must have previously engaged in other practices which have also shaped who I am. Thus, not everybody is allowed to take up any role in any practice. In order to understand a practice we need to study who engages in it, which sort of people are allowed to do so and why. This, of course, also applies to other practices for the production and transmission of knowledge. One of the tasks of the epistemologist is to evaluate which exclusions from practices are acceptable and which are not. This is one of the reasons why it matters epistemically whose knowledge we are talking about.

On these issues the contrast with traditional analytic theories of knowledge could not be starker. They have consisted in attempts to formulate universal accounts of knowledge which ignore the social contexts within which knowers are located. Recent analytic epistemology has been more attuned to the social aspects of knowledge, but it finds it difficult to shed its individualist character. Historically, analytic philosophers are led to this position by the conception of knowledge as adequate representation. Knowledge is conceived as something which, like a mental representation, an individual has or possesses. One might need to look outside the individual to determine the meaning of his representations.[18] It certainly is not sufficient to look inside the head to decide whether a given representation is adequate, whether it is knowledge. In any case what matters is the representation or belief, the grounds or reasons for that belief, and whether the representation is true.[19]

The focus on the individual knower is a legacy of the Cartesian tradition in epistemology. Both Descartes and Locke take individual cognitive autonomy as a fundamental epistemic value. They both stress that achieving knowledge is an individual feat. Locke, for example, claims that when somebody relies on the testimony of others what he acquires is 'borrowed wealth, [which] like fairy money, though it were gold in the hand from which he received it, will be but leaves and dust when it comes to use' (Locke, 1975: I.iv.23).

When Locke and Descartes emphasize the importance of autonomy for knowledge, they are not merely stressing the importance of thinking independently. Rather, they have in mind a conception of the autonomous self as an individual who can achieve knowledge by employing only his own will, and by having control over what contributes to this achievement.[20] This too is a consequence of the representational theory of knowledge when it is combined with an outdated Lockean theory of mind. Only a subject who resists any external social influence and keeps in check his emotions may hope to achieve representations that mirror external reality. Both feminist and some mainstream philosophers have shown that, once we abandon the conception of the mind as a mirror of nature, there is no epistemic reason for requiring this sort of autonomy.[21] Furthermore, as I discuss in chapter 2, feminists have pointed out that there are strong connections between autonomy so conceived and Western notions of masculinity (Keller, 1985: 76).

Although there is a trend in analytic epistemology toward an appreciation of the social character of knowledge, it is correct to say that individualism in epistemology still has paradigmatic status. Mainstream continental philosophy, instead, has been for a long time much more attentive to social considerations. Continental epistemologists have, since Hegel, been acutely aware of the relevance of subjectivity to knowledge. In disagreement with Kant they have held that the subject who has knowledge is historically and culturally located. Hence, they have emphasized the social and perspectival character of knowledge.

Marx, for example, stresses the importance of the social position of the knower for an evaluation of the validity of her claim to know. This conception of knowledge as perspectival has been crucial to much feminist epistemology as it has been developed in the Anglo-American world. Marx had claimed epistemic privilege for the perspective of the proletariat. According to him, because of its social location the working class was better placed than any other class to provide an adequate account of social reality in a capitalist system. In more recent times some feminists have made similar claims on behalf of the feminist perspective on social reality under patriarchy (Hartsock, 1983). Standpoint theory of knowledge, as this view is commonly known, is not without its feminist critics. The debate over its formulation and validity is one of the most lively areas in the feminist study of knowledge. This debate will be discussed in chapter 6.

The claim that all knowledge is the product of socially and historically located subjects has led continental philosophers to appreciate that knowledge is the result of human practices and that it is connected with political interests. These two features of knowledge are at the core of the epistemologies developed in the twentieth century by both German critical theorists like Jürgen Habermas and French post-structuralists like Foucault. These two philosophical positions are radically different from each other, but they both focus on practices by means of which knowledge is achieved and on the relevance of politics to these practices. It is this focus that makes continental epistemologies much more hospitable to feminist thinking than their analytical counterparts.

Nevertheless, even continental philosophy has on the main failed to achieve the necessary break with the conception of knowledge as representations. I have already given an example of this phenomenon when I mentioned Lyotard's position above. The rejection of the representationalist framework which I intend to explore will require a thorough investigation of the role of the subject in epistemology.

Besides their disagreement concerning the importance of social factors to an understanding of knowledge and of the knower, there is another related difference between the projects pursued respectively by feminist and mainstream contemporary analytical epistemology. The latter is primarily concerned with the nature of justification. It attempts to find that property or quality which all and only justified beliefs have. Since knowledge is conceived as something possessed by an individual, it seems natural to look for a feature of those true representations which constitute knowledge, but which is not shared by other true representations.[22] One wants to distinguish knowledge from lucky guesses. The difference is made by justification. The practice of justifying our claims is, of course, of crucial importance to knowledge. But analytic philosophers tend not to think about justification in term of practices. Since for them knowledge is a special sort of representation, justification will be a feature of these representations. Analytic epistemologists want to find out which feature justification is. Some have explained it in terms of causes: a justified representation or belief is one which has been produced in the right way, typically its cause is what the representation is about. Others have explained it in terms of reasons: a justified representation is one which is supported by other representations which are also justified.[23] In either case social considerations will be relevant only if the justified representation is about social issues.[24]

Mainstream epistemology is not concerned with the norms or methods embedded in the practices for achieving knowledge in a given context.[25] Instead, it considers self-evident and rather simple examples of knowledge from which it attempts to learn which is the property they all share and that makes them examples of knowledge. Feminist epistemologists, on the other hand, are more concerned with finding out, and improving, the practices that help us to achieve knowledge. The narrow focus on the metaphysics of epistemology is a recent development even within analytical philosophy.[26] It marks a radical departure from Descartes's concern with the methods and rules of inquiry. Insofar as feminists discuss questions of methodology, it appears more correct to see feminist epistemology rather than analytical theory of knowledge as continuing this tradition of inquiry.

It is mainly due to the focus on the metaphysical question described above that mainstream epistemology appears so unsatisfactory and so irrelevant to our concrete intellectual inquiries. It seems irrelevant because it never considers complex cases where what is at issue is whether one knows or doesn't. It also seems unsatisfactory because it does not even attempt to be a guide for our intellectual endeavors. These criticisms of current mainstream epistemology are being voiced from several quarters even within analytical epistemology itself. Mark Kaplan, for example, claims:

> The problem is that a theory of justification thus purified, a theory of justification deprived of any role in methodology or the conduct of inquiry and criticism, is a theory that divorces epistemology from the very practices that furnish it with its only source of intuitive constraint. It is epistemology on holiday. (1991: 154)

Because feminist epistemology discusses methodology and the conduct of inquiry it is not epistemology on holiday.

A similar concern with appropriate conduct of inquiry is present in the work of those philosophers, belonging to the continental tradition in epistemology, who claim that knowledge bears the marks of the partial perspectives from which one attempts to achieve it. During the nineteenth century philosophers such as Hegel and Marx thought of this partiality of human knowledge as a limitation that must be transcended in order to achieve complete and absolute knowledge of reality.[27] They also believed that their dialectical method provided the tools for achieving this superior form of knowledge. Twentieth century continental thinkers have abandoned any hope of achieving complete and absolute knowledge, and have settled instead for historically contingent knowledge. They are, thus, committed to fallibilism: the view that whatever we claim to know might always (be shown to) be mistaken. It does not follow that epistemic evaluations of our limited perspectives are pointless, but it does follow that both knowledge and theories about it are the subject of continuing evaluation.

Furthermore, since these continental thinkers view every claim to knowledge as an historical product, they have explored in depth the relevance of interests and desires to human knowledge. German thinkers, such as Theodor Adorno and Max Horkheimer, have criticized the traditional view that instrumental reason is the best method to achieve knowledge. They point out the connections between means–ends reasoning and the desire for control and domination typical of the Western culture.[28] This line of thought has also been pursued by feminist epistemologists; I discuss it in chapters 7 and 8 of this book.

I have so far isolated three issues that divide feminist and mainstream analytical epistemology, while bringing the former closer to continental epistemology. Firstly, feminist theories of knowledge are concerned with social practices; analytic epistemology, instead, is individualist partly because it implicitly subscribes to the model of knowledge as representation. Secondly, feminists engage in new investigations about the subject who has knowledge; analytic philosophy still employs a conception of the subject that abstracts from social considerations. Thirdly, feminists attempt to formulate an epistemology that helps to guide intellectual inquiries; mainstream analytic theory of knowledge has very little to say about this.

These two traditions in epistemology are not, however, totally divorced. There already exist analytic philosophers who are critical of the dominant epistemic paradigm in their tradition. Some of their proposals can be employed fruitfully by feminists. With respect to continental philosophy there seem to be even stronger reasons for convergence, since it appears to have critical aims which are to some extent similar to those espoused by feminists.

Furthermore, it has not gone unnoticed by feminists that

remaining in dialogue with the 'mainstream' offers certain strategic advantages [since] . . . it avoids the pitfall of advocating a separate, feminine epistemology, with its inevitable privatization, ghettoization, and consequent devaluation. (Code, 1991: 122)

Although feminist theorists who refuse to enter a dialogue with mainstream epistemology are not necessarily advocates of an essentialist 'feminine epistemology,' it is probably true that their positions would be interpreted as such by mainstream theorists. Furthermore, it is only by engaging in a critical dialogue with the 'mainstream' that feminists can avoid the danger of being ignored and devalued.

The belief that there are good theoretical and strategic reasons for feminists to engage in a debate with 'mainstream' epistemologies informs this whole book. This is a belief that is shared by many feminist thinkers about knowledge. For example, there is an increased feminist interest in naturalized epistemology which is currently in favor among analytical philosophers. Feminists have not appropriated this approach uncritically, but have engaged in a fruitful dialogue with its mainstream supporters.

The Study of Scientific Knowledge

The study of scientific knowledge is another important area of debate and conflict for feminist epistemology. There is, at the moment, no single working paradigm within this field. That is, there seems to be no agreement about which issues need to be addressed and which methods are to be employed when reflecting on science.[29] It is, consequently, quite difficult to map out the territory of this field of study. Broadly speaking, there are three often competing approaches to the study of scientific knowledge. The first is philosophical, its practitioners believe that the study of scientific knowledge should consist primarily in a philosophical evaluation of scientific theories and practices. The second is sociological, its supporters hold that since science is a social phenomenon it should be studied scientifically using the tools developed in the social sciences. The third is cultural, its supporters hold that since science has been developed mainly within Western cultures it should be understood by subjecting it to a kind of cultural critique.

These three approaches would seem at first sight to complement rather than compete with each other. Although there are scholars who employ a combination of these approaches, most tend to subscribe to one of them as a rival of the others. Each of the three approaches encourages a very distinctive way of thinking about science. For example, if one thinks that science is a social phenomenon, one could be led to conclude that sociology provides a complete account of it. There is nothing there for philosophers to point out which could not be better explained by sociologists. I believe that it is because of this sort of conviction that the three approaches I have described are taken as competitors.

While the study of science as a cultural phenomenon is a fairly recent addition to the debate, the division between philosophical and sociological accounts of science has dominated the scene in the 1970s and 1980s. What is at stake in the discussion between these two approaches is the autonomy of science. Philosophers tend to provide an account of the development of science which appeals only to factors internal to science itself. For example, they focus on evidence, rationality and scientific method. For this reason their approach to science has been called 'internalist' (Fuller, 1993: 13). Sociologists, instead, prefer an externalist approach. They attempt to explain the development of science in terms of social factors such as the interests of the groups involved, personal rivalries, and state funding policies, to name but a few. These accounts are called 'externalists' because they appeal to factors external to science itself in order to explain its development (Fuller, 1993: 9).

Despite their apparent opposition, these two approaches share many common assumptions. For example, they focus their analyses on scientific theories rather than on the practices of scientific activity. They also accept that there is a reasonably clear demarcation between what is internal to science and what is external to it. The cultural approach to science challenges, among other things, the existence of such a clear-cut boundary. It shows how science acquires its significance only against the background of broader cultural and social practices. For this reason it is particularly attractive for feminist engagements with science.

Feminist have employed all of the above-mentioned approaches to science. Helen Longino's work (1990), for example, is best seen as belonging to the philosophical tradition, while Kathryn Pyne Addelson's (1990) mainly pertains to sociology. However, most feminist thinkers employ methods and concepts belonging to more than one of these approaches. For example, Sandra Harding (1991) employs both philosophical and sociological concepts in her analysis of scientific knowledge. Elizabeth Potter's (1993) discussion of the importance of negotiation in science is informed by the history and the social-anthropology of science, and engages in both cultural and philosophical analyses of her object of study.

In what follows I delineate the characteristics of the philosophical, sociological, and cultural approaches to science. My accounts are inevitably sketchy; nevertheless, I hope they succeed in bringing out the conflicts between these different ways of understanding science.

A. Philosophy of science[30]

Although the philosophy of science has become, I believe, a field of studies with very porous boundaries, it can still be characterized in terms of a loosely shared set of concerns. First, it tends to concentrate on scientific theories rather than on the practices of scientific inquiry.[31] Philosophers think of science primarily as an enterprise for the production of theories. Second, they see this enterprise as goal directed, although they are divided about the nature of its goal or goals. For example, scientific realists argue that science aims to produce true theories, while instrumentalists believe that the goal is the production of theories which allow us to predict and manipulate phenomena. I shall say more about these two accounts of science below. Despite their disagreements over the aims of science, philosophers tend to agree that they are desirable, and that science should be seen as the rational pursuit of these goals. Philosophers, therefore, provide accounts of the development of science which give prominence to rationality and evidence. This emphasis on rationality is a third shared concern in philosophy of science. Fourth, philosophers, until recently, have assumed that one account could be given for all the sciences. In other words, they believe in the unity of science in so far as goals and scientific method are concerned.

Within the analytic tradition the philosophy of science has developed recently in ways that distance it from mainstream epistemology. The theories of scientific knowledge that philosophers have developed do not share the purified character of dominant epistemologies; instead, they are very much concerned with methodological issues. Nevertheless, contemporary philosophy of science, like analytic epistemology, is not of much use when we are concerned with improving our practices for the achievement of knowledge. Nowadays, philosophers seem more concerned with vindicating science rather than evaluating it. This attitude gives rise to a certain 'quietism,' which, perhaps surprisingly, is shared by sociologists of knowledge (Rouse, 1996: 4).[32]

The recent developments in analytic philosophy of science are in great part due to Thomas Kuhn's *The Structure of Scientific Revolutions* (1970). That book was highly instrumental in the creation of a non-positivistic philosophical reflection on scientific knowledge. Kuhn's historical account of science, as a discipline which does not advance by accumulation of knowledge but by means of revolutions, led philosophers to take a closer look at the activities of scientists. Previously, philosophers had not felt the need to investigate such activities because they were more concerned with the rational reconstruction and justification of scientific theories. They were not interested in what scientists did, but in what they ought to have done.

Philosophers of science drew a sharp distinction between the factors involved in the discovery of theories and those involved in their justification. The 'context of discovery' includes all those elements that play a role in the discovery of theories, they can be factors of any kind. For example, the ambition of some scientist, his hatred of competitors, and the luck involved in stumbling upon a crucial article in an obscure journal might all figure in a causal account of how a scientist arrives at the discovery of a theory. Philosophers found the context of discovery of no philosophical interest. In their opinion only those factors that contribute to the justification of a theory are worthy of philosophical consideration. These factors constitute the 'context of justification'; they are restricted to the evidence in favor of or against a theory.

For example, logical positivists adopted this approach because their main goal was the sharp demarcation of science from non-science; they achieved it by classifying as science only those claims to knowledge that are empirically verifiable. They held that only statements which could be confirmed or disconfirmed by experience are scientific.[33] Hence, positivists subscribed to empiricism: the view that all synthetic knowledge is empirical knowledge, that is, knowledge which is based on the evidence of the senses. For them, a claim is scientific only if one could justify it by means of experience. Thus, the context of justification is all that matters. Before Kuhn, philosophers of science agreed on this conclusion, even when they had rejected logical positivism.

Since Kuhn, this traditional approach to science has been subjected to severe criticisms. A testimony to this fact is that it is almost impossible to name a well-known contemporary philosopher of science who can be taken as pursuing this approach. Feminist philosophers too have engaged in a critique of this account of science. Harding, for example, criticizes its empiricism. Empiricism, she points out, is a theory that sanctions the primacy of observations, and which claims that scientific justification is only a matter of empirical adequacy. Harding argues at length that empiricist philosophy of science is inadequate. She claims, for example, that it is 'hostile to theories of belief formation within which gender could be understood as a part of science's conceptual schemes' (1986: 35). Other feminist critics of logical positivism have supported a modified form of empiricism while rejecting the claim that only empirically testable claims are meaningful, and the allied claim that each scientific statement faces the tribunal of experience in isolation (Longino, 1990: 185).[34] I shall discuss the uneasy relation between feminist philosophy of science and empiricism in chapter 4.

I have claimed that one crucial feature of traditional philosophy of science was a lack of interest in the social and historical aspects of science. The reception of Kuhn's work among philosophers has changed this. It is now impossible to ignore what scientists actually do when attempting to provide a philosophical account of science. In other words, it is widely agreed that such an account should contain a descriptive component.

There are at least two reasons why philosophers did not consider how science is done. First, as I said, they exclusively focused on verification in their attempt to demarcate science from any other enterprise. Second, they assumed that, at least most of the time, scientists pursued scientific methods, and avoided any influence by non-scientific factors. Thus, although these philosophers were concerned with how science ought to be done rather than with how it was done, they also assumed that actual scientists followed the methods which they had prescribed. Kuhn's historical work showed that this second assumption was misconceived. He showed that historically science has not proceeded in the way philosophers had assumed it had.

There is considerable dispute over the lesson to be learned from the history of science. *Prima facie* Kuhn's accounts show that even when science is successful seemingly social factors play a crucial role in the discovery, and in the justifications offered for theories. Although one may remain untouched by historical accounts, and simply claim that science has hardly ever been done as it should, the general response among philosophers has been to accept that an evaluation of science cannot be completely divorced from a description of how it actually proceeds. However, while sociologists take Kuhn to have shown that only causal accounts of the social factors involved in scientific activities can explain the results of science, philosophers, among whom Kuhn himself, have drawn a different lesson. They have not taken his work to show that one cannot provide a rational account of scientific knowledge. Instead, they interpret it as demonstrating that the nature of scientific rationality is different from what was previously thought.

Many philosophers of science share the internalism of the traditional account. They argue, however, that social factors play a positive role in the development of science. They hold that their presence in science can be explained rationally; they can be seen to further science's achievement of its goals. The image of science as an eminently rational activity is therefore preserved. This new approach not only continues the internalism of the tradition, in some respects it also constitutes a step in the wrong direction. Despite all their defects, logical positivists, for example, were not afraid to criticize the activities of scientists. The new, historically informed philosophy of science lacks any critical edge. It assumes that whatever scientists do when they do successful science is rational, and should not be challenged.[35] This is not an attitude which is shared by feminist philosophers of science.

The lesson they have drawn from Kuhn is that all sorts of factors play important roles in science. These factors should not be left unscrutinized. Harding, for example, criticizes the traditional view of scientific method for its lack of self-reflexivity. 'Cultural agendas and assumptions are part of the background assumptions and auxiliary hypotheses' which, she claims, function as evidence in favor of or against a theory. Hence:

If the goal [of scientific methodology] is to make available for critical scrutiny all the evidence marshaled for or against a scientific hypothesis, then this evidence too requires critical examination within scientific research processes. (1991: 149)

Harding's critique of traditional scientific rationality is directly linked to her rejection of empiricism. Since she holds that some evidence relevant to a theory is not empirical evidence, she concludes that the traditional scientific method is inadequate because it is incapable of evaluating relevant non-empirical evidence. Instead, she proposes a different account of scientific methodology that invokes new 'standards [which] are more rational and more effective at producing maximally objective results' than the ones associated with the traditional methodology (1991: 159).

Broadly speaking there are four different programs in philosophy of science: instrumentalism, historical rationalism, scientific realism, and social constructivism.[36] Although these programs have much in common, they differ with regard to the aims, the value, and the methods of science. Scientific realists hold that science aims to describe the world as it is independently of us. Instrumentalists take science to be concerned with the correct prediction of phenomena; control and manipulation rather than truth are the twin aims of science. Historical rationalists see science as a self-directed activity whose aim is to improve its theories and goals over time. Constructivists, instead, think of science as constructing to some extent the reality which it claims to discover, and do not attribute to science a unique aim. For example, Rouse remarks that 'much scientific research is occasioned not by the felt need to resolve known difficulties . . .

but by the concern to take advantage of the available resources in equipment' (1987: 87).[37]

The debate over the aims of science is intrinsically connected to the ontological issue concerning the nature of reality. Usually philosophers who engage in this debate assume one of two apparently exhaustive and mutually exclusive positions. Realists hold that our best theories are approximately true, and that the reality these theories describe is independent of our thoughts and commitments.[38] The anti-realist camp tends to be divided between empiricists, who are not concerned with truth but only with saving the phenomena, and constructivists who believe that we have no unmediated access to reality. Empiricists believe that talk of non-observable entities like electrons is in a sense a useful fiction. There are no electrons, but it could still be useful to use this notion in scientific theories that are good instruments for the prediction of phenomena.[39] The anti-realism of constructivists has a different character. They hold that the reality science purports to describe is not independent of our thoughts, and commitments. At times, they go as far as claiming that reality is a completely social construct.[40] Feminists have usually tried to debunk the dichotomy of realism and constructive anti-realism. They object to the stark opposition between subject and object which is posited by realists, while at the same time refusing to give in to the relativist flavor of constructivist theories.[41] The Heideggerian account, which I sketched in the first section, offers one way to occupy this middle ground.

Analytic philosophers of science have taken it for granted that science is directed at desirable aims. But, feminist and continental philosophers of science have explicitly discussed whether science is a socially valuable activity. Marxists, for example, have discussed the emancipatory potential of scientific knowledge. Some feminists and Heideggerian philosophers have argued that science fosters alienation from nature and from fellow human beings. Other feminists have discussed the, often negative, social effects of science on the lives of women.[42] It is a characteristic of thinkers involved in evaluations of this sort that they reject a sharp separation between a value-free pure science and technology. Instead, they argue that science and technology are inextricably connected, and that neither of them is a value free enterprise.

The thorny question of scientific method constitutes another focus of discussion in the philosophy of science. A somewhat instrumentalist way of framing this issue is to say that it concerns the methods which best serve science's achievements of its aims. Because philosophers generally agree that science pursues its goals rationally, this interpretation seems entirely appropriate. However, since they disagree about the aims of science they also disagree about how best they are achieved. There are several interconnected issues that are debated under this heading. A first topic concerns the relations between theory and observations. This issue is of extreme importance to empiricists who believe that the only evidence for theories is empirical or observational evidence. Contemporary empiricists argue that an observation is evidence for a theory only within the context of some background assumptions. It is primarily through these background assumptions that values enter into the justification of theories (Longino, 1990: 81). Harding, as I have already mentioned, is a critic of this sort of empiricism.

Depending on their understanding of the goals of science, philosophers have given different accounts of the rationality embodied by scientific activity. For example, historical rationalists like Larry Laudan attempt to extrapolate the norms of scientific method from past historical examples of good science. They tend, however, to interpret and classify selectively as cases of good science those instances that appear to support the philosophical prejudice that the best science is autonomous from other sorts of social considerations. That is, the best science is done when scientists engage in purely rational assessments of the empirical evidence. This view has led to Laudan's arationality assumption: the philosophers study the scientific methodology employed by scientists when they do good science; the sociologists, on the other hand, study those cases where due to the influence of external social factors science goes wrong (1977, ch. 7).

Many feminists have been engaged in the project of debunking 'internalist' accounts of scientific method typical of much contemporary philosophy of science. Harding, for example, follows sociologists of knowledge in advocating that the same sort of account should be provided for scientific error and success. She rejects Laudan's arationality assumption that sociological explanations are adequate only when science fails. Harding explicitly argues that true beliefs, as well as false ones, have social causes which are relevant to their epistemic evaluation (1991: 81–2). Furthermore, she holds that the falsity of internalists' accounts of science entails the falsity of objectivism. Objectivism is to be understood as value-neutral objectivity, which is the objectivity achieved by the use of reason alone, unaffected by emotions and human interests.[43] Many feminists have argued, instead, that true objectivity is achieved through an apt employment of emotions and a critical reflection on interests.

Other feminist critics have derived a very different lesson from the failure of objectivism and absolute realism. Due to the influence of postmodernism they have come to doubt the practical utility and theoretical validity of the whole epistemological and philosophical project. These sentiments have been expressed, for example, by Jane Flax (1993). Although her position permits different interpretations, she appears to support a rather strong version of relativism which undermines the epistemological enterprise itself, since epistemology survives only if we admit that there is a difference between knowledge and non-knowledge. It is not only postmodernism that appears to have threatened the philosophical study of scientific knowledge, another strong opponent is to be found in the most sociological strands of the sociology of knowledge.

B. The sociology of knowledge[44]

The sociology of scientific knowledge emerges in the 1970s, and is characteristic of the lesson learned by sociologists from Kuhn's work. While philosophers have argued in favor of a different understanding of the rationality of science, sociologists have argued that science, like any other human activity, is better understood causally using the tools of the social sciences. They have also given prominence to Kuhn's claim that mature scientific disciplines have gone through different and incommensurable paradigms. Kuhn himself had argued that real science is a matter of problem solving within a paradigm, but sociologists have tended to see paradigm shifts as more characteristic of the nature of scientific inquiry.

Kuhn had pointed out that changes in any area of science are brought into being by the creation, through a revolution, of a new paradigm which is a set of assumptions and doctrines that together constitute a new worldview.[45] These different paradigms cannot be compared since they set for themselves very different sorts of problem. Furthermore, since the paradigms lead their supporters to see the world in very different ways, there is no neutral evidence by means of which their disputes can be adjudicated rationally. Sociologists have drawn relativistic conclusions from these claims, they have argued that science is not at all a rational enterprise.

The sociology of science has been developed in opposition to philosophical internalist accounts of this area of human inquiry. Sociologists give accounts of the development of scientific knowledge which invoke external factors, and tend to be at least skeptical about the rationality of science. Sociological explanations were first developed by Barry Barnes and David Bloor, who founded in Edinburgh the school known as 'the Strong Program in the Sociology of Knowledge' (Barnes, 1977). This program is labeled 'strong' because it supports the symmetry hypothesis: namely, the view that the same social factors account for both bad and good science.

Usually supporters of the Edinburgh school focus on the macrosocial aspects of scientific inquiry;[46] they find causal links between the contents of the theories advanced by scientists and the interests of the relevant groups. They believe that the scientific community comes to accept those theories that best serve the political interests of the dominant classes to which scientists belong, because they serve those interests. Although, of course, scientists themselves might not be aware of this phenomenon. Furthermore, supporters of the Strong Program hold that good science is not different from bad science in this respect. Hence, the Strong Program supports social constructivism about science, according to which the aim of science is neither to explain an independent reality nor to develop powerfully predictive theories. Rather, science, which is made up by scientists as they go along, constructs the reality it purports to explain.

During the late 1970s Bruno Latour's work initiated a new ethnographic approach to the study of science (Latour and Woolgar, 1979), characterized by a focus on the everyday activities and interactions of scientists within the laboratory. This new approach shares the social constructivism of the Strong Program, but uses new sociological methods and focuses on social interactions in the everyday environments of scientists, rather than on the structure of society at large. Sandra Harding has criticized this latter aspect of the sociology of knowledge. In her opinion it leads to a view of scientific communities as isolated from the larger social context. The focus on the micro-processes in the laboratory excludes any consideration of race, gender, and class relations from the analyses of science (1991: 162). Harding herself supports some of the tenets of the sociology of scientific knowledge. She subscribes to the symmetry hypothesis advanced by the Edinburgh school, but she criticizes this school for exempting from analysis their own productions of scientific knowledge of the social world (1991: 82).[47]

Although the sociology of scientific knowledge seems radically opposed to philosophical accounts of science, these two approaches share many features. First, they are both very timid about providing critiques of the actual practices of scientists. Philosophers refrain because they take them to be rational; sociologists, instead, because they antagonize the authority given to science, and concern themselves simply with exposing the social character of this form of inquiry. In this respect feminist reflection on science, even when sympathetic to sociological approaches, shows a marked difference from dominant trends. Instead of rejecting or accepting science *tout court*, it is involved in a rational critique of scientific activities.

Second, both philosophers and sociologists view science as a unitary activity. They believe that it is possible to give a general account of what makes some activities scientific. The third and most important shared feature between these two approaches is their almost exclusive concern with scientific theories rather than practices. This is not to say that activities are ignored altogether; instead, they are considered only for their contribution to the production of theories. Furthermore, with a few exceptions, both philosophers and sociologists think of scientific theories in terms of the representational model I have described in the first section of this chapter. In my opinion this view of science is doubly mistaken: first, it ignores that the development and confirmation of theories are not the only aims of scientific practice; second, it fails above all to see that theorizing is also a practice. Knowledge should be understood in terms of engagements with the world.[48] In the last few years some sociologists have argued for the necessity to provide accounts of scientific practices. However, since they see practice as opposed to knowledge, they fail to realize that knowledge is just one sort of practice. They do not abandon the representational account of knowledge.[49] The last approach to science, I discuss, is instead characterized by a move exactly in this direction.

C. The cultural study of scientific knowledge

Cultural studies of scientific knowledge are a recent addition to the reflection on science. This approach has been developed in recent years by feminist philosophers such as Susan Bordo and Elizabeth Potter, historians of science like Donna Haraway, anthropologists like Sharon Traweek, and scientists such as Evelyn Fox Keller.[50] They have applied to the study of science the whole range of critiques and analyses which are appropriate for many other cultural phenomena.

Scientific knowledge, as we know it, has mainly been developed in Western societies. It is unlikely that this is a pure coincidence. It is much more likely that the cultural climate of these societies has been a contributory factor to the emergence of the natural sciences. This simple consideration strongly suggests that a cultural approach to science is a worthwhile activity. Third World critics, for example, have drawn illuminating parallels between the Western system of beliefs about the natural world and eurocentrism. Feminists have pointed out that culturally entrenched stories about science rely on a series of dichotomies that exclude 'woman' from the class of knowers. In particular the association of the feminine with passivity and with nature as opposed to the masculine which is active and part of culture has been the object of much feminist reflection.[51] Often feminist analyses of these dichotomies and their association with gender have employed the whole range of critical tools made available by cultural studies, including psychoanalytic theory.[52]

This new approach challenges the belief in the existence of a clear-cut boundary between what is internal and what is external to science. It should not be understood as a mere extension of the sociology of knowledge to include general features of Western culture among the *causes* of science. Instead, the cultural approach to science aims to make explicit the background of social practices within which scientific activity gains its significance. Because the supporters of the cultural studies of science do not believe that their object of inquiry can be sharply separated from the rest of culture, they are not inclined either to vindicate the whole of science, or to reject completely its authority. Donna Haraway is a good example in this regard: her accounts are science-friendly without being uncritical. This approach represents a break with the 'quietism' of so much philosophy and sociology.

The cultural approach also encourages one to think about science in terms of practices which are to some extent local and which have a material element to them. It supports the view that knowledge as a kind of practice is always situated (Haraway, 1988). The cultural critic's cognitive practices are not exempt from this consideration; therefore, her position should also be the subject of analysis (Traweek, 1992: 435). In turn, this move, by bringing out the voice of the author within the text, instead of obliterating it behind the neutral language of facts, furthers the development of new ways of writing about science. Style, for Haraway and Traweek, matters; it is not just empty rhetoric.

The emphasis on practices characteristic of the cultural approach to science makes possible an enhanced sensitivity to the heterogeneity and open-endedness of this form of activity. As such, it has been argued by Rouse (1996), cultural studies encourages us to re-think the coherence and significance of scientific work in terms of an 'ongoing reconstruction of contested narrative fields' (1996: 169). Following Haraway he argues that scientists perceive their activities as part of an ongoing process because they continually produce new narratives about how results in their area fit together, and where the discipline is going. There is no appeal to widespread background beliefs, or to unrealistically uniform communities of scientists. This approach, besides doing justice to the variety of positions within scientific communities, opens up new ways of understanding how science, like any other human activity, acquires its significance only in a broader cultural context.

These scattered observations cannot aspire to be a satisfactory introduction to this new interdisciplinary approach. I hope, however, that the following chapters will succeed in showing how feminist cultural critiques have been deployed in different areas of science.

Further Reading

A useful introduction to analytic epistemology is Jonathan Dancy's *An Introduction to Contemporary Epistemology* (1985). Perspicuous summaries of the main positions held by continental epistemologists can be found in Linda Alcoff's 'Continental Epistemology' (1992) and in Charles Mills' 'Alternative Epistemology' (1988). Lorraine Code's 'Feminist Epistemology' (1992) provides an overview of feminist theories of knowledge.

Chapter 1 of Steve Fuller's *Philosophy of Science and its Discontents* (1993) outlines the different positions held by philosophers of science, while Andrew Pickering's 'From Science as Knowledge to Science as Practice' (1992) provides a useful overview of the sociology of science; the cultural approach to science is explained in the last chapter of Joseph Rouse's *Engaging Science: How to Understand Its Practices Philosophically* (1996). Donna Haraway's 'The Promises of Monsters: A Regenerative Politics for Inappropriate/d Others' (1992) puts it into practice.

Notes

1 There are epistemic issues that, so far, have been explored only by feminist philosophers. No more than this needs to be read into my claim.

2 Interest in the history of analytical philosophy has increased in recent years. Although scholars appear to agree that Gottlob Frege, a German mathematician, is probably the founding father of this tradition in philosophy, it is in the Vienna Circle that one finds the origins of the kind of epistemology and philosophy of science practiced by analytical philosophers.

3 It is perhaps a mistake to think of continental philosophy as a tradition, since the label is of use only to analytic philosophers when they characterize the work of those who do not fit in their own tradition.

4 There are also feminists whose work can be placed squarely within one tradition. Louise Antony (1993), for instance, identifies herself as an analytic philosopher. Luce Irigaray could be considered a continental philosopher.

5 For him 'philosophy will have no more to offer than common sense [supplemented by the natural and social sciences] about knowledge' (1979: 176).

6 Strictly speaking the claim I have attributed to Lyotard could be read along Quinean lines. I believe such an interpretation to be farfetched. If this were what Lyotard meant, he would have talked of the human condition rather than the postmodern one.

7   This point is made by Sellars (1997: 75–9).

8   My suggestion, therefore, amounts to a rejection of both foundationalism and coherentism. The latter is the view that justification is always a matter of inference.

9   For example, Hegel criticized any notion of immediate knowledge.

10   Descartes uses 'thought' as a general term which includes perceiving and willing (1980: 63). This use of the term indicates that he sees all our cognitive abilities as essentially involving representations.

11   Supporters of this view are too many to mention, but they include some of the leading philosophers in the field such as Jerry Fodor and William Lycan.

12   A clear formulation of this position can be found in *The Will to Power* (1968) sect. 480.

13   My account of Heidegger's position is especially indebted to Taylor (1987), Haugeland (1982), and Brandom (1983).

14   For a discussion of this issue, see Ginzberg (1987).

15   Antony makes the same point in a different context. She gives a baseball as an example of a socially constituted entity (1995: 163).

16   Some have discussed the social features of individual knowers which have epistemic relevance (Code, 1991: 4). Others have argued that the primary subjects of knowledge are social groups rather than individuals (Nelson, 1990: 255).

17   Code phrases this point in terms of the relevance of the identity of the knower (Code, 1991: 2). This is a stronger claim than the one I have made about the relevance of social locations. It is also a claim that commits Code to the theoretical fruitfulness of a problematic notion of identity. Code's point about the situatedness of knowledge and the consequent epistemic relevance of the subjectivity of the knower does not, however, need to be cashed out in terms of identity.

18   This is a widely held opinion among contemporary analytic philosophers.

19   This is the tripartite analysis of knowledge as true, justified belief that has dominated twentieth-century analytic philosophy.

20   This is not a view which is shared by contemporary analytic philosophers. It finds its origin in the belief that knowledge is something we achieve rather than something that happens to us. I discuss these views in chapter 2.

21   See among others Keller (1985) and Schmitt (1987).

22   The search for the common property is not just a feature of analytic epistemologists. Often sociologists have looked for common defining features of all the interactions which lead to the production of knowledge.

23   Recently some have dispensed with justification altogether and given a purely causal account of knowledge. William Alston, for example, holds this position (1989: 181).

24   Social factors may, of course, enter in the explanation of error. They may be the reason why a given representation is not justified.

25   I talk of methods here because it is quite common to conceive of practices as rule-governed activities. This is not my understanding of them, but it is useful

to bring to light the discontinuities between contemporary analytical episte-mology and the Cartesian tradition.

26   This approach to epistemology was initiated by Roderick Chisholm, and it is probably a consequence of the importance attributed to the rational recon-struction of science by the Vienna Circle.

27   I am indebted to Alcoff (1995/6) for these points.

28   They hold this position in *Dialectic of Enlightenment* (1991).

29   The disagreements are so severe that they have led to the production of new disciplinary discourses. This phenomenon is exemplified by the creation of new departments in universities: for example, departments of science studies, and of history and philosophy of science. They host groups of thinkers who share the same concerns and methodological assumptions.

30   In this section I am much indebted to Fuller (1993) and Rouse (1996).

31   Ian Hacking's work is an exception in this regard. See e.g. his *Representing and Intervening* (1983).

32   For more on this see section B below.

33   They also held that only claims of this sort are meaningful.

34   This is one of the two dogmas that Quine criticizes in his seminal paper 'Two Dogmas of Empiricism' (1961).

35   This point is forcefully made by Rouse (1996, ch. 4).

36   Eminent supporters of these programs are: Bas van Fraassen (instrumentalism), Larry Laudan (historical rationalism), Richard Boyd (scientific realism), and Bruno Latour (social constructivism).

37   Rouse is keen to emphasize that he is not a constructivist. However, he admits that his views bear close resemblance to that position (1987: 129).

38   This view has been adopted by Boyd (1991), and by Hacking (1983).

39   Van Fraassen (1980) is the most prominent supporter of a similar instrumen-talist view.

40   This view is usually supported only by sociologists of science. Mulkay (1990) is a good example.

41   See, for example, Code (1991), Harding (1991), and Nelson (1990) among others.

42   Marxist analyses of science were, for example, conducted by the left-wing scientists Hilary Rose and Steven Rose (1976); Merchant (1980) claims that Western science involves the exploitation of both human and natural resources; while Elizabeth Fee (1983) has analyzed the consequences of current scientific attitudes for women's everyday lives.

43   Several feminists have presented arguments against this conception of objectiv-ity. For example, Harding (1991), Code (1991), Keller (1985), Bordo (1987), Haslanger (1993) in the North American context. In the French context Irigaray has developed a powerful critique of the kind of rationality required by objectivism (Irigaray, 1985).

44   For a brief history of this program see Pickering (1992).

45   This is the traditional interpretation of Kuhnian paradigms as shared sets of beliefs. This interpretation is criticized by Rouse, who holds that Kuhnian

paradigms are best seen as a set of shared practices rather than shared beliefs (1987: 31).

46   On the other hand, the Bath school led by Harry Collins focused on the micro-aspects of the sociology of scientific knowledge.

47   She rejects, however, Steve Woolgar's solution to this problem faced by the Strong Program because it leads to embracing a totally unhelpful relativism (1991: 82). Nevertheless, Harding follows him in giving a central role to reflexivity about one's own knowledge production (1991: 163). Woolgar's own account of reflexivity is found in (1988a).

48   This is not say that there is no propositional knowledge in science. Scientific theories provide representations of the world. However, representations are tools we use to deal with the world. Rouse (1996) is wrong to attempt to deflate content.

49   This attitude is exemplified by Andrew Pickering (1992).

50   See, for example, Bordo (1987), Potter (1994), Haraway (1989) and (1992), Traweek (1992), and Keller (1985).

51   For example, see Keller (1985), and Bordo (1987).

52   In the United States, feminists working in the philosophy and history of science have mainly used object relations theory (Keller, 1985). French feminists have, instead, preferred Lacanian psychoanalysis (Irigaray, 1987).

2

Feminism and 'Malestream' Epistemology

In chapter 1 I provided an overview of epistemology, and discussed some aspects of continuity and difference between traditional and feminist theories of knowledge. Some of the basic assumptions made by many feminists in this field differ from those adopted by most mainstream philosophers. For example, I have mentioned that feminist thinkers usually reject the individualism typical of traditional approaches to knowledge. What characterizes feminist epistemology in its broadest sense is the belief that gender is a category which is relevant to the study of knowledge. Social and political factors, in other words, matter to knowledge. They matter epistemically; that is, they can play a role in what gives support to a claim. Other, more traditional, sorts of epistemology have, instead, assumed gender to be epistemically irrelevant. In this chapter I discuss several feminist critiques of the commitments and views accepted by philosophers working within the framework of traditional analytic thinking. These are views and commitments that are responsible for the inability to theorize the importance of gender which is a characteristic of mainstream epistemology.

Feminist opposition to mainstream thinking combines internal and external criticisms. That is, feminists are engaged both in revealing internal tensions and contradictions within mainstream theories, and in bringing to light those dimensions of knowledge that have been ignored by traditional epistemologists. In this chapter I discuss two related aspects of traditional epistemology which have undergone particularly severe criticism by feminist thinkers: its individualism, and its conception of the subject who has knowledge. Feminist criticisms of these features of traditional theories of knowledge have taken very different forms; I concentrate on *philosophical* critiques of individualism, and *psychoanalytical* elucidations of the traditional subject of knowledge. These two kinds of criticism, I argue, are best seen as complementing each other. They elucidate the shortcomings of the picture endorsed by traditional epistemology.

Feminist Criticisms of Individualism in Epistemology

Several feminist thinkers have remarked on the individualism of traditional epistemology. This individualism encourages a conception of the knower as an isolated individual who achieves knowledge thanks only to his own efforts. Such a conception places an undue emphasis on the importance of autonomy as a precondition for knowledge. It also downplays the importance of social context in the process of knowledge acquisition. It thus makes it impossible to appreciate the importance of social factors, like gender, for the theory of knowledge.

It is rather difficult to spell out what is individualistic epistemology. As a consequence, some philosophers have come to think of this sort of epistemology merely as non-social theory of knowledge.[1] It is probably better thought of as a loosely connected family of approaches to knowledge. It would be a mistake to think that epistemology has not undergone several changes in the last three hundred years. Nevertheless, it is possible to provide an account of the connections between different individualistic approaches. This I aim to do in this section by using the work of feminist and other cultural critics of theories of knowledge. On the basis of this account, I assess whether and to what extent contemporary epistemology is still individualistic. Finally, I produce some arguments for the rejection of some forms of individualism in the theory of knowledge.

A word of caution is necessary before I introduce an analysis of individualism. I rely throughout on the implicit assumption that to understand this approach to the theory of knowledge one must consider the social contexts within which it was developed. I may therefore seem to beg the question of its validity. Readers with this sort of worry can bring the distinction between discovery and justification to bear on my analysis. They may treat what I have to say about the characteristics of individualism as pertaining exclusively to the first context. What I have to say about the feasibility of this approach to knowledge will, I believe, stand nevertheless.

For readers of a different sensitivity I can offer another motivation for my interpretative stance. When one accepts that social factors are epistemically relevant to knowledge, one cannot treat epistemology, knowledge about knowledge, differently. Social factors equally matter to it; epistemology, too, is socially situated. One cannot assess any theory of knowledge unless one considers the factors that led to its emergence and its continuation. These considerations do not automatically open the door to nasty forms of epistemological relativism. The methods which maximize knowledge might differ depending on social circumstances. Suppose that I find myself in a context of extreme competition, I have no reason to believe that others will tell me what I need to know or that they won't try to mislead me. Given this social context, the best epistemology is one that recommends that I find out by myself what I need to know. On the other hand, in a different situation it would be better to ask others who have more experience about the issues. The characteristics of the society for which a theory of knowledge is elaborated should be taken into account when assessing that epistemology.

Individualism in the theory of knowledge first emerged in the early modern period. Many critics of this approach see Descartes as its forefather.[2] It has, however, also a distinctive empiricist strand. It does not seem inappropriate, therefore, to take Locke as a co-founding father of epistemological individualism. These philosophers lived in times of social and religious unrest. One of the characteristics of the sixteenth and early seventeenth centuries is an extensive questioning of the legitimacy of traditional sources of authority: the church and the king. The reformist movement, for example, had called into question the authority of the pope. Locke lived through a civil war between parliament and King Charles I, at the end of which the king was brought to trial and executed.

The widespread challenge to established political authority was instrumental in the development of a new account of how knowledge is best acquired and evaluated. But to see how this worked one needs to make a step backward. In the Middle Ages the scholastics considered claims to belong to one of two epistemic categories: demonstrative knowledge or opinion. The first concerned what could be deduced from first principles; the second regarded what was only more or less probable. However, 'probable' meant that authoritative people approved of it (Hacking, 1975: 22). Thus, there was no equivalent of the contemporary notion of probability that takes a claim to be probable if it is likely to be true. By the time Descartes appeared scholastic categories had come to grief. In particular, the many challenges to received authorities made it impossible to rely on them to acquire knowledge.[3]

One could not, however, trust only those authorities whose claims were most likely to be true, since this attitude presupposes a notion of probability that was not available at the time. The concept of evidence also requires a grasp of probability, since the evidence for a claim is provided by those considerations that increase the likelihood of its truth. Without a clear notion of evidence, there was no sense that one may assess the testimony of others in terms of their intrinsic credibility. The only alternative to complete trust was wholesale rejection. Thus, one could only go on one's own in the search for knowledge. This is what Descartes did. Cartesian epistemology, hence, fits the bill of the most common characterization of individualism, which, according to Alison Jaggar, sees 'the attainment of knowledge as a project for each individual on her or his own' (1983: 355).[4]

Lorraine Code also traces the beginning of individualism to Descartes. In particular, she discusses the autonomy which he attributes to reason. Code holds that there are two ways in which, for Descartes, reason is autonomous. Firstly, its proper employment requires that the individual undertakes his inquiries alone; secondly, it is properly employed independently of other human cognitive faculties (1991: 112). Descartes inaugurates the view that knowledge can be achieved only if one is not influenced by traditions or by the community. Knowledge requires autonomy as absence of external interference. Notoriously, Descartes claimed to have found in the cogito a new secure foundation on which to rebuild knowledge. This foundation was located in the privacy of one's own mind, and could only be discovered by the unfettered use of reason.[5]

The next stage in the history of individualism is its transformation in the hands of empiricists like Locke and Hume. As Michel Foucault points out (1970: 61), around this time a new understanding of the notion of sign had been developed, which included the distinction between natural and conventional linguistic signs. This made two moves, essential to Lockean empiricism, possible. First, nature itself could provide testimony through its natural signs, it did not have to be interpreted through the lenses of authoritative books or other sources. It was thus possible to rely directly on the testimony of the senses. Second, conventional signs were taken to be outside nature. This second fact, when combined with the notion that ideas belong to a inner private space, gives rise to the sort of representationalism which I have discussed in chapter 1.

The distinction between two kinds of sign makes it possible to draw a parallel distinction between sources of epistemic authority: the testimony of nature, and the testimony of others. At the same time, as Ian Hacking has convincingly argued, we observe the emergence of the contemporary notion of probability (1975: 44, 47). The latter would have allowed for a middle ground between Cartesian rejection of external authority and slavish obedience to it. It would have made it possible to evaluate the credibility of human testimony on the basis of nature and of the opinion of tradition. Empiricism prevented this development toward a more social epistemology, since it was committed to accepting only the authority of the senses (Stout, 1981: 74).

Epistemology thus remains firmly individualistic. The pursuit of knowledge can be successfully accomplished only when one is free from external human interference. The basis of knowledge is to be found in the deliverances of the senses; that is, representations which, within the individual, mirror nature outside. Furthermore, individualism acquires a new dimension: the facts alone can provide evidential support for our claims, any other sort of evidence is either ruled out or it must be based on factual evidence.[6]

I would like to interrupt this historical account to make a comment on Jaggar's explanation of epistemological individualism. Although she is aware of the differences between early modern and twentieth century theories of knowledge, she does not, in my opinion, spell them out sufficiently. For example, Descartes was interested in how to acquire knowledge, while more contemporary epistemologists investigate the nature of the relation between the evidence and what it is meant to support. Since Cartesian epistemology is focused on methodological questions, it does not share the very purified concerns of twentieth century analytic theory of knowledge.

Jaggar claims that contemporary analytic theories of knowledge constitute the culmination of an individualistic tradition initiated by Descartes and developed by the logical positivist movement. The logical positivists, she holds, endorsed the possibility of reducing all knowledge to physical knowledge. They claimed that science is the only source of knowledge, and that all sciences can be reduced to physics. Knowledge, they held, requires objectivity. Scientists must attempt to adopt a value-neutral attitude, which would secure the absence of bias. They must be detached from their values, emotions, and interests. Therefore, Jaggar concludes 'the good scientist of positivism is the abstract individual of liberal political theory' (1983: 356). This is the individual stripped of any specificity deriving from social and cultural location.

Jaggar suggests that, as a consequence of its individualism, traditional epistemology fails to see that knowledge production is always socially situated. It assumes an understanding of objectivity as value-neutrality according to which knowledge is achieved only if knowers keep in check their subjectivity. It also makes metaphysical assumptions about the nature of reality; that is, it assumes that reality is physical and exists independently of the knower. Jaggar, thus, paints a picture of the tradition in the theory of knowledge according to which we acquire knowledge by forming representations of a pre-existing reality. Our knowledge is a mirror of what is known, the result of any subjective input is a distortion on the reflecting surface.

I have claimed in chapter 1 that there are links between individualism and the view that knowledge essentially involves representations. One must, however, be very careful not to confuse these two features of traditional epistemology with the empiricist conception of the mind as a passive mirror of external mind-independent reality. For example, Kant subscribed to individualism, but he did not take the mind to be passive. The Copernican revolution he took himself to have initiated, centered precisely on the claim that the object of experience is partly constituted by the mind itself. Our representations do not represent a reality of things in themselves which exist independently of us. Rather, the mind constructs these representations.

A similar problem with Jaggar's account is raised by Louise Antony; she argues that it grafts a Cartesian theory of mind onto a Lockean empiricist theory of knowledge (1993: 194). The Cartesian rationalist tradition takes epistemology to provide the method which each individual must follow to achieve knowledge. This method involves the autonomous use of reason which for the rationalists constitutes the essential feature of the human mind. However, the view that all knowledge is ultimately derived from the impression of experiences onto a passive mind belongs only to Lockean epistemology. Empiricists claim that any trace of subjectivity must be erased in order to achieve knowledge. Rationalists, like Descartes, were, instead, aware that bias might be inevitable. Rationalists, that is, knew that the constitution of the human mind constrains the development of knowledge. Antony concludes that Jaggar's critique distorts and oversimplifies the early modern tradition because it confuses the empiricist conception of value-neutrality with rationalist views about reason, and method (1993: 193). Although Antony might be correct, her criticism is not fatal for Jaggar's position. If we take the latter to describe the dominant conception of knowledge in our culture, it is entirely possible that this cultural product is the result of combining several theories and traditions into an, often incoherent, whole.

Nevertheless, I find Jaggar's account unsatisfactory for at least two reasons. First, her explanation of individualism fits perfectly only Locke's epistemology. Individualism goes hand in hand with the view that knowledge is a matter of representations, but it does not require the Lockean conception of the mind as passive. Second, Jaggar forges too tight a connection between individualism and the problem of objectivity.

It is to this second point that I now wish to turn. Code joins Jaggar in finding a conceptual link between individualism and the notion of objectivity as value-neutrality. She claims that 'only a knower who is autonomous . . . could be as objective as that stark conception requires' (1991: 112). I think this is a mistake, objectivity is not a problem only for individualistic epistemology. Furthermore, if by autonomous knower we mean somebody who does not allow any external factors to influence her judgment, there is no reason why such a knower should not employ values as long as those too have been arrived at autonomously. True, the conception of objectivity as value-neutrality has characterized traditional epistemology. But this is an empiricist feature, it is not a consequence of individualism.

Some feminists have presented a different sort of argument for the intimate connection between the autonomy required by individualism, and the posture of detachment necessary for value-neutrality. The nature of this connection according to them, however, is not conceptual. Rather, as Evelyn Fox Keller points out in *Reflections on Gender and Science*, these features of traditional epistemology are unified in a psychoanalytic account of the emotional needs of a specific kind of subject (1985: 124). I discuss this issue in the second section of this chapter.

I now return to the historical development of individualism in epistemology. In particular I want to look at how it has been transformed in the eighteenth century by the work of Kant. In his answer to the question 'What is Enlightenment?' Kant characterizes the Enlightenment as the way out of immaturity (1986: 263). The latter is the state of our will to accept the authority of others in matters concerning the employment of reason alone. Individuals are responsible for their own state of immaturity, since they can escape it by bringing about a change in themselves. To do so involves having the courage to know autonomously.

Kant has thus fleshed out a new, stronger notion of the kind of autonomy required to acquire knowledge. Freedom from external interference is not sufficient, doing as one chooses or wishes is as important. The autonomous individual is someone who does things, rather than somebody to whom things happen. Thus, autonomy is linked to control and to the responsibility that goes with it. For Kant, we are under an obligation to become autonomous epistemic subjects. This is a state each person can bring about by using her own will.

Another aspect of Kantian epistemology is also relevant to the history of individualism. It regards a new conception of the self who is capable of knowledge. Kant's account of the transcendental subject in the *Critique of Pure Reason* is formal in nature. Very roughly speaking the transcendental subject is what makes it possible for the knower to be self-aware. In turn, self-consciousness is, for Kant, a necessary feature of any form of awareness. Thus, as Code remarks, 'the analysis Kant offers is of the knowledge of a "standard knower", undifferentiated from any other knowers by any of his particular traits' (1991: 113).

These two features of Kantian epistemology have contributed to shaping the individualism of twentieth century theories of knowledge. Analytic epistemologists have often explained the difference between knowledge and a lucky guess in terms of fulfilling one's epistemic obligations. One should not rush to judgment. One must try to gather all the relevant evidence, consider whether it sufficiently supports one's beliefs, withhold opinion in dubious cases, and so forth. This view, according to which justification is a matter of how one stands *vis-à-vis* epistemic obligations, is commonly known as the deontological conception of justification.[7] It presupposes a Kantian notion of autonomy with regard to holding beliefs. It makes no sense to talk about epistemic obligations unless we can be held responsible for fulfilling them. In turn, this makes sense only if it is within our control to do so.

The deontological conception of justification motivated the adoption of internalism. This position can be formulated in several different ways, but it always concerns some sort of constraint about what could justify a belief.[8] Typically it claims that what justifies a belief must be something the subject can become aware of simply by means of reflection. The motivation for this restriction comes from the deontological conception. It would seem that, unless the evidence for our beliefs is something we can be aware of, we could not be held responsible for failing to check whether it stands up to scrutiny.

Twentieth century analytic epistemology also inherits the formalism of the Kantian approach. When it comes to justification, the relation between reasons and what they support, one can abstract from all those features which distinguish one knower from any other. This is the sort of individualism which employs the formal conception of the person that, as Jaggar remarks, is at the basis of liberal political theory.

More recently, mainstream analytic epistemology has changed in many respects. Most notably it has taken a naturalistic and externalist turn.[9] This sort of naturalism, which Quine has advocated, can assume different forms. However, it always involves demarcating knowledge from lucky guesses in terms of the causes of belief. One may still talk of reasons for belief, but this talk should at least be expressible in terms of causes. Naturalism holds that how a belief is arrived at contributes to determining whether that belief is knowledge. It is also externalist because it abandons any internalist constraints. In other words, naturalism makes knowledge dependent upon the context of discovery, and it rejects the view that we know only when we have autonomous reasons for believing what we believe.

Antony (1993) sees this approach as making a clear break with traditional epistemology. I believe that this is true only up to a point. Naturalists, for example, are not committed to thinking of knowledge acquisition as a solitary pursuit in the way Descartes did. Naturalists also reject the more Kantian aspects of epistemology. They abandon the voluntarism and the formalism of deontological theories of justification. I do not want to undervalue the importance of these features of naturalized epistemology. In particular, I find it a particularly useful tool when attempting to make it plausible that gender may matter epistemically.

Some of the methods that people use to form their beliefs are socially acquired. Social circumstances influence which methods an individual might learn to use. They are also relevant to the reliability of the methods used. Hence, if, as many naturalists hold, knowledge is reliably acquired true belief, these social circumstances make a difference to the knowledge one has. In the same way in which reliable eyesight gives one visual knowledge, a reliable ability to discriminate cases of sexual harassment gives one some knowledge about sexism. Individuals differ in their discriminatory abilities; in some cases their social circumstances play an important role in the acquisition of reliable methods for the production of belief.

This more socialized conception of knowledge has, for example, been developed by Philip Kitcher, a contemporary analytic philosopher who adopts a reliabilist account. Kitcher holds that whether an individual has knowledge might depend on features of other individuals or of the community to which that individual belongs (1994: 113). This is a minimal conception of how knowledge is social, since it at least rejects the individualist tenet that knowledge is achieved only by individuals who do not rely on others for their knowledge. When knowledge is, thus, socialized some topics ignored by traditional epistemology take on center stage: for example, the issues of division of cognitive labor and of consensus formation within communities of knowers (1994: 114).[10]

Once it has been granted that social arrangements and relations make a difference to knowledge, it is but a short step to claim that gender is a relevant factor in theories of knowledge. Kitcher, thus, rephrases feminist standpoint epistemology in the language of analytic philosophy. I shall discuss standpoint epistemology in chapter 6; for now it suffices to say that it claims that the social locations of knowers make a difference to the extent and nature of their knowledge. Kitcher, who is a reliabilist, holds that knowledge is a matter of true belief acquired by means of processes which are reliable, that is, which more often than not give us true rather than false beliefs (1994: 113). Kitcher offers this way of incorporating feminist approaches into the more mainstream but socialized account:

> Feminist epistemology offers important insights in its recognition that each of us occupies a standpoint, and that standpoints make epistemic differences . . . The claim that a particular standpoint is preferable to others can thus be recast in terms of the relative reliability of the processes that standpoints make available. (1994: 124–5)

The social locations of knowers, that is, make a difference to the processes they employ to acquire knowledge and some of these processes are more reliable than others. Gender is, for Kitcher, one of the relevant factors that might make a difference to the reliability of belief acquisition; he cites as an example the developments in primatology, the study of primates like gorillas, since the 1970s.

Despite these considerations, I believe that naturalistic analytic epistemology is still mainly individualistic. One should not forget that, for Quine, naturalism showed that traditional epistemology should be substituted with individualistic psychology. Most important, however, is the tendency within naturalistic epistemology to see the social factors of knowledge as parasitic on its individualistic aspects.[11] Since knowledge is true reliable belief, there are only two ways in which social factors can be crucial for the reliability of belief-forming methods. Firstly, a person's social location plays a crucial role in the experiences she may have. These have an influence on the reliability of some of the methods this person acquires. But, social factors are relevant in this case only insofar as they are part of what causes the acquisition of reliable individualistic knowledge. Secondly, since some methods of belief acquisition rely on the beliefs of others, their reliability will depend on the reliability of the methods employed by other people. For example, if I adopt the method of relying on my doctor's diagnoses in matters of health, the reliability of my method will depend on that of the processes employed by the doctor in reaching her opinion. In this case too the social dimension of knowledge is factored out in terms of an individualist approach. Compare normal vision with vision aided by a microscope. In the first case, I rely only on my eyesight, in the second also on the reliability of the instrument. The microscope is a way of extending my individualistic knowledge processes. Kitcher's account reduces the social aspects of knowledge to an extension of its individualistic aspects.

Reliabilism, I believe, can never give us the basis for a thoroughly social epistemology. Its individualist commitments flow out from its representationalism. Reliabilists might hold that the content of individual representations depends on the social environment of the subject. The content of belief is not determined by what is in the head. They might also hold that the reliability of the processes for the acquisition of belief depends on the social location of the believer. Nevertheless, they are committed to the view that knowledge is not essentially social. An individual who exists independently of any society could still have at least some knowledge.

At this point one may ask whether individualism in epistemology must be rejected. There is no doubt that a very crude picture of individualism is totally unsatisfactory. As David Hull remarks:

> The reason that epistemologists have not been able to justify knowledge-claims in their sense of 'justify' is that no such justification exists. . . . They view knowledge acquisition in terms of an individual subject who confronts objects of knowledge in total isolation from other knowing subjects. On this view, languages mirror the world, but the 'world' is the sensations of the isolated knowing subject. . . . This epistemological stance places obstacles in the path of knowledge acquisition that are all but insurmountable. (1988: 13)

But epistemologists do not subscribe any longer to this picture. Can less extreme forms of individualism be preserved? Analytic philosophers who argue for the demise of individualism usually claim that it fails to account for much of the knowledge we possess, and which we have acquired merely by trusting other people (Webb, 1993). This is correct. Testimony is an independent source of evidence. Nevertheless, a critique of individualism, which is limited to making this point, will still accept the existence of some individualistic knowledge. It will not view knowledge itself as socially constituted. The framework I have presented in chapter 1 provides instead the basis for such a view. It holds that a claim can count as knowledge only against the background of social practices. I shall return to this toward the end of this section.

Furthermore, if we merely expand our theory of knowledge to include testimony as a further source of knowledge, we might still be captive of the severe restrictions that individualism imposes on epistemic evaluation. While it is not correct to say that we always need independent grounds to believe what other people say, it would also be a mistake to hold that only the actual reliability of other people matters. All sorts of moral, political, and epistemic evaluations are made when we rely on other people's opinions. Traditional epistemology fails to give them the necessary consideration.

Lynn Nelson advocates an even more radical move away from individualism than the one I have discussed.[12] I have not questioned that individuals are the primary subjects of knowledge. Communities have knowledge only in a derivative sense; that is, only insofar as their members have it (Kitcher, 1994: 113). Nelson, instead, holds the converse view. She argues that it is communities rather than individuals that, in a primary sense, have beliefs and knowledge. For her knowledge is always social. Nelson does not deny knowledge and belief to individuals, but she holds that they individually know and believe only in a derivative sense (1990: 256). She grounds her claim on the social public character of the conceptual apparatus which is a precondition for having beliefs (1990: 108). Furthermore, for Nelson knowledge depends on evidence, and the latter, she claims, is communal (1990: 255).[13] As I argue in chapter 4, I don't think that Nelson succeeds in establishing that communities are the primary subjects of knowledge, but she shows that individuals couldn't know if they were not members of a community. The two points are rather different. An example might make this clear: without a football team there could be no goalkeeping; nevertheless, it is the individual goalkeeper who keeps goal, not the team. Nelson considers objections of this sort, but, I argue in chapter 4, does not answer them satisfactorily (Nelson and Nelson, 1994: 497).

Some philosophers, for example John Hardwig, have argued for a position similar to Nelson's by considering some actual cases of acquisition of scientific knowledge. These are cases where, due to practical circumstances, it seems reasonable to claim that a community knows what none of its members knows in its entirety. This is a rather different claim from Nelson's much stronger assertion that in principle knowledge is a matter for communities. Instead, it simply asserts that in a limited range of examples we have communal knowledge which is in practice not reducible to individual knowledge. Nevertheless, it would seem that, at least in principle, even in these cases reduction to individual knowledge is possible. It is made practically unachievable by the finitude of our life spans.

In particle physics, and other highly theoretical sciences, it is rather common to see articles in specialist journals authored by more than ten people. These scientists did not, of course, write the article together, but they each contributed to some part of the research that produced the results divulged in the article. There are several reasons why research in these areas is done by teams rather than individuals. First, it would take an individual an enormous amount of time to carry out the whole of the research; in many cases, it would actually be impossible to do it within one's lifetime. Second, different parts of the research require different specializations which could not all be acquired by a single individual. Thus, in these cases it would seem that no individual member of the research team has the knowledge to carry out every part of the research, or even the knowledge to understand it all.

In these cases each member of the team relies on the claims made by others about their results. Thus, Hardwig argues that no individual is in the position to know or even understand the whole of the evidence which supports the claims they present as knowledge in their published article. If one knew only when that individual had the relevant evidence, then in these cases no individual scientist would know what they have published. Nevertheless, at least in some cases these communal efforts produce knowledge, knowledge which, it is argued, is possessed by the research team as a whole rather than by each of its members.[14]

This argument is mistaken. It is true that no single individual is in possession of all the necessary evidence in support of the claims made by the research team as a whole, but this fact does not prevent individuals from having knowledge. To suppose otherwise, is to assume that in the case of individual knowledge individualism is correct. It is only if one subscribes to the individualism of old-style mainstream epistemology that one can safely derive from the fact that an individual does not possess all the relevant evidence, that the individual does not know. But if knowledge is seen as social, an individual can be said to know even when he or she relies on evidence possessed by others for that item of knowledge. Hence, not even these examples support Nelson's claim that the primary subjects of knowledge are communities.

There are ways of arguing that knowledge is essentially social without denying that it is primarily individuals who have knowledge. Naomi Scheman, for example, has focused her criticisms on the philosophy of mind subtending individualistic epistemology. She denies that psychological states, like beliefs, can be understood in the manner required by the representationalist picture. In 'Individualism and the Objects of Psychology', Scheman argues against an individualistic assumption that 'the objects of psychology – emotions, beliefs, intentions, virtues and vices – attach to us singly', which is pervasive in contemporary psychology (1983: 226).

It is not very clear, however, what the assumption is. Scheman's first characterization suggests that she is attacking the view that the content of a belief can be determined by what is in the believer's head. She says that according to this view beliefs are individualist states of mind, in the way in which being five feet tall is an individualist feature of a person. Instead, she appears to suggest that we should liken belief to relational states such as being divorced (1983: 226). The marital status of an individual is a state of the person, but it is a state one can not be in unless one is related to others. Similarly, a relational view of belief says that the content of a belief depends on relations to what is outside the believer's head. Twenty years after her paper was written Scheman's view that the content of belief is not in the head is very popular in analytic philosophy. But, as Antony (1995) has pointed out, the individualist assumption that Scheman wants to get at goes beyond a mere rejection of internalism about the contents of psychological states.

In the same article Scheman also claims that psychological individualism is 'a realist thesis (emotions, beliefs, and so on are really there as particular states)' (1983: 232). Similarly, she sees it as making 'the assumption that my pain, anger, beliefs, intentions, and so on are particular, (in theory) identifiable states that I am in, which *enter as particulars into causal relationships*' [my italics] (1983: 226). These claims have prompted Jean Grimshaw to interpret Scheman as arguing against the view that it is individuals who have beliefs (1986: 164). I don't think this is Scheman's position. Closer to the mark is Antony (1995). She understands Scheman as opposing psychological realism (1995: 161). Antony assumes that psychological theories provide explanations of behavior in terms of their mental causes. Psychological realism is the view that beliefs and other mental states exist, and cause our behavior. Antony interprets Scheman as denying the existence of psychological states, because Scheman denies that they figure in causal explanations of behavior. Antony's conclusion is unwarranted. Scheman's position must be understood in its Wittgensteinian context: rational explanations of behavior are a matter of making intelligible patterns of behavior. Scheman, thus, is not saying that beliefs do not exist. They are simply not the sort of thing which can be understood causally. For Scheman, 'actual psychological explanations – from the commonsensical to the scientific – explain behaviors in context. Our ordinary psychological vocabulary, in particular, is ineliminably interpretative and normative' (1996: 152). Beliefs and desires, for Scheman, are patterns which emerge 'only from distinctive perspectives, in the light of distinctive social interpretative practices' (1996: 151).

Individuals, for Scheman, have beliefs. Nevertheless, psychological states are socially constituted. We define beliefs in terms of their content. The belief that Rome is in Italy, and the belief that Paris is in France are different beliefs because they have different contents. Thus, the content of a belief is what makes it the belief it is. Content, that is, is constitutive of belief. For Scheman, we attribute beliefs with given contents to individuals in order to make sense of their actions. Which beliefs we attribute to them will depend on what they do. But, actions are not the same as physical movements. The same physical movement could be either a bath or a baptism; these are two very different actions. Actions are categorized in terms of their significance, which they acquire only against the background of social practices. Since attributions of belief with a given content occur in the context of explanations of actions, and actions are partly constituted by social practices, beliefs will also be socially constituted. In particular, since beliefs are the psychological states we attribute to individuals when they make assertions, the social practice of giving and asking for reasons plays an important role in their constitution.[15] If I claim that Rome is in Italy, you attribute to me a belief with that content. My act counts as an asserting with that content, however, only if I have at least some mastery of what would follow from that claim, and what would count as a reason for it. Otherwise, you will be tempted to say that I do not know what I am talking about. Thus, a performance can count as an asserting only against the background of the social practice of giving and asking for reasons. Since beliefs are expressed by assertions, this particular social practice is crucial to an account of this kind of psychological state. Scheman's views about belief have important consequences for the theory of knowledge. Since knowledge is often understood as true justified belief, if belief is socially constituted, knowledge must also be so constituted. This view amounts to a complete rejection of individualism about the knowledge possessed by individuals.

To summarize, individualism as the view that knowledge is achievable only by a fully autonomous and separate knower has been subjected to severe criticisms by feminist philosophers. More recently some analytic philosophers have modified their individualism to admit that social factors are relevant to knowledge. These philosophers have claimed that it is individuals who have knowledge, but the social location of these individuals is relevant to how much and what knowledge they have. Although this is a step in the right direction, I have claimed that it does not go far enough. Social factors in these accounts are among the causes of knowledge. They can be part of what causes individuals to acquire some of their beliefs. They can also have a causal influence on the psychological makeup of individuals. In turn, differences in psychological character will make a difference to the reliability (or the justifications) of beliefs. These accounts, however, do not make social factors essential to knowledge.

Some feminists, like Nelson, have gone even further by claiming that knowledge and belief are primarily properties of communities rather than individuals. I have also considered an argument formulated by Hardwig in favor of the claim that communities can have knowledge that no individual possesses, but I have found it unconvincing. Finally, I have discussed Scheman's anti-individualist theory of mind. This approach is opposed to the framework presupposed by traditional epistemologists. I have argued that in Scheman's account social practices are constitutive of belief. Therefore, this account provides the basis for a truly social epistemology.

Feminist Objections to the Traditional Epistemic Subject

Traditional epistemology, I have explained, is individualist. This individualism, I have argued, does not always require a view of the mind as a passive mirror of outside reality. This is why epistemic individualism has outlived this old-fashioned theory of mind. Nevertheless, some common assumptions about knowledge, for example, that it requires emotional detachment and value-neutrality, have also been preserved despite the demise of the account of the mind that justified them.[16]

Some feminists have claimed to have found the connections between individualism and value-neutrality in the emotional needs of the epistemic subject: the knower. Value-neutrality does not follow from individualism or vice versa, but they are both symptoms or typical attitudes of the same kind of knowing subject. If the link between individualism and emotional detachment, as these feminist argue, is not conceptual, something other than philosophical reflection is required to unearth it. Psychoanalysis, which gives prominence to the role of desires in its account of the subject, seems to provide useful tools for this purpose.

The critique of traditional conceptions of the subject, and the attempt to develop alternatives to it, have been central to many feminist theories of knowledge. In this section I discuss some arguments in favor of the claim that the alleged universality of the traditional subject of knowledge is a mask. What is presented as a universal human ideal is in reality male.

There have been several interpretations of the kind of subject who would feel it necessary to be totally autonomous and value-neutral to achieve knowledge. For Richard Bernstein this is a subject who suffers from 'Cartesian Anxiety'. This is the anxiety that imposes the necessity of an Either/Or. Either knowledge has a fixed support, or we are prey to madness, intellectual and moral chaos (1983: 18). Keller has provided a more detailed analysis of the epistemic subject in her 'psychosociology of scientific knowledge' (1985: 13). Keller relies on psychoanalytic object relations theory to delineate the kind of subjectivity implicitly attributed to the epistemic subject in traditional theories of knowledge.[17] Object relations theory proposes an account of the development of the self both in terms of innate drives and of early experiences of relations to other individuals. Hence, the structure of the family and of the society in which children develop has an effect on the nature of this development.

In order to achieve full emotional and cognitive maturity, children need to develop a sense of themselves as separate from the surrounding environment. That is, they need to achieve personal autonomy. Although, this is required in children of both sexes, and there are similarities in the ways they achieve it, there are also important differences. In our society it is women who care for children, as a consequence children first develop their autonomy by demarcating themselves from their mothers. This is a process of demarcation which produces a longing to undo the differentiation, and an anxiety that one's autonomy may be threatened by a return to the undifferentiated stage. The need for separation from the mother is more acute in boys because it does not only serve the purpose of establishing oneself as a different individual from the mother, but also of establishing oneself as an individual of a different gender from that of the mother (1985: 88). Boys, because they undergo a double process of demarcation, have a stronger need for separation, and are consequently prone to more anxiety about undifferentiation.

In a society like ours where masculinity and femininity are seen as opposites, boys are subject to cultural pressures to develop a masculinity which must erase any traces of femininity. They are, that is, encouraged to see themselves as being completely different from women. They are thus led to see their separation from their mothers as a matter of radical independence. Boys develop a heightened and rigidified sense of autonomy, according to which autonomy is preserved only when there is total independence from others (1985: 97). This need for an exaggerated separation from others in order to preserve autonomy is a consequence of the construction of masculinity as that which contains not even a trace of femininity. Such a need engenders a self who must suppress any longing for the early stage of undifferentiation. The product is a self who is always anxious about his autonomy, for whom any loosening of the ego boundaries is equivalent to loosing the sense of oneself and precipitating into chaos. Furthermore, since temporary relaxations of the boundaries between self and other are necessary for emotional growth, the masculine subject comes to acquire an unemotional posture in his relations to the environment (1985: 82).

The cognitive development of the child is also related to the development of personal autonomy. By separating themselves from their environment children come to conceive of reality as external to them. They acquire a capacity for objectivity, that is, 'for delineating subject from object' (1985: 80). Objectivity is, thus, necessary for coming to know one's environment, and be able to satisfy one's needs. Consequently, 'objectivity . . . is the cognitive counterpart of psychological autonomy' (1985: 71). Autonomy is the result of emotional separation from the mother, objectivity is the result of cognitive separation from external reality.

'Objectivism,' which takes objectivity to be a radical separation between the knowing subject and the known object, corresponds to autonomy as total independence (1985: 97). The kind of subject, who needs to have total autonomy to preserve its sense of itself, requires a severance of subject from object in order to relate cognitively to external reality. Knowledge would thus require a total separation of subject from object. Furthermore, for Keller, since this sort of subject is defined as masculine, the reality or nature from which he is totally separated comes to be conceived of as feminine (1985: 79).

The issue of autonomy is also correlated to questions of power. Autonomy is the 'psychological sense of being able to act under one's own volition instead of under external control' (1985: 97). For Keller, the mindset which confuses autonomy with total separation also confuses objectivity with objectivism. The latter confusion arises from taking objectivity to require domination (1985: 98).

The preservation of autonomy requires a sense of power, of ability to control; a sense that one is an effective agent who is not under the control of external forces. However, when autonomy is conceived as radical independence, the boundaries between the ego and others are subject to constant monitoring which reveals, as I said before, a persistent anxiety. The issue of control, of not being under the control of others, becomes a dominant concern. The preoccupation with control is transformed into a preoccupation with domination and mastery through 'psychological assimilation of autonomy with external authority' (1985: 103). The sense of power which is necessary to autonomy, comes to be interpreted solely as power over others (1985: 97). When this conception of power is combined with a perception of the world as containing an already established hierarchy, dominance and submission become the only modes of relating to other individuals. To claim control, thus, becomes equivalent to claiming dominance.

The perception of the world as containing an established hierarchy is engendered by the child's encounter with adult authority in the figure of the father (1985: 109). Autonomy as separation from the maternal is offered to boys through identification with the father who offers 'the future prospect of domination of the maternal' (1985: 109). The child perceives the world as one where fathers have authority, an authority which receives legitimization both in the public and in the familial spheres. Thus, boys learn to conceive of autonomy as the achievement of domination over the feminine. Girls, on the other hand, learn from the father's authority submission as a technique of seduction (1985: 111).

When objectivity is confused with domination, as in the case of masculine subjectivity, the relation between the knowing subject and the known object becomes one of mastery and domination, that is, of objectification.

Keller's account attempts to show how the traditional epistemological requirements of individualism and value-neutrality can be seen as resulting from the cognitive posture of a personality which needs constantly to police ego boundaries. The cohesion between individualism and value-neutrality would not be intellectual; it would lie instead in the emotional needs of a certain kind of subject (Keller, 1985: 124). In other words, the traditional conception of what makes knowledge possible is designed for a certain kind of subjectivity; since this is a masculine subjectivity conceived as transcending anything feminine, the epistemic subject of traditional theories of knowledge is masculine.

Keller is not denying the importance of the search for reliable knowledge of the world, she is not claiming that women should reject science and objectivity altogether. Instead, she is trying to uncover the ideology of modern scientific knowledge and demonstrate the importance of gender in the development of this ideology. She is aware that her psychoanalytic account of gender identity is always in danger of being read as presenting gender as a natural, stable, and universal category (1985: 71). But what she is attempting to do is show how the ideology of gender influences psychological development, and how this ideology shapes the kind of personality that belongs to the knowing subject of traditional epistemology. In other words, she is arguing that science and socially constructed male gender identity seem to be made for each other.

I have presented Keller's position as an account of the connections between the male gender and the features of the subject presupposed by traditional accounts of knowledge. According to my reading Keller is talking about real men and women. This is an interpretation Keller would partly resist. She claims:

> It is important to emphasize that what I have been discussing is a *system of beliefs* about the meaning of masculine and feminine rather than any either intrinsic or actual differences between male and female. (1985: 87)

Keller here claims that she does not intend to provide an account of the character of real men and women. Instead, she wants to explain Western beliefs about what sort of personalities men and women should have. She claims to be talking about cultural sexual stereotypes, not real people. But her intention is frustrated by her use of object relations theory. The latter is a theory that purports to explain actual gender differences.[18] She is, of course, not talking about 'intrinsic' or biological differences between men and women; but it is hard to dispel the impression that Keller is discussing those differences between men and women which are generated by their different socialization.

Keller is right to assert that feminist accounts about the maleness of the subject of knowledge should focus on the cultural meanings of masculinity. But she is not sufficiently careful about the relations between sex, gender, and cultural symbolism to provide a detailed account of the metaphorical maleness of knowledge. Keller's account fails in two respects. First, she attempts to sever completely gender from bodily differences. She thus reproduces a sort of mind–body split that has been justly criticized by feminists. Second, she does not distinguish enough between social gender and cultural meanings to provide a detailed explanation of their interactions.

The convergence between Keller's account and Bernstein's diagnosis of traditional epistemology as suffering from 'Cartesian anxiety' is made explicit by Susan Bordo in her account of the Cartesian masculinization of thought. Bordo reads Descartes's work as a 'psychocultural story' (1987: 5) tracing the birth of the modern world out of the mother-world of the Middle Ages. This birth is characterized by 'a separation anxiety,' which is .

compensated by a need for a total separation from the maternal (1987: 58, 100). This flight from the feminine gives rise to objectivism, and to an attitude of detached mastery over nature which continues to be seen as feminine. Bordo traces in Descartes the birth of a new characterization of the epistemological stance which is required to achieve knowledge, and the simultaneous emergence of a new sort of masculine subjectivity.[19] Transcendence from the feminine, thus, becomes the central feature of both modern masculinity and the modern subject of knowledge. Bordo applies object relations theory to understand the development of the whole modern Western culture, thereby adding an historical dimension to Keller's psychosocial characterization of the ideology of scientific knowledge.

Bordo's account of the emergence of the modern epistemic subject has been criticized by Code for its troubling romanticism and its essentialism (1991: 53). While the charge of romanticism is correct,[20] that of essentialism needs to be carefully rephrased. To believe that Bordo's arguments rest on 'attributions of essential maleness [which] efface differences among men and claim a natural necessity for characteristics that are in fact typical only of an elite group of white men in specific situations of power, property, and political privilege' (Code, 1991: 53) is to misunderstand her point on several counts. Firstly, Bordo's argument traces the social construction of a new kind of masculinity, hence it is far from understanding it as a sort of natural necessity. It would be a mistake to read her as a biological essentialist. Secondly, Bordo's argument is about masculinity not individual men. Many individual men will not conform to this ideal masculinity, and they will be judged to be less manly because of this. Nevertheless, Bordo's employment of object relations theory faces the same difficulties encountered by Keller.

These accounts are, in my opinion, marred by an ambiguity. Sometimes Keller and Bordo provide causal accounts of the influence of social structures on the development of the psychological makeup of individuals. These structures have often caused men and women to develop different psychologies. They note that the methods which suit male psychology have been highly praised. These are the methods which are meant to give us scientific knowledge. They also point out that methods which would suit female psychologies have been unjustly undervalued. This unhappy situation can be resolved if we can find out which methods are more reliable. Once this has been discovered, social structures must be changed so that all children can develop the psychological makeup which will allow them to gain reliable information about the world. Thus, these accounts demonstrate why current child-rearing practices must be analyzed and modified.

There is, however, another aspect to these accounts. This other aspect is in evidence when Keller and Bordo focus on the cultural meanings attached to femininity and masculinity. They claim that gender norms, which are implicit in social practices, are part of the background against which science gains its significance. This is not a causal account of the relevance of gender to science, it is a cultural account of the significance of gender symbolism for science. I believe that Keller's and Bordo's reliance on object relations psychoanalysis could be at the root of this confusion. This psychoanalytic theory presents itself as scientific; it aims to give causal accounts. What we should try to make explicit, instead, is how gender norms or meanings are constitutive of scientific practice.

Critics of object relations theory usually have highlighted other problems with this approach; they have focused on its implicit social determinism (Moi, 1989). This sort of psychoanalysis sees masculinity and femininity as resulting from an internalization of social relations concerning parenthood; thus, it 'points to a social, rather than a natural, biological foundation for sexual identity' (Brennan, 1989: 8). However, if gender identity is an internalization of existing social norms, exceptions to gender stereotypes are impossible. Object relations theory can explain why men from different cultures and class backgrounds are different from each other, but it cannot explain the differences between men belonging to the same culture, race, and class.[21]

Object relations theory has been particularly under attack for its elision of the tension between psychical and social reality. For many feminists, who are convinced of the importance of psychoanalysis, object relations theory with its reduction of psychical reality to social reality gets things back to front. For them sexual difference is the foundation of the symbolic order, and as such it 'is not only the result of socialization but its condition' (Brennan, 1989: 8). Object relations theory, instead, provides an account of gender as floating free of bodily differences.

Luce Irigaray employs a psychoanalytic account of the symbolic and of the cultural imaginary to develop her critique of the epistemic subject in Western culture. The notions of 'the symbolic' and of 'the imaginary' were first developed by the French psychoanalyst Jacques Lacan. For Lacan the symbolic and the imaginary are opposed but interdependent terms. The imaginary is a moment in the formation of subjectivity insofar as it provides the conditions for becoming a subject. The baby through seeing the image of its own body reflected in a mirror (or by seeing itself as mirrored in an adult) first experiences itself as a whole. The imaginary is thus the stage when one transforms the image of others (or of a double) into a representation of oneself. Hence, Lacan refers to this stage as the mirror stage. At a cultural level the imaginary can be understood as providing the social representations of the self. Opposed to the imaginary is the symbolic. The symbolic is the stage when one achieves the position of a subject, this is done through an encounter with the Law of the Father. The child at the imaginary stage begins to differentiate itself through its relation with the Mother, but on realizing that she lacks the Phallus the child enters the stage of the symbolic. The Phallus is not, for Lacan, a sexual organ (penis), it is rather an emblem of language. It is what he calls a signifier; that is, a linguistic element with no fixed reference to external reality. The symbolic is the domain of language and of the social; the subject acquires its identity at the level of the symbolic: it acquires identity by being positioned by language as an 'I.'

Irigaray does not merely borrow Lacanian psychoanalytic theory; instead, she produces a sustained critique of its fundamental notions. Irigaray psychoanalyses Lacan's psychoanalytical theory to demonstrate that the unconscious images that subtend it are masculine and inevitably support the view of the female body as a defective male body (1985: 89).[22]

While she disagrees with the inevitability that Lacan attributes to his account of the formation of the subject, Irigaray also asserts that at the moment the symbolic order is male, which makes it impossible for women to achieve the position of subjects. Irigaray thus holds that the creation of a feminine symbolic and imaginary are the primary task of feminism.

For Irigaray, Western society is dominated by a mono-sexual (masculine) symbolic and imaginary. The masculine imaginary and symbolic are constructed through an exclusion of the feminine in the function of the mother. Men project their egos onto the world, thereby seeing themselves everywhere. Women, as mothers, are instead the matter through which men represent themselves, women thus never get represented. While men see their own images in a mirror, the mother is instead the mirror itself, she is therefore never represented. Thus, the unrepresented mother is that which makes a masculine imaginary possible. It is through this act, which is the equivalent of matricide, that the masculine imaginary of our society is constituted (1987: 84).[23]

In addition to the lack of recognition of the mother, women also fail to be represented as women. In our traditional conception of the family the mother is uniquely mother; thus a child has no image of woman, and therefore no image of sexual difference (1979: 44). That is, he or she has no representation that there are two sexes, rather than merely defective and fully fledged variants of the masculine sex. There is therefore no image of woman in the Western cultural imaginary. Since imaginary and symbolic are interdependent, there is also no feminine symbolic. As Margaret Whitford points out, without the imaginary the symbolic is empty of content, but without the symbolic the imaginary has no structure (1991: 91). Because there is no feminine symbolic, women, for Irigaray, are denied the position of subjects-in-language, and instead are relegated to the position of objects. Furthermore, since the subject is structured by language, women are denied access to subjectivity.

The ideology of science is for Irigaray the most obvious and dangerous manifestation of the masculine cultural imaginary of Western society. Like the other feminists I have discussed in this section, Irigaray believes that a feminist critique of epistemology should start with understanding the notion of the epistemic subject. She claims

One of the places most likely to provoke a questioning of the scientific landscape is that of the examination of the subject of science and its psychic and sexed implications in discourse, discoveries and their organization. (1987: 79)

First of all, Irigaray calls into question the supposed neutrality of the subject of science.

Given that *science* is one of the last figures, if not the last figure, used to represent absolute knowledge, it is – ethically – essential that we ask science to reconsider the non-neutrality of the supposedly universal subject that constitutes its scientific theory and practice.

In actual fact, the self-proclaimed universal is the equivalent of an idiolect of men, a masculine imaginary, a sexed world. (1993: 121)

The subject which knows scientifically, who has the authority of science, far from being neutral and universal is, for Irigaray, a masculine subject. To understand this claim one must first recall that to be a subject is to assume a certain speaking position in language. That is, one becomes a subject by being positioned as an 'I' in language. For Irigaray this sort of position is denied to women, who therefore have no access to subjectivity. This is particularly true for the case of the subject of scientific activity. The epistemic subject is for Irigaray the subject positioned in a speaking role in a specific discourse which is the language of theory, the constative language of description. This language is characterized by the impersonal form taken in it by claims: instead of saying 'I believe,' scientists claim 'there is.' But,

Irigaray holds, this move is equivalent to using the 'there is' as 'one more mask for the I' (1993: 137). A move such as this 'uses the edifice of language to blur the enunciation. And denies also who it is who has produced this grammar, this meaning, and the rules governing them' (1993: 137).

As a result, the language of science hides behind a supposed neutrality the fact that it is a product of sexed beings: that is male beings. The move to the impersonal covers up the fact that the subject of science is sexed as male. Science is a particularly extreme manifestation of the existence of only one possible speaking position in language, a position which despite its pretenses is never neutral but always sexed as male.

What is excluded without acknowledgment by means of the supposed neutrality of the subject who speaks in the language of science is the role of the Mother who has made possible the cultural imaginary on which science is built. One important task for feminist epistemology would then be to acknowledge this exclusion. To make such an acknowledgment would involve, against traditional epistemology, a recognition that 'one should not have to give up love in order to become wise or learned. It is love that leads to knowledge' (Irigaray, 1993: 21).

Since there is no subjectivity in science – 'neither *I*, nor *you*, nor *we*' appears in science (1987: 66) – the subject is required to separate from himself and his desires; he must keep science and politics apart. Above all he must ignore the questions which Irigaray insistently asks, namely: 'what desire (individual or social) is at stake in him or her when they do science, what other desire when they make love?' (1987: 68).

To acknowledge that scientific discourse is spoken by sexed subjects, who are constituted through the exclusion of the feminine, is to acknowledge the subjectivity of science, and therefore the relevance to science of desires and interests. Far from being neutral, the subject of science brings to it interests and desires which he denies. To acknowledge the role of passion in science would make it possible to see how love leads the way to knowledge.

Currently, however, the role of desires and interests in science is hidden by the impersonal form taken by scientific discourse. This impersonality makes it impossible to raise the ethical question of responsibility concerning scientific statements. When the role of the subject is masked by the impersonal, the speaking subject does not have to take responsibility for his claims. In this way it becomes impossible to interrogate scientific theories from a moral viewpoint. Since science supposedly speaks the truth, it will reply to any questioning as to the morality of its claims by saying that it is just telling the facts as they are. This reply, however, hides the fact that science, like every other human activity, is produced by subjects who have political interests. These interests make a difference 'in what science takes or does not take as the stakes of its research' (1987: 75). To be clear about the non-neutrality of the subject of science makes it possible to ask moral question about what is at stake in pursuing a certain line of research, say about the links between race and IQ, rather than another.

Irigaray claims that the language of science is neither neutral nor universal, but is instead an expression of the masculine cultural imaginary. Its supposed neutrality is damaging because it makes it impossible to raise ethical issues about the claims of science. Irigaray's attitude toward science is not, however, totally negative. She does not advocate a feminist rejection of the notion of the epistemic subject. Instead, she believes in the importance of the creation of differently sexed epistemic subjects capable of producing a science which is not completely masculine.[24] She does not suggest that we can devise a truly neutral and universal language of science; what she advocates instead is a language of science which admits a feminine speaking position, which acknowledges the cultural debt to the maternal function, which permits ethical questioning, and which makes it possible to see that love leads to knowledge.

There are problems with Irigaray's denial of the possibility of a universal subject of knowledge. Although she is probably right that, given current conditions, any assertion of universality would end up privileging a masculine position, I believe that it is still possible to think of some universality as embodying a hope for the future. It is a hope, though, which must be compatible with feminist claims that all subjects (and the whole of knowledge) are socially located.[25]

Further Reading

For a critique of the individualism of traditional epistemology see chapter 11 of Alison Jaggar's *Feminist Politics and Human Nature* (1983), and chapters 1, 2, and 3 of Lorraine Code's *What Can She Know? Feminist Theory and the Construction of Knowledge* (1991). Evelyn Fox Keller's *Reflections on Gender and Science* (1985) is still a good example of psychoanalytic critique of the traditional notion of the epistemic subject.

Notes

1   This understanding is on the surface of Schmitt (1994: 1).
2   For example, Code (1991: 112) and Stout (1981: 25).
3   On these issues see Stout (1981, ch. 2).

4   A similar account of individualism in epistemology is provided by Addelson and Potter (1991: 263–4).

5   Descartes, thus, marks the beginning of another aspect of individualism. For him, the foundations can guarantee knowledge only if they are within the direct cognitive grasp of the subject.

6   Locke exemplifies the first attitude when he denies any credibility to the testimony of other people; Hume adopts the second because he accepts testimony only when there is inductive factual evidence that the witness is reliable.

7   For a critical discussion, see Alston (1989: 185–226).

8   Often internalists have also formulated higher level constraints about justification. For example, some have required that the subject also have a higher order justified belief that one's evidence for lower order beliefs actually justifies them. These higher order constraints often lead to vicious regresses. I shall ignore them here.

9   I discuss naturalized epistemology in chapter 5.

10   These are discussed in detail by Addelson (1983) and, following her, by Nelson (1990).

11   For example, for Alvin Goldman socially acquired belief-forming methods can give knowledge, but only if one's acceptance of the methods themselves results from the employment of an individualistic belief-forming process. I can be said to have learnt the method for deriving mathematical square roots from somebody who taught me, but only if I have independent individualistic ways of checking that the method is reliable (Goldman, 1986: 91). One can accept the testimony of others, provided one has independent factual evidence that such testimony is reliable.

12   But in another dimension less radical, since she is a naturalist.

13   I discuss Nelson's theory of evidence in chapter 4.

14   These points have been made by Hardwig (1985, 1991).

15   Here I ignore the case of playing devil's advocate.

16   One may wish to assert that these assumptions have a different source of justification. Perhaps. What remains surprising is how few arguments have been provided to this end.

17   The main feminist sources of Keller's account are Nancy Chodorow's *Reproduction of Mothering* (1978), and Jessica Benjamin's work which appeared as a book under the title *The Bonds of Love* (1988).

18   A useful analysis of these issues is presented by Soble (1994).

19   Scheman (1987) has argued along similar lines that the problem of skepticism, which is central to Cartesian concerns and to traditional epistemology, also finds its origin in the separation anxiety which characterizes the emergence of a new masculinity in the sixteenth century. She finds this new problematic exemplified in Shakespeare's *Othello* and in Descartes.

20   I address this problem in chapter 7.

21   For a detailed critical analysis of the intersection of class, gender, and race in object relations theory see chapter 4 of Spelman (1990).

22   On this point, see Whitford (1991: 65). For my discussion of Irigaray I am heavily indebted to Margaret Whitford's excellent account.

23   Irigaray's account of the exclusion of woman from the cultural imaginary has been criticized for its ahistorical character and its lack of subtlety by Michèle Le Doeuff. See, for example, her discussion of the exclusion of women from philosophy in 'Long Hair, Short Ideas,' in Le Doeuff (1989).

24   It is for this reason that Naomi Schor claims that Irigaray's attitude to science is ambiguous (1994: 53).

25   I argue in chapter 9 that reason need not be irredeemably male.

3

Feminism and Science

Science, in Western society, is widely regarded as the best way to gain reliable information about the world. This belief is largely true. Even its critics recognize that science is a source of knowledge. This is not to say that all is well with science. One does not have to be anti-science to recognize that it raises several problems. Feminists have, for example, argued that sexism permeates scientific activity at many levels (Rose, 1994: 12). Similarly, Western cultural biases have deeply influenced the development of science. These claims should not be surprising. Science is a human activity. It is unlikely to be unaffected by the social contexts within which it has developed. Since society is permeated by gender and Western biases, these are in all probability reflected also in science. While this conclusion might shatter the traditional image of science as the supremely rational human activity, it could be readily accepted, as it stands, even by the more traditional philosophers of science. They only need to concede that good science is rarer than it is commonly presumed.

In this chapter I discuss some of the analyses of science provided by thinkers influenced by feminist concerns. I do not explore full-blown oppositions to science as a means for the acquisition of knowledge. Instead, I present those views that acknowledge that science is a fundamental source of knowledge. Nevertheless, these critiques of science often show scientific theories to be flawed. They demonstrate that these theories are not immune from the gender and cultural biases present in Western society at large. Values – good and bad – permeate science in different ways, and along several dimensions. A few examples might help to illustrate the multiplicity of this phenomenon.

In the first instance, gender and cultural biases might lead scientists to pursue some lines of inquiry rather than others. For example, research on the biological basis of intelligence is thriving. It often tries to find out whether men are more intelligent than women, whites than blacks. Some of the literature produced on this topic is bluntly sexist, and racist. Of course, these are not necessary features of all studies in this area. Nevertheless, given the inconclusive nature of much of this research, it is hard to believe that it continues to receive funding in virtue of its scientific achievements. It seems more probable that its appeal with institutions lies in its ideological value. Be that as it may, the questions this branch of biology attempts to answer could only be thought of in a society where men are taken to be more intelligent than women, whites more intelligent than blacks. These questions could not be dreamed of in a culture where 'intelligence' is seen as an umbrella term for many abilities which are possessed in different measure by individuals. Thus, sexism and racism might have an influence on which questions are taken to be worth pursuing in science.

They might also affect which answers are given to scientific questions. For example, they can influence the formulation of hypotheses. This influence can take different forms. Scientists might simply explore the hypotheses they assume to be natural about, for instance, the behavior of male and female primates. Furthermore, scientists might be guided by metaphors about male activity and female passivity in the study of human fertilization. Thus, the prejudices of scientists might have a direct effect on which hypotheses they formulate. Or, more subtly, they may inform the preferred metaphors scientists employ when they are trying to come up with a view to explain reality.

Further, sexism and racism might be relevant to the confirmation of hypotheses, not just their formulation. Scientists might ignore some of the relevant evidence, fail to notice it, or have no access to it. For example, they might fail to include women in a case study about the use of aspirin to prevent heart attacks in human beings. When they do so, as they have done, they ignore relevant evidence. Alternatively, scientists might not pay any real attention to the behavior of female primates. When this happens, as it has done, they fail to notice some of the evidence relevant to their theories about the behavior of apes. Finally, and famously, male anthropologists, for example, have no access to women-only spaces such as the menstruating hut of some cultures. As a result they were led to foolish hypotheses about the length of the natives' menses, when the women prolonged their stay simply because they dreaded everyday chores. In this case (some) scientists, in virtue of their sex, have no access to some of the relevant evidence.

Sexism and racism have, at times, an effect on the selection of the problems which are perceived to require an explanation. They are relevant to the hypotheses which are brought forward as explanations. Finally, they influence the selection of the evidence that warrants hypotheses. But they are not merely relevant to scientific theories; their influence on science can also take other forms. For example, philosophers have been concerned with the demarcation between science and other ways of gaining knowledge. They have often drawn the line so as to exclude women's activities from the realm of the scientific. This exclusion goes hand in hand with the excessive importance attributed to theory over practice in science. And, although it might be idle to postulate a direct influence of sexism on the preference for theory, this provides an example of how values are relevant to shared conceptions of what makes an investigation scientific. Similarly, the drive for unity in science, and the importance attributed to universal exceptionless laws might be, at least in part, motivated by typically Western values.

These examples suggest that science is dependent on social context in a variety of ways. Yet, these dependencies can often be accommodated by defenders of traditional conceptions of science. They can accept that values play a role in the discovery of theories by influencing the selection of problems to be investigated, and the formulation of hypotheses. They can also admit the presence of values in the confirmation of theories whenever such presence gives rise to examples of bad science. Nevertheless the exploration of these phenomena is of fundamental importance. Firstly, it leads to better science by laying bare some of the mistakes made in the past. Secondly, it undermines the common conception of science as autonomous from its social context. These examples do not tell us how science ought to proceed; they do not show whether social values can be beneficial to science. However, they suggest that the influence of values might be inevitable. I discuss these examples in the first section of this chapter.

The second section presents more explicit challenges to traditional conceptions of the autonomy of science. In this section I discuss arguments for the claim that social values are important to good science. If this claim can be adequately supported, it would show that autonomous science is not merely unachievable, but also undesirable. It comes as no surprise that many feminists have provided arguments to this end. After all, they have attempted to establish their belief that holding good feminist values helps rather than hinders the pursuit of good science. These arguments often go beyond the debate between internalist and externalist conceptions of science typical of the past decade. Internalism is the view fostered by many philosophers and scientists alike. It holds that good science is independent of social context. This is not say that scientists are immune from social influences. It entails, however, that when science is done properly confirmation proceeds only through the use of reason, the evaluation and the collection of evidence. According to this view, in good science only factors internal to science itself should motivate a change of theory. Externalism, mainly adopted by sociologists of science, is opposed to internalism. It holds that social factors influence every example of science. As I pointed out in chapter 1, even though externalists are critical of the authority of science, their stance leads to a sort of quietism about the activities of scientists. Since they call into question the rationality of all science, they often refrain from making a distinction between good and bad science. Thus, externalism does not have much to say about how to improve science. Feminists, on the other hand, have often pursued precisely this goal.

They have done so in different ways. For example, some feminist thinkers have adopted Quine's thesis that theories are underdetermined by empirical evidence to argue for a less internalistic conception of science. This thesis states that more than one theory will always be compatible with all the empirical evidence. Social values contribute to the confirmation of theories, since empirical evidence alone cannot determine uniquely the choice of one theory. Although several feminists, notably Sandra Harding, have followed externalists in the belief that the relation between values and science is one of cause and effect, they have never refrained from evaluating science. These evaluations are discussed in the second section of this chapter.

Sexist Science

We have all at some point read sensationalistic newspaper reports about the alleged superiority of boys in mathematics, of girls in verbal communication. More recently, a great deal of ink has been spilled hypothesizing the existence of a gay gene. Often, journalistic reporting is much cruder about the alleged findings than the specialist articles they purport to divulge. However, the scientists themselves tend to forget their caution when talking to the press. They might do so for a variety of reasons, including the fact that notoriety brings funding, and journalists need definitive results for their front page headlines. But, even if we ignore the exaggerations of the press, research on the biology of human beings and on their evolutionary history often embodies sexist and racist assumptions.

In this section I discuss some examples of this phenomenon. I begin with cases that, from an epistemological viewpoint, should appear unproblematic. The theories examined do not satisfy the criteria imposed on research by the scientific method as paradigmatically understood. In other words, these theories are, even by traditional standards, instances of 'bad' science. Research on the so-called sex differences in cognitive abilities provides a good example. It is commonly believed that boys outperform girls in spatial visualization. There might be some truth in this claim. It is difficult to be sure since experiments were not set up to screen out the influence of other sex-related factors. Anne Fausto-Sterling describes the rod and frame test which is commonly used to investigate this skill. The subject is in a dark room alone with the experimenter. She is facing a luminescent frame bisected by a lighted rod. The experimenter tilts the frame, and the subject must ask him to adjust the rod so that it is vertical to the room. The subject must ignore the immediate context of the tilted frame (1992: 30). Apparently, scientists ignored the possibility that female subjects might have felt uneasy about being alone with a male scientist in a dark room. They have also ignored the possibility that less assertive people, as women often are, might hesitate to continue asking the experimenter to make tiny adjustments (1992: 32). Since experimenters have failed to notice factors which are evidentially relevant, their conclusions can be open to question. Only persons that are unaware of the complexities of gender relations could be blind to the necessity to look out for these influences.

Suppose, however, that a sex-related difference in spatial visualization exists. It would be quite small. Only 5 percent of the variation in ability in a mixed population could be linked to gender, while the remaining 95 percent would be due to individual differences (Fausto-Sterling, 1992: 33). Nevertheless, scientists have used a lot of resources in the attempt to explain this result. They have almost always attempted to find a biological origin for these differences. This research provides a clear illustration of the multiple ways in which sexist values can influence science.

First of all, one may question the belief that sex differences in cognitive abilities are to be explained biologically. Given the enormous differences in the way male and female children are reared, a sociological explanation should seem equally plausible. And yet, there has been very little research exploring this hypothesis. It would seem that scientists have been guided by the assumption that differences between men and women are 'natural' when trying to explain different abilities in spatial visualization. In this case, the selection of the hypothesis, which is taken to offer more promise for a satisfactory explanation, has been influenced by sexist values. This impression is also confirmed by the existence of evidence that visual-spatial abilities are, at least in part, learned skills (Fausto-Sterling, 1992: 34).

Furthermore, evidence that might suggest a social origin of these differences is consistently ignored. Sex-related differences in spatial visualization vary in different cultures. For example, there are no differences among Eskimos, where girls are allowed more autonomy than in other cultures. Women's visual-spatial abilities vary in accordance with the degree of freedom they have (Fausto-Sterling, 1992: 35). It would seem that, since we are talking about a small difference in an ability which is at least partly learned, there is no need to search for a biological explanation. Nevertheless, the search continues because the evidence for a social cause is ignored or underestimated. It is hard to believe that, having discovered a positive correlation between spatial ability and throwing accuracy, scientists go on to suggest that past selection on hunting skills in males might explain their superior skill today. And yet, this is what they have done. It hardly needs to be mentioned that boys might have learned to throw by playing soccer or basketball with their fathers and playmates. Boys, more than girls, are carefully trained to perform well in these sporting activities. This explanatory hypothesis seems less far-fetched than the evolutionary one. Nevertheless, scientists have latched on to the hypothesis that makes difference 'natural,' a fact of life that one must simply accept.

Several candidates have been presented as the possible biological cause of women's inferior visual-spatial abilities. They include space genes, and brain lateralization. The studies on lateralization have provoked much interest and remain one of the dominant views on this issue. Nevertheless, as Ruth Bleier has pointed out, these studies are inconclusive. Thus, some scientists have claimed to have discovered that women use both hemispheres of the brain to perform verbal and spatial tasks. Women would, therefore, be less lateralized than men. They conclude that women are inferior in spatial visualization because these tasks require hemispheric lateralization. However, the only evidence they have that these tasks require lateralization is that women are inferior at performing them, and they are less hemispherically specialized. Other groups of scientists have, instead, claimed that women are more lateralized than men, and concluded that women are less capable in spatial visualization because it requires the equal use of both hemispheres (1984: 93). Scientists have no independent evidence that hemispheric lateralization has anything whatsoever to do with these abilities. Hence, even if it is true that men and women differ in hemispheric lateralization, it is impossible to make any inference about visual-spatial skills.

More recent studies on the biological basis of homosexuality provide another good example of how cultural assumptions influence science with often disastrous results. This work is, of course, predicated on the assumption that there is a particular kind of person -the homosexual – who is different from the heterosexual. The belief that people can be so categorized is a rather recent one. It became fully formed only in the nineteenth century, as Foucault, among others, has persuasively argued (1978: 101). For example, when in 1534 the Reformation Parliament in England created the new felony of buggery, it referred to a sexual act defined in terms of anal penetration independently of the gender of the penetrated. It is possible that the classification of acts into homosexual and heterosexual did not seem at the time as important as the distinction between natural and unnatural sexual practices. It does not follow that such a distinction cannot be made and be used to describe past acts. Similarly, even if there was no available concept of the homosexual before the nineteenth century, it might still be true that there were homosexuals. It would be true, if homosexuality were a reasonably well-defined property which is possessed by gay people today, and could be attributed to some people living in the past. A good candidate for such a property would be some genetic or anatomical feature that pertains to homosexuals alone. Both of these hypotheses have been explored in contemporary work on the origin of homosexuality.

The mere fact that 'homosexual' is a recent concept does not show that it cannot be a biological category. Nevertheless, the questions asked in the research about homosexuality could not even be formulated in a society that did not have this concept. Furthermore, in contemporary Western culture this category is not value-neutral. It carries connotations of deviance, or wrongness. The conviction that something must have gone wrong in the development of individuals who engage in same-sex sexual practices must be one of the motivations for finding out what causes this behavior.

Sexist assumptions, and stereotyping of gay men, are often present in recent research on the biological basis of male homosexuality. In 1991 Simon LeVay announced the finding of anatomical differences in the hypothalami of gay and straight men. LeVay's argument of why the hypothalamus should matter is fraught with biased assumptions. The hypothalamus is a region at the base of the brain which also produces hormones that regulate the hormonal output of the pituitary gland. LeVay relied on studies of rhesus monkeys that seemed to show that tampering with the hypothalamus caused changes in sexual behavior. These studies, as Fausto-Sterling shows, did not provide any evidence about sexual orientation. Male monkeys often present their rump to other males, but researchers define this normal male behavior as a female sexual response (1992: 248). The monkeys, whose brains had been tampered with, did this more often than the other males. The researchers concluded that they manifested an increased tendency to assume a female role. This conclusion is unwarranted. Since all male monkeys assume this role sometimes, it makes no sense to classify it as female. In a more recent popular work on scientific theories about homosexuality, LeVay still indulges in this kind of reasoning, when considering studies about rats. He says that mounting behavior 'can be shown on occasion by rats of the "wrong" sex' even when they have not been subjected to hormonal manipulation (1996: 133). One is left wondering about who decided that females rats, which, on occasion, mounted other rats, were behaving inappropriately for their sex.

Nevertheless, on the basis of these claims, and on the basis of an unconfirmed claim about differences between men and women, LeVay formulates the hypothesis that gay men have a female hypothalamus. Thus, when LeVay found a difference in the hypothalami of the dead men he examined, he concluded, on the basis of the studies on monkeys, that the difference was linked to sexual orientation rather than to other factors. What are we to make of this hypothesis?

First of all, one must notice that without making several value-laden assumptions no one could even dream of formulating it. For example, one must think that there are different sexual behaviors appropriate for the two sexes. One must also believe that orientation toward women is typical sexual behavior for men, while orientation toward men is typical of women. Otherwise, it is difficult to understand why one would think that gay men may have a female brain. In other words, one must implicitly rely on the belief that gay men are inverts; they are female brains (rather than souls) in male bodies. One must also assume that the appropriate behavior is heterosexual. The heterosexism inherent in the hypothesis should make us suspicious about its truth.

Furthermore, even if we grant that there is a difference between the hypothalami of straight and gay men, the evidence that LeVay has provided from studies on monkeys and rats, does not warrant the claim that this difference is the cause of sexual orientation. LeVay has always granted this point in his scientific writings, but he does not mention that his work is

compatible with the possibility that the alleged difference in the hypothalamus might have nothing to do whatsoever with sexual orientation (1996:
146). It is not simply possible that sexual orientation causes the difference
rather than being caused by it, it is also possible that the cause might be
found in something else altogether. For example, gay men have on average
many more sexual partners than straight men. For all we know, this fact
could cause differences in the hypothalamus. Instead, the only alternative
LeVay explicitly considers is fraught with heterosexist assumptions. Since
his first study only included gay men who had died of AIDS, he speculates
that his sample may not be representative of the entire gay population. He
goes on to say that they might have had a stronger preference for receptive
anal intercourse (1996: 144). Even if we ignore the fact that people might
get infected by engaging in other practices, this speculation remains deeply
troubling. It encourages a distinction between two kinds of gay men. The
biological gay would be the one who engages in 'feminine' sexual behavior.
This hypothesis once again relies on the ugly stereotype that the true gay
man is an invert.

What is most surprising in this work that relies on a long list of
heterosexist assumptions, strange hypotheses, and tenuous evidence, is
LeVay's throwaway remark that no one has ever replicated his results
(1996: 146). In other words, no one else has ever found a difference in the
hypothalami of straight and gay men. And yet, all the dubious assumptions
I have described have been presented to explain this fact![1] Other aspects of
LeVay's work are also troubling. He is willing to speculate that lesbians
might have a masculine hypothalamus, while admitting that neither him
nor anyone else has ever done any work on the subject. Furthermore, he
seems to present sex-related differences in cognitive abilities as a well-
established scientific fact. He mentions in passing that some feminists have
objected to these claims. But he presents Germaine Greer as an example
(1996: 140). Whatever one thinks of her work, she is not a biologist. The
books by Fausto-Sterling, Ruth Bleier, and Ruth Hubbard are not mentioned. What we get, instead, is the standard list of possibly hormonal,
anatomical and evolutionary reasons on why men are better than women
at spatial visualization among other things. The possibility that such
differences in skills might be due to socialization is hardly ever mentioned.
Furthermore, after several pages where LeVay has described these differences as a matter of objective fact, he simply announces that: 'It should be
emphasized that both the existence and the causes of cognitive differences
between the sexes are still disputed' (1996: 154). I do not know whether
the reader is meant to infer from this that those who dispute these issues

are nutty, or whether she is meant to infer that LeVay has carelessly presented as fact what has not been established.

Unfortunately, these bad scientific theories also have a pernicious self-confirming effect. Even if there is little or no difference in ability between men and women, a belief that it exists and is biological will lead parents and educators away from encouraging girls to do better. Consider the case of mathematical ability which has been persistently linked to spatial visualization. If it is commonly believed that girls are not mathematically gifted, they are unlikely to be encouraged to do well, and to develop self-confidence in their abilities. As a result girls will consistently underachieve. Therefore, belief in the natural inferiority of women breeds poor performance in girls. The quality of this performance will be taken to confirm the theory which produced the results it presumed to explain. Similarly, one may argue that scientific theories of homosexuality created the category of people they were meant to explain.[2]

These two examples suffice to show how some science is riddled with sexist and heterosexist values. These values affect the choice of questions to be pursued, and the hypotheses that are put forward. They are also relevant to the evidence. Some evidential connections are not noticed or ignored; observations are described in a highly contentious way. The list could go on and on. Research on sex differences in cognitive abilities and on the biological basis of homosexuality might not be particularly bad, since researchers often caution their readers that they have not in fact established anything. Nevertheless, one concurs with Fausto-Sterling that when these criticisms of these views are pointed out, they will seem correct even to those who conducted this research (1992: 11). The criticisms I have discussed so far should be acceptable also to traditional philosophers of science. These objections present examples where values have influenced scientists for the worse, and have led them to engage in less than optimal science.

However, even these examples of bad science can be used to make a case for the claim that feminist values are instrumental to better science. In the context of a community which does not hold these values, feminism can provide an alternative angle of vision (Fausto-Sterling, 1992: 11). It helps to discover unwarranted assumptions, and formulate new hypotheses. Evidence that others have ignored or failed to notice might be unearthed by feminist scientists. These claims too, as we shall see, can be explained by traditional accounts of science.[3] They can be so accommodated because values are only said to be relevant to the discovery of evidence, they are not themselves part of the evidence. In other words, although values might help to find out what justifies scientific claims, they do not themselves figure in the justification.

It is now time to turn to the traditional accounts of science that can accommodate the results presented so far before discussing more complex instances of the influence of values on scientific research. These accounts are deeply influenced by empiricism. They also draw a sharp demarcation between science and non-science (Boyd, 1991: 5). One reason for insisting on this separation is the shared conception of science proper as an autonomous enterprise.

At the beginning of this century the Logical Positivists hoped to provide an empiricist account of science as a matter of induction from sensory experience. According to this view scientific theories are generalizations on the basis of past experience; thus, we claim that free bodies fall, because we have observed it to be the case in all of our past experiences. This account was soon rejected because of numerous problems encountered in the formulation of a logic of induction, and because experiences are not conceptually independent of theories (Nelson, 1990: 46). In its place a new post-positivist account of science was formulated by Carl Hempel and Ernest Nagel. Their account gained paradigmatic status for many decades and is still a very powerful component of lay conceptions of science. According to this account, science is characterized by the employment of the hypothetical-deductive method. Scientists are not engaged in induction from experience; instead, they creatively produce hypotheses which are subsequently confirmed or falsified by experience. The focus here is on science as a body of theories, which are sets of claims formulated in technical and mathematical language; very little consideration is given to science as a practice involving training, experimental procedures, and other forms of know-how. Scientific theories, according to this account, logically entail claims about observations. The truth of these claims can be verified by means of the observations themselves, while the theoretical claims are confirmed when all, or more practically very many, of their observational consequences are found to be true.[4]

Another notorious feature of the Hempel–Nagel account of science is the already mentioned distinction they draw between the production and the justification of scientific knowledge. The first process, which is known as the context of discovery, concerns the various factors which influence scientists when they formulate the scientific hypotheses to be tested; the second, the context of justification, is concerned only with the confirmation of scientific hypotheses. Hempel and Nagel focused on this second context as that which distinguishes science from any other activity, and generates the objectivity which pertains to scientific knowledge.

They also believed that only the context of justification is relevant to an epistemology of science; while discovery is not a proper object of philosophical investigation. One reason for this sharp distinction, which Locke and the other early empiricists did not make, is to be found in the concern with method. Since Descartes it was generally agreed among philosophers that true knowledge can only be achieved if one's thinking is governed by a set of rules, by a method. Hempel and Nagel had claimed that there was no method for the formulation of hypotheses, because this was an eminently creative activity. The method, however, was to be found in confirmation; hence, it was confirmation that conferred to science the earmark of knowledge, and it was by studying confirmation that philosophers could pursue the traditional epistemological project of formulating the rules, the method, for achieving knowledge.

The emphasis on confirmation based on observations makes Hempel and Nagel's hypothetical-deductive account of science the heir of Locke's empiricism because it takes experience alone to provide the justification for the whole of science. Furthermore, the exclusion of the context of discovery from the province of what makes a claim an instance of scientific knowledge plays in Hempel and Nagel's account the same structural role played by the conception of the mind as a passive receptor in the account provided by Locke. Locke had ruled out the relevance of subjectivity to knowledge by asserting that the mind is passive. Hempel and Nagel claim, instead, that the mind is creative, but hold that this subjective aspect of the production of knowledge is not relevant to the philosophical reflection on knowledge. Instead, they claim that methodological confirmation removes from science any subjective influence that might have permeated it through the context of discovery. Thus Hempel and Nagel, like Locke, are committed to the exclusion of values from knowledge.

According to this view, good science requires value-neutrality; it is only when values are screened out that the objectivity proper to scientific knowledge can be achieved. The examples I have presented above are compatible with this interpretation of how science ought to proceed. In these cases the influence of values on science produces bad results. The biological theories I have considered remain unconfirmed. The traditional view of scientific method can also accommodate the modest claim I have made about the positive influence of feminist values on scientific research. This influence would be restricted to the context of discovery. Values would be instrumental to the formulation of good hypotheses, but they would not be part of the evidence in their favor. They might, however, help to design experiments which test scientific hypotheses. For example, a scientist who holds feminist values might be alert to some features of the experimental circumstances that another person would ignore. Thus, in the frame and rod experiment I mentioned above, she would consider the effect of women's lack of assertiveness on the result.

It can be argued, however, that even the relatively non-controversial examples of the influence of values on scientific theories, which I have already discussed, present problems that cannot be resolved simply by adherence to the hypothetical-deductive method. This method might not be sufficient to screen out all biases. That is, it might fail to achieve the purpose for which it was designed. I shall consider this possibility in the second section of this chapter. I now turn to a new set of examples of the multifarious influences of values on scientific activities.

These examples are concerned with the role played by metaphors in science. Biological theories about human fertilization are a good starting point. Since Aristotle women have been conceived as passive, and men as active. These metaphors have guided the formulation of hypotheses in biology. Thus, the female egg has been understood as passive, while the spermatozoon has been seen as active. The traditional account of fertilization focuses on the activities of the sperm. It tells us that one ejaculation releases millions of them in the vagina. Millions of them die in the inhospitable female genital tract, but some find their way into the oviduct. Finally, one penetrates the egg, and fertilizes it. In this story the egg does not do anything, it simply waits to be penetrated. Often, as members of the Biology and Gender Group have shown, this tale is told in highly evocative language. Sperm is thought of as an army, the egg as a seductive whore (1988: 65). Views about the behavior appropriate to the two genders have been imported into the biology of fertilization, and applied to sperm and egg. They have guided the selection of the tale I have presented, and made it seem natural. It is only in more recent times that biologists have started to hypothesize that the egg clasps the spermatozoon, it is not just penetrated by it. Some evidence for this phenomenon had been available since 1895, but it had been largely ignored (1988: 66). Similarly, the sperm probably needs to be activated to become capable of fertilizing the egg. Secretions of the female genital tract appear to play an important role in this process. This possibility was not explored presumably because it did not fit preconceived ideas about female passivity.

In this example metaphors of female passivity have mis-guided scientific research. The intrusion of bias has had a bad effect on science. Masculinist assumptions have caused scientists 'to focus on certain problems to the exclusion of others, and they have led [them] to make particular interpretations when equally valid alternatives were available' (1988: 62). In this case too, values have been instrumental to the production of bad science. Hence, also this example can be accommodated by supporters of internalist conceptions of science. External factors have had a negative effect on the rationality of the choice of theories made by scientists.

The roles performed by metaphors in science cannot be so neatly described when they affect our understanding of nature as a whole. This phenomenon is exemplified by the conception of reality formulated for the first time by scientists in the seventeenth century. This conception still influences contemporary theories on these matters. Proponents of mechanistic science, such as Robert Boyle, proposed a corpuscular theory of reality. According to this view, reality is ultimately constituted by little parcels of matter, which are called 'corpuscles'. These corpuscles are intrinsically inert; they can be put into motion only when they receive an impulse from outside. Thus, material reality is newly conceived as passive and in itself without life.

In *The Death of Nature* Carolyn Merchant argues that the new science of the seventeenth century introduced a conception of nature as a lifeless mechanism. This conception replaced a view of nature as a living organism. She holds that the mechanistic conception is responsible for the exploitative attitude toward nature which has led to contemporary ecological disasters. Furthermore, she claims that due to the long-standing stereotypical identification of woman with nature, the new science has had disastrous consequences for women.

Merchant identifies several contradictory metaphors and preconceptions at work during the seventeenth century: on the one hand, nature continues to be thought as female, but the metaphor of the earth as a nurturing mother (1980: 20) is substituted by a vision of nature as unruly and chaotic. The wild character of nature was associated with female lust and sexuality; both, it was claimed, had to be subdued and kept in their place (1980: 132). On the other hand, nature, which was previously conceived as a live organism, becomes associated with ideas of passivity, hence:

> The Aristotelian and Platonic conception of the passivity of matter [and of the female sex] could . . . be incorporated into the new

mechanical philosophy in the form of inert 'dead' atoms, constituents of a new machine-like world in which change came about through external forces. (1980: 20)

This view of matter as passive and female is particularly explicit in the writings of Robert Hooke, Boyle's assistant, who wrote that the female principle is rightly called '*Materia*, Material Substance, or *Mater*', and that it is 'in itself without Life or Motion' (quoted by Potter, 1988: 27). Nature is, thus, conceptualized as both extremely unruly and intrinsically passive: it is, however, conceived as female in both cases.

There were many causes for the seventeenth century adoption of the view that matter is corpuscular and passive, some were linked to 'internal' scientific considerations, but others were certainly influenced by 'external' social factors. Boyle and his contemporaries lived in a period of social unrest when women actively participated in political movements such as that of the levelers.[5] Scientists in Boyle's circle, instead, shared a conviction that the natural order reflects the moral order which sees man as superior to woman. Furthermore, they were influenced by the Aristotelian association of woman with passive matter. These considerations must have had an effect on their understanding of matter as passive, and of science as the manipulation of it. After all, as Elizabeth Potter points out:

At least for those cases in which a particular generalization is under-determined by the data, as the generalization that matter is dead was when Boyle considered it, the decision as to which generalization to adopt must be based on other grounds than simple observation. (1988: 30)

Potter is not claiming that Boyle's generalization is false, but only that at the time he endorsed it, he must have been guided by unquestioned assumptions about the proper place of women in society. Furthermore, Potter does not derive from this claim that Boyle was engaged in 'bad science'; instead, she claims that 'the dichotomy between "good science" and "bad science" . . . hinders rather than helps a feminist understanding of science' (1988: 28). She takes her analyses to show, instead, that accounts of science and knowledge are not 'politically innocent' (1994: 46). I shall return to this issue in the second section of this chapter. For the time being I only want to mention the interpretation of Boyle's account of matter as passive which is available to the proponents of internalist conceptions of science. They can claim that Boyle struck it lucky, although he was guided by unpleasant preconceptions about women, and about nature as female. Bad values influenced the formulation of Boyle's theory. Nevertheless, these values have been screened out in subsequent years when new evidence emerged that confirmed his theory. Potter, as we shall see, would not endorse this interpretation herself.

Despite the similarities in their accounts, Potter and Merchant seem to disagree on a number of issues. Firstly, while Potter does not think that it is particularly useful to label scientific theories that have been used in ways that are damaging for women as 'bad science,' Merchant appears to endorse this position.[6] Secondly, Merchant is not sufficiently critical of the association of woman with nature as opposed to cultural man. Thus, she appears to approve of the association of woman with earth conceived as a nurturing mother (1980: xvi). This approval is extremely problematic because it acquiesces in the idea that there is a female essence which is inextricably linked with women's reproductive functions. But, this idea of woman has been produced in a deeply sexist society and, as such, it should be regarded with suspicion. For example, it reinforces the stereotype that (white middle-class) women should be mothers, caring, and non-competitive. This stereotype has been used for centuries to keep women in their place, and feminists should be very careful unquestioningly to endorse it. They should also be careful to support a view that preserves the exclusive dichotomy between female and male natures.[7]

Thirdly, Merchant also tends to equate the ideal of objective knowledge with the allegedly value-free knowledge prescribed by empiricism. Similarly, Elizabeth Fee seems to endorse the association of the dichotomy between objective and subjective with the man/woman gender dichotomy. Hence, she concludes that 'the attributes of science are the attributes of males; the objectivity said to be characteristic of the production of scientific knowledge is specifically identified as a male way of relating to the world' (1983: 13). Fee does not attempt to undermine the gender dichotomy; instead, she turns it on its flipside, and endorses those features which are usually associated with woman. While Fee does not advocate abandoning science altogether, since she believes that traditional science has made some important achievements, she appears to hold that belief in the objectivity of science stands in the way of the development of less sexist science (1983: 23). I believe this judgment to be far too one-sided, but I shall not discuss the issue here. I present feminist alternatives to traditional conceptions of objectivity in chapter 7.

So far I have explained some of the ways in which values influence scientific theories. I have also highlighted how supporters of traditional accounts of science can come to terms with these examples. However, values permeate all the dimensions of scientific activity. Furthermore, even the examples I have already provided can be interpreted in ways that go beyond internalistic interpretations. I turn to these novel interpretations in the second section, where I also discuss the influence of values on other dimensions of scientific practice.

Science and Values

I have presented most of the examples I discussed above as clear-cut examples of bad science. This presentation has been, to some extent, too simplistic. While it is plausible to argue that many of the scientific theories discussed above should ultimately be rejected, this fact alone does not warrant the claim that they constitute instances of bad science. A little reflection on the history of science should support this belief. Most theories ultimately become superseded. It would be futile to characterize all past rejected theories as examples of bad science. Otherwise, we would have to come to the conclusion that science is usually badly done.

This comment, however, could easily lead us to conflating two separate issues. Bad science is often contrasted with 'science as usual.' It is thus suggested that bad theories are the result of unusual scientific practice. Some of the work done on the biology of sex differences could not be classified in this way. Instead, it belongs to normal science when it is considered in the context of the larger research projects within which it has been developed (Longino, 1990: 112). Potter's comment that the distinction between 'good' and 'bad' science does not help feminist accounts should be read in this context. Scientific research informed by values, including sexist values, is not unusual. It is not different in kind from normal 'good' science. The distinction between science as usual and bad science, however, is different from the normative distinction adopted in traditional internalist accounts of science. Supporters of these views could reach the conclusion that normal science is bad. For instance, if 'good science' should be value-neutral, but most scientific research is permeated by values, an internalist will conclude that science is usually badly done. Internalism could, thus, be defended.

There is, however, a high price to pay for this defense. There is no point in claiming that science should be value-neutral if this goal cannot ever be achieved. Internalist prescriptions appear futile when there is no way in which scientists could fulfill them. Traditional conceptions of science must presuppose that science often results in value-neutral knowledge. Otherwise, their supporters would be committed to the claim that good science is impossible. As a consequence, they would be forced to deny that science has any epistemic authority. They would have to admit that science is not a source of knowledge.

Feminists have provided several arguments for the claim that internalist conceptions of science are inadequate. These conceptions subscribe to the myth which holds that science, unlike any other human activity, can be made intelligible outside its cultural and social context (Fuller, 1993: 35). Feminists show that the belief in the autonomy of science is unwarranted. They also argue that the internalist myth has consequences. First, it leads to complacency. It prevents examination of the possibility that established 'knowledge' might serve the interests of the dominant groups in society (Jaggar, 1983: 378). Second, it encourages the dismissal of feminist analyses of the influence of gender assumptions in instances of good or successful science. For example, it could be used to dismiss Potter's explanation of the influence of a gender model on Boyle's atomistic hypothesis concerning the ultimate structure of physical reality (Potter, 1988). Those who are committed to an internalist account of science can understand Potter's analysis only in one of two ways, both of which she explicitly rejects. They could understand her if she claimed that Boyle's hypothesis is an instance of bad science because he was influenced by his sexists values and beliefs. They could also understand her if she claimed that Boyle's theory is correct, despite the fact that he was influenced by sexist values, because it has been confirmed. Although values played a role in Boyle's formulation of the theory, this would be a purely contingent fact that can be screened out in the context of confirmation. Potter, however, is not making either of these claims; rather, she discusses those social factors which influenced Boyle, but she does not believe that Boyle was necessarily doing bad science or that values can be screened out. Thus, the internalist account of science makes some of the feminist discussions of science philosophically unintelligible.

Feminist critiques of internalism take different forms. In what follows I shall examine four different arguments for the view that science is not autonomous. These are arguments that attempt to show that values always permeate science. The first two arguments establish that values cannot in practice be screened out from science. These arguments do not show directly that internalism is mistaken. Instead, they conclude that value-neutral science is a chimera. If internalists were to be convinced by these arguments they could either preserve their internalism and reject science, or abandon their internalism to preserve belief in science. Presumably, they would opt for the second choice. Internalists would, thus, follow feminist philosophers. They would agree that values cannot be eradicated from science, and conclude that these values must always be subject to scrutiny. Some values might even contribute to better science. The other two feminist arguments I shall discuss make this last point. If successful they show that some values, but not others, play a positive role in science. These arguments do not merely attempts to establish that values are inevitable, they also try to show that some values are desirable in science.

There are at least two ways to flesh out the view that values cannot be screened out in science. First, one might hold that values are part of the evidence that supports theories. Values, therefore, would play an essential role in the confirmation of theories. Second, one might point out that in practice no theory is ever definitely confirmed. Rather, scientists tend to endorse the hypothesis which, among its extant alternatives, appears to have more evidence in its favor. Confirmation, therefore, involves comparisons between alternative hypotheses (Okruhlik, 1992: 73). Thus, if the same values are presupposed by all the theories under consideration, they will not be screened out in the process of choosing which hypothesis is best supported by empirical evidence. For this reason Fee suggests that 'we should expect a sexist society to develop a sexist science' (Fee, 1983: 9).

Helen Longino has presented an argument of the first kind. She relies on Quine's thesis that theories are underdetermined by empirical evidence to support her view. Observations, according to Quine, are not sufficient to determine the choice of one theory. There is always more than one theory which is compatible with all the empirical evidence. Longino employs this thesis to argue that observations can function as evidence for theories only relative to background assumptions which might involve values (1990a: 151). I shall discuss the details of her argument in the next chapter. If successful, this argument would demonstrate that values can be part of the evidence used to confirm a theory. It could, thus, be taken to show that values can play a positive role in science. They would not merely guide us in the formulation of hypotheses, values would also be relevant to the justification of theories. Longino, however, does not seem to draw the same conclusion from her argument.[8]

The second argument for the impossibility of value-neutral science takes a different form. It does not show that values function as evidence for theories. Rather, it attempts to demonstrate that traditional accounts of scientific method cannot achieve their stated aims. Widely shared values might be embedded in every hypothesis considered by scientists. In this case, even the best available theory will presuppose values whose influence on science remains unchecked.

The logic of confirmation alone, as endorsed by Hempel and Nagel, fails by its own standards, since it does not deliver what it promised. That is, it does not screen out every bias derived from the influence of values on the content of scientific theories (Harding, 1991: 144). It is, therefore, necessary to include the context of discovery within the province of legitimate philosophical reflection on science. A proper assessment of science requires a critical analysis of the assumptions which implicitly or explicitly guide scientists in the formulation of scientific hypotheses.[9] These are assumptions which, everybody agrees, are influenced by social factors.

Some feminist philosophers, notably Lynn Nelson, have further argued that the very distinction between the two contexts of discovery and justification is unwarranted. Following Quine's naturalized epistemology, she claims that 'the task of epistemology is discovering how the beliefs we have are acquired' (1990: 84). Hence, the theory of knowledge is a study of how our beliefs are arrived at, it cannot produce an independent logic of confirmation since ' "justification" of our beliefs and theories is not going to be supplied from outside of science' (1990: 83).

It would be possible to take these criticisms on board and conclude that, while science should and can screen out values, the model adopted by Hempel and Nagel fails to explain how this happens. This approach appears to be endorsed by Bleier in some of her papers on scientific research on sex differences in cognitive abilities. Bleier points out how time and again results based on scarce evidence are presented as scientific fact; how research in this field is done ignoring alternatives which would be equally supported by the little evidence available. As a result 'few of the hypotheses and assumptions [of sex differences research] have independent scientific support but together, supported by each other, they create the illusion of a structure with weight, consistency, conviction, and reason' (1986: 149). If this is indeed a defect of such theories, it is not one which can be entirely avoided by adherence to the hypothetical-deductive method. What is required is closer attention to the ways in which social values infiltrate the work of scientists (1986: 148).

The route taken by most feminist philosophers is, however, a wholesome rejection of internalist accounts of science. Harding, for example, claims that no method can insulate science from politics and the general social context. Awareness of this phenomenon should be conducive to better science because it would lead to a critical examination of the values which are unavoidably implicated in scientific research. Thus, no scientific theory whatsoever is politically innocent; however, politically influenced scientific theories are not necessarily instances of bad science.[10] Values are not merely an inevitable part of science, some values help its development. The issue is, 'once we've acknowledged the necessity and legitimacy of partiality, *how do we tell the good bias from the bad bias?*' (Antony, 1993: 189).

This is, I believe, a crucial question in the ongoing tradition of feminist philosophical reflection; arguably, what distinguishes three main approaches to feminist epistemology is their position on this issue. According to feminist empiricists, a good bias is conducive to empirical adequacy; standpoint theorists take it to be the bias of an oppressed standpoint,[11] while postmodern feminists emphasizes the contingency of the notions involved in the distinction.

So far I have illustrated two ways in which values play a role in science. Firstly, one could argue with Longino that values are part of the evidence for theories. Values would not merely be inevitable, they could also help the confirmation of hypotheses. Secondly, one might hold with Harding that not all values can be screened out in the process of confirmation. Values cannot be eradicated from science. Further, a scientist who holds progressive values is in a good position to unearth the implicit assumptions made by conservatives colleagues. In this case too, values play a positive role in science. It must be noted, however, that Harding's argument does not show that values can constitute part of the justification for a theory. It merely supports the claim that social and political commitments can cause scientists to spot gaps in the views endorsed by others, and to formulate new hypotheses. Hence, Harding's position is less innovative than it might seem at first sight. If pushed, even internalists might concede that values play these roles in science. A more revolutionary view would hold that values are in part constitutive of the evidence for theories.

An example might help to explain the difference between causal and constitutive relations. A scientist who holds feminist values might gain more reliable information about primates than her sexist colleagues. Her values cause her to formulate hypotheses which are better confirmed by empirical evidence than previous views. Values in this example are not part of the evidence for the theory, but they are one of the causes that led to its formulation. However, when a feminist scientist interprets women's poorer performance in the frame and rod experiment as evidence of their lack of assertiveness, values are part of the evidence. They function as the background that enables observations about performance to constitute evidence for a claim about assertiveness.

The arguments presented by Longino and Harding are rather different.

Nevertheless, they are also similar in important respects. Firstly, they rely on the assumption that, in principle, we can always tell the difference between social values and scientific fact. Second, they use Quine's under-determination thesis to show that empirical evidence is not sufficient to determine a unique theory. For Harding values cause us to choose one among empirically equivalent theories. For Longino, they constitute the background that makes one theory better confirmed than its otherwise equally warranted rivals. Quine's thesis, however, is not unproblematic. For example, Ian Hacking has argued that tinkering with scientific instru-ments often helps to determine scientific theories. When scientists get empirical results that are consistent with more than one theory, they may change their equipment so as to get a result that definitely supports one rather than another theory (1992: 53). Because Quine only considers the relations between observations and theories, he ignores most of what constitutes the practice of science. But when these practical activities are considered, theories look much less underdetermined than Quine takes them to be. This is not to exclude that values also play a part here, but this part should be understood in terms of their influences on the practices of scientists.

A third feminist argument against internalism is deeply influenced by the sociology of science. The internalist model endorses a division of labor between the philosophy of science and the sociology of knowledge, since it holds that a sociological study of science is appropriate only when something has gone wrong. The philosophy of science, instead, would be relevant only when science is successful. Supporters of the internalist account of science do not bluntly deny that scientific activity is a social phenomenon. Rather, they claim that what makes a research project an instance of good science is not to be found in its social characteristics, but in its relation to normative structures: methods, standards of evidence, experimental procedures and so forth. In other words, a sociological study of science would not further our understanding of what makes an instance of scientific research good rather than bad.

Harding rejects this tenet of internalist accounts of science; she holds that the view that the content of 'good' science has no social causes is mistaken, and unscientific. Instead, following the sociologists of knowledge, she claims that 'a fully scientific account of belief will seek causal symmetry; it will try to identify the social causes (as well as the natural ones) of the best as well as the worst of beliefs' (1991: 82). It is true that all beliefs, both good and bad from a scientific viewpoint, have social causes. However, this claim does not counter the internalist position, which does not deny that scientifically good beliefs have social causes, but only holds that these causes are not what makes them good. Harding's claim for symmetry in causal explanations of belief is, nevertheless, valuable, since it reminds us of the importance of considering factors belonging to the context of discovery as pertinent to philosophical reflection on science.

Harding, however, is not merely claiming that social causes, which can only be detected at the level of the context of discovery, can have negative effects on the content of science. Rather, she wants to claim that some social causes have a positive effect on science; that is, she holds that some biases are good. Thus, she asserts that 'certain social conditions make it possible for humans to produce reliable explanations of patterns in nature, just as other social conditions make it very difficult to do so' (1991: 83). This claim is also true. All kinds of social factor have an effect on which processes for the acquisition of beliefs one may learn, and on their reliability. For example, being trained in particle physics makes one more capable to produce reliable explanations in this field. The same point, however, can be made about, for instance, gender and class. One could claim that on some issues women are more reliable than men because of the way they have been socialized. I doubt the truth of these universal claims. There are sufficient differences among women to make such generalizations implausible. It is more likely, however, that holding feminist values might cause one to become the sort of person who, for example, is more reliable than others on a variety of issues. Hence, one may agree with Harding that 'not all social values and interests have the same bad effects upon the results of research. Some have systematically generated less partial and distorted beliefs than others' (1991: 144).

This argument presupposes that knowledge is reliably formed belief. Justification becomes a matter of the causal history of belief. The argument is an instance of naturalized epistemology; among feminists, it has been adopted by Harding and Nelson to name but a few. Traditional views about knowledge enforced the conviction that our beliefs are based on the facts alone. Given this picture social factors can play no positive role in the justification of beliefs which are not about society. Naturalism, instead, can lead to the claim that a variety of social factors can make a difference to the reliability of the methods employed by scientists.

Nevertheless, this is achieved by side-stepping the important issue of the rationality of theory choice. The normative dimension of knowledge, justification and rationality, is ultimately made dependent on factual issues about the causes of belief and the reliability of the processes involved in arriving at them. The internalist conception of science is, instead, at least partly motivated by a desire to preserve an irreducibly normative dimension in explanations of science. I subscribe to this motivation, without endorsing the internalist solution to it; I will give some arguments against naturalism in chapter 5.

However, to preserve the irreducibility of normative studies of science to sociology, one does not have to subscribe to the view that sociology has nothing to say about what makes good science good. To say that there is a sociological dimension to what makes research an instance of good science requires only that we take seriously the common sense belief that science is done by communities rather than individuals in isolation.[12] Even if it is individual scientists who have knowledge, they do not settle on their beliefs without discussing their results with others and without being influenced by others in many ways. I suppose it is not uncommon for postgraduate students to find themselves holding the view advanced by their supervisors without having compared it with its extant rivals. As Miriam Solomon points out, the mistake made both by internalist philosophers of science and relativist sociologists of knowledge is to assume that if there is rationality in science, it is to be found in the decision-making processes of each individual scientist (1994: 336).[13] In other words, the problem lies with one of the forms of individualism which I discussed in the previous chapter. If we take rationality in science to be instantiated by communities rather than individuals, we can see how the community, as a whole, could behave rationally even if individual scientists are biased. For example, each scientist might give more importance to her observations, but their different biases might balance out overall. Once we take seriously the claim that theory choice is done by an entire community, the relevance of the social arrangements within this community to an evaluative discussion of science becomes quite obvious. Similarly, the incompatibility between good science and the influence of politics on the individual scientist's decisions disappears. It becomes clear that science 'does not require that scientists be unbiased, only that different scientists have different biases' (Hull, 1988: 22). One can claim that science provides reliable information about the world, and at the same time hold that scientists are always influenced by social considerations in their decisions (Hull, 1988: 4). Hence, there is always a need for scientists to scrutinize the sexist and racist biases of some of their colleagues.

These considerations provide a fourth argument against internalist accounts of science. The internalist view of science as an enterprise which ought to proceed rationally is preserved, but it is argued that this is compatible with, or may even require, less than rational behavior on the part of individual scientists. Longino, for example, has formulated such an argument, and Nelson has also used considerations of this sort.

Although these arguments against traditional conceptions of science are correct, they do not go far enough in questioning those conceptions. In particular, they go along with them in merely assuming that rationality itself is not social, although it might be embodied by social groups. For example, the fourth argument I have presented above assumes that the rationality of science is always a matter of instrumental (means–ends) reasoning. These arguments, thus, rely on the view that what counts as a reason or a justification cannot have a social history. They can explain that what people think counts as a reason may change, but this just shows that some people have false beliefs about reason and justification.

Another problem with these arguments is their exclusive concern with scientific theories, they hardly examine the roles played by values in other aspects of science. Instead, it is important to remember that science is also an eminently practical activity that often involves the use of instruments in laboratories. Shifting the focus from science as theory to science as practice might help to see novel ways in which values permeate science. The account of practice I have sketched in chapter 1 provides the framework for this shift in focus.

Tools, I have claimed, are socially constituted. They are defined in terms of the significance they have for us. If we want to explain what a detector of high energy particles is, we describe its purpose. We say what it is appropriately used for. Laboratory practices that involve the use of this tool make it what it is. Outside the context of these practices there are no detectors, although there could in principle be objects that are physically identical to them. Thus, scientific equipment, like detectors, is constituted by the value it has for us. Our practical engagements with these tools bestow upon them the significance that makes them what they are. The values that constitute tools often are internal to science, they include precision and stability of results. But values of a different kind can also be relevant. Laboratory mice are an example of this phenomenon. These mice are scientific equipment, although they may be more than that. They are constituted by their significance, which they acquire through their employment in laboratory practices. Some mice have even been genetically mutated in the laboratory. I am inclined to think that, sometimes, experimentation on animals is acceptable. But, whatever one believes about the morality of these activities, practices involving mice invest them with a significance that has a moral dimension. Scientists experimenting with mice take it to be appropriate to treat mice as tools. Moral values, which might be objectionable, constitute mice as a piece of equipment.

I have argued in chapter 1 that an observation, such as a reading of the temperature, acquires its significance only against a background of other knowledge. One must know what thermometers are for, and be able to recognize them. Observations made using more sophisticated tools require skill and theoretical knowledge. They might also require a background of social practices. Suppose that in the process of human reproduction the egg clasps the sperm that fertilizes it. Using microscopes it is possible to see a mound of small finger-like projections, the microvilli, on the surface of the egg (Biology and Gender Study Group, 1988: 177). However, in the context of a society in which anything female is conceived as passive, it would be impossible for this phenomenon to be seen as a clasping of the sperm by the egg. This observation becomes possible only when a community of individuals challenges sexist social practices. Thus, a change in the social background gives to an observation a new significance. Like a toddler, who cannot read the temperature when she looks at a thermometer, a scientist steeped in sexist prejudice cannot see the egg clasping the sperm when he looks through the microscope.

This example shows how knowledge can be socially constituted. Social values do not merely cause scientists to discover new knowledge. They function as the background that constitutes it. In the absence of feminist practices no observation of the egg would count as seeing it clasping the sperm. The analogy, I have used in chapter 1, should be of help to grasp this point. I have claimed that no immersion in water is a baptism outside the context of religious practices. Religious belief does not merely cause people to be baptized; religion creates a new significance for an old act. Water is now taken to clean the soul, rather than the body. Similarly, in this example feminist practices endow the physical event of an observation with a new significance. They do not only cause it. Furthermore, the example, I have provided, is an instance of non-inferential knowledge. Thus, it would be a mistake to believe that feminist values merely contribute to inferential justification.

Similar claims, of course, can be made about theoretical knowledge. The justification of theories makes reference to observational knowledge – if the latter is socially constituted, the former will inherit this feature. Moreover, social factors might be relevant to what counts as a justification. It is possible that the social context makes a difference about what sort of claims can be treated as evidence, which forms of reasoning are taken to be appropriate. I have claimed in chapter 2 that, before the early modern period, individuals had no notion of evidence. No assertion could have counted as providing evidence for a claim. The notion of evidence only appeared with the emergence of probability. Changes in underlying economic practices and advances in mathematics made this emergence possible. Once the notion of probability had been grasped, a new epistemic practice was created which attributed to assertions the significance of giving evidence in favor of claims. This practice has been subject to modifications over the years. For example, it was assumed that claims made by women could not count as evidence. This epistemic practice, we would want to say, was mistaken. Changes in the underlying social practices have made some corrections possible. Much still needs to be changed, but women are now granted some epistemic authority. In other words, the current social context is one in which, sometimes, assertions made by women have the significance of justifications in support of some claims.

To summarize, I have claimed that the internalism of traditional empiricist conceptions of science is inadequate. I have shown why post-positivist beliefs about the autonomy of science, and the exclusive importance of the context of justification, must be abandoned. I have also discussed four different arguments that feminists have provided in favor of this rejection. The first two presuppose the value-ladenness of every theory, and the third relies on naturalized epistemology. The fourth argument is based on considerations about the rationality of scientific communities. Finally, I have proposed a supplementary argument in favor of the social constitution of knowledge.

Feminists, as is clear from this discussion, have been among the most prominent critics of internalism and of empiricism. These criticisms have prompted Harding to provide a rather negative assessment of a feminism that would endorse empiricist views. It is a testimony to the vitality of feminism that, as soon as Harding published this assessment, new and more engaging sorts of feminist empiricism have emerged. The task faced by these epistemologies, as by any other, is, I have argued, to explain how knowledge is possible, not despite value and political engagement, but in part because of them (Mitroff, 1974: 591).

Further Reading

Anne Fausto-Sterling's *Myths of Gender: Biological Theories about Women and Men* (1992) provides a highly readable and very comprehensive discussion of sexist biases in science. Helen Longino's *Science as Social Knowledge: Values and Objectivity in Scientific Inquiry* (1990) and Sandra Harding's *Whose Science? Whose Knowledge?* (1991) contain powerful arguments against conceptions of science as a source of value-neutral knowledge.

Notes

1   Admittedly, LeVay's belief that his biological speculations might help the cause of gay rights is also fairly surprising. It is, however, not unusual in the North American context.

2   This latter point is forcefully argued by Hacking (1990).

3   Harding (1986: 94) seems to believe that feminists who make these points are committed to the view that scientific methodology is not problematic as it stands. I believe this judgment to be unfair. When one points out that several scientific theories fall short of current standards, one has not automatically accepted those standards.

4   This brief description greatly simplifies the Hempel–Nagel account of the hypothetical-deductive method. For example, it makes no mention of the crucial issue of bridge laws. The supporters of this account recognized that often theoretical scientific claims included a vocabulary that referred to entities, such as the electron, which cannot be observed; thus, no observational claim will make reference to electrons. Hence, it would seem impossible to confirm any claim about these entities. It is because of this problem that they introduced the notion of a 'bridge law' which formulated definitions in the vocabulary of observations for terms that referred to entities which cannot be observed. The seminal texts on the hypothetical-deductive method in science are: Hempel, *Aspects of Scientific Explanation* (1965), and Nagel, *The Structure of Science* (1961). There are many texts which explain this approach to science, in particular see Nelson (1990: 43–60); for more details see Longino (1990).

5   The activities of women in this movement are described in some detail by Potter (1988: 24–6).

6   Much is at stake here; for example, the very possibility of feminist empiricism. I shall continue this discussion in the next chapter.

7   Nevertheless, we should not forget that 'caring' is an important moral virtue and one that is unjustifiably underestimated in our current society.

8   I discuss her position on this issue in the first section of chapter 4.

9   The importance of taking the context of discovery into account is emphasized by Harding (1986, 1991), Longino (1990), Nelson (1990), and Okruhlik (1992), among others. Claiming that both contexts should be subjected to philosophical reflection is not the same as saying that the distinction between the two contexts is unwarranted.

10   This is a view held by many feminists: Nelson (1990), Potter (1988), Harding (1986, 1991), Longino (1990), Code (1991), to name but a few.

11   Although they do not necessarily claim that what ultimately makes the bias good is just the fact that it belongs to a given standpoint.

12 There is also a growing non-feminist literature on the importance of the social to science. For example, the papers by Hardwig (1985, 1991) and by Kitcher (1994) that I discussed in the previous chapter, but also Kitcher (1990).

13 The claim that the rationality of theory choice emerges when one takes into account the whole scientific community rather than the decision of individuals is not equivalent to Nelson's claim that communities are the primary subject of knowledge. The first claim simply requires that individual knowledge may depend on evidence possessed by others, and on the social organization of the community to which the knower belongs. It does not require that it is communities that have knowledge.

4

Feminist Empiricism

In the previous chapter I discussed the relations between feminism and mainstream philosophy of science. Usually feminists have been rather critical of traditional philosophical accounts of science. In particular, they criticize the internalism which is inherent in most of them. Instead, they argue for a more social understanding of science. Often, however, their arguments have been explicitly directed against empiricism, which they take to be wedded to both individualism and the internalist myth about science. Although many traditional forms of empiricism are indeed antithetical to feminist accounts of science, an empiricism which admits that social factors influence the content of good scientific theories might be sympathetic to a feminist model of science. In this chapter I explore this more social feminist empiricism.

We owe the term 'feminist empiricism' to Sandra Harding, who characterizes it as one of three possible answers to the issue of how politicized research can be more scientific than allegedly value-neutral work. The other two replies are: feminist standpoint theory, and feminist postmodernism (1986: 24).[1] These are, for Harding, three forms that a feminist epistemology could take. They are epistemologies in the sense of providing a normative account of the justification of theories. They are feminist because they are concerned with the grounds for the justification of feminist claims (1986: 24).

Harding's tripartite distinction is now widely employed within the field of feminist epistemology. It is, however, doubtful whether any feminist thinker fits perfectly within any of these labels. Nevertheless, Harding's distinction is still useful as a way of delineating three possible feminist positions on the relation between politics and knowledge, especially scientific knowledge.

These points are particularly pertinent to the case of feminist empiricism as it is characterized by Harding. To my knowledge no self-defined feminist thinker has wholeheartedly endorsed the position Harding describes as feminist empiricism, even though one can notice strands of this way of thinking in the work of some writers.[2] Nevertheless, Harding's characterization has proved itself fruitful since it has provided the stimulus to produce some fully developed feminist empiricist theories which avoid the pitfalls previously highlighted by Harding herself.[3]

Harding characterizes feminist empiricism as an attempt to rectify the sexism and androcentrism of current science by arguing that these are 'social biases correctable by stricter adherence to the existing methodological norms of scientific inquiry' (1986: 24).[4] The existing methodological norms Harding is referring to are those advanced by Carl Hempel and Ernest Nagel, whose model of scientific knowledge I have discussed in the previous chapter.

More than once her reader feels inclined to think that for Harding the very notion of a feminist empiricism is a contradiction in terms. Often she almost claims that empiricism is incompatible with feminism. This should not come as a surprise, since feminist empiricism is meant to explain the epistemic virtues of politically informed research while adhering to a methodology which requires value-neutrality. This is not strictly speaking a contradiction in terms; nevertheless, it requires an erasure of feminist values from the justification of knowledge in order to avoid infringing the requirement of value-neutrality. Feminist values would be confined to the process of discovery, which is not governed by scientific methodology and is irrelevant to what makes a scientific theory good rather than bad. Hence, feminist empiricism would be forced to admit that feminist values make no contribution to the achievement of science proper.[5]

It would be unfair, however, to criticize Harding for having set up a straw-woman, since one of the achievements of her analysis is to have brought to light the tensions between the traditional empiricist project and the tradition of feminist thinking. Nevertheless, Harding is thus forced to claim that the challenging work of feminist empiricists has been to develop arguments which ultimately undermine the key assumptions of empiricism itself and demonstrate its internal incoherence (1986: 162). For example, Harding claims that feminist empiricists have challenged the stark empiricist distinction between the contexts of justification and of discovery (1991: 116); consequently they have also criticized the internalism of traditional philosophy of science (1986: 40). Hence, for Harding, feminist empiricism as an epistemology has a 'transitional character' because it shows the way to more radical positions. Harding does not reject feminist empiricism altogether, but for her its virtues mainly reside in the fact that 'it is effective at explaining the successes of feminist-inspired research to certain important audiences for this work' (1991: 114). The audiences in question are those composed by non-feminist scientists. The virtues of feminist empiricism are characterized mainly as pragmatic; they are located in its ability to sustain a dialogue with mainstream science and philosophy.

Harding's rather negative assessment of the prospects for feminist empiricism has prompted a renewed interest in this topic. At the moment there are two kinds of feminist empiricism: contextual empiricism and naturalized empiricism, which have been developed respectively by Helen Longino and Lynn Nelson.

These approaches differ from each other in more than mere matters of detail, but they share a rejection of some features of traditional empiricism. First, they acknowledge that science is a human social activity and that it would be a mistake to reduce scientific practice to the theories it produces (Longino, 1990: 17; Nelson, 1990: 10–11). Since they recognize that science is primarily an activity which is pursued by groups, they realize that any adequate account of knowledge would have to consider its social dimension. This is an aspect of science that had been ignored by old-style empiricism because of its commitment to individualism.

Second, because they view science as a social activity, both Nelson and Longino claim that a philosophical account of science cannot limit itself to an analysis of the justification of theories, but must also consider those factors which are traditionally taken to belong to the context of discovery. However, while Nelson holds that her naturalistic account of evidence undermines the very distinction between the two contexts (1990: 264), Longino preserves the distinction and includes analyses of both contexts in her account (1993: 102).

Third, they reject the presumed value-neutrality of science characteristic of traditional empiricism, and show how values are inevitably employed in the justification of theories.[6] Although both Nelson and Longino claim that values play a part in what counts as evidence for a scientific theory, their accounts of evidence and of the role of values differ quite substantially. It is mainly this difference that makes Nelson's account naturalist and Longino's contextualist.

Despite their rejection of traditional forms of empiricism, both Nelson and Longino characterize their positions as empiricist because they hold that the evidence for knowledge claims is mainly (or only) empirical evidence (Longino, 1990a: 150; and Nelson, 1990: 21). This is, according to them, the central tenet of empiricism. Thus, although both Longino and Nelson believe that many feminist criticisms of traditional Lockean and post-positivist empiricism are warranted, they hold that empiricism can still be preserved once these criticisms have been taken on board.

The starting point of these new forms of empiricism are two theses whose importance in empiricist philosophy has been highlighted by Quine: observations are theory-laden, and theories are underdetermined by empirical data. The first states that observations are not conceptually independent of theories because the latter provide those concepts which are necessary for observations. For example, suppose I look at the mercury column of a barometer and see that it registers a given pressure. In a sense it is true that even a child with no conception of barometers can do this; however, this child will not recognize the barometer as a barometer, she will not be able to read the pressure from the barometer. Hence, the child will not observe the value of the pressure. It is this latter kind of observations which, for Quine, are important to science and presuppose some knowledge of theories.[7]

The second thesis claims that theories are underdetermined by empirical data; that is, there will always be more than one theory which is compatible with all the available empirical evidence.[8] This thesis has been taken to refute foundationalism, since it claims that experience is not enough to guide our choice of one theory over another. It is not clear whether this is correct, but in any case this thesis, if true, would show that empirical evidence is not sufficient to determine uniquely the choice of the best theory.

Contextual Empiricism

Longino's contextual empiricism is a modification of the Hempel–Nagel model of the confirmation of scientific theories on the basis of a qualified subscription to the two Quinean theses mentioned above. Longino accepts that 'some data (or evidence) may only be conceived or sought in the context of investigating some hypothesis' (1990: 56). She does not, however, subscribe to a Kuhnian interpretation of the consequences of this phenomenon. For Thomas Kuhn incommensurability of different theories follows from the theory-ladenness of observations, since the meanings of terms employed in observations are relative to the theory one adopts. There cannot be any neutral evidence to adjudicate conflicting theories.[9] As a consequence, in the Kuhnian model the description of data presupposes the truth of the theory for which they serve as evidence (1990: 56). Following Mary Hesse, Longino claims instead that, although there is no theory-neutral language of observations, it does not follows that observations cannot be used as independent tests of theories. She points out that there will be some overlap between supporters of different theories, and that the theory which informs the meanings of the terms used to describe a given observation might not be the same as that for which the observation is a test (1990: 55–6).

The theory-ladenness of observations, Longino points out, highlights the fact that what functions as evidence for a theory are not 'raw' data but always experiences which are informed by theoretical considerations (1990a: 150). The example of the barometer mentioned above makes this phenomenon explicit. Longino further claims that

> as a consequence of theory-ladenness, a more prudent empiricism treats sense experience not as the sole legitimator of knowledge claims, since other sorts of considerations may be relevant to establishing the content of observation and the proper articulation of data. (1990a: 151)

Thus, experience does not constitute the whole of the evidence for or against scientific theories.

The underdetermination of theories by data, according to Longino, shows that observations function as evidence for theories only relative to a set of background assumptions or auxiliary hypotheses (1990a: 151). That is, 'why one takes some state of affairs as evidence for one hypothesis rather than for another, depends on one's other beliefs, which we can call background beliefs or assumptions' (1990: 43). Longino's model of theory confirmation still follows Hempel and Nagel insofar as it takes theories to function as hypotheses which are to be confirmed by observations. It differs from their approach in the claim that it is only against the background of other beliefs that observations can provide evidential support for theories.

This is not a small difference, because it shows how science is inevitably value-laden. Background assumptions or auxiliary hypotheses, which are essential to the confirmation of theories, might embody or presuppose values. Furthermore, the method of scientific confirmation is not sufficient to screen out the influence of these values.[10] These values which are part of the justification of theories are not just the constitutive values of simplicity, consistency, etc. which are derived from the goals of scientific research. They are also contextual values; political and moral values that belong to the social and cultural environment in which science is practiced (1990: 4).

While rejecting the traditional empiricist tenet that good science is autonomous from politics, Longino upholds the empiricist view that science is about formulating hypotheses which must be tested against experience. She does not claim, however, that empirical scientific method is sufficient to eliminate oppressive political values from the fabric of science. To achieve this, it is also necessary to scrutinize the background hypotheses which enable the data to function as evidence for scientific hypotheses. Furthermore, given the context dependence of confirmation, it is only intersubjective criticism which 'assures that idiosyncratic beliefs, values, and interests are excluded from the body of what gets to count as scientific knowledge' (1990a: 152). Since the method of confirmation does not automatically screen out the influence of subjective values, this screening process can only be achieved if science is practiced and criticized within a varied community of individuals who do not share the same interests and political outlook. In a scientific community of this sort it is more likely that somebody will spot the values embodied in the background beliefs employed by somebody else to confirm scientific hypotheses. Scientific knowledge, therefore, is social knowledge because it can be properly achieved only by individuals working in a varied community.

To summarize, for Longino empirical testing is what validates scientific knowledge claims, but validation cannot erase the influence of values on science because values are an inevitable part of the context of justification. It is only when we conceive of science as a social phenomenon pursued by a socially varied community that we can hope to minimize the influence of values in science. Nevertheless, at any time some values are likely to remain hidden from view, and it remains the task of intersubjective criticism to make them visible and available for evaluation (1990: 223).

Longino's account is important not simply because it provides a detailed explanation of how empiricism is compatible with a rejection of pretense value-neutrality and of the individualism characteristic of its earlier versions. It is above all important because it makes intelligible feminist claims that even good science might embody values.[11] Thus Longino has shown that empiricism is not committed to an internalist account of science, instead it is compatible with understanding science as a social phenomenon. Longino's empiricism therefore avoids many of the problems raised by Harding in her analysis of feminist empiricism.

Nevertheless, Longino's account appears unsatisfactory at least to those feminists who, like Harding, believe that holding a certain set of values makes one a better knower than those who hold a different set (Harding, 1991: 83). It is not easy to formulate this criticism precisely. In a sense Longino would agree with this claim, since she would hold that in a deeply sexist society non-sexist scientists are in a better position than others to spot and criticize the role of sexism in the background assumptions of current theories. Just the same, Longino believes that scientists should aim to screen out all social values from science;[12] this, of course, can never be completely achieved, but it is still a regulative ideal for science. She holds that objectivity is achieved by inclusion in science of all perspectives because they are likely to cancel out each other's subjective partiality; objectivity, therefore, is a matter of 'maximal minimization of subjective (whether individual or collective) preference' (1990a: 152).[13] Hence, for Longino, feminist values are external to the methodology of science; nonetheless they are useful to counteract dominant androcentric values.[14]

Naturalized Empiricism

Nelson's feminist empiricism shares some of the features of Longino's contextual empiricism but also departs from it at several junctures. Nelson, like Longino, accepts that observations are theory-laden and that theories are underdetermined by the data. However, Nelson's account of the notion of empirical evidence is rather different from Longino's. Consequently, their interpretations of the two Quinean theses mentioned above are also different.

Nelson's account of science is greatly influenced by Quine's version of empiricism in science and of naturalism in epistemology. Like Quine, Nelson rejects the dichotomy between analytic truths, which are true in virtue of meaning, and synthetic truths, which are true in virtue of facts. Instead, she holds that every truth is true because of both how the world is and what the words we use mean (1990: 91). Nelson also rejects the view that statements taken individually can be confirmed by empirical evidence. She claims, instead, that whole theories, rather than individual statements, are confirmed or disconfirmed by experience (1990: 90). Thus Nelson rejects two important tenets of traditional empiricism: she rejects the claims that some statements, for instance logical and mathematical ones, are immune from revision, and that observations confirm statements in isolation.

Nelson also follows Quine in claiming that scientific theories are 'bridges of our own making.' They are artefacts of our own creation, and serve to bridge sensory stimulations: by doing so they explain and organize experience (1990: 108, 310). This understanding of scientific theories is deeply connected with several central aspects of Nelson's empiricism.

Firstly, it reflects her belief that 'theories, including scientific theories, are tools for organizing, explaining, and predicting experience' (Nelson and Nelson, 1994: 488). This is an expression of the typical empiricist position on the aim of theories. While for scientific realists science aims to provide a true description of the world, empiricists prefer a more instrumentalist characterization of science as a tool for prediction and explanation.[15]

Secondly, it expresses Nelson's holism about theories and their empirical contents. She views theories as networks which connect experiences with other experiences by explaining how they hang together and by predicting future experiences on the basis of past ones. The metaphor of the bridge or network for theories derives from Nelson's commitment to holism. She claims that statements can neither be confirmed nor have meaning in isolation. A holistic view of confirmation is a direct consequence of the rejection of the second tenet of old-style empiricism, according to which observations can confirm isolated statements. Holism about meaning follows because Nelson holds that the meaning of a statement is its empirical content (1990: 88; 1993: 155). The empirical content of a claim is given by the sensory stimulations (experiences) that would confirm it; since no statement can be confirmed by experience in isolation, no statement has empirical content or meaning in isolation. This is an account of meaning as a matter of confirmation (or verification) which Nelson shares with Quine and which, besides being holistic, is not very different from old-style logical positivism or empiricism.

Thirdly, it reflects Nelson's conviction that science is primarily a human activity which consists of constructing and evaluating theories, and of positing objects. For Nelson the objects of scientific theories are 'posits.' She takes this notion to undermine the dichotomy between social constructionism and realism about knowledge and about the objects included in the domains of theories. Objects are posited by us to organize experience; our success in doing so constitutes the evidence we have for these objects. Thus objects are not discovered prior to theorizing, rather they are proposed and evaluated with the theories about them (1990: 106). For Nelson, posits are not unreal, pure social constructions, but they do not exist independently of theories either. Instead, the dichotomy between social construction and discovery is undermined because there is 'no sense to be made of distinction between the objects we talk about and the ways we talk about them' (1990: 102). I believe she is mistaken on this point. An object is posited if its existence is required by a theory; its status as a posit is a reminder of what kind of evidence can be mustered in its favor. The notion of a 'posit' is epistemic, it tells us nothing about the kind of existence which is attributed to posited objects. For example, when scientists posit an object, they usually assume that it exists independently of their theories about it. The notion of a 'posit' does not undermine the ontological distinction between socially constructed entities and things which exist independently of us. Nevertheless, Nelson's view that objects are posits entails that ontology – the study of what there is – is to be conducted scientifically. There is no vantage point outside science from which to conduct this study; instead, the results of science must be taken at face value.

Nelson's theory of evidence derives from her commitments to holism concerning the empirical content of scientific statements, and to empiricism as a theory of evidence. A theory of evidence is, for her, a theory about what justifies or warrants scientific claims (1990: 292; 1993a: 177). Initially she proposed a coherence account of evidence, according to which 'coherence – to our experiences and others of our theories – is the overarching standard we use in judging whether theories and beliefs are warranted' (1990: 28). Subsequently she has come to see evidence as having a further aspect which concerns the explanatory power of the theory or assumption under scrutiny (1993: 139).

A theory is empirically adequate if there is substantial evidence in its favor; that is, if it coheres with experiences and other currently accepted theories, and if it helps to explain experiences and the links between other less general theories. This account of evidence is not the result of armchair reflections on Nelson's part. Following Quine, she believes that there is no first philosophy which could prescribe the conditions for the justification of theories. Instead, she holds that there is no significant boundary between science and epistemology (1990: 106). As a consequence:

> standards of evidence are historically relative and dynamic, emerging concomitantly with the processes through which knowledge is generated, rather than having been laid down prior to these processes. (1993: 122)

Nelson's theory of evidence is itself an empirical scientific theory, which is to be judged in terms of its empirical adequacy. It is to be evaluated on the basis of its explanatory power and its coherence with experience and other current theories (1993a: 179). This is a task which Nelson attends to when she argues that her account explains the practices of science and the import of feminist criticisms, and that it coheres with experiences and other theories.[16] The scientism implicit in Nelson's position is not, however, without problems (a matter which I also take up in the next chapter).

In Nelson's account evidence is communal (1993: 124). She also argues that, since knowledge always requires an appeal to communal standards of evidence, the proper subjects of knowledge are communities. Individuals have knowledge only in a derivative sense (1990: 255). Nelson's claims that both evidence and standards of evidence are communal are not altogether clear. Firstly, she holds that evidence is communal because 'experience [which is part of evidence] . . . is fundamentally social' (Nelson and Nelson, 1994: 496). There are no immediate experiences, because experiences or observations are theory-laden; that is, 'we never experience a world "untheorized"' (1990: 24). Hence, 'our sensory experiences are themselves shaped and mediated – indeed they are made *coherent* – by numerous specific theories' (1990: 22). The theory-ladenness of experiences shows, *contra* traditional Lockean empiricism, that 'sensory experiences are not, and cannot be, foundational' (1990: 22).

As in the example of the barometer presented above, experience of the kind which is relevant to science is possible only when somebody has acquired a given conceptual apparatus; that is, only when somebody has at least partly understood some specific theory expressed in a public language.[17] Thus, it is the emergence of theories that makes experiences possible; for example, according to Nelson, experiences of protons became possible only when particle physics was developed (1993: 138). This claim should not come as a surprise, since protons are theoretical posits which are never directly experienced. Furthermore, only those who understand some of the relevant theory can have these experiences. Thus, an experience is always relative to a community within which the necessary concepts for the experience have been developed (1990: 110).

It would seem that, even if experiences were possible only when a given public theory has been formulated, it is nevertheless individuals who have these experiences. This impression appears to be confirmed by Nelson's claim that 'experience (so our best theories tell us) will be cashed out, in the end, as the firings of sensory receptors' (Nelson and Nelson, 1994: 496). These firings are, of course, physical states of individuals. However,

Nelson immediately adds that 'we do not *experience* those firings' (Nelson and Nelson, 1994: 496). Nelson is thus arguing that it is likely that we will explain phenomenological experiences in terms of firings of sensory receptors, while at the same time making clear that the notion of experience which she employs in her theory of evidence is phenomenological: what matters is what we experience. This characterization of experience does not, however, dispel the impression that it is individuals who have experiences; this impression is also confirmed by Nelson's frequent reference to individual experiences.[18] It is, however, only in the context of a community that it is possible *to recognize* a sensory experience as *relevant* to a given body of knowledge (1993: 138). This characterization suggests that for Nelson experiences can function as evidence only when they are brought into the public domain through expression in a public language.

Another constituent part of evidence is the whole body of our current theories. This does not just include scientific theories but also so-called 'common sense.'[19] These theories are our body of knowledge, and knowledge is, for Nelson, social since it is communities that are the primary bearers of knowledge. Thus, evidence is communal because both the experiences and the theories that constitute it are social. Standards of evidence – the standards by which we judge whether something is evidence for a theory – are also communal because they are essentially shared by a community (Nelson and Nelson, 1994: 497). These standards evolve dynamically in accordance with the construction of theories (1990: 105; 1993a: 173). It is only against the background of a community which shares a conceptual apparatus, scientific methods, and evidential standards that, according to Nelson, observations can function as evidence for theories. Therefore, Nelson concludes, it is communities rather than individuals which are the primitive bearers of knowledge.

This argument is not convincing. At most it establishes that individuals cannot know unless they are part of a community; it does not show that it is communities which are first and foremost knowers. Nelson appears to be aware of this problem when she restates her point as 'none of us knows what no one else could' (1993: 142). Her argument does indeed support the view that membership in a knowing community both limits and enables which knowledge we have, so that whatever one knows it is possible for others in the community to know it.

There is another strand to Nelson's thinking which also gives support to the view that individuals have knowledge only as members of a community. Suppose an isolated individual had claimed centuries ago that the earth rotates around the sun, but that her claim did not come to be accepted. Centuries later the scientific community comes to accept the heliocentric view of the solar system but without relying on the experiments and methods of that isolated scientist. In a case such as this one, Nelson holds, we would not attribute knowledge to the isolated individual unless we made her an honorary member of the scientific community that later developed.[20] This analysis might be convincing when we apply it to those Greek philosophers who advanced the heliocentric hypothesis. One could be quite reticent to attribute to them scientific knowledge of the fact that the earth rotates around the sun. Their methods seem to have been too primitive, too different from ours to attribute to them the knowledge we have. This example introduces a temporal historical dimension to the theory of knowledge.[21] Nelson, however, does not discuss this issue. Because she provides a causal account of knowledge, she fails to capture the historical dimension of science as a human practice that is always endowed with new meanings.

We do not attribute knowledge of the earth's rotation to those ancient Greek philosophers because their theories have no connection to ours – there is no relation between the two. It is not sufficient that we seem to say the same things about the solar system: to attribute our knowledge to them it would also be necessary that the background against which their claims acquire significance is suitably related to the background of practices and beliefs provided by our community. If this is true, what somebody could know would depend also on which communities she belongs to. Nelson does not provide this argument herself, but what she says about knowledge can be used to develop this line of thought. None of these arguments, however, supports Nelson's claim that it is communities that have knowledge in a primary sense.

Nelson's sophisticated theory of evidence provides a new framework for the analysis of the role of moral and political values in science. She argues that since science is not autonomous from common-sense beliefs and theories, science is not autonomous from values. Common-sense theorizing is not separate from our political and moral views; the values implicit in it filter through to science which is dependent on common sense itself (1990: 247). Furthermore, values shape our experiences of the world. They are part of the evidence for scientific theories because they are inherent to experiences and to other theories with which any theory must cohere to be evidentially supported. This assessment of the role of values in science is further confirmed by the underdetermination of theories by observations: since more than one theory is compatible with experience, the choice of one candidate over others is guided by considerations of coherence with our whole worldview. Furthermore, since science is pursued by communities which practice divisions of intellectual labor, the content of scientific theories is also informed by those values that guided the division of labor (1990: 174).

Nelson's account substantiates the claim that values permeate scientific enquiry. This phenomenon does not, however, undermine the objectivity of science because values themselves can be evaluated. Thus, ideology does not necessarily have a field day (1990: 306). Values themselves can and should be subjected to empirical controls (1990: 248). That this is possible is, for Nelson, a consequence of relinquishing the dichotomy between facts and values. Instead, she encourages us to appreciate that 'how things are in part determines how things ought to be, and . . . how things ought to be determines in part how we take things to be' (1990: 317). As a result of a scientific evaluation of values, 'we are in a position to see that not all values . . ., not all politics . . ., are created equal' (1990: 316). That is, values are not just a matter of subjective preference, they are objective.

Nelson's explanation of the role of values in science, thus, overcomes some of the problems with the account provided by Longino, but creates new problems of its own. Although Longino holds that contextual values play a role both in the formulation and in the confirmation of scientific hypotheses, she conceives of values as subjective preferences which must be minimized: their erasure remains a regulative ideal for the scientific enterprise. Nelson, on the other hand, attributes objectivity to values; therefore, she claims that correct values and politics have a positive place in science. But, as I argue in the following chapter, for Nelson these values have to evaluated by scientific standards, rather than vice versa. Objectivity is, for her, not 'maximal minimization of subjective preference'; instead, it is achieved by a critical self-reflection which includes an evaluation of values in order to understand which values are more defensible than others (1990: 308).[22]

Nelson's account provides the grounds for a powerful argument against leaving the evaluation of scientific theories to professional scientists alone. If evaluating scientific research includes an assessment of the values underlying it, then it is a matter for the whole community to engage in (1990: 308). Nevertheless, these evaluation would have to be done in accordance with those scientific standards that apply to the whole of science of which values are a part. This consequence of Nelson's position unwarrantedly limits the range of acceptable critiques of science because, I argue in the next chapter, it makes scientific discourse become a sort of master narrative. In other words, science is capable of being criticized only from within science.

Nelson's acknowledgment that values are not totally separate from fact, however, permits the development of an empiricism which includes explicitly political feminist goals as part of its methodology; Longino's empiricism, which is closer than Nelson's to the traditional post-positivist account of confirmation, does not deal satisfactorily with this issue.[23]

On the other hand, Nelson's acceptance of a quasi-verificationist theory of meaning, which has its roots in logical positivism, generates a different set of problems. The view that statements and terms have their empirical contents holistically, when combined with the interdependence of theories and observations, raises problems about the evidential relations between them. As Longino points out, if theories shape observations, it would seem that experiences presuppose the truth of theories and, therefore, cannot function as evidence for them. Nelson disagrees with Longino on this point. Firstly, she does not believe that observations must be independent of the theory for which they are meant to provide evidence. Rather, she interprets this requirement as being probably a remnant of foundationalism. Thus, she believes that the evidence for a theory can be radically interdependent with that theory. She acknowledges that this move gives rise to a circularity, but she does not believe that this circularity has to be vicious (1990: 9).

Nevertheless, Nelson is also keen to avoid the incommensurability between competing theories which, according to Kuhn and Longino, would follow from an interdependence between theory and experience. Incommensurability is avoided because there is always common ground between the disagreeing parties: either because scientists agree on some other theory which is not under discussion, or because they agree on common-sense views that are adopted by the society of which they are members. Insofar as we do not assume that theories are isolated from each other, and that science is autonomous from social beliefs, the interdependence of theory and observation does not threaten us with incommensurability (1990: 238).

Nelson is right to claim that Kuhn's view of incommensurability is far-fetched, and that there is always likely to be common ground between scientists who belong to the same society. Nevertheless, she seems to miss the point of Longino's (and Kuhn's) worry about incommensurability: once we adopt a thorough holism with regard to the meanings of terms

within theories and abandon the analytic/synthetic distinction, any disagreement will reverberate throughout the whole network of theories.
Suppose that, with Nelson, we believe that there is no principled distinction between what is true just as a matter of meaning, and what is true as a
matter of fact. There are no pure analytic truths or pure synthetic truths,
but every truth is true because of both how the world is and what the
words we use mean. Also, suppose that we believe that what a term means
is a matter of its relations to the meanings of every other term. It follows
that any disagreement, no matter how small, will have an effect on the
whole network of theories: on the meanings of the words we use, on
which facts our claims are meant to describe. Partial agreement is never
possible. Of course, this is an implausible position, and Nelson is right to
point out that it never occurs. Nevertheless, her views on the meaning of
scientific terms commit her to this implausibility, and to avoid it she must
abandon some of her commitments. This is not, however, a fatal problem
for Nelson's position since much of what she says can be preserved without
subscribing to the theory of meaning she borrows from Quine.

Be that as it may, the forms of empiricism developed by Longino and
Nelson do not encounter the problems raised by Harding for traditional
empiricism. Instead, it would seem that these criticisms of empiricism do
presuppose some old-style empiricist assumptions that both Nelson and
Longino are keen to reject.[24]

The Limits of Empiricism

The work of Nelson and Longino shows that individualism, the distinction
between context of discovery and justification, and the fact–value, distinction are not essential parts of empiricism. They demonstrate that many
feminist criticisms of empiricism, discussed in chapters 2 and 3, apply only
to logical positivism and to the hypothetical-deductive method developed
by Hempel and Nagel. Nevertheless, the new kinds of empiricism developed by mainstream and feminist philosophers are not completely satisfactory. They mark an immense step forward insofar as they abandon the
internalism which characterizes older empiricist accounts of science. But
they fail to capture fully the meaning of science as a human practice with
an historical and cultural dimension. Although both Nelson and Longino
acknowledge that science is a practice and should not be identified with
the theories it produces, their analyses are characterized by a lack of

attention to the activities of science. Instead, they produce theories of evidence, that is, theories about the evidential relations between theories and observations.

This is due to a limitation which is intrinsic to empiricism. Nelson is right when she claims that empiricism should be seen mainly as a theory of evidence. But because evidential relations are relations between theories and observations, empiricism is committed to what Joseph Rouse has called a 'theory-dominant' understanding of science; that is, an understanding that 'is not tied to our *practical* involvements with the world' [my italics] (1987: 69). This kind of approach to science encourages us to see systematicity in scientific knowledge, and sustains the belief that it is possible to abstract from the practices of individual scientific disciplines a common core of standards to which all of them adhere. Both Nelson and Longino accept this view and attempt to provide theories of evidence which are adequate for every natural science. It does not occur to them that different sciences might have very little in common. In any case, unless one views science as a systematic body of knowledge, there is no reason to assume that each discipline employs the same or even similar notions of evidence.

I shall return to these questions in the last chapter of this book. For now it suffices to say that the Heideggerian approach I have sketched in chapter 1 suggests that the theory-dominant approach endorsed by empiricists is wrongheaded. However, even if empiricism provides an at least partly adequate account of scientific knowledge, it remains severely incomplete. This incompleteness is due to its inability to deal with scientific knowledge as a matter of know-how.

That science involves practical abilities is a fact well known to any aspiring scientist whose training requires not only learning theories but also learning to find her way about a laboratory. To become a scientist it is not sufficient to know theories, one must also know how to do several things. Without this know-how the scientist would fail in her attempts to produce knowledge. Hence, a philosophical theory of knowledge will not be complete without an account of scientific know-how and of the contribution of this practical knowledge to the production of theories. This empiricism is badly equipped to do.

This problem with empiricism reveals a value judgment which is implicit in many empiricist theories: namely, that practical knowledge is only second best to theoretical knowledge. The latter but not the former can make a claim to being knowledge in the strictest sense of the term. Historically this is a judgment that has been employed to devalue the knowledge produced by women.[25] Their knowledge has often been denied the title of science because of its highly practical character. The problem with this sort of approach is not simply that it discriminates against women. More crucially, a theory-dominant approach distorts our understanding of scientific knowledge. Knowing how is important for scientific practice, even in the highly theoretical discipline of particle physics. Accelerators of particles must be built and run by technicians and experimental scientists; these activities require many complex skills.[26]

Empiricism, thus, is at best an incomplete theory of knowledge, and at worst a mistaken one. In chapters 6 and 10 I discuss alternatives to this approach; but before that I consider what has become a rather popular feminist approach to epistemology and has been adopted by several empiricists. This approach is naturalized epistemology.

Further Reading

Sandra Harding discusses feminist empiricism in *The Science Question in Feminism* (1986), which provides an accessible introduction to empiricist views. Both Helen Longino's *Science as Social Knowledge: Values and Objectivity in Scientific Inquiry* (1990) and Lynn Nelson's *Who Knows: From Quine to a Feminist Empiricism* (1990) contain fairly technical discussions which might be difficult for readers who are not versed in philosophy of science. They are, nevertheless, worth struggling with. Richmond Campbell's 'The Virtues of Feminist Empiricism' (1994) provides a useful survey of some of the main issues raised by feminist empiricism.

Notes

1   I discuss empiricism in this chapter. Standpoint theory is the topic of chapter 6 and postmodernism of chapter 10.

2   This impression is further confirmed by the fact that Harding almost never refers to the views of individual feminists when she delineates the empiricist position. The only reference is to the introduction of Millman and Kanter (1975).

3   In particular Nelson (1990), Longino (1990), and Duran (1991).

4   For a similar definition, see Harding (1991: 48).

5   For a discussion of this argument, see Campbell (1994: 93–4).

6   I have discussed these arguments in the second section of chapter 3.

7   For discussions of the theory-ladenness of observations, see Quine (1990), Longino (1990: 55–6), and Nelson (1990: 86–91). In chapter 1 I presented a similar argument against foundationalism which was first developed by Sellars (1997: 75–9).

8   See Quine (1990). This is a rather controversial thesis; even its formulation by

Quine has undergone several changes. Furthermore, this thesis appears to be at odds with some forms of empiricism, since some empiricists are committed to the view that formulations of theories which have the same observational consequences are just linguistic variants of the same theory.

9   See Kuhn (1970). Longino provides her interpretation of his position in (1990: 26–7).

10   Suppose we have a theory T containing terms about unobservable entities like electrons. The observations used to confirm it will, of course, make no mention of electrons; instead, they will be about traces, bubble chambers, and other observable entities. Hence, an observation e will confirm a claim a about electrons only relative to other hypotheses t which are part of the theory T. Observation e functions as evidence which directly confirms a, if instances of a are deduced from e and the auxiliary hypotheses t. However, it is impossible to rule out, without greatly impoverishing science, that some hypotheses t will neither be directly confirmed relative to T, nor be independently established. These hypotheses will be confirmed only insofar as they are necessary for the direct confirmation of other claims that belong to the theory; that is, only insofar as they are relevant to the explanation of the phenomena by the theory. Nothing, however, rules out the possibility that value-laden claims might be necessary for the confirmation of a certain theory. For the claim that this is a consequence of the best model of how the confirmation of theories by empirical evidence works, see Longino (1990: 49–51). The model she has in mind has been developed by Glymour (1980).

11   For example, Elizabeth Potter's account of Boyle's discoveries which I have discussed in chapter 3.

12   In her more recent work, however, Longino seems to attribute a more positive role to contextual values in science (1993: 112–13).

13   For a critical, but perceptive, account of Longino's use of the notion of objectivity as grounded on intersubjective criticism see Sharon Crasnow (1993).

14   Campbell (1994) provides a useful discussion of these issues. He claims that some feminists hold that the relation between values and empiricism is only external, and argues that this position depends on the fact–value dichotomy .

15   I discussed this issue in chapter 1. Longino is also opposed to scientific realism (1990: 28–32).

16   See chapters 5 and 6 of Nelson (1990).

17   The Sellarsian account I have presented in chapter 1 entails that nothing can have the significance of an observation outside the context of other background knowledge. This claim is different from Nelson's since it makes no reference to knowledge of theories.

18   See, inter alia, (1990: 277) and (1993: 150).

19   Nelson follows Quine in claiming that there is no principled boundary between scientific and common-sense theorizing (1990: 96).

20   Nelson considers a similar hypothetical case in (Nelson and Nelson, 1994: 497–8).

21 For the claim that one should understand science historically see Richard Bernstein (1983: 25).

22 I discuss these issues at greater length in chapter 7.

23 For a discussion of these issues with feminist empiricism, see Campbell (1994).

24 I am indebted to Campbell (1994) for a discussion of this issue.

25 For an insightful analysis of this phenomenon especially as it applies to the case of midwifery, see Dalmiya and Alcoff (1993).

26 Sharon Traweek (1992) provides a detailed account of particle physicists, their lives and activities.

5
Naturalized Feminist Epistemology

A recent phenomenon in feminist epistemology is the emergence of a new alliance with some strands of mainstream theories of knowledge. The focus of this alliance is the development of naturalized versions of the theory of knowledge. I have already mentioned in previous chapters some of the points of convergence between naturalized and feminist epistemologies. They mainly concern attention to the importance of the concrete features of knowers, and to the relevance of the social context in the study of knowledge.

Feminists have criticized traditional epistemology for its disregard of the situatedness of the knower, and of the specific circumstances in which knowledge is acquired. Naturalized epistemology does not ignore these factors. Instead, it is concerned with describing how knowers acquire knowledge. While traditional epistemologies viewed the justification of a belief as a matter which is largely independent of the ways in which the knower arrives at that belief, naturalized epistemology makes knowledge dependent upon the causal processes that led to its production.[1]

Naturalized epistemology appears sympathetic to feminist concerns not only because it permits an account of the locatedness of all knowledge, but also because it marks the breakdown of the distinction between the contexts of discovery and of justification. Social factors cannot any longer be ignored in an account of what makes good science good. Insofar as both feminist and naturalized epistemologists are opposed to post-positivism, there seems to be enough common ground to develop a useful alliance. The emphasis that naturalized theories of knowledge put on the study of the causes of belief also provides a starting point for the kind of interdisciplinary work with sociologists of knowledge advocated, for example, by Sandra Harding.

Feminist routes to naturalism in the theory of knowledge have been varied, but they gain some of their impulse from Quine's criticisms of the traditional epistemological enterprise, from a cross-fertilization with the sociology of knowledge, and from a reevaluation of pragmatism. Some feminists, for example Lynn Nelson (1990) and Louise Antony (1993), explicitly refer to Quine's 'naturalized epistemology' as the source for their approach. Others, like Jane Duran (1991) take as their source the naturalism of mainstream epistemologists such as Hilary Kornblith. Others still, for example Elizabeth Potter (1993) and Kathryn Pyne Addelson (1993), find the roots of their naturalism in the sociological study of knowledge.

What motivates mainstream analytic philosophers to embrace naturalized epistemology is rather different from what most feminists find valuable in it. The current popularity of naturalized epistemology in analytic philosophy is primarily due to a commitment to scientism. Naturalism is taken to provide explanations of the reasons for belief in terms of causes of belief. In other words, it makes the legitimacy of a belief depend on how the belief has been acquired or maintained. It transforms questions about why one believes something into questions about how one forms and sustains the belief. Explanations of this sort naturalize the mind because, if successful, they would show that the realm of reasons belongs to the natural world. This is the physical world which can be completely described in terms of causes and effects. Since science provides the best accounts of the natural world, if knowledge is just another causal (natural) phenomenon, it too should be explained scientifically.

In a word, scientism is the driving force of naturalized epistemology in analytic philosophy. Reasons, like all other sorts of causes, are better understood scientifically. Nelson, for example, holds that the core of Quine's proposal about naturalized epistemology and philosophy of science is that they should be viewed as continuous with their object of study. In particular, they should 'abandon the pretense of providing an "extra-scientific" explanation of or justification for science' (1995: 401). This characterization captures perfectly what naturalism is about among analytic philosophers; the source of my disagreement with Nelson concerns whether this is the best approach to the philosophical study of knowledge. I shall argue in the first section of this chapter that naturalism so understood is neither theoretically tenable nor politically desirable.

Nelson, however, is an exception among feminists who advocate naturalized epistemology. The motivation for feminist naturalism in the theory of knowledge is usually rather different from the one outlined above. Unfortunately, however, some recent literature manifests a conflation of different kinds of naturalism. I shall discuss this issue in the first section before providing a critical analysis of Nelson's position. In the second section of this chapter I discuss the influence of the sociology of knowledge on feminist naturalized epistemology. I argue throughout this chapter that the naturalism required by feminist epistemology should be seen to have very little to do with what has been advocated in analytic theories of knowledge.

Feminism and Naturalized Epistemology

The word 'natural' has at least two distinct meanings. In the first sense, the sense in which it is opposed to supernatural, it refers to whatever belongs to this world. In the second sense, when it is opposed to conventional or cultural, it refers to what is not-social, to what is not constructed by human beings.

Naturalism in the first sense is the commitment to explain phenomena that occur in our concrete world without appealing to the existence of anything outside it. Thus, naturalists reject, for example, Cartesian appeals to a magnanimous God to explain why we can trust our senses. Similarly, they do not invoke Platonic forms. For naturalists reason and knowledge are phenomena whose explanation does not involve appeals to transcendent notions. Instead, they emerge out of human practices and can be explained entirely in terms of them. Naturalism, so understood, is the rejection of Platonism and, perhaps, of Kantianism. This is the sense in which, since Hegel, many philosophers have been naturalists. Feminist epistemology, also, is (and should be) naturalistic in this first sense. Knowledge, it holds, is a 'thing' of this world and it should be understood as such. The best context for its study is what Wittgenstein has called the 'natural history of human beings.' This is the sort of naturalism which is endorsed by Sabina Lovibond (1989: 13). It involves studying knowledge in terms of human epistemic practices; it is based, as Lorraine Code claims, on ' "desublimating" reason' (1996: 9).

The naturalism of feminist epistemology would amount to a rejection of accounts of knowledge that employ transcendent notions. It would start by looking at the varied human practices, it would attempt to evaluate and explain them in all their cultural richness as phenomena with a history. It would hold that justifications and reasons cannot be reduced to power relations, but should be understood as emerging out of practices.

Many analytic philosophers also reject supernaturalism. They too are naturalist in the first sense I have discussed so far. However, they implement the 'desublimation' of reason by taking it to be natural also in the second sense I have defined above. Reason is a 'thing' of this world; but this is the 'natural' world of causes and effects. Thus, reason does not have a history, because it is not a cultural phenomenon. Instead, like all 'natural' occurrences it is to be explained scientifically in purely causal terms. It is this second form of naturalism which is endorsed by analytic philosophers like Quine and Kornblith. This form of naturalized epistemology is not, I will argue, one feminists should embrace. So far, however, these varieties of naturalism have been conflated in ways that hinder the development of the study of knowledge.

For example, Lorraine Code thinks that naturalism opens up new possibilities for feminist epistemology. She approves of desublimating reason and of studying real-world epistemic practices (1996: 1). She argues against the scientism of analytic naturalized epistemology. Science, she holds, should not be turned into a master narrative which provides the standards for its own legitimacy (1996: 13). Her conclusion is correct, but her arguments are unconvincing because she fails to deploy the distinction between the two senses of naturalism mentioned above. Instead, she uses 'natural' to indicate both what normally occurs, and what can be causally explained. Code argues that there is something un-natural (non-normal) about analytic naturalized epistemology. She objects to its exclusive employment of empirical psychology in the study of how knowledge is produced. She points out that the scientific study of human psychology is often conducted in laboratories. This is not a natural setting; normal conditions are very different from those that obtain in the lab. Therefore, the results obtained by psychologists are, at least in part, the product of the way in which experiments are designed (1996: 10). The 'natural' cognitive processes scientists claim to describe are, in fact, artificially provoked. These are processes that would not occur 'in nature' in exactly the same way.[2] Suppose Code is right, and I certainly think she is, what follows from it? It follows, perhaps, that experimental psychology should not be the only science we deploy in doing naturalized epistemology. Her argument does not show that some combination of sciences is not the ultimate arbiter about knowledge.

I share Code's sentiment that science does not 'have the credentials to

dictate how philosophy – and hence epistemology – should be carried out'
(1996: 4). However, it is not sufficient to say that one should not use the
results of science to justify science, since a naturalist will have to start by
taking for granted that we have knowledge in order to study how we do
it. Similarly, it won't help to show that the results of experimental
psychology cannot be generalized to real world situations, because one
would just make recourse to other sciences. As long as naturalism in
epistemology is understood as the project of giving causal accounts of
knowledge it will have to be based on science, which, after all, is the best
way we have of studying causal regularities in the world.

Code decries the un-naturalness of individualism in much naturalized
epistemology, and I share her convictions. Any study of human cognitive
processes should take into account our interdependence on other human
beings in the acquisition of knowledge. This dependence is, as Code says,
'natural' (1996: 12). However, I take this naturalness to mean that it is
normal, and that it can be explained without talk of supernatural notions.
Code, instead, also thinks it can be explained causally.

Code's own version of naturalism in epistemology is based on an
ecological model. There are two incompatible strands in Code's account.
On the one hand the ecological model is just analytic naturalized epistemology without individualism. On the other, she wants an account of
knowledge that has a historical and cultural dimension. The first strand is
apparent when she views her account, which foregrounds social relations
between individuals in the joint pursuit of knowledge, as relying on good
natural science. She believes that her model 'must draw on the best
available scientific and social scientific evidence' (1996: 12). Code seems to
support a version of naturalism which relies also on the social sciences to
provide causal accounts of knowledge. Perhaps, however, Code does not
take social sciences to provide causal explanations. Up to a point this is
certainly correct. Nevertheless, it displays Code's ambiguity about naturalism. She presents her model as an extension of analytic naturalized
epistemology, minus its scientism. She also claims that her ecological model
is scientific. She is, thus, committed to a causal account of knowledge. It is
hard to see how such an account would not be scientistic.

These tensions in Code's account evince a conflation of the two senses
of naturalism I have distinguished at the beginning of this section. This is
most evident when Code claims that:

In a cultural climate where reason is 'irrevocably desublimated,' *it is
puzzling that* 'the naturalistic turn' and 'the interpretative turn' should

amount to turnings away from one another, usually in antagonism. (1996: 10) [my italics]

But this is not at all puzzling, it is exactly as it should be. The 'interpretative' turn is only naturalistic in the first sense. It is characterized by the claim that meaning and reason emerge out of human practices, and could be understood only in this context. Interpretation, as a kind of understanding, is opposed to the causal descriptions offered by natural science. The interpretative or hermeneutic turn rejects the view that knowledge is natural in the second sense. It holds, instead, that reason and knowledge are not natural, they are cultural phenomena. 'The naturalistic turn' in analytic philosophy, instead, is characterized by the belief that causal accounts of knowledge are appropriate. The two views are incompatible; this fact may remain hidden when the two senses of naturalism are not clearly distinguished.

Code is on the right track when she holds that naturalism should be historical and cultural (1996: 2; 5). Desublimated knowledge is the result of human practices. I shall discuss whether interpretation as description is sufficient to understand these practices at the end of this chapter. For now, it suffices to notice that Code's hope in the development of 'productive and interactive dialogue between interpretative and naturalistic forms of inquiry' (1995: 232) is misplaced. I do not suggest that epistemologists should not take into account what people and scientists actually do when they acquire knowledge. Epistemologists, however, do not have to describe these doings in terms of causes and effects. I do not believe that causes, especially social causes, are epistemically irrelevant. Instead, I think that they are not the whole story; in fact, they are not even half of the story.

If, as I am urging, knowledge is constituted by practices, it is crucial that epistemologists study these practices. This is a sort of naturalism, because it rejects rational reconstructions which invoke ahistorical notions of reason and justification. Several feminist philosophers have highlighted the importance of studying the activities of scientists. For example, Elizabeth Potter claims that philosophers of science must look at what scientists actually do (1993: 167). She also argues that philosophers must not ignore the influence of social and political considerations on the work of scientists (1995: 436). She concludes that historical and sociological accounts of science are a necessary part of philosophy of science (1995: 438). This is just a consequence of the importance of studying the activities of scientists. However, Potter readily assumes continuity between science and the philosophy of science. She claims that 'in its descriptive aspects, a philosophy of science is very like a history or sociology of science and, with them, similar to work in natural science' (1995: 436). This claim is not self-evident; supporters of the interpretative turn would certainly object to it.

One can argue that philosophers need to provide descriptions of the activities of scientists. These descriptions would show that science has social and historical dimensions. However, it does not follow that these descriptions should be scientific. There is no reason to believe that one must describe what scientists do only in terms of the causes and the effects of their behavior. There are descriptions which are not concerned with picking out causal regularities in patterns of behavior. Instead, an epistemologist might describe our epistemic practices as practices. She would not try to produce causal accounts of the behavior of individuals and communities. Rather, she would describe the standards of appropriateness which are implicit in our epistemic practices. In other words, she would be concerned with the significance or meaning of the activities of scientists. Thus, she would describe which behaviors, attitudes, and responses scientists take to be appropriate under certain circumstances. This approach, which I have discussed in chapter 1, is naturalist only in the first sense of the term. It is not scientific.

Potter, nevertheless, does not completely subscribe to the scientism typical of naturalized epistemologists. For her, the philosophy of science has a normative component. Potter believes that causal descriptions of what scientists do cannot provide the whole story about the sort of rationality embodied in scientific practice. This is apparent when Potter claims that philosophers of science must make rational choices about whether to consider 'a bit of work to be "irrational" . . . when scientists themselves deem it "good work"' (1995: 437). This claim would not make sense if Potter believed that the philosophy of science is only concerned with descriptions.

Nevertheless, Potter, like Code, relies on naturalized epistemology to argue that social factors can be part of an explanation of good science. She assumes that philosophers can unearth the social character of knowledge by describing the behavior of scientists. Since she also assumes that these descriptions are similar to those provided in natural science, she must take them to express causal relations. This conclusion is also supported by the examples provided by Potter. She chooses to mention social, political and professional interests as prime instances of social influences on knowledge (1995: 436). It seems rather obvious that the relations between interests and beliefs are causal. Of course, knowledge has social causes. Potter's account is not mistaken, but it is limited. The social involvement of knowledge runs deeper. Social factors can be constitutive of knowledge. This is a possibility that Potter does not explore.

Neither Code nor Potter wants to naturalize epistemology in the manner of analytic epistemology. There are, however, some feminist thinkers who explicitly follow this project. They, therefore, make reference to the work of Quine or of other analytic philosophers to develop their accounts. Three related aspects of Quine's views about naturalizing epistemology are relevant in this context. They concern his scientism, his reliance on individualistic psychology, and his ambiguous position about the status of normative concepts, such as reason or justification.

The latter point can be brought into focus when we consider Quine's oscillation between two opposite claims. Sometimes he holds that, since we cannot deduce knowledge of the external world from sensory evidence, we should settle for a factual psychological account of how we produce theories on the basis of sensory experiences (1969: 75). That is, he suggests that we should abandon epistemology and replace it with psychology. Quine's reason for this claim, however, sounds peculiar, since no philosopher of science, at least after positivism, has ever thought that scientific knowledge is logically deducible from sensory experiences.

On the other hand, Quine also claims that 'epistemology still goes on, though in a new setting and a clarified status. Epistemology, or something like it, simply falls into place as a chapter of psychology and hence of natural science' (1969: 82). He believes that we must abandon traditional epistemology in favor of empirical psychology. But, while at times he suggests that epistemology needs to be abandoned altogether, other times he claims that psychology provides a new way of doing epistemology. This oscillation betrays Quine's uncertainty about the status of normative notions. At times, he thinks that we should cease to talk about reason and justification, and start talking about psychological causes. On other occasions, he holds that we can explain reasons in terms of patterns of causal interactions.

Quine firmly believes that the study of knowledge is a chapter of empirical psychology. Quine's naturalized epistemology is, thus, conceived as a scientific theory of knowledge. He claims that it is a chapter of science, rather than a first philosophy which, from outside, gives legitimacy to every scientific claim. He thus betrays the view that the scientism of causal accounts is for him the only alternative to supernaturalism. He does not even consider the possibility that one may be against transcendent reason, but still oppose the identification of reasons with causes. Furthermore, he takes this sort of epistemology to be a chapter of a specific discipline, namely empirical psychology. As Nelson points out, this move betrays the individualism typical of much thinking in the analytic tradition (1990: 284; 293).

Some feminist versions of naturalized epistemology adopt Quinean individualism – for example Antony's (1993). Duran (1991), who finds inspiration in the work of analytic naturalized epistemologists such as Kornblith, also subscribes to individualism. At first glance one might think otherwise because of her insistence on a communicative mode of knowledge. Nevertheless, her optimism regarding the reduction of epistemology to empirical psychology suggests a commitment to reducing the social characteristics of knowing to purely individualistic ones (1991: 128). Furthermore, Duran does not explicitly address the issue of the role of values in epistemology; instead, she repeatedly claims that her epistemology aims to give a purely factual account of how we justify our claims (1991: 117). She appears to want to rule out all talk of reasons and norms.

Nelson' s version of naturalized epistemology is based on Quine's position, but she rejects his individualism. She also retains talk about justification, although she explains this notion in causal terms. Like Quine, she holds that epistemology consists in 'providing an account of how we go about theorizing, and of the relationship between that theorizing and the evidence we have for it' (1990: 280). Epistemology is, then, a matter of describing how theories are discovered, and of analyzing the relation between theory and evidence. Nelson, also like Quine, is not concerned with the apparent circularity involved in this approach to the theory of knowledge. Neither is worried to use science to study justification in science. Quine is not very explicit about why this circularity is not problematic. His attitude, however, seems to be that science is all we have to go by, and we should use it to provide the best possible scientific account of how theories are constructed (1969: 76). Nelson is clearer on this point: circularity does not matter because she 'do[es] not demand that an epistemology justify our theorizing and theories' (1990: 9). This claim also captures Quine's motivation and attitude; the circularity involved in naturalized epistemology is not vicious because this is not a theory of knowledge which aspires to stand outside and legitimize our entire body of knowledge.

Insofar as naturalized epistemologists point out the unattainability of a God's eye epistemology which stands outside its sociocultural contexts, they are to be applauded. Their mistake is to take scientism as the only alternative. Naturalism, as it is formulated by Quine and Nelson, renders science a self-legitimizing enterprise. Science thus becomes what Lyotard has dubbed a master-narrative, a mode of knowledge which supports itself and provides its own criteria of legitimacy.[3] Ultimately, this makes science autonomous from any other enterprise, and unaccountable because it cannot be subjected to external criticism. Nelson partly remedies this problem when she departs from Quine in holding that absolutely any way of thinking about anything is a part of science, although in some instances of bad science. Thus, science includes morality, politics and any other form of reflection about values (1990: 134; 243). Because Nelson rejects a sharp distinction between fact and value, her account permits political criticism of scientific results. For her politics is, after all, part of science. Nevertheless, my objection still stands. Science can be criticized from a political viewpoint; however, these critiques are legitimate only if they meet scientific standards. Nelson is right to say that her account does not make science autonomous from, say, politics. But this is true by default, since there is nothing from which science could be autonomous, nothing that stands outside it. The result is that science, with its own criteria for what counts as a good argument, stands as the only legitimate mode of critique. Thus, feminist critiques of science are not, in Nelson's account, declared illegitimate; rather they are called scientific, so that they would have to be judged by the standards of the scientific mode. In order to see whether this conclusion is warranted, what is required is a fuller analysis of Nelson's position about what epistemology is and does. Nelson explains her views on the issue when she claims:

> I am denying that an epistemology can do the job of justifying any claim or theory. *We begin* . . . with the assumption that what we believe is *true*. It is the ability to make sense of what we experience and to predict our experiences that will, in the end, justify any theory or claim. What we are concerned to do in constructing an epistemology is to offer *causal explanations* [my italics] for how theories, beliefs, and claims have been arrived at, explanations that are in keeping with what we experience. Because, for example, we have been successful at theorizing, an adequate epistemology will need to be able to explain why and how, and this is why I have insisted that epistemologies that do not (or cannot) provide an account of how theories are constrained by evidence are inadequate. (1990: 292)

According to Nelson, the theory of knowledge provides causal explanations of the genesis of beliefs and theories, but does not justify them.

Thus, epistemology is not a first philosophy.[4] There are no fixed and absolute criteria of justification. Nelson holds, instead, that justification is always internal to science. There is, she explains, no absolute Justification which the theory of knowledge bestows upon some scientific claims but not others.[5] That is, there are no transcendent criteria of Justification; instead, we have changing criteria of what counts as evidence (justification) for a theory. These are criteria that emerge with science, and are modified within it. Epistemology itself is part of science (1990: 106).

Nelson interprets this rejection of absolutist epistemology naturalistically as the claim that theories about evidence are themselves scientific. Hence, although epistemology does not lay down absolute principles of Justification, justification is still part of its remit as a theory of evidence. I have claimed that naturalized epistemology in analytic philosophy is concerned with factual accounts. This point is in evidence when Nelson claims, in the passage quoted above, that: '[what] we are concerned to do in constructing an epistemology is to offer *causal explanations* for how theories, beliefs, and claims have been arrived at' [my italics] (1990: 292). It would seem that for Nelson the sole purpose of epistemology is to describe the causes of theories and of beliefs. If this is correct, and I shall argue that it ultimately is, Nelson provides a reductivist account of evidence or justification in terms of natural (psychological and social) causes. Nelson, however, is not always forthcoming on this issue because she holds two apparently incompatible theories of evidence or justification.

Nelson is keen to distinguish her account of evidence from the sociology of knowledge, and to emphasize that evaluation has a legitimate place both in epistemology and in science. Nevertheless, she ends up providing a factual account of justification. There is a strange ambivalence in Nelson's position. On the one hand, she holds that epistemology is concerned both with an account of how we theorize and with a theory of evidence, thereby suggesting that these are distinct concerns (1990: 280). On the other, she claims that causal accounts of theory production are the sole purpose of epistemology (1990: 292). These two claims are not irreconcilable: they can both be accommodated if we interpret Nelson as claiming that a causal account of how theories are produced also functions as a theory of evidence. This is, in fact, Nelson's position, but it is not reached without tensions in her overall theory.

These tensions are apparent, for example, when she draws the distinction between epistemology and sociology of knowledge:

I have not suggested that the *only* causes for beliefs are social causes. I am not advocating that sociology of knowledge is all there is, or could be, to epistemology. 'Knowledge' is socially constructed through and through – but the construction is constrained by evidence. (1990: 295)

This passage illustrates the fundamental ambiguity of Nelson's position about justification. At first, she suggests that epistemology is not reducible to sociology of knowledge because it studies all the causes for belief, not only those social causes which are the concern of the latter. Epistemology would thus seem to be, like sociology, interested in a factual account of the causes for belief. This conception of the theory of knowledge is consonant with Nelson's claim that epistemology is a matter of giving a scientific account of how we go about theorizing. The second part of the quote, however, points in a different direction. It is peculiar that what is socially constructed is 'knowledge'; that is, knowledge in scare quotes, so-called knowledge. It would seem that 'knowledge' becomes knowledge proper only if it is supported by adequate evidence. A causal account of how a belief is produced would constitute only a part of what epistemology is about; the remaining part would be a theory of evidence. But, causal accounts are meant to provide a theory of evidence, hence the timidity of the quotes appears odd.

Furthermore, Nelson's unremarked transition from a factual distinction between types of causes to a normative one between causes and evidence should alert the reader that the situation is more complex than it appears. This suspicion is borne out by Nelson's theory of evidence. She claims that 'there is a world that shapes and constrains what it *is reasonable* to believe, and . . . it does so by impinging on our sensory receptors' [my italics] (1990: 20). The world by impinging on our sensory receptors causes sensory experiences, which function as evidence for our beliefs; that is, they make them reasonable or justified. These experiences are evidence for belief insofar as they are causes of belief. Thus, following Quine, she holds that, 'in the end, empirical evidence is sensory stimulations' (1990: 95). Sensory stimulations are nervous stimulations. Basically, they are the reaction of the individual's nervous system to external input. Sensory stimulations are the causes of our beliefs, and, for Nelson, they also provide the evidence for beliefs. This causal theory of evidence would be an integral part of an epistemology whose sole concern is to provide causal accounts of how theories and beliefs are produced.

This, however, will not do as it stands. Presumably there are perfectly coherent causal accounts of how beliefs in the power of the evil eye are produced, even though there is no evidence to support them. These beliefs have causes, however, like anything else. Therefore, the causes of some beliefs do not constitute evidence in their favor. Nelson would agree. But, to make this latter point she uses a different theory of evidence. She adopts a pragmatist account which holds that a theory is warranted if it coheres with our other theories and our experiences, it has explanatory power, and it is helpful to predict future experiences.[6] These two rather different accounts of evidence are also found in Quine whose theories constitute Nelson's starting point.[7] Nelson, like Quine, oscillates between them within one paragraph as the long quote above makes explicit. This ambiguity allows her to gloss over some problems with her position. Firstly, the theory of evidence seems an empirical scientific theory only if we understand evidence in causal terms. The pragmatist account suggests instead that a theory of evidence is not purely empirical, even though it is not transcendent first philosophy. Secondly, Nelson and Quine oscillate between 'experience' and 'sensory stimulations' as the primitive notions in their accounts of evidence. They both talk of experience, in the loosely phenomenal sense of feeling, when they employ a pragmatist account of evidence: what theories explain and predict are experiences. It would be odd to say that theories explain and predict those sensory stimulations which give rise to experiences.

Suppose I have a 'common sense' theory about vegetables. I know that tomatoes are green when they are not ripe, and red otherwise. This rather minimal theory is supported by empirical evidence. It explains why when I taste a green tomato I find it to be not ripe; that is, it explains the feeling I have when I bite into the tomato. The theory also helps to predict that if I leave a green tomato on the plant, it will probably become red. It predicts that I will have the feeling of seeing a red tomato. This theory, however, does not explain my sensory stimulations when confronted with a green tomato. That is, it says nothing about the state of my sensory receptors when I look at the tomato, only a theory about human neurophysiology could do that.

On the other hand, both Nelson and Quine talk of sensory stimulations when they are concerned with a causal account of evidence – it is our sensory stimulations that cause us to adopt certain beliefs. Thus, when Nelson takes the evidence for a theory to be a matter of what the theory explains and predicts, she must be talking about experiences in a phenomenal sense. But when she talks of evidence as the cause for the production of theories, she is talking about sensory stimulations. This is not a trivial point, because Nelson needs the pragmatist theory of evidence to provide a credible account of this notion, while she needs the causal account to give credibility to the view that epistemology is just another chapter of science.

It might be possible to naturalize the pragmatist account of evidence offered by Nelson, but this project requires the formulation of criteria for distinguishing between those causes which count as evidence and those which do not. Nelson briefly hints at a solution of this problem when she claims:

> Because, for example, we have been successful at theorizing, an adequate epistemology will need to be able to explain why and how, and this is why I have insisted that epistemologies that do not (or cannot) provide an account of how theories are constrained by evidence are inadequate. (1990: 292)

Those causes that count as evidence are the kind of causes that generally characterize successful theorizing. That is, a theory is well supported by evidence if it has been caused by factors that typically lead to successful theorizing.

This solution to the problem of naturalizing evidence is not dissimilar to that employed by mainstream thinkers who hold a belief to justified only if it is the product of a method or mechanism which reliably produces true rather than false beliefs (Goldman, 1985: 100). Yet this option does not seem available to Nelson. Even if it is plausible to claim that all good scientific theories are coherent with experience and our whole body of theories, have explanatory powers, and help to predict experiences, it looks much less plausible to claim that they all have similar causes. There is no reason to believe that we will find useful similarities in the causal histories of successful theories that distinguish them from unsuccessful ones. Rather, the history of science points in the opposite direction.

Nelson's willingness to reduce the whole of knowledge to something which can be fully explained in causal terms permeates also her account of values. Nelson's makes a decisive break with Quine's naturalism about the issue of moral and political values. While Quine believes that values stand outside science, Nelson holds that they are part of it. She also holds that these values should be subject to critical scrutiny (1990: 5). For Nelson, 'values emerge within and shape a community's practices and theories, and many of these values are political in nature and consequence' (1990: 14).

These values function as evidence for theories, and are also a consequence of the changes in our viewpoints which are generated from the theories themselves. Values in science, however, should not go unchecked. Rather, like everything else, they are subjected to empirical controls (1990: 248).

Nelson shares with others the conviction that values have always had an influence on science, and the belief that, unless their presence is recognized, they will go unchallenged (1990: 307). However, since she has rejected the existence of any sort of critical reflection besides that dictated by the standards and methods of empirical science, she concludes that values themselves are subject to empirical controls. This, she thinks, is possible because values are grounded in how things are (1990: 133). Nelson's naturalism suggests that she might be willing to go even further and claim that values, like facts, are objective. Evaluative judgments could be empirically tested to show that some values are more adequate than others. Nelson's commitment to objectivism about values has the merit of fending off the specter of relativism. It does mean, however, that she abandons the fact–value distinction at the price of assimilating values to facts. The result is that: 'A "value judgment" on "values" *is issued within* science' (1990: 133). This is, however, a dangerous move. Science is an inherently instrumentalistic enterprise. It requires a mode of thinking which is concerned only with finding out the best means to predetermined ends. What Longino calls the 'constitutive values of science' – explanatory power, simplicity, and predictive ability – are exactly that: namely, constitutive. Any practice that pursues other ends is not scientific. In light of the many critiques, voiced by several philosophers, of the overall dominion of instrumental reason in Western society, Nelson's implicit acceptance that instrumental thinking can provide adequate evaluations of values is rather problematic.

My critique of Nelson's position on values is just one aspect of the criticism I have raised before about her conception of science as a self-legitimizing enterprise. Nelson appears to believe that her version of naturalized epistemology is the only alternative to a traditional epistemology which would function as a first philosophy. I have argued that there is, however, no reason to believe that this is true. To admit that epistemology itself is socioculturally situated is not the same as claiming that it is a scientific theory. It is only if one is already convinced of the power of science to explain everything that one might not see that there are other options. The problems with Nelson's account which I have discussed above are consequences of her scientism, which is an immediate consequence of the way in which epistemology is naturalized in the context of analytic philosophy.

Sociology and Naturalized Epistemology

In sociology supporters of the strong program developed by David Bloor and Barry Barnes hold that even true scientific theories and beliefs have social causes. This is not controversial since almost everything has a cause. The strong program goes further; it asserts that knowledge can be *explained* in terms of its social causes. Traditional sociology only provided accounts of scientific error. It invoked social causes and influences to explain why scientists go astray. Thus, sociology explained what made a scientific failure a failure. But, in line with post-positivist thinking, traditional sociology was taken to have nothing to say about what made a scientific success a success. No one denied the possibility of giving a sociological description of an instance where science proceeded successfully, but it was believed that such a description would not contribute to an explanation of why in that instance the result was good. Supporters of the strong program deny all this. Instead, they hold that sociology can explain both error and knowledge.

The strong program in sociology can be seen as an effort to naturalize knowledge. While philosophers like Quine suggest that we employ empirical psychology to give a full account of knowledge, Bloor and Barnes propose to use another scientific discipline, namely sociology. The underlying principle, however, is the same; we can fully account for knowledge in terms of its causes. Quine believes these causes to be psychological, the others believe them to be social. The difference seems to result in part from the lingering individualism in Quine's philosophy.

Harding finds some aspects of the strong program in sociology useful for a feminist epistemology. In particular, she notes that both hold that knowledge is socially situated, and is generated in the context of political and other struggles (1991: 12). She thinks that the central tenet of the strong program is especially valuable. It claims that:

The same kinds of causes that are cited to explain the generation and acceptance of false beliefs must be used to explain the generation and acceptance of 'true beliefs'; . . . 'causal symmetry' should be the goal of maximally scientific accounts of belief acceptance. (1991: 166)

In accordance with naturalized epistemology Harding holds that in order to understand both knowledge and error we need to look at the causes that have led to the formation of beliefs and theories. Harding draws substantial conclusions from this position. Since the social circumstances that are among the causes of their emergence contribute to making some theories examples of knowledge, some social arrangements are more beneficial to knowledge production than others. Furthermore, since social arrangements are promoted by groups of people who hold some but not other social and political values, it follows that social values can contribute to the growth of knowledge (1991: 65). This is a claim that goes beyond what the originators of the strong program asserted. Harding, for example, criticizes supporters of this program for failing to consider the relevance to knowledge of issues of class, gender, and race. These issues are central to discussions of social values, and these are values which can facilitate or impede the growth of knowledge. For Harding, the supporters of the strong program ignore these issues because they consider scientific research communities to be isolated from society at large. Therefore, they have restricted their analysis of the social causes of theories to the processes which involve only the research community (1991: 162).[8] It should go without saying that at a time when scientists need increasingly expensive technology to pursue their research this restriction is artificial and rather unwarranted.

From what I have said so far, there emerge some similarities between Nelson's fully naturalized epistemology and Harding's qualified support of the sociology of knowledge. They derive from their causal analyses of knowledge the conclusion that some social values rather than others facilitate the production of knowledge. This shared understanding of the role of social values in science, and of the importance of causal accounts in epistemology, constitutes the common ground between Nelson's empiricism and the standpoint theory of knowledge which is endorsed with some reservations by Harding.[9] Standpoint theory, for Harding, differs from the strong program because 'it requires causal analyses not just of the micro processes in the laboratory but also of the macro tendencies in the social order, which shape scientific practices' (1991: 149).[10]

Nelson and Harding also share a belief that epistemology should be scientific. In the previous section I argued that Nelson derives her scientism from Quine. Harding's position is different. For her, 'maximally scientific accounts of belief-acceptance' recognize that cultural agendas function as background assumptions of scientific theories while 'extending the notion of scientific research to include systematic examination of such powerful background beliefs' (1991: 149). Thus, Harding shares with Nelson the view that social criticisms of science can be internal to science itself, but does not commit herself to the totalizing view that everything needs to be judged by scientific standards.

Harding rejects fully naturalized epistemology because she is suspicious of its scientism. For her, the theory of knowledge is not a chapter of science. Thus, while for Nelson justification is always internal to science itself, Harding believes that 'no conceptual system can provide the justificatory grounds for itself' (1986: 49). For Harding, epistemology provides justificatory strategies for theories and beliefs. It is a theory about how to formulate and evaluate justifications advanced in favor of some theory or other. Nelson, on the other hand, takes the theory of knowledge to describe how successful theorizing is done in science. Hence, radical critiques of the scientific understanding of 'justification' and 'evidence' become impossible.

Harding is also very explicit in rejecting the eliminativist tendency, present in Quine, which she thinks is endorsed by the supporters of the strong program in the sociology of knowledge. Harding criticizes their refusal to engage in epistemic evaluations and their inability to go beyond descriptive accounts. She points out that to preserve the normative dimension of epistemology is not to fall back on traditional foundationalism because 'once we allow reasons to be causes, there is no contradiction in affirming that beliefs can be simultaneously socially and rationally caused' (1991: 168). Naturalizing epistemology does not require giving up talk of evidence and justification as supporters of the strong program seem to believe. Instead, if one takes reasons to be one kind of causes, it is possible to say that 'scientific beliefs, like those that feminist standpoint theories justify, are held for *both* good reasons and social causes' (1991: 168).[11]

Harding seems to believe that critics of naturalized epistemology merely object to those versions of it which abandon talk of justification altogether. She does not seem to realize that those critics would find the identification of normative patterns with causal regularities equally problematic. To say that reasons can be causes, would not placate these critics; quite the contrary, this is exactly the move they object to. There are rare occasions when Harding distinguishes normative evaluations from causal descriptions. For example, when she says that in epistemology, we need

to think critically about how beliefs are formed and why they are adopted, and to develop such thought as a *logic* of belief that carries normative values, not just as 'scientific' description of what in fact occurs. (1991: 169)

Here, Harding drives a wedge between good reasons and social causes. Scientific descriptions of causes do not tell us which reasons are good. Harding does not pursue this line of thought, but it opens up new possibilities.

While Harding wants to preserve the evaluative character of the theory of knowledge, Addelson develops an epistemology which is descriptive but not normative. She holds that this epistemology 'serves as a way of testing, in practice, the usefulness and adequacy of whatever normative epistemologies feminist philosophers cook up' (1993: 266). Her descriptive (meta)epistemology would provide the means for testing the empirical adequacy of feminist normative theories of knowledge.

Addelson's starting point is that any adequate epistemology should take social organization as fundamental to knowledge. She asserts that scientists have cognitive authority which they exercise both within and outside their research communities (1983: 165). That is to say, they are treated as experts about certain features of natural or social reality. Not every scientist, however, is granted the same amount of authority; rather, social arrangements within the science community, and the society at large, influence the ascendancy of some researchers, but not others, to more powerful positions from where they dictate the agenda for their discipline. As a consequence which theories become accepted at any time is in part influenced by social factors. Furthermore, since scientists are consulted by governments and other organizations for their expertise, they also get to define, at least in part, the way in which all of us understand our world. Science is, therefore, always politicized insofar as the acceptance of any theory over its competitors is in part determined by social factors that give more power and attribute more authority to some researchers rather than others. These are important factors in scientific activity which should not be left unexamined in epistemology (1983: 182).

Addelson defines her theory of knowledge as an instance of descriptive epistemology. It is a sociological theory that describes how science is practiced, and what consequences this has on society at large. She holds that in order to change things 'we must know how the social organization of knowledge has supported male dominance. . . . We must know precisely and practically how our work operates to undermine dominant elites' (1993: 268). It is for these reasons that 'feminist epistemology must have a central descriptive component, grounded in appropriate empirical science' (1993: 268).

Addelson's claim that epistemology should at least in part be descriptive and grounded in empirical science brings her position closer to that of naturalized epistemology. Her descriptive theory of knowledge is a scientific account of the complex causal social interactions which play an important part in scientific activity. It would seem, however, that such a theory is *not* what is needed to see, for example, how current modes of knowledge production support male dominance. The very notion of 'male dominance' is evaluative, in order to classify an activity as an instance of male dominance we need to invoke some value judgments. Thus, a descriptive theory of knowledge must be supplemented with a theory of moral and political values. This is a point that Addelson, I believe, would accept.

Addelson's approach might also appear to be similar to other naturalized theories of knowledge in treating science as a self-legitimizing activity, and as our best way of understanding any aspect of reality. Although Addelson is quite critical of the unexamined authority which is currently granted to scientists, she assumes that the scientific mode of investigation is most apt for understanding the issue of knowledge production. According to her,

> normative epistemologies have to be taken as rhetoric or as ideologies that are embedded in our folk understandings . . . We must understand even the feminist, normative epistemologies as rhetoric-proposals for new ideologies. (1993: 287)

These epistemologies play a role in our creative processes of knowing and doing but 'understanding the process of knowing and doing requires a descriptive epistemology, not a normative one' (1993: 288). Although normative epistemologies are useful as rhetoric to be used at times for some purposes, they do not contribute to our understanding of the real process of knowledge production. Addelson seems to believe that only a description of what goes on in science could do that.

However, Addelson understands sociology as the study of a human world endowed with meanings: meanings which are always in the process of being constructed (1990: 121). There exists no untheorized world which the scientist could simply describe. Instead, description is a matter of interpretation of the meanings embedded in the social world. Nevertheless, sociology is an empirical science because it strives in its interpretations to 'remain faithful to the empirical world' (1990: 135). Consequently, Addelson is not suggesting that we see epistemology as a chapter of science as traditionally understood. Epistemology is, for her, descriptive and scientific, but it is part of a science of interpretation, not a science whose sole concern is a description of causal processes. It aims to promote understanding rather than to provide causal explanations. It studies features of reality, such as actions and social roles, which it takes to be endowed with meaning. It attempts to interpret these meaningful 'objects' within the social context which functions as the background that enables them to be meaningful.

Addelson's position is a descriptive hermeneutics of the processes involved in the development of knowledge. This approach is naturalistic only in the first sense, since it rejects the view of epistemology as first philosophy. It is not naturalistic in the second and causal sense. Therefore, it does not adopt the scientism which is present, for example, in Nelson's naturalized epistemology. Addelson, thus, shows the way toward an epistemology which is attentive to the actual practices and activities involved in the production of knowledge without assuming that the best way to study these practices is to describe chains of causation. However, she is wrong to dismiss normative epistemology as mere rhetoric. If we want to change things, we need to create new practices. Epistemic evaluations of current activities provide one way in which this can be achieved.

Feminist epistemology, I believe, should not appeal to anything outside our concrete world to explain knowledge. It should be naturalized only in the first of the two senses I distinguished at the beginning of this chapter. Knowledge is thus seen as the result of human practices. Addelson is right to insist that the phenomena studied by epistemology are always endowed with meanings. The theory of knowledge must include a description of epistemic practices as practices. Addelson's account, however, must be supplemented with an evaluative dimension. On the other hand, Harding is correct to insist on the importance of normativity, but she is mistaken in thinking that justification can be identified with causal relations. Social causes are not irrelevant to the justification of theories. Nevertheless, if we want to understand how values are relevant to the constitution of knowledge, we must go beyond causal accounts.

Widespread acceptance of sexist values might have been among the causes that led biologists to formulate false theories about human fecundation. Similarly, adherence to non-sexist values might have led some primatologists to formulate good accounts of the behavior of apes. However, values do not merely cause scientists to prefer some hypotheses to others. Often, values are constitutive: they contribute to the significance of scientific hypotheses. One might even say that an assertion counts as a bit of science only in the context of a society that has adopted specific practices.

I have said in chapter 1 that an immersion in water can be a baptism only in a society that has religious practices. Of course there are immersions in water without religious practices, but they are not baptisms. Further, religious practices do not merely cause the baptism. They constitute its significance; they invest it with meaning. We cannot understand what a baptism is, unless we understand its significance. The values embedded in religious practices are thus constitutive of baptisms. The same considerations apply to scientific activities. Observing, experimenting, and theorizing are all events invested with significance. They could not exist without a complex background of practices. The values embedded in this background are likely to include social and political values. Thus, a change in the political practices of a society might result in a change in science. It would be a mistake, however, to believe that we can give a purely causal account of these phenomena. For example, I have pointed out in chapter 2 that before the sixteenth century 'probable' was used to indicate the approbation of received authority. The contemporary notion of evidence emerges after this time of political turmoil, when the received authority of king and church was strongly opposed. It thus becomes possible to view a claim as probable when there is evidence that makes it likely to be true. It would be far too simplistic to claim only that political changes caused changes in epistemology. This is partly true, of course, but it fails to get to the heart of the matter.

In the Middle Ages people, presumably, trusted one another on many matters. Nevertheless, the claims made by ordinary people would never be treated as knowledge. They could not be assessed for their intrinsic credibility. On the other hand, the claims made by received authority were, by definition, probable. In this case too, however, probability had nothing to do with intrinsic credibility. There was no epistemic category under which both kinds of claim could fall. Political changes in the early modern period made the emergence of new practices possible. Assertions acquired a new significance; they came to be treated as a way of providing evidence. They also started to be taken as the sort of thing for which evidence may be needed. It was considered to be appropriate to respond to the claims made by authorities by trying to assess whether they were likely to be true. Although the word of the king or of the pope might have been given more initial authority, the claims made by ordinary people could also be treated as knowledge. They did not have this significance before; they acquired this new meaning in the context of changed cultural practices.

In conclusion, feminist epistemology should take knowledge to be cultural, it should not treat it as natural. It should investigate the relevance of sociocultural phenomena to cognitive practices. But, it should not limit itself to studying the causal effects of social circumstances on the activities of knowers. It should, instead, acknowledge that its objects are always endowed with meanings, which must be interpreted. However, epistemology does not merely attempt to discover these meanings, it also aspires to be a motor for change. A purely descriptive epistemology is, therefore, not sufficient.

Further Reading

Quine discusses his position in 'Naturalized Epistemology' (1969). Lynn Nelson's book, *Who Knows: From Quine to a Feminist Empiricism* (1990), provides an exposition of Quine's theory of knowledge as well as developing Nelson's own position. Andrew Pickering gives a useful summary of the history of sociological studies of scientific knowledge in 'From Science as Knowledge to Science as Practice' (1992). For an example of the approach to knowledge adopted by the strong program, see Barry Barnes, *Interests and the Growth of Knowledge* (1977). Sandra Harding discusses the sociology of knowledge in *The Science Question in Feminism* (1986) and *Whose Science? Whose Knowledge?* (1991).

Notes

1   This is only roughly correct since, of course, one could continue to hold a belief for causes other than those which led one to acquire it in the first place. These new causes would determine whether the belief continues to be justified.

2   That is to say, they would not occur in the same way in their normal social settings.

3   For an account of master-narratives, see Lyotard (1984: 34).

4   In chapter 1 I distinguished two senses of epistemology as first philosophy. I take Nelson to reject both of them.

5   'Justification' (with a capital letter) refers to a transcendent notion of justification, while 'justification' refers to a notion of justification which is always internal to our cognitive practices.

6   For a discussion of this aspect of Nelson's position see the second section of chapter 4.

7   I take this point, and the argument for it, from Ken Gemes's 'Epistemological vs Causal Explanations in Quine' (unpublished manuscript).

8   Although this may be a fair criticism of the Bath school, it does not apply to the original Edinburgh school.

9   Other aspects of the convergence between Nelson's empiricism and standpoint theories have been noted by Nancy Tuana (1992). Nelson is, however, very keen to contrast her approach with that of standpoint theory rather than to point out possible agreements.

10 In chapter 10 I argue that the emphasis on causal theories of knowledge is a
problem for some versions of standpoint epistemology.

11 Harding's causal account of knowledge differs from others because she
identifies reasons with causes without reducing the normative theory to a
causal theory. For this reason, it would not be completely correct to take her
theory of knowledge to be an example of fully naturalized epistemology.

6

The Importance of Standpoint in Feminism

When people look at things from different perspectives, what they see is likely to be different. This platitude is the starting point of one of the most popular feminist approaches to knowledge, namely standpoint epistemology, according to which there is a distinctive perspective on reality which pertains to feminists or to women. They have a distinctive outlook because their experiences are different from those of people who occupy other positions in society. This feminist or womanly perspective, furthermore, is not merely different from, say, a masculinist perspective, it is also a privileged perspective. It is a perspective that makes it possible to understand reality better, perhaps to understand it as it really is.

What I have given is only a rough sketch of standpoint epistemology from which more sophisticated versions diverge on several accounts. Nevertheless, it is already evident that standpoint epistemology employs notions such as 'experience' and 'privileged perspective' which require a closer scrutiny. In this chapter I first discuss formulations of standpoint based on the notion of women's experience, and then several problems which later formulations of standpoint attempt to resolve.

What is a Standpoint?: Beginning from Women's Experience

There are at least two constitutive aspects of the several versions of standpoint epistemology: first, the notion of a standpoint or perspective; second, the notion that some perspectives are epistemically privileged. Thus, this sort of epistemology needs to establish that there is a distinctive perspective which pertains to women or to feminists, and that this perspective is privileged.

Feminist standpoint epistemology finds its ancestor in the Marxian notion of a standpoint of the proletariat. According to Marx the positions occupied in society by different classes give them distinct perspectives on social reality. These positions constitute different standpoints which provide dissimilar understandings of social relations. These standpoints are not only different in content, they also differ in accuracy. The understanding of society available from the standpoint of the working class is less distorted than those offered by other perspectives or standpoints.

For Marx, knowledge emerges through active engagement with social and natural reality. Thus, knowledge does not pertain to a theoretical sphere which is independent of practical activities. Rather, understanding of the social and natural world results from individuals' labor; that is, from their involvement in the process of production. What, for Marx, characterizes the capitalist political system is the class division of labor. In this system intellectual and manual labor are kept strictly separate, so that some economically privileged individuals perform only intellectual work. It is these individuals alone who are recognized as producers of knowledge, whereas the knowledge possessed by manual laborers goes unacknowledged. Marx, however, does not merely claim that the working classes possess knowledge which is not usually recognized. He also claims that the working class has a distinctive understanding of social reality under the capitalist system, an understanding which is more accurate than the understanding available to members of the other economic classes.

The perspective of the working class is distinctive because it emerges from their practical activities. The class division of labor ensures that some manual productive work is done only by members of the proletariat; thus, working-class people's lives are systematically different from those of the members of other classes. This difference grounds or gives rise to a distinct perspective on social reality. This unique perspective of the proletariat in a capitalist system is privileged from an epistemic viewpoint because the working class plays a crucial economic function in preserving the system while it has no vested interest in its continuation. In other words, for Marx, it is possible to gain a more accurate understanding of the social reality of capitalism from the perspective of that class which is socially marginal but economically central. The social marginality of this class ensures that its members have no vested interest in preserving the system and are, therefore, not likely to be blind to its shortcomings. Its economic centrality guarantees that the members of this class have first-hand acquaintance with the workings of the capitalist system.[1] Thus understood, Marxian epistemology claims that to acquire accurate knowledge of a phenomenon one must be in a position to experience it and its effects, and one also must have no vested interests, no biases, which would lead to a distorted understanding.[2]

Some standpoint feminist epistemologists, notably Nancy Hartsock (1983), Hilary Rose (1983), and Dorothy Smith (1988), have explicitly modeled their theories on this Marxist account. In particular, they have developed explanations of the division of labor which ground the claim for a distinctive perspective pertaining to women or to feminists, and have supplemented these with analyses of social reality which show women to be both central and marginal in relevant ways.

Feminist critics of Marxist political theory have notoriously exposed the gender blindness of its crucial notions. In particular, they have noted that the Marxist focus on systems of production excludes and naturalizes those systems of reproduction which are central to many women's lives. Similarly, the exclusive focus on capitalism as an economic system ignores the system of patriarchy, a distinct set of social relations, which contributes to the continuation of women's oppression.[3] These concepts of 'reproductive labor' and 'patriarchy' can provide the tools to formulate an account of standpoint epistemology within a feminist context. Women's reproductive labor provides them with a distinctive perspective on reality; their socially marginal role under patriarchy, when combined with their essential function in its preservation, guarantees the epistemic privilege of their perspective.

These tools have been employed by Hartsock (1983) in her formulation of a feminist standpoint. Starting from the Marxian tenet that the material conditions of a person's everyday life inform the understanding of society developed by that person, Hartsock finds in the specificity of women's experiences the basis for a distinctive perspective.

For her a feminist standpoint emerges from what she calls 'the sexual division of labor' (1983: 284). She chooses the term 'sexual' instead of 'gendered' to remind us that 'there is some biological, bodily component to human existence' (1983: 289). This bodily component is deeply linked to one of the aspects of life which distinguishes women's work from men's: namely, their production of other human beings, their reproductive capacities. Childbearing and childrearing are complex social activities which give rise to distinct experiences (1983: 294).[4] Even in the sphere of the production of goods for subsistence, women's activities differ structurally from men's. Women spend more time than men in the production of goods in the house, goods which are not sold as commodities (1983: 292). In both cases, women's labor is distinct from men's and involves an unification of mind and body. Hence, as Hartsock remarks, 'women's lives differ structurally from those of men' (1983: 284).

Hartsock is not alone in believing that the distinctiveness of women's work grounds a notion of women's experience which differs structurally from men's. This experience is the basis of women's distinctive understanding of the social and natural worlds. Similar claims have also been supported by Rose (1983), who adds that women's work concerning reproduction is distinctive especially because it is a 'labor of love' (1983: 83–4; 1986: 164–6). Women's caring work, for her, does not just unify hand and brain, as Hartsock claims, but also the heart (1983: 83). A crucial aspect of feminist standpoint epistemology is for Rose an acknowledgment of the central role of emotional involvement in the process of knowledge acquisition: this is an aspect of feminist epistemology that opposes the abstract and depersonalized character of traditional science (1983: 84).[5]

Both Rose and Hartsock find in the division of labor by sex-gender[6] the origin for the character of women's experience; an experience that differs structurally from that of men. Women's experience is, as Rose remarks, a 'subjective shared experience of oppression' (1983: 88).

This focus on experience as the basis of a feminist standpoint is also present in the sociological theory of Smith. For her, to acquire knowledge in the way recommended by standpoint epistemology is 'to begin our work from our experience as women' (1988: 78). Division of labor accounts for the difference between men's and women's experience since women do the work which makes it possible for men to engage in intellectual work (1988: 83). In other words, women's work releases men from any concern with care of bodies and their needs.

What characterizes women's experience is, for Smith, 'a point of rupture,' 'a line of fault' (1988: 49). This line of fault is the perceived 'disjuncture between experience and the forms in which experience is socially expressed (becoming thereby intelligible . . .)' (1988: 50). It is, that is, a perceived mismatch between what one actually experiences and the conceptual framework socially available to put one's experiences into words.[7] The cause of this experiential rupture is found in men's oppression of women, or, more precisely, in patriarchy as a set of oppressive social relations (1988: 51).

For Smith what makes women's experience valuable from an epistemic viewpoint is their dual marginal and central position in the current set of social relations. Women's position is central because they do the work which sustains the current patriarchal system and also produce the invisibility of such work as work (1988: 81). They are marginal because they do not occupy a position of power within the system. As a consequence, 'for women (as also for others in the society similarly excluded), the organization of daily experience, the work routines, and the structuring of our lives through time has been and to a large extent still is determined and ordered by processes external to, and beyond, our everyday world' (1988: 65). Thus, women occupy the position of insiders/outside: insiders because they are crucial to the continuation of the current system, but also outsiders since they have no power within it.

It is because they occupy this dual social role that women's experiences reflect more accurately than men's the reality of current relations. From their position relations which are invisible from dominant positions become visible. Since women have a direct experience of what is invisible to men, they come to perceive a rupture between what the world is like for them and what dominant views say about it. It is this line of fault which alerts women that something is amiss. Starting from their experiences it is possible for them to expose those aspects of social reality that are invisible from other positions.

Thus, Smith does not only argue for the distinctiveness of women's standpoint but also for its epistemic privilege. Before addressing the problematic nature of Smith's appeals to women's experience, I would like to return to Hartsock's argument for the epistemic privilege of that distinctive feminist standpoint which, she has explained, is based on women's experiences.

Hartsock draws an explicit parallel between the feminist standpoint and that of the proletariat. She holds that

> just as Marx's understanding of the world from the standpoint of the proletariat enabled him to go beneath bourgeois ideology, so a feminist standpoint can allow us to understand patriarchal institutions and ideologies as perverse inversions of more humane social relations. (1983: 284)

Hence Hartsock also exploits the Marxian argument that those who occupy a position which is central to the preservation of a social system, but are oppressed by it, have a better understanding of the real nature of the system in question. Even if we accept this argument, however, the scope of its application is limited to knowledge of society and cannot be automatically extended to other domains.

Hartsock's argument could only establish that the reality of the patriar-chal system is better understood from the feminist standpoint; the same argument could not justify a claim for the superiority of the feminist standpoint in knowing other aspects of the world.[8] This is reflected in Smith's use of her formulation of standpoint as the methodological basis of a sociology of everyday life. The perspective of women's experience is granted an epistemic advantage only concerning matters that have to do with social relations shaped by the system of patriarchy.

Rose and Hartsock, on the other hand, aspire to provide greater applicability to the notion of a feminist standpoint. To do so, they need to argue both for the distinctiveness of women's perspective in other fields of inquiry, and for the epistemic privilege of that perspective in these fields. It is, I believe, possible to find arguments for a broader distinctive feminist perspective in both Rose and Hartsock, although they do not explicitly take these arguments to fulfill such a purpose.[9] Crucially, for standpoint theorists women's experiences, grounded in the sex-gender division of labor, give women access to knowledge which is denied to members of other groups. That is, under patriarchy women have experiences of social relations whose content is different from those of men's; furthermore the content of women's experience reflects more adequately this social reality. For exam-ple, men might experience women's childrearing as involving nothing more than the deployment of instinctual attitudes, but women's own experience of childrearing reflects the fact that socially acquired skills are involved in this activity. Considerations of this sort indicate that women's experiences about some social relations under patriarchy are more reliable than men's. However, these considerations cannot, as I said, be automatically extended to other fields of inquiry. It is at this point that both Rose and Hartsock modify the nature of their claims: instead of holding that women have experiences whose content differs from the experiences of members of other groups, they hold that women have a different way of experiencing, or more precisely a different cognitive style from that employed by men. Thus, for Rose, women's caring labor endows them with an affective way of knowing; Hartsock employs psychoanalytic object relations theory to a similar effect. She holds that there is a distinctive female subjectivity with a specific way of being in the world. Girls develop a 'female sense of self as connected to the world' (1983: 295) which informs all their experiences. Object relations theory therefore explains how the sexual division of labor gives rise to a distinctively female way of experiencing.[10]

It thus becomes possible for Rose and Hartsock to hold that the distinctiveness of women's perspective has general application, since what makes it distinct is women's cognitive style rather than just the specific contents of their experiences.[11] Of course, to say this is not to unearth a contradiction in Rose and Hartsock, rather it becomes now possible for them to claim that women's different cognitive style is the cause of the difference in content of their experiences. Nevertheless, an invocation of a distinctive cognitive style that belongs to women makes it rather difficult to explain why this style would be epistemically privileged for the whole range of its application. The Marxist claim that oppressed groups, central to the system of their oppression, have a better understanding of that system cannot in this case provide an adequate explanation. Instead, one perhaps could argue for the superiority of this female cognitive style over traditional ones by showing how it embodies certain epistemic virtues which are absent from the traditional masculinist approach. There is, however, little evidence for this claim which does not seem to possess much initial credibility. Further, even if one could provide a convincing argument in its favor, this claim would constitute a move away from the Marxist origins of standpoint epistemology.

Be that as it may, there are serious feminist objections to talk of a distinctively female cognitive style. Genevieve Lloyd has pointed out that the view that women have a distinctive way of reasoning is an unintended consequence of Descartes's mind–body dualism. While men were seen to possess Reason, conceived as 'a highly abstract mode of thought,' women were associated with a different sort of intellectual character, one that involved emotional and practical thinking (1984: 49). Although a reevaluation of these latter cognitive functions is overdue,[12] Lloyd doubts that an endorsement of the division by sex-gender of ways of thinking is either empirically correct or politically useful.[13]

This is only one of several objections that have been raised against the version of standpoint epistemology developed by Hartsock (1983), Rose (1983), and Smith (1988). Other objections include: (i) the charge that this theory of knowledge rests on the assumption that there is a female nature or essence; (ii) arguments against the assumption that there are enough experiences all women share which could constitute the basis of a standpoint, (iii) arguments against grounding knowledge on the notion of experience. These three objections are interrelated and I shall discuss them together in what follows. Another set of objections focuses on the understanding of marginality implicit in the versions of standpoint epistemology discussed so far; these criticisms, voiced by Bat-Ami Bar On (1993), assert that: (i) marginality should be understood as a locus of resistance rather than primarily as a matter of being victims of oppression, and (ii) people at the margins are not free from the dominant ideology. I shall also consider these objections, and argue that they derive in part from a misunderstanding of standpoint. Nevertheless, they point toward the need for more reflection on the notion of marginal position.

Several critics, including Sandra Harding (1986 and 1991) and Bar On (1993), have remarked that standpoint epistemology appears to entail false essentialisms and universalizations. To claim that there is a unique cognitive style or set of experiences which pertains to women seems to presuppose that women have essential features and to ignore the many important differences among women.[14]

It is true that, as Harding remarks, standpoint theorists 'tend to center a difference between the genders at the . . . expense of clearly focusing on differences between women or between men in different races, classes, and cultures' (1991: 178). That is, standpoint thinkers, like Smith, talk about the position of 'women in general' (1988: 86), or about 'women's oppression,' and ignore the differences between the positions occupied, and the oppressions experienced by, women of different races, classes, and sexual orientations. However, unless we support what Susan Bordo has aptly termed 'a new skepticism about the use of gender as an analytic category' (1990: 135), this observation alone is not sufficient to reject standpoint theory. A recognition of differences among women should not automatically lead to the assumption that there is nothing useful to be said about women in general. A recognition of the importance of, say, race and sexual orientation in the lives of some women, does not mean that every feminist analysis of some aspect of social reality should focus on all these dimensions (1990: 139). This is exactly the position held by Hartsock who, with regard to her Marxist strategy, says

> I adopt this strategy with some reluctance, since it contains the danger of making invisible the experience of lesbians or women of color. At the same time, I recognize that the effort to uncover a feminist standpoint assumes that there are some things common to all women's lives in Western class societies. (1983: 290)

Hartsock is aware of the risks involved in focusing on commonalties at the expense of differences among women, nevertheless she believes in the theoretical fruitfulness of using gender as a category in this context. To believe in this fruitfulness is to believe in the separability, at least in thought, of gender from other dimensions such as class and race. Unless this is, at least sometimes, possible, gender cannot be a useful analytic category. It has been argued by Elizabeth Spelman that this view entails what 'we might call tootsie roll metaphysics: each part of my identity is separable from every other part, and the significance of each part is unaffected by the other parts' (1990: 136). Spelman claims that it is not possible to abstract from the racial identities of white and black women in order to focus on a certain 'womanness' they have in common (1990: 135). Spelman, who is white, supports her claim by asking us to consider the following counterfactual (contrary to fact) situation:

> we should have no trouble imagining that had I been Black I could have had just the same understanding of myself as a woman as I in fact do, and that no matter how differently people would have treated me had I been Black, nevertheless what it would have meant to them that I was a woman would have been just the same. (1990: 135)

Although Spelman is correct to point out that we cannot assume that what it means to be a woman is the same for white and black women, this does not necessarily mean that we cannot ever abstract from race to consider issues of gender. Such an abstraction does not commit one to the view that there is an essence all women share. Similarly, we are not embracing essentialism when we abstract from all other features to claim of a group of people that they are all students in British universities. This claim does not even commit one to the view that being a student means the same to each one of them. Nevertheless, it is still possible to say a few politically important things about all these students, such as that they are likely to have financial worries since their grants have been cut, and therefore are likely to have a part-time job.

Similarly, to recognize that gender, race, class, and sexual orientation are not neatly separable does not entail that nothing can be said about gender without mentioning all other aspects.[15] It means, however, that this is possible only in limited and carefully chosen contexts. In particular, it means that it is not easy to make generalizations about women's experience because this is a context where the other dimensions of one's identity seem to make an important difference. Women belonging to different social classes, races, and sexual orientations face very different problems, and encounter different forms of oppression. While it is reasonable to claim that we all are 'victims' of racism, insofar as racism affects in negative ways everybody's life, the experience that non-white people have of racism is, of course, very different from what is experienced by whites. Furthermore, the institution of racism has consequences on the division of labor: non-white people usually do less well paid menial work, they face discrimination in the workplace, and tend to be excluded from professional occupations. More importantly, given Hartsock's claims, black women's experience of childbearing and childrearing are likely to be different from that of white women. If we do not conceive reproduction as a purely biological set of activities, we quickly come to realize that it is deeply affected by social factors such as wealth, family structure, and cultural assumptions, to name but a few. Raising a black child in a racist society is very different from raising a white child. One could also notice that it is often black women who take care of bodies so as to free white women from these chores. Therefore, neither Smith's nor Hartsock's assumption that it is possible to talk about women in general in the context of these aspects of social life are empirically correct. Instead, we are drawn toward the opposite conclusion that the life of a black woman is likely to be structurally different from the life of a white one. There are enough relevant differences in the conditions of women's lives to make it impossible to talk meaningfully about the experiences of women in general as the basis of standpoint.

Hartsock has managed to overlook these facts partly because she implicitly assumes that all women share some experiences in virtue of having a female body. It is this biological fact of embodiment, a fact she highlights in her preference of the term 'sex' over the less biological category of 'gender,' which I believe guides Hartsock's thinking in these matters. However, even if it is necessarily true that we are embodied, and biologically true that bodies are sexed, it does not follow that people with the same kind of body must have the same experiences of embodiment. This would only follow if one assumed that experiences are not mediated by social factors. Furthermore, even if having a female body were a source of identical experiences for all women, we still could not derive from this a standpoint unless we assumed that these experiences, which would have a purely biological source, were crucial to being a woman. Unless, that is, we assume that there is a female nature which is somehow grounded in facts about embodiment. Since Hartsock subscribes to Marx's opposition to a fixed human nature, she could not hold this position; nevertheless it is only by giving a crucial role to a female nature that one could support her claim that women have the same experience of reproductive labor.

To summarize, the version of standpoint theory based on shared experiences seriously underestimates the importance of differences between women. It thus runs the risk of essentialism; furthermore, since it employs unwarranted generalizations it is also in danger of making invisible the experiences of women who are poor or black or lesbians. Standpoint theorists like Hartsock took these dangers to be avoidable, but they were mistaken in doing so.

We must, however, also be careful to avoid the opposite error of putting too much emphasis on differences among women. Firstly, because this attitude tends to construe people with identities other than ours as complete and mysterious 'Others' with whom we have nothing in common. When we do this it becomes easy to fall prey to all sorts of generalizations which merely reflect our prejudices: e.g., that all black people must be poor. Secondly, an emphasis on difference may lead one to claim that people can only talk on behalf of their own group. Thus, although it may appear to be a step in the right direction to state that, say, only lesbians can talk for the lesbian community, the result is that claims such as this one are often taken to entail their converse. Thus, lesbians would be entitled only to talk about themselves. This is what Gayatri Chakravorty Spivak has called 'clinging to marginality' which, by teaching a person to speak for oneself, works 'precisely to contain the ones whom this person is supposed to represent' (1994: 162). In other words, if persons belonging to groups which are taken to be marginal in society can only speak for themselves, what they have to say is taken to be relevant only to their groups and can, therefore, be safely ignored by everybody else.

What I have said so far suggests that shared experience might not be the correct starting point for a feminist epistemology. And, indeed, there are versions of standpoint epistemology which do not rely on this notion: an example is the theory developed by Harding which is the topic of the next section. The notion of 'experience' itself has been the focus of intense criticisms, especially by feminists who are sympathetic to post-structuralist views. What feminists like Joan Scott find objectionable is not 'experience' in its colloquial sense; rather, they argue against the philosophical conception according to which experience is the basis of all human knowledge. Although Scott is explicitly concerned with historical knowledge, her critique of experience is couched in general terms and is easily applicable to knowledge in many other fields. Scott criticizes the use of 'experience' as a 'foundational ground' of knowledge (1992: 26). In this sense experience would function as the ultimate and 'uncontestable evidence' for a claim to knowledge (1992: 24). Scott rightly argues that experience is fallible, and therefore contestable. Further, she claims that experience cannot be taken as a ground for all other knowledge, because this would amount to ignoring 'the constructed nature of experience' (1992: 25). Usually post-structuralist claims about the construction of a given entity carry several ontological commitments, but in this context it is possible to read Scott simply as endorsing anti-foundationalism. Thus, it is not possible merely to have an experience, one must also somehow conceptualize what is happening, and hence what one experiences will depend on the concepts available to that person.[16] This is a position which is widely accepted also in analytic philosophy, and which I discussed in chapter 4. As that discussion has I hope made clear, anti-foundationalism does not require abandoning the notion of experience altogether, but it involves both accepting that experience is fallible and that it is not independent of theory.[17]

Most standpoint theorists do not adopt a conception of experience as untheoretical or immediately given. Hartsock, for example, is quite explicit in her claim that the 'vision of the oppressed group must be struggled for and represents an achievement which requires both science . . . and education' (1983: 285). The experience of oppression as oppression is not something which is immediately available to the oppressed; instead, it represents an achievement obtained by thinking and producing theories about one's situation.[18] On the other hand, Smith appears to appeal to a notion of immediate experience when she distinguishes between experience and the categories for its expression. Thus, she believes that there is a world which is immediately and directly experienced (1988: 55). Experience is employed here to give some authority to the views held by people occupying marginal positions, but, as Scott has argued, foundationalist accounts of experience are ultimately incorrect.

Besides being criticized for its universalism and for its use of experience, standpoint epistemology has been accused of misconceiving the notion of marginality. Bar On suggests that we understand it not in terms of oppression but, as has been done by bell hooks, as a matter of resistance (Bar On, 1993: 87). Bar On also points out that even practices of resistance are tainted by the dominant ideology from which it is impossible to escape completely (1993: 94). Bar On is correct on both counts. These points, however, help to articulate further the notion of standpoint – they do not oppose it. I discuss these issues in the next section. For now, it suffices to say that both points had already been acknowledged by Hartsock when she claims that a struggle is necessary to achieve a standpoint and that the 'vision of the ruling class (or gender) structures the material relations in which all parties are forced to participate' (1983: 285).

In conclusion, the versions of standpoint which start from women's experiences discussed so far have enormous problems because they assume that there are experiences shared by all women. What is needed, it would seem, is a standpoint which is based on something other than experience.

Starting from Marginal Lives

A fruitful attempt to provide such an alternative notion of standpoint epistemology has been developed by Harding. She claims that there are several reasons why it is not possible to use experience as the basis of standpoint. First, she makes the same point raised by Scott (1992) which I discussed above: women's experience cannot provide the foundations of knowledge because 'experience itself is shaped by social relations' (1991: 123). Second, women's experiences are not homogeneous. It is, she adds, possible to understand different sorts of feminism as based on the experiences of different historical groups of women. Hence, she concludes that 'both "women's experiences" and "what women say" . . . would not seem to be reliable grounds for deciding just which claims to knowledge are preferable' (1991: 123).

Harding does not deny the importance of experience, but she holds that:

> For a position to count as a standpoint, rather than as a claim – equally valuable but for different reasons – for the importance of listening to women tell us about their lives and experiences, we must insist on an objective location – women's lives – as the place from which feminist research should begin. (1991: 123)

Experience is a useful pointer toward the correct starting point for feminist research, but the grounds of feminist knowledge are theories and observations that 'start out from, that look at the world from the perspective of, women's lives' (1991: 124). In this way Harding attempts to avoid basing feminist knowledge on a notion of experience conceived as immediate and infallible. Instead, she stresses that even experiences are shaped by social reality. For example, one experiences a remark about one's body from a work colleague as either a normal form of interaction between men and women in the workplace, or as an instance of sexual harassment. Thus, what we experience is influenced by our understanding of social relations. Similarly, in the case of natural science what I experience as mere lines on a surface, a physicist may experience as the traces of the path of an elementary particle. In both cases, experiences are not something that we just have; instead, there is a lot that needs to be learned before we are capable of having them.

Harding shares with those standpoint theorists whose views I discussed in the previous section a belief that the lives of women and of people belonging to marginal groups differ structurally from those of men in dominant groups. She also believes that these differences are a source of new understandings of social reality. She holds, however, that research should start from the objective facts of these lives rather than from the experiences of those who conduct such lives. She makes this move because she wants to avoid the problems encountered by early versions of standpoint theory. As I said above, for Harding these problems are centered on the problematic notion of immediate experience and on the risk of erasing differences among women. Starting from women's lives rather than experiences contributes to a solution of both problems. First, it recognizes that experience is not immediately given but presupposes some theory and understanding. Second, it acknowledges that women belonging to different groups lead different lives.

Harding provides an indication of some resources available when one starts research in this fashion. Looking at social reality from the perspective of women's lives permits a recognition of the partiality of dominant understandings (1991: 121). Due to the nature of many women's activities, their lives are the ideal ground for understanding both the processes which have created our social reality (1991: 128) and the cultural character of phenomena which current ideology takes to be natural (1991: 131). That is, women's work in childrearing and in the general care of bodies makes it possible for others to dedicate themselves to socially recognized activities; but, since such work is invisible from the dominant perspective, social theories fail to recognize the indispensability of women's labor for our current social arrangements. The invisibility of women's work as work makes possible current ideological conceptions of it as a natural and instinctual activity.

Furthermore, starting research from the lives of oppressed groups makes possible an understanding of the mechanisms of oppression (1991: 126); it also increases the objectivity of the results of research in many areas of inquiry because it is only through social struggles to change the current social reality that we come to understand previously hidden aspects of social relations (1991: 127). Finally, the position of marginal lives as outsiders within the social order is a valuable source of understanding because it brings to 'research just the combination of nearness and remoteness, concern and indifference, that are central to maximizing objectivity' (1991: 124).

A concern with a stronger notion of objectivity is prominent in Harding's later work, and it is the contribution of standpoint to achieving such objectivity that she finds most valuable. She holds that scientific method as traditionally conceived is incapable of identifying and screening out the ideological values of dominant groups in society and scientific communities.[19] What is instead needed is an approach which, like standpoint, scientifically studies those assumptions that appear unremarkable from dominant perspectives (1991: 150).[20]

Harding's account of standpoint builds upon the work of other feminist thinkers, in particular she adopts Patricia Hill Collins's notion of the position of 'outsider-within.' This is the position occupied by people who are within a community or society but inhabit its margins. Within academia, for example, 'black women remain outsiders within, individuals whose marginality provides a distinctive angle of vision on the theories put forth by . . . intellectual communities' (1991: 12).

The perspective of marginal people, such as black women, is a standpoint. It provides a preferred stance to understand oppression because it is less likely than dominant perspectives to deny the links between its claims and political ideological interests (1991: 234). Each marginal group has its own perspective, and each of these is partial (1991: 234). As Collins says: 'No group has a clear angle of vision' (1991: 234). Thus, no group can legitimately claim to possess that unique standpoint which permits a completely adequate account of social reality.

While Hartsock and Smith seem to take a standpoint to be capable, at least in principle, of offering a complete account of social oppressive relations, Collins denies the possibility of such completeness. She criticizes these earlier Marxist accounts of standpoint for sharing 'the positivist belief in one "true" interpretation of reality' (1991: 235). There is, however, more than one way of interpreting claims about the partiality of any standpoint. One may follow Harding's talk of perspectives which are less false than others, claiming that not even 'our "best" representations of the world are transparent to the world' (1991: 185). That is, our best claims are themselves situated. None of our claims can represent the world as it is in itself independently of human interests. Nevertheless, some perspectives furnish less distorted understandings of the world of human concerns. A perspective is, thus, partial because it is not a transparent representation. One could, however, provide a different account of partial perspectives according to which what counts as 'true' is simply a matter of negotiation and agreement between those involved in discussion. This might amount to some sort of relativism, and it is rightly rejected by Collins (1991: 235).

For Collins, although every perspective is partial, not all claims to knowledge are equal. Instead, the standpoints of 'outsiders-within' are to be preferred to that of dominant groups.[21] Collins holds that each marginal group has its own partial perspective. Her approach envisages a coalition among marginal groups.

> Each group speaks from its own standpoint and shares its own partial, situated knowledge. But because each group perceives its own truth as partial, its knowledge is unfinished. Each group becomes better able to consider other groups' standpoints without relinquishing the uniqueness of its own standpoint or suppressing other groups' partial perspectives. (1991: 236)

Acknowledgment of the partiality of one's own angle on reality encourages a politics of solidarity in the awareness that one does not have a complete knowledge of social reality: one may thus be disposed to learn what other marginal standpoints have to offer. This approach does not only have political advantages, it also facilitates more accurate knowledge of social relations. Its epistemic superiority originates from awareness that systems of oppression are deeply related. It is only through the combination of the insights of different standpoints that it is possible to study how these systems interconnect, so that each needs the others in order to function (1991: 222).

The account of standpoint epistemology provided by Collins, thus, avoids some of the problems encountered by its earlier versions. First, since she recognizes that each group has its own perspective, she does not erase differences among women. There is, for instance, a black lesbians perspective, one that pertains to poor latinas, and so on. Second, she avoids additive analyses of oppression. The search for a unique privileged standpoint may lead one to assume that it must belong to the most oppressed group of all.[22] Such an assumption would betray a mistaken understanding of oppression as composed of separate layers rather than deeply related phenomena (1991: 207). As Collins points out, oppression is a matrix with no pure victims and no pure oppressors. All groups have some different amount of privilege and underprivilege depending on the context. There is no group which is the most oppressed of all, because oppression is not quantifiable in this manner. Instead, we are all partly victims and partly oppressors to a varying degree depending on the situation. Furthermore, each system of oppression – along the axes of gender, race, class, and sexual orientation – is interlocked with all others without which it could not function in the way it does. Thus, Collins's approach has the double advantage of making explicit that it is not possible to understand one kind of oppression independently of all others, and that the members of no group can be seen as pure victims of oppression. On the other hand, earlier standpoint epistemologies encouraged both the view that the oppression of women can be understood in isolation, and the belief that women do not themselves oppress anyone.

Further, Collins's understanding of oppression as a matrix is combined with a conception of marginal positions as sites of resistance. Marginal positions thus become sites of, using bell hooks's apt phrase, 'counter-hegemonic discourse' (1984: 15). They are both locations of oppression and resistance (hooks, 1990: 151). If margins, all margins, are sites of resistance, we do not need Marx's account of standpoint as pertaining uniquely to that group which is both oppressed by a system and central to its continuation. What for Marx was the result of occupying a double central and marginal position is for hooks and Collins proper to all marginal positions. For them the very condition of marginality provides the materials for understanding oppression. And since there are different marginalized groups, there will be different standpoints.

Marginality can by itself be a source of knowledge because it is not seen just as the position occupied by victims; it is instead the space where oppressed people organize their resistance. Hooks and Collins rightly insist that the experiences of oppressed people are not just experiences of oppression and powerlessness, they are also experiences of struggle to preserve one viewpoint, to resist oppression (hooks, 1990: 150). Thus, they avoid what has been perceived as early standpoint theory's tendency to view women as victims rather than agents of resistance.[23] This non-Marxist conception of marginality finds support in Foucault's conception of power. Power stops being seen as the unique property of institutions to limit the liberty of individuals, and it becomes also a positive force or ability to make new freedoms possible. Power does not just work top-down, but is a force permeating every level which enables new possibilities while impeding others.[24]

Collins's standpoint theory, thus, avoids those problems encountered by earlier standpoint theory. Nevertheless, she employs the notion of lived experience as a crucial source of knowledge. At times her position may seem similar to Harding's, for example when she suggests that we look at African-American women's family lives to denaturalize the notion of the nuclear family (1991: 223). In this case the starting point of her research appears to be the lives of marginal people rather than their experiences of those lives. More frequently, however, Collins explicitly claims that the primary source of knowledge is provided by the experiences of marginal people. These experiences give rise to a concrete wisdom developed in the struggle for survival and which is opposed to the knowledge of dominant groups (1991: 208). Collins does not, however, understand experience as something which is infallible, immediately given and untheoretical. If it is correct to say that Collins's account avoids those problems encountered by early versions of standpoint even though she relies on the notion of experience, the source of trouble for standpoint is not its use of 'experience' but rather the assumptions made by early theorists. They assumed that women have the same experiences, and Smith also assumed that these are infallible, immediate and independent of theory. Once these assumptions are rejected, it becomes possible to put the notion of experience to fruitful employment. Thus, more recently some feminists have tried to rethink experience in new ways.

Morwenna Griffiths, for example, has recently argued that feminist epistemology cannot dispense with experience because of its concern with subjectivity. What characterized traditional epistemology was its willingness to hide the role played by the subject in the process of achieving knowledge.[25] The contribution of the subjectivity of usually white male knowers was thus left unchecked. On the contrary, what characterizes many feminist theories of knowledge is a recognition of the role played by subjectivity in the process of knowledge acquisition (1995: 59). Hence, experience is necessarily a starting point for acquiring knowledge – one must start from a perspective. Experience is, of course, only a starting point since it must always be subjected to a process of critical revision (1995: 6). While Griffiths argues for the indispensability of experience Oshadi Mangena provides an account of how true universality, the mark of adequate knowledge, can emerge from a recognition of concrete experiences in all their very specific differences.

For Mangena there is no common experience as a consequence of gender to which race and class can simply be added on (1994: 281). These dimensions of identity are inextricably linked and, as Collins also points out, can be better understood by foregrounding their relations. Furthermore, gender itself is thoroughly relational. Hence, 'we cannot examine the experience of woman in society without taking into account the fact of their interconnectedness with men' (Mangena, 1994: 280). This is especially true in African societies where both men and women are oppressed, and where these oppressions, although systematically different, are inextricably linked. Similarly, the condition of women in the South of the planet must be linked to the global condition of women. The concrete experiences of individuals belonging to different groups not only differ in very specific ways, they are also interrelated. The causal processes underlying those experiences can be therefore adequately represented only if we understand them as processes of interaction (1994: 280). We can understand social reality only if we look at it in a global manner taking into account all the relations that constitute this reality.

Mangena's emphasis on experience is based on her acknowledgment that subjectivity always colors scientific knowledge (1994: 227). Experience cannot, therefore, be excised from knowledge. What characterizes traditional science is that the, usually male, investigator considers only his experience of reality. This very specific form of experience is then invested with the title of knowledge. Because the investigator has the exclusive right to the process of objectification that transforms experience into knowledge, what is usually termed 'knowledge' is a collection of falsifying universalisms. What results is abstract universality, a false universality achieved by giving universal character to only one form of experience.

Instead, for Mangena, feminist epistemology should indicate how to achieve true or concrete universality (1994: 278). Such universality can be obtained when we assume 'a holistic approach to knowledge in the sense that both subjects and objects of experience are together involved in the process of formulating human knowledge from their distinct but interrelated situational experiences' (1994: 278). Knowledge is a process by means of which experiences are represented and objectified, and human experiences are always situational insofar as they emerge our of our relations with others. Thus, adequate knowledge requires a sort of participatory democracy. Everybody must be invited to participate to the process of objectification of experience so that all experiences are taken into account. In this manner, we can produce theories which represent the whole situation since they reflect the interrelated character of the experiences themselves (1994: 280). This participatory process gives rise to a concrete universality because it is possible to bring together all these different perspectives as a coherent whole (1994: 281). The resulting claims would have true universal applicability 'in the sense that they would refer to a multiplicity of concrete experience, although in general terms' (1994: 281).

To summarize, in recent years some feminists have claimed that experience can be a useful tool for epistemology as long as it is not understood as giving us an immediate and infallible access to the object of knowledge. Starting from experience is a sound starting point of inquiry if it is understood as a matter as starting from a perspective which is inevitably partial and subject to revision. The problem encountered by earlier versions of standpoint epistemology can be avoided if we acknowledge differences among women. We can, thus, admit the existence of multiple standpoints, which can perhaps be unified as Mangena suggests. Even if this unification is impossible, the multiplicity of viewpoints need not lead to relativism. We can admit the legitimacy of more than one perspective without claiming the all perspectives are as good as any other.

What is characteristic of all the very different versions of standpoint epistemology which I have discussed is the belief that objectivity can be achieved from partial perspectives. This claim requires that the very notion of 'objectivity' is given new meanings. It this issue which constitutes the main topic of the next chapter.

Further Reading

The best example of the early version of standpoint is Nancy Hartsock's 'The Feminist Standpoint: Developing the Ground for a Specifically Feminist Historical Materialism' (1983). Sandra Harding provides discussions of this position and the problems it faces in chapters 6 and 7 of *The Science Question in Feminism* (1986) and in chapters 6 and 7 of *Whose Science? Whose Knowledge?* (1991). Bat-Ami Bar On's 'Marginality and Epistemic Privilege' (1993) provides a useful critique of the political dimensions of standpoint. For revaluations of the notion experience which bring to the fore rather than hide differences among women, see Patricia Hill Collins's *Black Feminist Thought: Knowledge, Consciousness, and the Politics of Empowerment* (1991) and part I of Morwenna Griffiths's *Feminisms and the Self: The Web of Identity* (1995).

Notes

1 For a good discussion of social marginality and economic centrality in the context of Marxist theory see Bar On (1993: 85–6).

2 Marxist theory of knowledge is, therefore, closer to traditional conceptions than one might expect, since it claims that lack of bias is a necessary condition for knowledge. This is an aspect of the theory which has been modified in some of its feminist reappropriations.

3 The debate over the need to supplement Marxism with accounts of patriarchy and of the sexual division of reproductive labor has been central to socialist feminist theories in the 1980s. Some feminists, for example Heidi Hartmann (1981), have argued for a dual theory of women's oppression in terms both of the structure of relations in society which constitutes capitalism, and of that which constitutes patriarchy. Others, such as Alison Jaggar (1983), have attempted to provide a unified theory which nevertheless takes into account the specificity of women's reproductive labor. For an overview of this debate,

see chapter 6 of Rosemarie Tong (1992); for a discussion of these issues in a specifically epistemological context, see Rose (1986).

4   For a theoretically sophisticated account of gender-specific experiences, see Vrinda Dalmiya and Linda Alcoff (1993).

5   I have already mentioned the importance of emotions for scientific knowledge when I referred to Barbara McClintock in chapter 1. I return to this issue in chapter 7.

6   Hartsock (1983: 284) talks of division of labor by sex; but, as Rose (1986: 176) notices, this sort of talk 'pulls her arguments too strongly back to nature' and extenuates the socially sanctioned character of this division of labor.

7   For this interpretation see Harding (1986:157). Although it seems quite clear that this is how Smith intends to characterize the experiential line of fault, her claim is too strong. If there truly were no way in our current society to give a name to one's experiences they could not constitute the basis for knowledge. We can, however, interpret Smith as claiming that it is not easy to give a name to one's actual experiences because they do not correspond to what, according to socially sanctioned norms, one ought to experience.

8   The issue here is made more complex by the Marxian rejection of a sharp dichotomy between natural and social worlds. Nevertheless, no feminist would argue that patriarchy is sufficient to explain every aspect of reality, therefore even complete knowledge about patriarchy will not be sufficient to have knowledge about other aspects of the world.

9   Thus, Rose (1994: 74) provides a very different explanation from the one I provide below of the role of object relations theory in standpoint epistemology.

10 For a discussion of object relations theory see the second section of chapter 2.

11 The notion of a distinctive cognitive style of women has been explicitly endorsed, for example, by Shulamit Reinharz (1983: 183). For a critical discussion of this issue see Harding (1991: 121–2).

12 One must not assume that, were such a reevaluation to take place, women's perceived intellectual status would be improved. When the romantic movement glorified emotions and passions, women were seen to be deficient because they did not have them as much as men (Battersby, 1989: 113).

13 As Judith Grant (1987) notices this division seems to reinscribe rather than challenge patriarchal assumptions.

14 Marnia Lazreg (1994) raises these objections and finds their origin in an underexamined acceptance of the empiricist conception of experience.

15 In this context, for ease of exposition, I have chosen to leave unquestioned the received view about identity claims. According to this view, identity attributions describe features that individuals possess in virtue of their psychology, or of the social role they occupy. I criticize this view in the second section of chapter 10.

16 Strictly speaking even a foundationalist can accept this point and argue that experience functions as evidence independent of theory, although one needs the theory to conceptualize experience.

17 Although Lazreg (1994) is right to claim that the notion of immediate

experience is an outgrowth of classical empiricism, it is incorrect to deduce, as she does, from this that the projects of a feminist standpoint or of a feminist empiricism must be abandoned. This unacceptable conception of experience is not essential to either.

18   Hartsock's view is similiar to Wilfrid Sellars's anti-foundationalism, which I explained in chapter 1. Although experiential knowledge is not inferential, it counts as knowledge only against the background of other knowledge.

19   This is a view defended also by Helen Longino; I have discussed her position in chapter 4.

20   I discuss Harding's account of objectivity in chapter 7.

21   I follow Collins here in using 'standpoint' as synonymous with 'perspective.'

22   This would, of course, go against Marxian accounts of epistemic privilege of a standpoint.

23   As I said above this criticism of early standpoint theories is not entirely accurate.

24   I discuss Foucault's notion of power in chapter 8.

25   I have discussed this issue in chapter 2.

7

Objectivity and Feminism

In science the imperative 'be objective' has often been taken to indicate a norm whose satisfaction is necessary to achieve knowledge. It is commonplace to believe that unless a scientist is objective, she will only utter mere opinions which bear the mark of subjectivity. Thus, objectivity is an issue for science. But objectivity does not figure prominently in discussions about knowledge in general. This is an important but rarely remarked upon fact. It is true that epistemologists often presuppose objectivity, but they do not see it as an issue over and above justification and evidence. This is not a mere coincidence. Traditional conceptions of objectivity have been deployed to demarcate scientific from non-scientific knowledge. They have been used to characterize and legitimize the specific kinds of representations of reality offered by modern Western science.

Donna Haraway has produced some of the most important work on objectivity written from a feminist perspective. In her article 'Situated Knowledges' (1988) Haraway begins to move beyond the traditional conception of scientific knowledge in terms of representations. She achieves a break with the tradition in 'The Promises of Monsters' (1992), where she develops an account in which scientific knowledge emerges out of practices. Her account is science-friendly, without holding that science needs no modifications. In this chapter I look at feminist critiques and reappropriations of objectivity through the lens offered by Haraway's work. I employ her insights on the debates about this notion to discuss how and why it has become a topic of feminist concern.

What is Objectivity?

In order to understand what 'objectivity' may mean we need to consider the influence of metaphors of vision on theories of knowledge. At least two of these metaphors have played a structuring role in discussions about objectivity. Vision is also the focal point of Haraway's work (1988: 581). In 'Situated Knowledges' she argues that a feminist notion of objectivity should be based on a new metaphor of vision: 'prosthetic vision.' Prosthetic vision is the sort of sight made available by modern technological science. It makes it possible for us to see how the world looks to the compound eyes of an insect, or to the camera eye of a satellite in space, or even to the eye of a microscope. Elsewhere Haraway shifts her focus from the optics of reflection, which has traditionally dominated these discussions, to one of diffraction (1992: 299). The latter is concerned with interferences, not with the reduplication of images typical of representation. I return to Haraway's alternative visions in the third section of this chapter. In this section I discuss those characteristics of the notion of vision which have been crucial to traditional conceptions of objectivity, and have influenced feminist reactions to them.

The first visual metaphor concerns representations. Vision is understood as the power of the eye to represent the world as it is, independently of the gaze. A passive eye merely reflects a passive reality. Everything can be represented by the eye besides the eye itself, which is, therefore, the only thing to stand outside the picture. This scientifically crude understanding of vision has provided a metaphorical model for knowledge characterized by objectivity. Knowledge, according to this metaphor, must exclude any subjective input, it must consist in a representation of how things are independently of us, and it must be a sort of view from nowhere. It is this account of knowledge which has generated the traditional equation between objectivity, value–neutrality, and a view which is not from any particular perspective.

The second metaphor of vision which is relevant to contemporary debates about objectivity is that of the power of the gaze. This is a metaphor about power. The eye is understood as capable of looking at an object which cannot stare back. Vision is conceived as an asymmetrical relation between an active eye and a passive object. Through vision the object is objectified: that is, it comes to be seen as devoid of meaning or purpose. The world as it appears to the objectifying eye is the disenchanted mechanical world typical of the new science of the seventeenth century.

These two metaphors of sight are at the root of the conception of knowledge as adequate representation. The traditional problem of objectivity, I argue, makes sense only in the context of this conception which, I hold, must be rejected. Although feminists do not endorse these two metaphors, often they fail to abandon them completely. They remain trapped within a representationalist framework. In this section I discuss the philosophical theories resulting from these metaphors, before discussing feminist engagements with them.

The contemporary debate structured by the first metaphor finds its origin in early modern philosophical theories. In this debate objectivity is treated both as an ontological and epistemological notion. In the first ontological sense objectivity pertains to reality as opposed to appearances. In the epistemic sense objectivity is a feature of those judgments that mirror reality. These two senses of the notion of objectivity are best understood in the context of the theory of perception, first developed by Locke, which is commonly known as 'indirect realism.'[1] This theory takes reality to be beyond the mental screen, the so-called 'veil of perception.' This screen is the only thing we are in direct contact with, and on the screen are representations of what lies outside. Thus, we are immediately aware only of appearances, the way reality seems to us, not of reality itself.

Locke's distinction between objective features of reality, which he calls primary qualities, and subjective features or secondary qualities, is based on this theory of perception. Locke starts by dividing things and their qualities into two groups: those which are mind-dependent and those which are not. What is mind-dependent would not exist unless there were minds; mind-independent are those things that exist independently of minds. There is no problem with this distinction *per se*. But indirect realism introduces the further distinction between a world of appearances or representations and the real world. While for Locke representations of primary qualities resemble features of the real world, representations of mind-dependent secondary qualities do not. For example, we represent the external world as colored, but the world in itself has no colors. Colors belong to the way the world appears to us. Since primary qualities exist in the real world, which is contrasted with the subjective world of representations, they are considered objective. Secondary qualities are, of course, subjective.

Primary qualities appear in the same way to everybody because we have representations that resemble them. Hence, Locke characterizes primary qualities as what does not vary from perceiver to perceiver. Secondary qualities are, instead, relative to perceivers and may, therefore, vary. The ontological notion of objectivity is introduced to distinguish between the properties and qualities that belong to the real world and those that exist in our inner representations but do not resemble anything outside us.

The view that reality exists beyond a mediating interface, which characterizes indirect realism about perception, has also generated the conviction that knowledge must be independent of the subject's perspective. Only representations that do not vary from perceiver to perceiver can be instances of knowledge of objective reality.[2] Furthermore, since knowledge is a matter of accurate representations, it can be achieved only by screening out any possible influence of the subject on the contents of the representations.[3] Knowledge, therefore, would require value-neutrality. Epistemic objectivity pertains to claims about which there can be agreement among perceivers. When the truth of a claim is the best explanation for the existing agreement, that claim is said to be objective. In this case, it is claimed, judgment is guided by the facts alone.

The 'absolute conception of the world' as discussed by Bernard Williams exemplifies this approach. What characterizes this conception is that it 'might be arrived at by any investigators, even if they were very different from us' (1985: 138). But, Williams continues, if all sorts of investigators can, at least in principle, converge on this conception despite their very different perspectives, it must be because the absolute conception represents how things are (1985: 136). For Williams the absolute conception is characteristic of science, and distinguishes it from other kinds of investigation.

Thomas Nagel has also argued that independence from any perspective is what characterizes the scientific enterprise. 'The wider the range of subjective types to which a form of understanding is accessible – the less it depends on specific subjective capacities – the more objective it is' (1986: 5). Objectivity transcends our particular points of view, and involves 'a more detached understanding of ourselves, of the world, and of the interaction between them' (1986: 5).

Objectivity, for both Williams and Nagel, is the mark of scientific knowledge. Its purpose is not to distinguish knowledge from non-knowledge in general. Instead, it serves to demarcate scientific knowledge from all other sorts of knowledge. Williams and Nagel are trying to capture what is distinctive about scientific knowledge. They identify this feature as matter of independence from human perspectives. However, since they adopt the ontological framework of indirect realism, they misunderstand the nature of the independence typical of scientific knowledge. A better account of the distinctive characteristics of this kind of knowledge can be provided in terms of Heidegger's distinction between the ready-to-hand and the present-at-hand.

The world of the ready-to-hand is the world imbued with human values. In this context, things are understood in terms of their usefulness to or obstruction of human projects. A hammer is an example of a thing of this kind. What makes a hammer what it is, is its proper use. In other words, a hammer is a piece of equipment which is defined in terms of its role in human practices. The world of science is, instead, the world of the present-at-hand. This world is characterized by its independence from human practical ends, since objects in it are not treated as tools. Instead, they are taken to exist independently of us, and to have objective properties. For Heidegger, however, the present-at-hand is dependent upon the ready-to-hand. He holds that to take something to exist independently of us amounts to instituting a special sort of dependency. It is a way in which we take things to be. Hence, the world of the present-at-hand is not a world which is independent of all human context, since there is no such world. Rather, it is a world dependent on a specific human context. The practice of giving and asking for reasons provides, according to Heidegger, this context. Thus when we take something to be present-at-hand, we treat it as the kind of thing to which it is appropriate to respond by making assertions about it.

Consider, once again, the example of a hammer. We take a particular hammer as belonging to the ready-to-hand when we respond to it by using it as a tool. We think of it in terms of how it can contribute to our practical ends. However, when we take that hammer to be present-at-hand, we adopt a different stance toward it. We treat it as the sort of thing about which we can make assertions. We thus place it within the context of human discursive practices. We do not attend to the object as something that satisfies human needs, but as something about which we can talk. Thus, the world of the present-at-hand is a world which is independent of human practical concerns. It is not, however, irrelevant to those concerns. For example, if a hammer does not work properly, we can switch our stance toward it. We can treat it as the sort of thing about which we make assertions, which will guide our practical repairing activities.

To summarize, for Heidegger the mark of scientific knowledge is a certain degree of autonomy from human practical ends. The objects of scientific knowledge are taken to be independent of human concerns, although they are not irrelevant to them. However, it would be a mistake to conceive the world of science as a world of things in themselves. Rather, it comprises things whose dependency on us is of a special kind. These objects are defined in terms of their social significance. But this is the significance they have for our discursive practices, rather than for our practical activities.[4]

Williams and Nagel assume, instead, that scientific knowledge is knowledge of things in themselves. While Heidegger encourages us to think of the detachment characteristic of the scientific attitude as a special kind of engagement, Williams and Nagel think of it as the attempt to gain knowledge independent of any human context. Hence, they take the objectivity of science to require value-neutrality and a view from nowhere. Williams and Nagel are captive to the conception of knowledge which is implicit in Locke's theory of perception. They postulate a world which is totally severed from human beings. They take knowledge to be a matter of representing this world. In this manner, they open up an epistemic gulf between the representations internal to the knower and the objects in the world, and invoke the notion of objectivity in order to bridge this abyss. But, I hold, since we cannot ever step outside ourselves, we cannot ever achieve a true view from nowhere. There is no value-neutral perspective from which we can glimpse at a world of things in themselves. What we can achieve, instead, is perspectival knowledge which is, sometimes, only indirectly connected to immediate practical concerns.

It is now time to turn to the second source of influence on feminist debates on objectivity: namely, the connection with objectification. One can trace this connection to a common reading of Hegel's master–slave dialectic which describes one stage in the development of the consciousness of self. At this stage the self defines itself as a subject by negating the subjectivity of a dominated other. The self, as an agent, differentiates itself from others who are objectified. That is to say, they are treated as objects which are devoid of intrinsic purpose and incapable of action. This conception of the relation between self and other has been employed by Simone de Beauvoir to understand the position of women:[5]

> She is defined and differentiated with reference to man and not he with reference to her; she is the incidental, the inessential as opposed to the essential. He is the subject, he is the Absolute – she is the Other. (1988: 16)[6]

This view presupposes that the relation between subject and other, against which the subject defines himself, is akin to the relation between the knowing subject and the object known. It is also assumed that the attitude of the knowing subject toward the other is one of domination. In a word, objectification is the result of adopting toward fellow human beings the objectifying attitude of the natural sciences. The traditional reading of Hegel's dialectics takes this form of domination to be a necessary step in the development of subjectivity. Oppression is, therefore, inevitable.

The importance in the objectivity debate of the metaphor about vision as an instrument of control and domination is also noted by Haraway. She rejects the model proposed by this metaphor and claims that:

> Situated knowledge requires that the object of knowledge be pictured as an actor and agent, not as a screen or a ground or a resource, never finally as slave to the master that closes off the dialectic in his unique agency and his authorship of 'objective' knowledge. (1988: 592)

Haraway clearly recognizes the Hegelian origin of this conception of the relation between subject and object. She goes beyond Hegel when she claims that the objectifying attitude of the natural sciences is always a sort of domination. We should not only refrain from adopting this approach toward other human beings, but also avoid it when we are trying to know non-human entities. On this point I disagree with Haraway. I do not think that trying to gain practical mastery of our environment is always a form of domination.

Objectivity and Objectification

The most radical feminist critiques of the notion of objectivity find their source in the connection between objectivity and oppression, that is objectification. Catharine MacKinnon, for example, explicitly relates objectivity to objectification. She sees the first as the epistemological stance which corresponds to the social process of objectification. It is a male epistemological stance which amounts to a denial of the subordination of women (1987: 136). A similar link between objectivity and domination is drawn by Evelyn Fox Keller.

Keller holds that the traditional notion of objectivity results from a conception of scientific thought which is associated with masculinity. She claims:

> Having divided the world into two parts – the knower (mind) and the knowable (nature) – scientific ideology goes on to prescribe a very specific relation between the two. . . . The relation specified between

knower and known is one of distance and separation. It is that between a subject and an object radically divided, which is to say, no worldly relation. Simply put, nature is objectified. (1985: 79)

For Keller, when the relation between the subject and the object is one of separation, the object is objectified. That is to say, the object is dominated, it is oppressed. It is this oppressive relation of objectification which, for Keller, characterizes 'objective' forms of knowledge as they are currently understood. Further, separation and distance are culturally associated with masculinity. As a consequence we have a 'culturally pervasive association between objectivity and masculinity' (1985: 71). Masculinity here 'connotes a radical rejection of any commingling of subject and object' (1985: 79).

For Keller 'objectivity . . . is the cognitive counterpart of psychological autonomy' (1985: 71). In particular, objectivity as separation is connected to a static sense of autonomy, which is associated with anxious concern about the boundaries between self and others (1985: 102). While psychological autonomy, as the sense of being in control of one's own actions, is necessary to the development of self (1985: 97), static autonomy leads to the adoption of an objectifying attitude. This form of autonomy is characterized by an excessive concern with control which, in a highly hierarchical society like ours, becomes an obsession for domination (1985: 103). Thus, for Keller anxiety about differentiation between self and others, which characterizes masculinity, promotes the pursuit of domination and oppression of others (1985: 112). It also encourages the adoption of a posture of emotional detachment, since to show emotion would amount to lack of control.

Individuals, who have developed a static sense of autonomy, relate cognitively to nature in ways that are similar to the way they relate to other human beings. They are anxious to preserve a separation between them and nature, and they relate to it in a manner that reflects a need for domination. For example, they consider objects only from the perspective of how they fulfill the needs of the knower (1985: 120). In other words, they treat nature instrumentally, consider it only in terms of how it can fulfill their own purposes.

Keller's alternative to dominant conceptions of objectivity is dynamic objectivity, which is the cognitive counterpart of dynamic autonomy. She does not reject the ideal of objectivity altogether because for her it merely indicates the pursuit of 'maximally reliable . . . understanding of the world around oneself' (1985: 116). Dynamic objectivity is characterized by an 'interaction between emotional and cognitive experience' (1985: 116). It does not involve a severance of the subject from the object (1985: 117), but makes use of subjective experience (1985: 117). It is a form of love, which enables a sense of oneness with the object (1985: 118).

There are several problem with Keller's alternative conception of objectivity. Firstly, although it is meant to combine reason and emotions, it still relies on a distinction between the cognitive and the emotional. As evinced in the short quote above, Keller thinks that emotional experiences are not cognitive. That is, she sees emotions as mere feelings. For example, when Keller discusses knowledge as a form of love she distinguishes between its purely emotional component (a mere feeling of 'oneness') and its purely cognitive aspect (a focus on the interests of the loved ones). This conception of emotions, as Alison Jaggar has pointed out, is deeply mistaken for several reasons. First, the same feeling can be associated with different emotions depending on context. Second, emotions can be appropriate to their context, while feelings are mere happenings (1989: 155). For example, we can be justifiably proud of our achievements, rightly outraged by oppression. A feeling of thirst is, instead, something that simply happens to us. Thirst is not something that can be appropriate or inappropriate. Finally, emotions are not necessarily associated with any particular feeling. Love, for example, need not involve any feelings of oneness.

A second problem with Keller's analysis of objectivity is her implicit equation of differentiation with domination. Oppression, thus, becomes a necessary consequence of self-definition, since each individual, in order to become a subject, must differentiate herself from everything else. Keller explicitly rejects this interpretation of her position. She claims that the need for control is not the same as the need for domination. While the first is necessary to a sense of autonomy, the second is the result of the hierarchical social relations of current Western society. However, she assumes that, in a more equal society, individuals would develop a dynamic sense of autonomy, which she conceives as 'an exquisite balancing act' (1985: 100). It is a balancing act between a sense of control, and a sense of continuity between self and other (1985: 100). Thus, dynamic autonomy is 'a product at least as much of relatedness as it is of delineation' (1985: 99). Keller takes control to be a matter of separation which needs to be balanced by a sense of continuity between self and others. But balance would be required only if there were something intrinsically wrong with control. Keller, I believe, implicitly makes this assumption which contradicts her explicit position.

The source of this internal tension in Keller's position is a conflation

between relatedness and continuity or lack of differentiation. Static autonomy leads to domination because it is typical of a self who thinks of himself
as totally unrelated to others. Such an individual is purely self-interested.
He behaves altruistically only if this behavior is ultimately in his own
interest. Therefore, this individual will exploit other people to pursue his
own ends. Dynamic autonomy, instead, is about relatedness. An individual
who has developed this sense of autonomy will be concerned with the
interests of other people. He will have these concerns because he does not
think of others as unconnected to himself. However, relatedness is not the
same as continuity. There is no reason why one would need to blur the
boundaries between self and other to experience relatedness. Similarly,
there is no need to relax control of oneself in order to care for other
people. Keller, instead, assumes that relation requires lack of differentiation.
This assumption is deeply problematic, since it amounts to saying that we
can care for others only if we ignore their independence from us. This
attitude, however, is also a source of oppression since it denies the
autonomy of the other person (Grimshaw, 1986: 182).

Thus, as Toril Moi points out, Keller's position amounts to a romantic
attempt 'to overcome the subject/object division by advocating some form
of communion between subject and object' (1989: 192). The continuity
between subject and object results in 'the subject engulf[ing] the object,
thereby radically destroying it as other' (1989: 192). Keller obviously wants
to avoid this consequence, when she claims that oneness does not destroy
differentiation, but her account of dynamic objectivity cannot serve this
purpose. Separation is for her a form of domination. It must, at least
momentarily, be put aside when engaged in the sort of love as a feeling of
oneness which she takes dynamic objectivity to require.

A similar romanticism about fusion with nature, sustained by the belief
embedded in object relations theory that any form of separation is a form
of oppression, can be found in Susan Bordo's critique of objectivity. Bordo
argues that the concern with objectivity is relatively recent, it is a
consequence of the early modern need to postulate a sharp separation
between subject and object (1987: 99). This should be seen as a reaction to
an anxiety about autonomy which leads to an emphasis on separation.
Here, Bordo romantically invokes 'the medieval sense of relatedness to the
world, . . . [which] had not depended on "objectivity" but on continuity
between the human and physical realms' (1987: 98). But, once again, it is
only if one unjustifiably believes that all forms of differentiation are forms
of oppression, that one may be drawn to dream of fusion and continuity

while forgetting the dangers they may contain. Ultimately, Bordo endorses Keller's notion of dynamic objectivity which, I argued, is doomed to failure.

Although I disagree with several aspects of Keller's account of what is wrong with traditional conceptions of objectivity, nevertheless I believe that her claim that objectivity has been traditionally associated with masculinity is correct. Genevieve Lloyd's analysis of the masculinization of reason is sufficient to make this point (1984: 50).[7] Objectivity has been traditionally associated with an unemotional way of reasoning which, as Lloyd shows, has often been conceived as masculine.

I have argued that Keller and Bordo base their critiques of objectivity on the unwarranted belief that all forms of differentiation involve domination. This is a belief that they share with some of their staunchest critics: namely, those feminists who ally themselves to post-structuralism and postmodernism. Susan Hekman, for example, holds that the notion of objectivity is essentially tied to the account of knowledge provided by the Enlightenment. A present-day version of this account is Williams's 'absolute conception of the world' which I mentioned above. According to Hekman, since the Enlightenment project is bankrupt, a 'feminist critique of masculinist science . . . must abandon objectivity along with the other trappings of Enlightenment science' (1990: 131).

For Hekman, this traditional conception of knowledge is based on a Cartesian notion of the subject which is generated by a split between subject and object (1990: 69, 73). The quest for objective knowledge, according to her, makes sense only within this framework. Hence, for Hekman, as for Keller and Bordo, the problem of objectivity is paradoxically a problem of subjectivity. It is only a certain kind of subject who thinks he needs objectivity to have knowledge. This is the early modern subject who is trapped within the realm of appearances. For a different kind of subject the problem of objectivity does not arise, or, if it does, it is in radically new ways.

While Keller and Bordo envisage a subject who is continuous with objects, feminists influenced by post-structuralism see the subject as constituted by discourse (Hekman, 1990: 84). The subject is not a given which would be always the same independently of its cultural environment. Instead, to be a subject is to occupy a certain position in a culture. It is to be accredited with certain abilities, to elicit a certain range of responses. In this sense, who counts as a subject depends on the signifying practices of a society. Further, these practices also give rise to the distinctive character of subjectivity. We internalize the expectations that society puts upon us. Cultural norms thus become part of our own understanding of ourselves.

The reference to signifying practices introduces a third term in the relation between subject and object. Since these practices construct both subject and object, they mediate between the two. The subject is, thus, neither a Cartesian subject, nor the partially undifferentiated subject of object relations theory. However, this post-structuralist account of the subject is still predicated upon the view that differentiation is always a form of domination. Hekman (1990: 83), for example, endorses Irigaray's claim that:

> Being's domination requires that whatever has been defined – *within the domain of sameness* – as 'more' . . . should progressively win out over its 'other,' its 'different' . . . and when it comes right down to it, over its negative, its 'less.' (Irigaray, 1985: 275)

Hekman interprets this passage to entail that any dualism of subject and object leads to domination. In particular, she endorses the view, which she attributes to Irigaray, that we must 'attempt to see woman as neither subject nor object' (1990: 83). Any attempt to achieve the status of the subject, Hekman believes, involves objectification of the other.

As a consequence, even within this account differentiation and control involve violence. But, as Moi has remarked, 'just as the child's attempt to impose control and order on its world cannot be equated with exploitative domination, it is singularly unhelpful to see all forms of intellectual mastery simply as aggressive control and domination' (1989: 192–3).

Objectivity, Values, and Responsibility

Criticisms of traditional accounts of objectivity as value-neutral and aperspectival characterize contemporary feminist thought on this topic. Typically, there has been no wholesale rejection of objectivity. Instead, feminists such as Sandra Harding, Helen Longino, and Lorraine Code have proposed new formulations of this notion. They have attempted to avoid what Haraway calls the contemporary 'dichotomy on the question of objectivity' (1988: 576). On the one hand there is the traditional account of science as providing a view from nowhere of an objectively existing reality. On the other hand there is complete social constructionism which rejects any notion of independent reality and reduces knowledge to power. According to this view all talk of knowledge and objectivity is a mere ideological disguise for attempts to gain effective power (1988: 576–7).

Haraway tries to find a position which does not collapse into either of the two poles of the dichotomy. One that still allows us 'to talk about reality' (1988: 577) while acknowledging 'all the rich and always historically specific mediations through which we and everybody else must know the world' (1988: 577). This position is embodied in her claim that 'feminist objectivity means quite simply *situated knowledges*' (1988: 581).

When objectivity is conceived as the result of situated knowledge, ethical issues come to the foreground. Knowledge always involves responsibility for what we claim to know. The ethical dimension of knowledge is one that is easily forgotten by supporters of the view from nowhere. To paraphrase Haraway, unlocatable knowledge claims are irresponsible (1988: 583). These are claims which cannot be called into account because, allegedly, they are value-neutral, merely determined by the facts. But if value-neutrality is unattainable, this appeal to the facts is, as Irigaray points out, 'one more mask for the I' (Irigaray, 1993: 137).[8] It is a mask for a subject who is unwilling to take responsibility for the values embedded in his claims.

Appeals to the supposed value-neutrality of science serve to foster the values and interests of the dominant groups in society in two ways. Firstly, it permits those scientists who endorse the values of the dominant group to avoid reflecting on the role played by these values in obtaining scientific results. Secondly, it justifies discrediting results obtained by scientists who openly endorse a political agenda critical of dominant views. Arguably, it is exactly because it helps silencing criticisms of the values of dominant groups that the conception of objectivity as value-neutrality is preserved despite its inherent flaws (Harding, 1991: 147).

In this section I explore some of the connections between objectivity as situated knowledge, responsibility, and values. I argue that the dichotomy on the question of objectivity can be avoided only when we think about knowledge as a matter of practices rather than in terms of adequate representations which are interposed between subjects and objects.

In *Science as Social Knowledge* Longino claims that 'the objectivity of science is secured by the social character of inquiry' (1990: 62). She distinguishes between epistemic and ontological notions of objectivity, and characterizes the former as a willingness 'to let our beliefs be determined by "the facts" or by some impartial and non-arbitrary criteria' (1990: 62). Longino adopts the view that in ascribing objectivity to a method of inquiry we are concerned with 'the extent to which it provides means of assessing hypotheses and theories in an unbiased and unprejudiced manner' (1990: 63). The debate over objectivity in traditional philosophy of science is, for her, a debate about whether individual scientists can achieve this sort of objectivity. For Longino this debate is a consequence of the mistaken belief that the scientific method is something which can be practiced by an individual in isolation. But once it is recognized that scientific method is practiced by social groups it becomes possible to see how science is objective (1990: 67). For Longino what counts as evidence for a theory is always dependent on background assumptions which will include value judgments. Nevertheless, intersubjective criticism makes objectivity possible in science (1990: 71). In particular, criticism of the background assumptions provides 'a way to block the influence of subjective preference at the level of background beliefs' (1990: 73). In other words, the joint effort of different scientists makes it possible for each to criticize the background assumptions presupposed by others; assumptions that tend to be invisible to those who employ them. Hence, although no individual in isolation can be value-neutral, community effort can succeed in neutralizing values. This effort, since it involves more than an examination of empirical issues, shows that 'it would be a mistake to identify the objectivity of scientific methods with their empirical features alone' (1990: 75).

Longino adopts a fairly conventional notion of objectivity. She, nevertheless, succeeds in showing that, although values are inevitable, they do not prevent objective knowledge, and that a scientist can be objective and a feminist. The objectivity of science is preserved because the influence of values can be canceled out through intersubjective criticism. A scientist can be a feminist because this puts her in an ideal position to criticize the influence of sexist values on the hypotheses of her colleagues. The result is that objectivity pertains to what can, after rational discussion has taken place, be accepted by all. Objectivity does not secure truth; nevertheless, it is the best way we have to achieve it.

Although there is much to be admired in Longino's socialized solution to the problem of objectivity, there are also some serious problems with it. Firstly, it presupposes that unhindered rational discussion can take place in the scientific community. It is possible, however, that such an ideal is not realizable. In this case, objectivity is once again unachievable. Longino is aware of this problem and, therefore, argues that objectivity is a matter of degrees: the closer we are to the ideal, the more objectivity we obtain (1990: 76). Perhaps, but we are left with an account where power relations always prevent the achievement of objectivity. This does not seem to be correct. Scientists are not and could not just be in a community of equals. Rather, this community always involves power struggles. In some cases the exclusion of individuals from the community for political reasons may be for the best in science. Just think of how much good biology could be done if feminist scientists did not have to spend all their time exposing the flaws of sexists theories.

Secondly, political values are still seen as something that must in the end be screened out. Although Longino recognizes the positive influence some values may have in guiding criticisms of dominant assumptions, she still holds that an adequate scientific account must be unbiased. Objectivity cannot be, for her, a matter of being guided by the facts alone since the influence of background assumptions is inevitable. Nevertheless, she holds that ideally the community of researchers should strive to neutralize the influence of political values on the results of research: objectivity is a matter of 'maximal minimization of subjective (whether individual or collective) preference' (Longino, 1990a: 152).

Another feminist philosopher who has discussed extensively the notion of objectivity is Harding. She has argued powerfully in favor of a conception of strong objectivity which must replace the traditional model of value-free, aperspectival knowledge. Her account provides the best example of how feminist epistemology's concern with objectivity is the result of subscribing to a representational theory of knowledge. To see how this is so, one needs to read Harding against what Michel Foucault has said about the modern episteme. Although Harding does not see herself as a supporter of this form of epistemology, and would probably resist such an interpretation, when we look at her work from this perspective we can understand why she is so concerned with objectivity.

Harding believes that objectivity is an indispensable notion in epistemology since it accounts for the necessary gap between how we want the world to be and how it is (1993: 72). We need objectivity to talk about reality, to avoid reducing knowledge to power. Science, otherwise, would have to be conceived merely as the rhetorical disguise used by the powerful to hide their efforts to make the world become as they want it to be.

What is needed is a transformed notion of objectivity, one that does not require value-neutrality. A new notion is required because the traditional one is inherently flawed. For Harding, it simply is not objective enough. Her critical target is what she calls 'objectivism': the view that objectivity is a matter of impartial, value-free and dispassionate research (1991: 143). According to this traditional approach, we achieve objectivity when we expunge any subjective input from scientific research. That is, we must attend only to the facts, to what is outside ourselves, and ignore anything which has its origin in us: emotions and values. So understood, objectivity applies both to a method used while doing research, and to attitudes. A method is objective when it prescribes that we ignore subjective factors. We assume an attitude of objectivity when we examine things in a dispassionate manner without being influenced by our emotions and our values.

Harding criticizes this conception of objectivity on two counts: (i) she argues that it fails in its stated objective of screening out all the influences of values on the result of scientific research; and (ii) she claims that it fails to recognize that 'not all social values and interests have the same bad effects upon the results of research' (1991: 144).

The notion of objectivity which complements the view from nowhere is thus both too weak and too strong. It is too weak because values inevitably play a role in research. Its failure to recognize this phenomenon means that the values shared by all researchers go unchecked (1991: 143). It is too strong because some values have a positive effect on research. These are the values embedded in research that starts from the lives of a marginal people. Traditional objectivity is too strong because it fails to recognize that not all perspectives are on a par; it ignores the existence of epistemically privileged standpoints.[9]

What is needed instead is a new stronger notion of objectivity – one that takes into account all the evidence available for theories, and does not refuse to acknowledge the influence of background values on scientific inquiry (1991: 149). Since the social locations occupied by scientists are crucial to the values they may endorse, strong objectivity involves a 'call for scientifically examining the social location of scientific claims' (1991: 142). In other words, objectivity is maximized when we scrutinize those background values which influence the formulation of a given theory, rather than pretend that they play no role. This is the sensible option once the myth of the value-neutrality of science is exposed.

Strong objectivity, however, is not limited to this. If it were, it would not go beyond Longino's social empiricism. Instead, strong objectivity also involves a recognition that some values are conducive to good science, while others have a negative effect on it.[10] For example, democratic values generate less distorted beliefs than values that are anti-liberatory (1993: 71; 1991: 149). For Harding there are two ways in which some set of values can generate good research. Firstly, objectivity is increased if we take the locations of marginalized people as the starting point of scientific inquiry. A research conducted in this way is less likely to endorse without question the dominant values shared by scientists who tend to come from socially privileged backgrounds (1993: 56). The values held by marginal groups, insofar as they differ from dominant values, make it possible to see the latter as values, which can be questioned, rather than as givens. Secondly, values which encourage reflexivity are also conducive to good science, since they lead to examining critically our own attitudes and our own values (1991: 161).

Since strong objectivity requires self-critical evaluation of values and the adoption of a standpoint, it involves a recognition of the situatedness of every claim to knowledge. But, as Haraway points out, 'positioning implies responsibility for our enabling practices' (1988: 567). Hence, objectivity cannot be divorced from responsibility. More strongly, responsibility promotes objectivity.[11] It is only when we acknowledge the role of values in science, and we take responsibility for our value-involving claims, that we can hope to be objective.

Objective knowledge is, for Harding, situated knowledge. Nevertheless Harding's epistemology is quite different from Haraway's. Both agree that all knowledge is situated; that is, it is essentially tied to a perspective. Consequently, epistemology, which is knowledge about knowledge, must also be considered as an example of situated knowledge. It is at this point that Harding's position differs from Haraway's. For Harding, the epistemology of scientific knowledge is fundamentally a science of science; it is concerned with scientific accounts of scientific knowledge. Since science provides causal accounts of its objects of study, epistemology should give causal accounts of the production of scientific beliefs (1991: 93). In particular,

> standpoint epistemology sets the relationship between knowledge and politics at the center of its account in the sense that it tries to provide *causal accounts* – to explain – [*sic*] the effects that different kinds of politics have on the production of knowledge. (1993: 55–6) [my italics]

This is indicative of Harding's partial adherence to the strong program in the sociology of knowledge. She believes that the same kind of causal account provides an explanation of both knowledge and error. She also holds that this symmetry of causal explanation applies both to the subject who knows and to the object which is known. In other words, 'the same kinds of social forces that shape objects of knowledge also shape (but do not determine) knowers and their scientific projects' (1991: 64). Thus,

Harding tends to assimilate subjects to objects insofar as both can be explained in causal terms.

Instead, Haraway encourages us to talk about the objects of knowledge in terms usually reserved for the subject. She wants us to think of 'objects' in the world as actors or agents (1988: 593). And, she sees this claim as a corollary of her position on the relation between epistemology and ethics. For her, 'politics and ethics ground struggles for and contests over what may count as rational knowledge' (1988: 587). There is a sense in which Harding could, and does, subscribe to this claim. For her too, politics grounds knowledge; but it does so by being one of the causes of the production of knowledge. Haraway, instead, is not committed to a causal understanding of 'ground'; and, I believe, she is best interpreted as not doing so.

Harding's insistence on causal accounts of the production of knowledge is at the basis of her assimilation of the subject who knows to the object which is known. It leads her to say that 'strong objectivity requires that the subject of knowledge be placed on the same critical, causal plane as the objects of knowledge' (1993: 69). Hence, she adds, the 'subject of knowledge . . . must be considered as part of the object of knowledge from the perspective of scientific method' (1993: 69). Harding's approach fits perfectly Foucault's description of the modern episteme. The subject of knowledge she envisages is the 'man' who is studied by social science.

Harding rejects Keller's romantic view according to which knowledge involves a fusion of the subject with the object. Strong objectivity requires valuing others' perspectives, but there is no merging of the self with the other (1991: 151). Harding also objects to classical conceptions of the subject. She notices that it is this model according to which 'the ideal mind as a mirror . . . can reflect a world that is "out there," ready-made' (1991: 157) which gives rise to the view that scientific research must be value-free. In other words, Harding rejects what Foucault has called the 'classical episteme.'

Harding, however, still holds that knowledge is a matter of representation, of beliefs matching the world (1991: 83). Of course, since the representing mind is not a mirror of reality, we have no representations of things in themselves. Instead, 'nature as-the-object-of-human-knowledge never comes to us "naked"' (1991: 147). Rather, 'trees, rocks, planetary orbits, and electrons always appear to natural scientists only as they are already socially constituted' (1993: 64). For Harding, scientists 'are destined to study something different (but hopefully systematically related to what is "out there")' (1993: 64). The objects of scientific knowledge, which are socially constituted, are thus distinct from a mind-independent reality which exists 'out there.' We only have knowledge of representations, the way reality appears to us.

Harding's conclusion is unwarranted. It is possible to argue that both everyday objects, like trees, and theoretical entities, like electrons, are socially constituted, without concluding that they have the reality of representations in the mind. For example, a tennis ball is a socially constituted object. We define tennis balls with reference to their role in the sport of tennis, which is a social practice. Yet tennis balls are not representations in the mind. They exist out there in the world of human engagements.

Since Harding takes knowledge to be a matter of representation, she needs criteria to distinguish between more and less accurate representations. This is what objectivity is meant to provide. However, since representations do not mirror an independently existing reality, objectivity is not a matter of value-free inquiry. Rather, representations are our constructions. What does the constructing is the subject. A subject, however, who, unlike the Kantian subject, is socially situated; that is, shaped by the society she lives in. Consequently, the representations produced by the subject are also socially situated. They are shaped by social factors, for example, the political values and interests of their creators. Political power, therefore, is never external to knowledge.

What shapes representations is not itself necessarily a representation. For example, knowledge is grounded on and made possible by social factors. Harding's epistemology is an example of the modern episteme, because it starts with a study of the subject. It is concerned with the forces that shape the production of representations within the individual. In accordance with nineteenth century positivism, it also assumes that knowledge production must be understood causally.

If the grounds of representations do not have the character of representations, they cannot function as reasons for what they ground. Only what has meaning can function as a reason, and only representations have meaning. By exclusion, the relation between grounds and representations must be causal. This in turn leads Harding to interpret reasons as a kind of cause. More precisely, reasons are those causes which are themselves representations, and, therefore, something the subject may be conscious of. The other grounds of representations are outside the consciousness of the subject, they are those features of the subject shaped by external social forces. 'There are,' Harding claims, 'some *causes* of scientific beliefs and practices that are to be found outside the consciousness of individual scientists; that is, they are not *reasons* for the acceptance or rejection of these beliefs and practices' (1991: 78). These causes of belief 'shape the activities and consciousnesses of scientists as well as of the rest of us' (1991: 78). They are causes which are embodied in the institutional practices of science and constitute a form of rationality which permeates our society.

Harding claims that our representations are sometimes caused by external social forces. She also holds that we understand knowledge when we study the causal histories of belief. Hence, epistemology as a theory of representation must investigate what in the subject is outside the conscious sphere, and also the social causes of these features of the subject. Thus, epistemology takes the subject as its object of study. It puts it on the same causal plane as any other object. Hence the primacy of the social sciences. We can evaluate those representations which constitute the knowledge offered by natural sciences, such as physics, only if we first understand how representations in general are produced. We can do this only if we look at the subject as an object in the manner of social science. Thus, Harding asserts that 'it can be illuminating to think of natural sciences as inside, part of, social science' (1991: 96).

Harding holds that knowledge requires strong objectivity which involves considering everything, including social causes, which have an effect in producing and sustaining a given belief or theory. Code, instead, holds that all knowledge involves both subjectivity and objectivity. Like Keller, she believes that the traditional account of objectivity is the expression of a peculiar kind of subjectivity (1991: 48). Like Harding, she holds that this traditional account which relies on a sharp fact–value distinction allows scientists to absolve themselves from any moral and political responsibility for their claims (1991: 35).

The plausibility of mainstream views about objectivity is in great part due to the choice of examples of knowledge which are taken as paradigmatic. Traditional epistemologists choose simple observational claims such as: 'there is a black mug in front of me.' Code changes examples. She suggests we take knowledge of other people as paradigmatic. What is characteristic of this sort of knowledge is that it admits degrees; it also involves the subjectivity of the knower (1991: 38). She rightly points out that knowledge of this sort plays an important role in our everyday life. More importantly, much of the knowledge we acquire in many instances depends for its 'epistemic credibility and validity on implicit appeals to knowing people' (1991: 40). But knowing other people requires emotional involvement not detachment. Hence, subjective factors are always involved in the acquisition of knowledge of this sort.

Objectivity, however, must not be abandoned when one takes subjectivity into account. There are, that is, some objective constraints imposed on knowledge. When Code talks about the continuing importance of objectivity what she appears to have in mind is the traditional ontological version of this notion. She gives as an example of objective constraints the limits on the range of experience dictated by our biological sensory equipment (1991: 42). Thus, she continues, 'the minimal constraints that derive from the "reality" of the world and of cognitive agency constitute a residual set of objective limits on adequate, responsible inquiry' (1991: 43). There is a fact of the matter about how things are; there is an objective reality which poses constraints on our knowledge. Or, as Code herself puts it, although knowledge is not purely objective, it does not follow that reality is socially constructed. There is a point in trying to discover how things are (1991: 43).

Code's version of objectivity offers an alternative to the view that knowledge requires mediating representations. For Code, knowing somebody is not exclusively or, perhaps even primarily, a case of 'knowing that.' Knowing a person, in other words, is not just a matter of knowing all the facts about that person (1991: 40). These examples of knowledge suggest that knowledge is not simply a matter of having accurate representations of facts. Unfortunately, however, Code does not develop her account in this direction.

Donna Haraway's work, instead, constitutes a real break with the dominant account of knowledge in terms of representations. Her writings belong to a new and heterogeneous field: the cultural study of science. For Haraway, 'science is culture' (1992: 296). In a sense this is obvious. What is not so obvious is the epistemological relevance of discussing science as a cultural activity.

It would be easy to assimilate Haraway's insistence on studying science as culture to easy postmodernist claims that there is nothing beyond representations or texts of our own making. Haraway's claim that 'scientific practice is above all a story-telling practice' (1989: 4) may even reinforce this interpretation. This reading, however, is mistaken in view of her 'nononsense commitment to faithful accounts of a "real" world' (1988: 579). Admittedly, talk of 'faithful accounts' suggests a conception of knowledge as representation. 'Situated Knowledges' (1988), I believe, is a transitional paper where Haraway has not completely freed herself from the representational model. But she preserves her commitment to the world even in a later paper where she has moved outside the traditional framework (1992: 313).

The motivation for seeing science as a story-telling practice is different. The conception of knowledge as representation gives unity to science. It sees science as a body of representations of a specific kind (Rouse, 1996: 207). An anti-representationalist view of science needs an alternative account of what gives it coherence and unity. Story-telling practices provide this alternative. Joseph Rouse makes this explicit when he claims that the significance of scientific work is established in relation to an always changing narrative about the history and development of a scientific area of research. An important part of proving the significance of one's work is to refashion the history of the field, so that one's results come to be seen as central to it (1996: 169–71). Similarly, for Haraway story-telling is what gives coherence to science as a practice.

Something must now be said about how to understand science as a practice. For Haraway, 'scientific practice may be considered . . . a rule-governed, constrained, historically changing craft of narrating the history of nature' (1989: 4). In previous chapters I have characterized practices as ways of doing things, as patterns of action. So understood, practice is not opposed to theory. Rather, theorizing is just one kind of practice. Haraway shares this broad understanding of the notion when she compares scientific practice to a craft.

A craft, such as carpentry, requires skill. It is a way of doing things which admits of a right and wrong. One acquires mastery of the craft by learning to respond in the appropriate way to the raw materials, and to use tools correctly. Crafts, then, are bundles of practices that embed implicit standards of appropriateness. It might, however, be a mistake to think of these standards in terms of rules, since practices are subject to change. It would seem that we cannot explain these changes in terms of rules about how to change underlying rules, because this explanation unwarrantedly limits the possibility of change.

For Haraway scientific activity is a craft also in a literal sense, since it generates artefacts. Facts about the world are among these artefacts. The etymology of 'fact,' Haraway points out, is the past participle of the Latin verb to make or to do (*facere*): a fact is what has been made or done (1989: 3). There is always the danger of interpreting claims of this sort in a social constructionist fashion. Haraway's willingness to undermine the dichotomy between fact and fiction unfortunately encourages this interpretation.

I suggest a different interpretation of her claim that scientific practice deals in artefacts. An artefact is something which is literally made by creatures that use tools. Further, artefacts are socially constituted. Its social significance for us is what makes an artefact what it is. Road signs provide a good example of the socially constituted nature of artefacts. Think of a double yellow line by the side of a road, which in Britain means that one should not park a car there. We can think of a culture where a double yellow line means nothing in the road traffic code. Nevertheless, there could be people painting double yellow lines to make roads more aesthetically pleasing. In this case double yellow lines would not be road signs. It makes no sense to say that double yellow lines are constructed out of representations or language, they are made with yellow paint. What it makes sense to say is that these yellow lines would not have the same significance outside the context of our driving practices. They would not be road signs. Artefacts, like road signs, exist only in the context of human practices.

Haraway's claim that science deals exclusively with artefacts, however, seems unwarranted. The equipment, which is used by scientists to conduct experiments, has without doubt the character of an artefact. It is also true that some of the phenomena which take place in laboratory conditions would not otherwise occur. It does not follow that these phenomena are, like artefacts, literally made by scientists. It might, instead, be true that these phenomena are socially constituted. That is, we might have to make essential reference to human practices and abilities to individuate them for what they are. For example, consider a ray of visible light. It can be something that human beings have not made. Yet, to say that it is a ray of visible light is to make a reference to what humans can see. In a world of blind creatures, there would not be rays of visible light.[12]

Social constructionism is a different matter, since it takes socially constituted objects to have the reality of representations. For example, Steve Woolgar, a leading exponent of this approach, claims that 'rather than pre-existing our efforts to "discover" them, the objects of the natural world are constituted in virtue of representation' (1988: 83). Claims like this one raise issues about the reality of the objects being talked about, since they take these objects to exist only in our representations. Woolgar is saying that our representations produce reality. Representations, however, cannot literally produce anything in the world out there. Thus, we either think that there is nothing outside representations and language, or we believe that there is something out there which constraints our representations but cannot itself be known. In either case, what is left out by these accounts is, as Haraway remarks, the world (1992: 313).

To think about knowledge as representation is to remain trapped within a world of representations. If one believes with Woolgar that we cannot escape representation, then there is no alternative but to follow him and attempt to 'provide new ways of *interrogating* representation' (1988: 94). But we do not have to think in this way. Instead, we can claim with Rouse that:

> Nothing mediates our interaction with the world, not experience, thought, language, meaning, or representation. Talk and perception are just further interaction, not a medium through which interaction is filtered. (1996: 209)

Knowledge as a practice emerges out of all these interactions in which, according to Haraway, the 'natural' world has an active role. For example, she claims that organisms, as natural objects, are not born, 'they are made in world-changing technoscientific practices by particular collective actors in particular times and places' (1992: 297). The actors in question do not include only human beings. A pebble is made to have its shape by the action of other pebbles, of water, of wind, of animals. Nature is , thus, made as a 'co-construction among humans and non-humans' (1992: 297).

Scientific knowledge, so understood, does not entail objectification. When Haraway talks about 'nature' as an artefact she envisages a process which is not necessarily one of commodification. She therefore rejects 'the postmodernist observation that all the world is denatured and reproduced in images or replicated in copies' (1992: 297).

In 'Situated Knowledges' Haraway holds that objectification is the main problem with the traditional conception of objectivity. This is a conception that finds its source in the metaphor of passive vision. I have claimed in the first section of this chapter that this metaphor entails a splitting of subject and object where the object is conceived as inert. The vision of 'the "eyes" made available in modern technological sciences shatters any idea of passive vision' (1988: 583). These prosthetic devices show that all vision builds 'on specific *ways* of seeing' (1988: 583). There is, therefore, no view from nowhere, all seeing is situated.

Haraway wants to resist viewing the world as passive; she holds that 'the world encountered in knowledge projects is an active entity' (1988: 593). But, as I have mentioned previously, in this article Haraway has still not shaken off the trappings of the representational theory of knowledge which introduces some social constructivist elements in her approach. She still distinguishes between the 'concrete, "real" aspect and the aspect of semiosis and production in what we call scientific knowledge' (1988: 589). Thus, we still have the real world on one side and human representations of it on the other. In her more recent work, however, Haraway abandons altogether the representational model. She says:

> Artifactualism is askew of productionism; the rays from my optical device diffract rather than reflect. These diffracting rays compose *interference* patterns, not reflecting images. (1992: 299)

Vision is not understood simply as a matter of prosthetic devices; what she focuses on is diffraction, the mapping of interference. She is not interested in replication and representation. What is of crucial importance about diffraction is that it does not objectify. It achieves this by not trying to represent what is other than oneself. Instead, it takes into account the effects, the interferences generated by the other (1992: 300).

Haraway shifts the subject in the discourse about knowledge; she moves from thinking about it in terms of vision, which encourages a conception of knowledge as production of images, to conceiving of it in terms of interactions which need no mediating screens. Knowing becomes a way of engaging with the world, and to understand it we must study the patterns created by interactions. It is a mistake to think that knowledge exclusively involves representations produced literally or metaphorically by rays of light reflected by the surfaces of objects.

Viewing knowledge as a way of interacting avoids the problem of objectification inherent in representations. For Haraway, representation 'depends on possession of a passive resource, namely, the silent object' (1992: 313). Interaction, on the other hand, makes it possible to see non-human entities as active. The main lesson taught by this new epistemic framework is, as Haraway claims, that 'the world is precisely what gets lost in doctrines of representation and scientific objectivity' (1992: 313). Since there is no gulf between us and the world, there is no need for the traditional conception of objectivity that attempted to bridge it.

Further Reading

Evelyn Fox Keller's *Reflections on Gender and Science* (1985) provides a good account of the connection which psychoanalytic theory claims to find between objectivity and objectification. Sandra Harding discusses her notion of strong objectivity in chapter 6 of *Whose Science? Whose Knowledge?* (1991) and in

'Rethinking Standpoint Epistemology: What Is "Strong Objectivity"?' (1993). Donna Haraway's views are presented in 'Situated Knowledges: The Science Question in Feminism and the Privilege of Partial Perspective' (1988) and in 'The Promises of Monsters: A Regenerative Politics for Inappropriate/d Others' (1992).

Notes

1 I came to see the importance of the notion of indirect realism about perception in this context by reading Putnam (1994).

2 There are at least two ways of understanding how representations must be independent of the peculiarities of the perceiver. First, one may require that representations be available from any perspective. These will be representations of objective reality. Second, one may require only that the representations be available to all those who share the same perspective. The first, stronger, reading of independence generates a notion of absolute objectivity; the second gives rise to a notion of positional objectivity. On the latter notion of objectivity, see Sen (1993).

3 With the obvious exception of objective judgments about one's own internal and peculiar states.

4 I owe this account of Heidegger's position to Robert Brandom (1983).

5 See chapter 1 of Allison Weir (1996) for a discussion of the influence on de Beauvoir of this reading of Hegel, and for an argument that it amounts to a misreading.

6 For what may seem a different interpretation of de Beauvoir, see Moi (1994: 184). I owe this point to Ruth Evans. I believe that Moi's interpretation ultimately collapses onto the one I have provided.

7 I discuss Lloyd's views about philosophical theories of reason in the first section of chapter 9.

8 See the second section of chapter 2 for a discussion of this point.

9 For Harding's formulation of standpoint epistemology see the second section of chapter 6.

10 I have presented Harding's arguments for this claim in the second section of chapter 3 and the second section of chapter 6.

11 For an extended discussion of the centrality of responsibility for objectivity, see Lisa Heldke and Stephen Kellert (1995).

12 I owe this example to Mark Lance.

8

Knowledge and Power

Knowledge is not politically innocent. If there is any claim that would find all feminists in agreement, this is probably it. Feminist critiques of traditional epistemology and philosophy of science, which I discussed in chapters 2 and 3, aimed to show that knowledge cannot be understood in isolation from the social contexts in which it emerges. Politics is, of course, part of that context. Philosophical accounts of knowledge must, therefore, analyze its connections with power, especially political power.

The view that there are connections between power and knowledge is not new. One of the ideals which we have inherited from the Enlightenment tradition is the optimistic belief in the empowering function of knowledge. It was thought that the truth will always liberate us. This is an ideal that played an important role in the second wave of the feminist movement: for example, consciousness-raising was an activity which aimed at a better understanding of oneself and of one's circumstances. It was believed that acquiring this sort of knowledge would be instrumental to liberation. The aim of these activities was to enhance an individual's chances to get to understand her true needs and desires, and to make her more effective in achieving their fulfillment. The working assumption underlying these practices was that knowledge makes life better.

Although it has become rather difficult to subscribe wholeheartedly to the belief that knowledge always improves human life, no one would deny that knowledge is a source of power in this manner. There is no doubt that knowledge, through its technological applications, makes us for better or worse more effective in transforming our environment. Electricity, telephones, cars all have increased the power of human beings. Governments and other institutions employ knowledge for several political uses.

One can mention the employment of advanced science in the construction of weapons by the military, in the surveillance mechanisms used by the police, in the so-called 'rationalization' of medical resources. Knowledge, therefore, is instrumental to power.

Conversely, it is also obvious that power is instrumental to knowledge. Scientific research requires massive financial backups. Without a certain amount of power, research institutions could not secure the funding necessary for the production of scientific knowledge. There are numerous interactions between the world of science and the world of politics. Without any doubt decisions about the directions of new research are always influenced by political considerations about state and private support, about finance, and so forth. Struggles for power also figure prominently in relations among research groups and individual scientists within a team. Securing funding requires a certain amount of leverage; what sort of research one can pursue will depend on the amount of power one has acquired.

These relations between knowledge and power are pervasive.[1] Nevertheless, they have been interpreted as merely external and contingent. This interpretation requires a sharp distinction between pure science and its technological applications. Thus, one could argue that, although once knowledge has been acquired it can be applied in ways which increase power over nature and other people, it need not be used in this manner, or, more strongly, it need not be used at all. This latter claim illustrates what it means to say that it is only contingently that knowledge produces power. Pure knowledge, according to this view, does not necessarily have power effects. Conversely, one might acknowledge that, as things stands, some exercise of political power is needed to produce knowledge. But, one can also argue that were society different, this would not have to be the case.

The view that scientific knowledge in its pure form is independent of power and human interests is popular among philosophers working in the Anglo-American context. It is, however, relatively rare among those belonging to either the French or the German philosophical traditions. Continental philosophers have, in general, recognized the existence of very tight connections between knowledge and power, or human interest. Their diagnoses of the failure of the Enlightenment to fully deliver its promises are centered on its theory of knowledge. That is, while analytic philosophers might see no connection between some of the horrors perpetrated in the twentieth century and the notions of reason and knowledge endorsed by the movement of the Enlightenment, continental thinkers adopt a different approach. For philosophers such as Michel Foucault and Jürgen Habermas these epistemic notions have direct political consequences, some of which have been completely negative.

Generally speaking, while analytic philosophers have kept epistemology and political theory separate, continental thinkers have seen this separation itself as a political act. This opinion has also been voiced by feminists, like Sandra Harding, when they notice that endorsing the alleged value-neutrality of scientific research amounts to quietism about current political relations. These thinkers hold that there are deep conceptual connections between knowledge and power.

The view that knowledge may be a form of power makes sense only if we think of it primarily in terms of practices. Unless we take knowing to be a way of intervening on, and interacting with, our environment there is no plausibility to the claim that power is intrinsic to knowledge. Traditional epistemology, however, has been concerned with the problem of the justification of representations. This view of knowledge as a matter of adequate representations forces one to think of power as external to it. Power may have something to do with the conditions under which we come to form representations; it may also be the case that possessing some representations is a condition for exercising specific forms of power. However, the representations themselves cannot be a kind of power. Instead, if one thinks of knowing as a practice, as a way of doing things, it becomes almost trivial to say that it is a form of power. Of course, much more must be added to make it even plausible that the sort of power involved in the practices of knowing has anything to do with political power.

But if knowledge can be innocent of power, in the way many analytic philosophers presuppose, there is no specifically epistemological problem in the relations between knowledge and power. It will be up to sociologists and social theorists to investigate the power effects of technology, and the effects of social relations on the production of knowledge. Of course much can be learned from these studies. However, they would not force drastic modification of the theory of knowledge.

In this chapter I want, instead, to explore the positions held by those philosophers who urge us to reject the view that knowledge can be pure of power and interests. In particular, I discuss Foucault's claim that power is constitutive of knowledge. I describe Foucault's accounts of disciplinary and bio-power, and show how they can be usefully employed to under-stand the tight connections between politics and scientific knowledge. My discussion mostly concerns 'laboratory science.' High particle physics, genetics, and molecular biology are all examples of this kind of science, since they are practiced in laboratories. They 'use apparatus in isolation to interfere with the course of that aspect of nature that is under study' (Hacking, 1992: 33). In other words, these sciences involve experiments conducted by means of equipment in artificial settings. They study phenomena that often occur for the first time under experimental circumstances.

I argue that laboratory science yields knowledge which is constituted by power relations. More specifically, I claim that the results obtained in the laboratory can count as knowledge outside of it, only when the external environment has been transformed so as to resemble laboratory conditions. In other words, laboratory knowledge cannot be exported without instituting new power relations in the world at large. It is only in this case that the phenomena these sciences claim to know can be made to occur outside the laboratory. My argument builds on Foucault's views about disciplinary power, and on the account of knowledge as practice that I have developed in this book. I present some examples that illustrate the multiple relations between science and political power. I focus my discussion on the biological sciences, since their impact on our lives is quickly expanding.

Some thinkers, for example Nancy Fraser, have argued that Foucault's account of power lacks normative force. Thus the account would not provide any reasons why oppressive practices should be resisted. Others, for instance Habermas, have claimed that Foucault's position leads to irrationalism. Knowledge disappears in favor of power. In other words, Foucault would be committed to saying that claims to knowledge are always imposed by force. There would only be a pretense of legitimation or justification. In reality, there would simply be power in disguise.

In the first section of this chapter I compare some features of Foucault's position with the view endorsed by Habermas. I argue that one can hold that power constitutes knowledge, and preserve genuine justification. This comparative discussion also serves as an introduction to the debate about reason within feminist epistemology which I shall explore in the next chapter. Moreover, it functions as a background to an analysis of the difficult relations between postmodernism and epistemology which constitute the topic of chapter 10. At the same time, this discussion furthers the arguments I have provided so far on why feminist epistemology must distance itself from representational accounts of knowledge. I hope that it also highlights some of the dangers inherent in causal accounts of knowledge, along the lines of naturalized epistemology. Finally, it provides another occasion to thematize the issues surrounding different conceptions

of the subject who has knowledge. In the second section, I explain
Foucault's accounts of disciplinary and bio-power, and provide examples
of socially constituted knowledge.

constructed?

Power, Knowledge, and Human Interests

It has become commonplace to contrast Foucault and Habermas. They are
often seen as occupying diametrically opposed positions. This simplistic
reading would lead us to interpret Foucault as a supporter of an irrationalist
postmodernism, and to understand Habermas as a defender of good
humanist values. Undeniably there are many differences between these two
thinkers. However, we must consider the similarities in their views to
understand the philosophical context within which they raise questions
about the relations between reason or knowledge and power.

Their starting point is the disappointment with the failure of the
Enlightenment project to deliver what it promised. Both Foucault and
Habermas see this failure as a consequence of the theory of knowledge
developed by Enlightenment thinkers, and of the notion of reason they
endorsed. Habermas and Foucault, however, disagree about the extent of
this failure, and about whether any part of the Enlightenment project can
be saved. Thus, they hold different views on whether there is some form
of rationality which is totally free from power relations.

In the preceding chapter on objectivity I have shown that Harding's
conception of knowledge exemplifies a sort of Kantianism in epistemology.
She abandons the view, which she characterizes as 'objectivism,' that the
knowing mind is a mere mirror of external reality. Instead, she holds that
the subject actively constructs her representations. Nevertheless, I have
argued, knowledge is for her a matter of representations. Harding's account
of knowledge is thus an example of what Foucault has called the 'modern
episteme.' Since she holds that knowledge consists of representations
produced by an active subject, she must find in that subject the grounds
for the validity of the representations. More precisely, she must hold that a
theory of the subject is a precondition for the study of knowledge. One
must investigate the processes employed by subjects to form representations
in order to identify those representations that count as knowledge. This
investigation might not be sufficient, but it would be an essential part of
the theory of knowledge.

Foucault points out that there are only two, equally unacceptable, ways to understand the subject who has representations. It can be seen as a transcendental subject sensitive to norms, or it can be understood as an empirical subject (1970: 319). The representations formed by a transcendental subject would be justified when that subject has followed transcendent rules to form her representations. An epistemology which relied on this conception of the subject would study these rules. Foucault rejects this first possibility because it presupposes a subject who is outside history and society. Harding also rejects this conception of the subject. She must, therefore, take representations to be the product of the activity of an empirical subject. It follows that, for Harding, the knower is an entity that can be studied scientifically like any other empirical object. Harding acknowledges this commitment when she claims that the subject must be thought of as on the same causal plane as the objects of her knowledge (1993: 69). It also follows that representations come to be seen as the causal result of processes occurring in the subject. Epistemology would study these processes as well as others that involve external social causes which have an influence on the psychology of the subject. Thus, Harding's position should be understood as a version of social naturalized epistemology. In chapter 5 I have already explained why this view is unsatisfactory, while in chapter 6 I have shown how it has influenced feminist standpoint epistemology. Now, I want to raise a different criticism which is voiced by Foucault. He holds that this approach involves an objectification of the subject of knowledge. In other words, it requires that we treat the subject as an object. The objectification of the subject of knowledge is a consequence of the view that it should be studied scientifically. For this reason, Foucault believes that the theory of knowledge implicit in the project of the Enlightenment has oppressive political consequences. He thinks that it leads to treating people as objects.

In *Knowledge and Human Interests* (1971) Habermas attempts to solve this problem without resorting to a notion of ahistorical subjectivity. He posits the existence of two modes of action which embody different human interests. These modes of action are the basis of human knowledge. The first mode, which is employed in the natural sciences, embodies technical interests, and is concerned with the manipulation of the non-human environment. The second, which is employed in social theory, embodies our communicative interests, and is concerned with understanding fellow human beings. The mode of action on which knowledge of the natural world is based, requires only the use of means–end reasoning. Instrumental reason is the only form of reason needed in science. But knowledge of the social world requires a different kind of reason which is not instrumental. It would be a mistake to identify knowledge of objects with knowledge as such.

This distinction between two kinds of knowledge offers a solution to the problem outlined by Foucault. We can find in the subject an answer to the question about the validity of knowledge, but the focus on the subject does not involve objectification. The study of the subject must be conducted using communicative rather than instrumental reason. This is an ingenious solution because it legitimizes science's use of instrumental reason without treating the subject as an object. In other words, Habermas grants that we must study the subject in order to assess the validity of her claims to knowledge. Yet he also holds that this study does not involve objectification. Habermas thinks that an investigation concerning the legitimacy of human knowledge should explain the nature of the subject because he adopts a representational model.[2] For him, there is a gap between the subject and reality. Representations are intended to bridge this gulf. They do not, however, mirror external reality. Rather, they function as a sort of tool for the effective manipulation of the environment. Knowledge of the empirical world embodies human interests.

Nevertheless, Habermas's approach is not entirely satisfactory. Firstly, it embodies a rather crude understanding of natural science. It is far too reductivist to assume that science is merely a tool for manipulation and prediction. Secondly, it might still involve treating the subject as an object. For these reasons, in his later writings Habermas has modified his position. In particular, like Foucault, he now believes that any attempt to find in the subject the grounds that legitimate knowledge is doomed to failure.

Habermas claims that a philosophy of the subject or of consciousness, which is essentially dependent on positing a gulf between subject and object, can only conceive reason as subject-centered. This is a 'rationality assessed by how the isolated subject orients himself to representational and propositional contents' alone (1987: 314). Rationality so conceived can only be judged in terms of its efficiency; it becomes instrumental reason. But efficiency is, for critical theorists like Habermas, a matter of control over nature. Hence, if this form of rationality is employed in our cognitive relations to other human beings, rationality becomes a tool of domination. Furthermore, when, as epistemology requires, we investigate the limits of reason, the employment of subject-centered reason for this purpose involves an objectification of the subject of knowledge. This use of subject-centered reason also seems to undermine reason itself. When the subject is treated as an object, it is seen exclusively as a part of the empirical world of causal relations. If so, the subject cannot be a source of genuine normativity. The 'why' of reason must be repressed in favor of the 'how' of causes. Thus, when we try to locate reason in the subject, we only find complex causal interactions. Supporters of naturalized epistemology, of course, would beg to differ. They would hold that reasons are causes.

For Habermas the contradictions which emerge when we try to use reason to draw the limits of its legitimate employment should not lead us to despair. We need not abandon reason altogether, and embrace its other: unreason. Rather, 'the paradigm of the knowledge of objects has to be replaced by the paradigm of mutual understanding between subjects capable of speech and action' (1987: 295–6). We must, that is, abandon a subject-centered conception of reason in favor of what Habermas calls 'communicative reason.' This is the sort of reason required by intersubjective understanding (1987: 311), one that does not privilege the objectifying attitude of the knowing subject (1987: 296). Habermas takes himself to be providing, like Foucault, a way out of the philosophy of the subject (1987: 301). But Habermas believes that he, unlike Foucault, avoids the problems inherent in a radical critique of reason because he holds steadfast to the attempt to secure the validity of at least some knowledge claims. Legitimation, ideally, is achieved when there is a mutual agreement among all concerned, which is reached by means of discussions which are free from any form of coercion.

Simply put, Habermas argues that Foucault's position cannot avoid debilitating contradictions because it tries to provide a non-irrational critique whose aim is to establish that reason, whatever form it may take, is merely grounded in power. Foucault would thus be trying to deny any validity, beyond the force to persuade, to knowledge claims while presupposing some legitimacy for his own claims. A similar criticism has been voiced by Fraser in her insightful work on the politics implicit in Foucault's writings. She claims that: 'it is essential to Foucault's own project that he be able to distinguish better from worse sets of practices and forms of constraint. But this requires greater normative resources than he possesses' (1989: 32). For Fraser, it is impossible, within a Foucauldian framework, to offer a justification for resisting oppressive practices. Resistance is, of course, something which Foucault himself valued. But, Fraser argues, he has no way of explaining why, in some cases, resistance is better than acquiescence. After all, Foucault avoids questions concerning the legitimacy of any form of political power.

This criticism should not be taken lightly. In particular, it cannot be dismissed simply by accusing the critic of nostalgia for foundationalism.

Those who remark that Foucault needs a conceptual apparatus to sustain normative distinctions, are not asking for infallible foundations; rather, they point to the need for revisable and contested ways of making judgments about what is acceptable and what should be opposed. I think that these criticisms are probably correct. Nevertheless, I believe Foucault's view that power constitutes knowledge can be preserved. The account of knowledge in terms of practices, which I have presented, can be used to respond to these critics, since it acknowledges that our practices are sometimes mistaken. This account, therefore, does not prevent us from making normative judgments for which one must gain entitlement. Foucault's analyses of power-knowledge can be used to complement this account, even if one grants that Foucault himself did not provide a sufficiently robust notion of justification or evaluation.

Foucault rejects a philosophy of the subject for reasons that are similar to those presented by Habermas. Thus, he holds that it is a mistake to take the subject as a starting point of epistemology or any other philosophical inquiry. 'What I refused,' he claims, 'was precisely that you first of all set up a theory of the subject . . . and that, beginning from the theory of the subject, you come to pose the question of knowing, for example, how such and such a form of knowledge was possible' (1988: 10).

Turning away from the search for the grounds of knowledge in the structure of consciousness, both Foucault and Habermas turn to social practices as the object of study for a theory of knowledge. Knowing is conceived by them primarily as an activity rather than as a state of mind. Because they see knowledge as a kind of intervention, they at least in part abandon the traditional framework according to which knowledge is a special kind of representation that has a privileged status. In other words, they move away from a representational account of knowledge. Their accounts take practices, including representational practices, rather than privileged states of mind, as their starting point.

Foucault's interest in the practices of knowledge is centered on the study of 'power-knowledge relations.' These are intrinsic connections between political power and knowledge; such connections are always present because 'power and knowledge directly imply one another; . . . there is no power relation without the correlative constitution of a field of knowledge, nor any knowledge that does not presuppose and constitute at the same time power relations' (1979: 27).

What Foucault claims is that knowledge is made possible by some relations of power. Conversely, knowledge contributes to the creation of other power relations. In the second section of this chapter I shall give some examples that help to make these claims plausible. Foucault himself gives the example of the hospitalization of the mad which was a precondition for the rapid development of clinical psychiatry. It became possible to monitor constantly the insane and thus develop a whole body of knowledge about them. The conditions which made such continuous observations possible had effects on the behavior of the observed. Thus, some of the 'facts' observed by the psychiatrists were themselves effects of the new situation and did not exist before.

Foucault is at pains to make clear that, although knowledge and power are always mutually implicated, neither is reducible to the other. He wants to resist being interpreted as saying that, since power is everywhere, claims to knowledge are merely devices for the concealment of power relations. Foucault has often been accused of doing away with truth and validity in favor of mere relations of power, but this is an interpretation he rejects. He claims:

> We can show, for example, that the medicalization of madness, i.e., the organization of medical knowledge around individuals labeled as 'mad,' has been linked, at some time or other, to a whole series of social or economic processes, but also to institutions and practices of power. This fact in no way impairs the scientific validity of the therapeutic efficacy of psychiatry. It does not guarantee it but it does not cancel it out either. (1988: 16)

For him there is an issue about the validity of claims to knowledge which has some independence from consideration of power relations. Thus, he would agree with Fraser that his work requires a normative dimension. It is fair to say that this dimension is underdeveloped in his work, and it might be true that, despite his intentions, Foucault has failed to provide an account of genuine evaluation. Nevertheless some of the things he says about power/knowledge can be incorporated into a normative account.

For Foucault justification cannot be reduced to power. At the same time the subject is not, according to him, the source of this normativity. Norms emerge out of practices which involve power relations. These practices also shape the subjects who engage in them. Modern power, according to Foucault, suppresses heterogeneity. It is a form of normalizing power. Foucault portrays a picture of the modern Western world as a place where instrumental reason runs riot. It is a world dominated by concerns with efficiency, utility, and quantification. In my account I shall try to temper the dystopianism which seems implicit in Foucault's work.

I have argued in this section that Habermas and Foucault share a rejection of the philosophy of the subject in their epistemological investigations. This turning away from the subject is open to misinterpretation. I argue in chapter 10 that many Anglo–American postmodern thinkers make this mistake. What Habermas and Foucault share is not a belief in the irrelevance of the subject – quite the contrary. Rather they claim that any thinker who is a naturalist, who opposes any appeal to Platonic transcendent entities, must acknowledge that the basis of the normativity of epistemology cannot be found within the subject. Any other approach will, eventually, lead to the objectification of human beings.

Disciplinary Power, Bio-Power, and Science

Foucault's account of the forms that modern power has taken in Western society has been discussed widely among feminist thinkers. Despite the problems inherent in some of its parts, there is much in this account which can be employed fruitfully to develop a political theory of knowledge and science. Showing how it can be done is the primary aim of this section.

I can only provide a brief sketch of Foucault's account of power; hence, my presentation won't do justice to the details of his position. Nevertheless, I hope that my outline will suffice to show how Foucault's thought on these issues supports the view that politics contributes to the constitution of scientific knowledge. Following Joseph Rouse, I argue that there are extensive parallels between the worlds of scientific laboratories and those created by disciplinary institutions, such as prisons, schools, and convents (1987: 212). Rouse is aware that Foucault's analyses of power-knowledge relations are devoted specifically to forms of power deployed over people rather than over things. Even if there are similarities between these two cases, it is possible to argue that only power that coerces people can properly be understood as political power. However, as Rouse shows, the techniques of power, first employed in the laboratory world, are subsequently exported to the world outside. This process of exportation can succeed only at the cost of implementing major changes in our lives. Hence, 'scientific practices and the knowledge they embody can act as forms of domination and constraint, helping *produce* us as the kinds of persons we are' (1987: 212). Scientific practices involve forms of power

which are deployed over human beings. Rouse provides low-level technological examples, like agriculture, of this phenomenon. Nevertheless, I
argue, these examples can be used to show that scientific knowledge in
itself has political consequences.

In *Discipline and Punish* (1979), in his interviews and lectures on power-
knowledge (1980), and in the first volume of *The History of Sexuality* (1978)
Foucault develops an extensive account of the innovations introduced by
modern forms of political power.[3] In light of these novelties, analyses based
on the notions of sovereignty and repression are outmoded.

Pre-modern power can be thought of as something exercised by the
sovereign, the king. It is repressive, and aims to force people inhabiting the
kingdom to submit. In this context establishing the limits of sovereign
power constitutes the fundamental political problem. The theory of rights
is designed precisely to delineate the boundaries of the legitimate exercise
of royal power (1980: 94). According to Foucault, we need a different
model to understand the forms taken by power in modern societies, 'we
need to cut off the King's head: in political theory that has still to be done'
(1980: 121). The question concerning the legitimacy of power should not
be the crucial issue for modern political theory. This claim is at the root of
Fraser's criticism that Foucault undermines the intellectual resources for
any effective political critique. Since he does not try to distinguish
legitimate from illegitimate uses of power, Foucault seems unable to justify
his claim that some forms of power, but not others, are oppressive.

I turn now to those features of Foucault's account of power which have
been used by Rouse to demonstrate its applicability to the study of natural
sciences. Broadly speaking, for Foucault, modern power takes two forms.
Firstly, it consists of disciplinary techniques. This is what is known as
disciplinary power. Second, it involves regulative methods. This Foucault
calls 'bio-power.' These two forms of power intersect in the politics of
sexuality (1978: 146). Rouse discusses how the world of the laboratory
relies on the techniques of disciplinary power, but he does not investigate
how science is connected to bio-power. This second form of power,
however, is equally important for the study of science, especially with
regard to reproductive technologies. In what follows I first present Foucault's account of disciplinary power and Rouse's employment of it. I then
discuss bio-power, since it involves power relations in which gender and
sexuality play prominent roles.

Foucault, without any doubt, had a very keen eye for the striking
example which lodges itself in the mind. He used the 'panopticon' to
illustrate what he meant by disciplinary power.[4] The 'panopticon' was

Bentham's design for the ideal prison. It was constituted by a central tower surrounded by an anular building. The outer ring was partitioned into cells which extended the whole width of the building; each cell had two windows: one in the outer, and one in the inner wall. The latter corresponded to a window in the tower. In this way, one guard placed in the tower could see inside the cells, each of which hosted only one prisoner. The prisoners were thus isolated, prevented from having any contact with each other. Furthermore, since the cells were illuminated by the sunlight coming from the outer wall, prisoners could not see what was going on in the tower. But, the guard in the tower could see inside each cell.

The form of power literally embodied in the architecture of the panopticon is about discipline. The ideal jail is a complex institution designed for the continuous surveillance of the inmates. This is the crucial difference between modern power and its predecessor. The latter was exercised through punishment, the former is exercised through surveillance or discipline.

Other differences between these two forms of power flow from this core one. Power based on punishment is essentially repressive; it functions through prohibitions and their enforcement. It is, therefore, a form of power which is only intermittently exercised. Disciplinary power is, instead, productive since it aims to modify behavior, to produce changes of comportment. This sort of power requires that its effects be present all the time. But a continuous exercise of the power of repression to achieve this productive aim would be far too costly. Hence, disciplinary power works by rendering its actual exercise unnecessary (1979: 201). It achieves constant surveillance by transforming the subjects, over which power is exercised, into their own guardians. Individuals must be turned into 'docile bodies,' who willingly supervise their own disciplined behavior.

Three distinguishing features of contemporary power emerge from this short description: (a) it is productive rather than repressive; (b) it operates at all levels, it does not just reside in the king or the state; (c) it has effects directly on people's lives without requiring that they are indoctrinated into false or ideological beliefs (Fraser, 1989: 18).

Foucault finds disciplinary power, driven by efficiency, embodied in many modern institutions including the monastery, the school, and the factory. They are all 'machines' for the production of disciplined, self-monitoring individuals who accomplish their tasks in the most efficient way. Thus, disciplinary power is normalizing power; it breeds homogeneity and conformism (1979: 183).

There are several techniques for training and disciplining which are employed in modern institutions. These techniques use three very simple instruments: hierarchical observation, normalizing judgments, and their combination in the examination procedure (1979: 170). First, power is exercised through making visible those who are coerced by it. Thus, in the panopticon the prisoners are always visible but the guard cannot be seen. This phenomenon constitutes a reversal of positions with respect to pre-modern times when those who exercised power, the monarchs, were highly visible. Second, another instrument of power is normalization, by means of which conformism is enforced. This is a technique which aims to punish deviations from the norm. It treats any sort of anomaly as an abnormality in its impulse to classification. Finally, the procedure of examination brings together the previous two techniques. It makes individuals visible and subjects them to the normalizing gaze. For Foucault, the ritual of the medical or scientific examination combines power and experiment, the deployment of force and the establishment of truth.

The operations of laboratory science bear a noticeable resemblance to those of disciplinary power. The similarities emerge when we think of scientific knowledge as being concerned primarily with intervention in 'natural' phenomena, rather than mere description. 'Scientific research' thus conceived 'is a circumspective activity, taking place against a practical background of skills, practices, and equipment (including theoretical models)' (Rouse, 1987: 95). Instead of thinking about science as a collection of theories, we take it to involve many complex practices. This is implicit in the conception of knowledge as practice which I have been developing.

The experiment is the paradigmatic example of scientific research, and it often takes place in the laboratory. Theory-oriented accounts of science have emphasized observing and recording as the main events involved in experiments. But a closer look at laboratories shows that many procedures are employed to achieve scientific results. For Rouse the laboratory is a microworld where objects are forced to reveal themselves in new ways (1987: 219). The world of the laboratory is different from the world outside. For example, it is cleaner and contains no extraneous fields of force. In the laboratory, also, everything is measured. In a different, untidier, situation scientists would get messier, uninterpretable results.

In the laboratory objects behave in unusual ways. Scientists work in this environment, they engage in practices which involve equipment. The activities of scientists, the tools used, and the features of the laboratory constrain the behavior of the entities under study. That is, together they institute a field of power relations. The phenomena 'observed' in the laboratory often have never occurred before. They are not less real because of this. These events are not made up by scientists, they are not illusions. Similarly, it would be too hasty to conclude that these phenomena are socially constructed. The mere fact that these events show up for the first time under the constraints of the fields of power instituted in the laboratory does not prove that they are human artefacts. However, the knowledge thus gained will not immediately count as knowledge of what happens outside the laboratory. It is only knowledge of the phenomena that occur in contrived circumstances. Yet science is meant to provide universal, rather than local, knowledge. Often this problem is glossed over by claiming that science explains what would happen in 'ideal' circumstances. In other cases this gloss will not solve the problem. Sometimes the external environment is made to resemble a laboratory so that scientific knowledge applies to it. In these cases one must institutein the world power relations which are similar to those at work in the laboratory so as to constrain objects to behave in the desired ways.

Rouse shows how the power relations instituted in the laboratory share the features of disciplinary power. Knowledge is achieved because reality is constrained through the techniques of hierarchical observation and normalization. Hierarchical observation is practiced in the laboratory by means of spatial enclosure and partitioning. This spatial structure makes phenomena visible. They isolate the world of the laboratory from unwanted causal interferences. The laboratory itself is spatially partitioned to avoid contamination. These precautions are necessary to obtain scientific knowledge, otherwise experiments would not yield information. Furthermore, scientists need to track processes, they do not merely record final results. Thus, the 'architecture' of the laboratory is designed to make this surveillance possible (1987: 221–2).

Foucault's technique of normalizing judgment also has a counterpart within the laboratory. This is the process of standardization which requires homogeneity among scientists in their procedures. Such a process assures that scientific results are repeatable, and, therefore, scientifically legitimate. Standardization is a force toward the production of stable laboratory procedures which, because they are less sensitive to individual circumstances, are more easily repeatable. Standardization, that is, helps to homogenize phenomena in the interest of stability (Rouse, 1987: 223–4).

The combination of techniques of observation and standardization makes the emergence of laboratory phenomena possible. Often the occurrence of these events cannot be produced in non-laboratory conditions. Furthermore, they do not happen spontaneously. Things must be forced to behave in this way. Laboratory techniques institute the necessary field of power relations. Thus, the knowledge acquired in the enclosed laboratory space is not universally applicable, it is instead local knowledge – knowledge of how objects behave under very specific circumstances. The results of science become applicable to the world outside the walls of the laboratory only if our everyday world is suitably changed. This world needs to be turned into something like a laboratory. Since scientific knowledge is local knowledge under experimental circumstances, those circumstances need to be reproduced outside the laboratory to make this knowledge applicable. In other words, since science tells us how objects behave within a very specific field of power relations, unless those power relations are reproduced, science loses its predictive power. The social environment must be shaped so that it can enact those power relations which are necessary for science as we know it. This shaping process requires decisions and acts that have a political import. Thus, political power is not just a consequence of the technological applications of science, it is in some sense a consequence of science *itself*. Or, to make the same point in a different way, all science – even so-called pure science – is technological.

It might, nevertheless, be objected that my argument concerns only the application of science, rather than science itself. This is not so. I have argued that unless the environment is suitably modified, laboratory science does not even yield knowledge of the world. Its descriptions and predictions would simply be false. My claim goes beyond asserting that technological applications cause changes in the environment. This second, weaker point is of course also true. Technology is a means for the development of new power relations. More importantly, however, modern laboratory science can be a way of knowing the world, only if it has already become a reality shaped by a field of power relations resembling Foucault's disciplinary power. Thus, it is no surprise that big laboratory science thrives under capitalist modernity. Scientific development is not necessarily better financed today, scientists are not smarter than their predecessors. Rather, the world has now been transformed into the sort of reality which Western science is suited to know.

At this point a word of caution is required. Firstly, my claim concerns only laboratory science. It does not apply to other sciences such as botany or astronomy. Secondly, I have not questioned the validity of science.

Rather, I have asserted its <u>dependency on power relations</u>. This phenomenon, I shall argue, is particularly evident in the case of the biological sciences.

The transformation of the world into one big laboratory has many political implications. The reproduction of scientific phenomena requires very precise transformations of the environment. One must reproduce the environment of the laboratory with its partitions and enclosures. One must also enact the procedure of continuous surveillance of the phenomena. In general, scientific knowledge can be extended to the world only at the cost of introducing new artificial complexities and new social organizations that manage the appearance of the desired phenomena. Because scientific phenomena emerge only under very specific circumstances there are many points at which things can go wrong. Things cannot just be let to happen, instead these new complexities must be monitored and managed all the time. Scientific results are, as Rouse points out, 'tightly coupled' with the organizations that manage them (1987: 230). The world, shaped so as to make scientific results reproducible, requires continuous surveillance. Due to the introduction of new complexities, there is very little flexibility built into the system.

Complexity and tight coupling do not merely have consequences for the environment. They also have consequences for human beings. The acquisition of scientific knowledge puts constraints on things and on people. Some individuals must become engaged in the process of monitoring and control necessary to make science applicable to the world at large. But engaging in these processes requires that discipline is imposed on the lives of those who must manage these systems. They must, like scientists, adopt specific routines.

Rouse provides two examples of the way in which science requires suitable social environments: agriculture, and obstetrical practice. Agriculture has recently seen many changes due to the introduction of hybrid varieties, first developed in laboratory, which are meant to be high-yield. But hybrid plants are high-response varieties, their yield is very sensitive to their environment. A small change in their circumstances can have a disastrous effect on their levels of production. Their use in agriculture has introduced a new artificial complexity. It has also introduced tight coupling: unless farmers manage their fields in a very precise predefined manner they will not obtain the desired results. Management of this sort is not possible in small farms. For example, it requires a lot of money to buy the necessary machinery. The machines themselves are better employed in large plots of land. Furthermore, high-yield varieties are riskier, since they are very sensitive to environmental changes. Only big farmers can remain in business after one bad year. For these reasons, the introduction of hybrid varieties has had major political consequences for agricultural communities (1987: 239). In general, it destroys subsistence agriculture, because it requires large farms to be implemented. The knowledge gained in the laboratory about high-yield varieties cannot be used to benefit small indigenous farmers. Either one takes it to be local knowledge which is of no use to agriculture, or one prepares the environment so that information obtained in laboratory becomes knowledge which is exportable. Bad technology cannot be separated from value-neutral pure science.

Similar considerations apply to the case of obstetric practice. The procedures that enable the medical profession to monitor and control birth introduce new risk factors and new complexities that make giving birth more dependent on the use of those very procedures (1987: 234). For example, fetal monitoring introduces a complexity which increases the possibility of fetal distress which in turn makes fetal monitoring more needed. It also increases the chances of a cesarean birth which in turn requires other highly scientific procedures such as anesthesia. These practices, of course, structure a field of power relations that affect the people involved in the process of birthing. It does not follow that all of these practices are necessarily bad for women. Nevertheless, one must be aware that they yield knowledge only in some social and cultural contexts. These contexts involve complex power relations.

This interpretation of scientific knowledge in terms of Foucault's account of disciplinary power casts new light on the relation between power and knowledge. It shows how the exercise of political power cannot be separated from pure science. Scientific knowledge as it developed in our societies is only one way of knowing among others. But it is a way of knowing that can be enacted only in a social environment with very specific characteristics. The drive toward scientific knowledge in our societies has had inevitable and very specific political consequences.

To summarize, I have argued that modern laboratory science requires configurations of power to yield knowledge. These configurations must be reproduced in the environment to export scientific knowledge. Specifically, the world must be shaped in accordance with the system of disciplinary power which is implemented in Western capitalist societies. Science and politics are, therefore, inextricably linked. This argument, however, has a limited application. It is relevant only to laboratory science which is intended to be exportable. Hence, it applies primarily to some biological sciences such as, for instance, genetics. The account of knowledge as practice which I have developed so far, however, supports a stronger claim. I have explained in chapter 3 that, according to this view, all knowledge is socially constituted. Therefore, politics is relevant to it. What is peculiar to exported laboratory science is the sort of politics it requires.

Since Rouse's account of the politics of laboratory science applies primarily to the biological sciences, it must be supplemented by taking into account what Foucault says about the other dimension of modern power, namely bio-power. It is a technology for the control and regulation of the human species based on the biological sciences. For example, in modern times there has been a flurry of state regulations and propaganda about levels of population. Governments have demonstrated a keen interest in natality rates. They have raised the twin specters of racial extinction and world overpopulation. More recent examples of the political centrality of the power over life offered by the biological sciences have been the debates about genetics and reproductive technologies.

For Foucault, bio-power is exercised over the human body conceived not as a machine, but as the basis of biological processes (1978: 139). The sovereign power of pre-modern times was power over death. The king could take the life of his subject. Modern power is, instead, power over life. It can prolong life, and manage its quality. It is exercised by means of policies over public health, migration, and reproduction. Bio-power, according to Foucault, 'brought life and its mechanisms into the realm of explicit calculations and made knowledge-power an agent of transformation of human life' (1978: 143).

Biological life comes to be seen as something which can be understood scientifically. This shift has several aspects. Firstly, life becomes the sort of thing about which there is a truth to tell. Second, science is conceived as the discipline which can uncover these truths. That is, scientific methods are thought to be appropriate in the search for truths about life. Finally, scientists gain epistemic authority about these matters. They are the individuals to be consulted on issues concerning biological life. Foucault characterizes these innovations as the emergence of a new 'truth regimen.' They manifest a shift in the 'politics of truth' present in society. Truth regimens for Foucault have several features. Firstly, they fix the distinction between discourses which are taken to be assessable with regard to truth and falsity and those which are not. Secondly, they determine the methods to use to distinguish truth from falsity. Thirdly, they specify the category of people who knows the truth (1980: 131). Bio-power institutes a new truth regimen because it creates the conditions for a science of life.

Furthermore, it bestows authority in these matters on scientists, and deprives other individuals of it.

This form of power is concerned with the management of life in accordance with scientific principles. Thus it <u>assumes that life can be quantified and manipulated.</u> The subsumption of life under science, according to Foucault, brings about a normalizing society (1978: 144). Modern science, he believes, treats every anomaly as something pathological, an abnormality. The <u>principles of science require that everybody be brought into line around the norm.</u> Hence, biological knowledge is not, for Foucault, politically neutral. It is made possible by a novel conception of the human body which subjects it to regulations. Under these conditions, a whole new range of political claims is taken to be acceptable while at the same time others are disallowed.

<u>Sex plays a central role in the deployment of bio-power.</u> It is the place where this form of power intersects disciplinary power. Sexuality is brought under the control of the regulative methods of bio-power and of the techniques of disciplinary power (1978: 146). This is particularly noticeable in the case of women's sexuality. The so-called 'truths' about health and population, which are an instance of the deployment of bio-power, motivate the medicalization of women's bodies and sex. That is, they induce the application of disciplinary techniques to the bodies of women (1978: 147). Hence, birth and other phenomena belonging to the sphere of female sexuality are seen increasingly as a matter for doctors to study, control, and tell us the 'truth' about.

Some aspects of Foucault's account of bio-power can be employed in feminist analyses of the political implications of new reproductive technologies. Thus Rosi Braidotti, for example, points out how these new technologies have been used to increase control over women's bodies while disempowering women themselves (1994: 70). This phenomenon accords with Foucault's claim that bio-power grants epistemic authority to the scientific expert. <u>Since scientists are meant to know best, they are given the power to make decisions that affect the lives of other people.</u> For example, often doctors decide when to give a cesarean birth without giving any choice to the woman concerned. Thus, women are denied control over an important aspect of their lives. This problem cannot be entirely solved by issuing new and stricter guidelines about informed consent. When reproduction becomes medicalized and highly technological, it is inevitable that doctors should be given power since they have knowledge of the appropriate techniques. Thus, high-tech reproduction makes a difference to attributions of epistemic authority. A new class of people, the doctors, emerge as the individuals who should be trusted on these issues. They become the experts, the truth-tellers in accordance with bio-power.

Furthermore, doctors can employ their knowledge only when the whole process of reproduction has been subjected to disciplinary techniques. For example, fetal development must be surveilled by means of scanning. This procedure makes the inside of a woman's body visible to the doctor. It forces this body to reveal itself in a new way. The institution of new practices, involving medical disciplinary techniques, for dealing with the female body invest it with new significances or cultural meanings. In other words, these practices introduce new ways in which it is supposedly appropriate to understand the female body.

There is a vast feminist literature concerning the reconceptualization of the body made possible by medical procedures. Feminists have focused their attention especially on ultrasound fetal imaging techniques. They have pointed out that, by making the fetus visible, these procedures grant it some sort of autonomy. They encourage us to see the fetus as an individual (Braidotti, 1994: 68). Thus they blur the distinction between baby and fetus. These techniques also give the appearance that it is appropriate to understand the female body as the environment for the fetus (Petchesky, 1987: 70). Thus the body is taken to be a mere container. According to Braidotti, this conception of the body leads to the identification of women with their uteruses. As a consequence, she claims, all women become interchangeable, since any uterus would do for the purpose of gestation (1994: 64). Braidotti's conclusion might seem too extreme. Yet it gains some support from the several cases of births from women kept on life-support machines. In these cases, although the women were brain-dead, their bodies were kept functioning until the fetus was thought to be viable. Perhaps, the women themselves would have wanted this to happen. Nevertheless, it remains surprising that hardly anybody questioned 'the ethics of using a woman's body in this way, without her prior consent' (Stanworth, 1987: 28). This attitude becomes less surprising if there is a tendency to consider the pregnant woman as a body which contains the baby/fetus.

The medicalization of reproduction has other consequences. For example, within this framework it makes sense to think of pregnant women and women who are trying to get pregnant as patients. Hence, both pregnancy and infertility acquire a new significance; they can be treated as illnesses. This phenomenon exemplifies the first feature Foucault attributes to bio-power, since it makes new claims assessable for their truth or falsity.

Before the advent of bio-power, the claim that pregnancy is an illness was neither true nor false. Feminists today, who do not see women's reproductive abilities as pathological, argue that this claim is false. Nevertheless, their objections take place within a background of medical practices that encourage treating pregnancy as a disease. Thus, feminists are forced to provide arguments against this belief. They cannot simply state that it is meaningless.

Foucault has also argued that bio-power institutes a normalizing society where what is anomalous is taken to be abnormal. In this context treating pregnancy as an illness amounts to treating it as something which is not normal. The underlying implication, however, is not that it is normal for women not to be pregnant. Infertility is also conceived as an illness. Rather, the implication must be that women are not the norm. Thus, the application of medical disciplinary techniques to women's pregnant bodies, which is one of the features of bio-power, re-enforces the assumption that the male is the human norm.

The case of infertility is even more complex. Treating it as an illness implies that there is something wrong with women who cannot get pregnant. This implication often lends support to the belief that motherhood is the natural function of women. Thus, it re-enforces stereotypes about the proper role of women. Male bodies, however, are not immune from bio-power. Hence, men's infertility is also seen as an illness. Nevertheless, since this attitude occurs in the context of cultural practices which do not define men in terms of fatherhood, its significance is not the same as in the case of women. This is not to say that infertile men are not made to feel inadequate. But they are not taken to be failing in their most important function. Given this framework it would seem appropriate for feminists to resist labeling infertility as a disease. Things, however, are not so simple. In the current socio-political context access to treatment is limited to those individuals who can afford to pay the bill for very expensive medical procedures. However, if infertility were taken to be a disease, in Britain, for instance, a claim could be made for universal coverage under the National Health Service. This consideration would not move those feminists who believe that infertility treatment is simply a means for the implementation of men's control over women's bodies. These feminists also believe that women allow such intrusive manipulations of their bodies, because they accept the myth of motherhood.[5] However, since this interpretation leads to a dismissal of some women's genuine desire to become pregnant, it seems wrong to endorse it wholeheartedly. One must resist positions that present these women solely as passive accomplices of their own oppression (Petchesky, 1987: 72; Braidotti, 1994: 70). Rather, it would seem more appropriate to claim that, while medical interventions within the current cultural background re-enforce many stereotypes about women, these practices could acquire a different, more positive, significance in a different context.

One should not conclude, however, that reproductive technologies are politically neutral. The problems with them do not merely lay in their implementation in a patriarchal society. Instead, it is important to acknowledge that these technologies can be successful only in situations shaped by the techniques of disciplinary power. These techniques enforce surveillance and standardization. In other words, reproductive technologies can operate only in the contexts of specific configurations of power relations. This is not to say that these medical procedures are inherently bad. They are, however, always dangerous.

Nobody, I believe, would deny that reproductive technologies are inextricably linked to issues concerning power. Some might, however, argue that the biological knowledge on which these technologies rely is immune from power. In light of the fact that many prominent biologists have commercial ties with biotechnological firms (Hubbard and Wald, 1997: 120), this claim would have to be taken as an expression of a possibility rather than a description of a reality. The commercialization of biological science is a serious problem which often gives rise to conflicts of interests. There is a need for stricter regulation of the corporate connections of scientists. Thus it is important to strive to isolate biological research from some power structures. It does not follow, however, that, were these changes implemented, biological knowledge would be pure of all power relations. Since biology is an example of laboratory science, it relies on disciplinary techniques to achieve its experimental results. The knowledge thus produced can be exported only to environments shaped by the distinctive power relations characteristic of disciplinary power. It would be hasty to conclude that this knowledge must necessarily have political consequences which are exclusively bad. For example, it is impossible to deny that reproductive technologies, from birth control to infertility treatments, have benefited some women. Nevertheless, it is important to maintain some degree of healthy skepticism about their success and their beneficial effects. For example, the genealogy of reproductive technologies should make us suspicious of their political implications. According to Foucault, the application of disciplinary techniques to women's sexuality was driven by the regulatory impulse constitutive of bio-power. These regulations were not devised to benefit women. A bad genealogy is not a conclusive proof of the nastiness of the phenomenon involved; it is, however, sufficient to raise questions about its political implications.

At this point two clarifications might help to dispel confusions about the argument presented in this chapter. Firstly, one might object that I have blurred the distinction between science and technology. This critic would be right. My argument, however, does not presuppose that such a distinction can never be drawn. For example, I have accepted that there is a difference between biology and biotechnology. However, I have also claimed that it would be wrong to think that the first is completely immune from power relations. Furthermore, I have argued that in some cases, for instance in the example of new developments in agriculture, insisting on the conceptual distinction between science and technology hinders the development of an adequate understanding of the situation.

Secondly, my argument does not support the view that every time disciplinary and bio-power come together they generate new genuine knowledge. Race provides a good example of this phenomenon.[6] Racialist thinking existed before the development of the biological sciences. Racialism thus predates the advent of bio-power. This way of thinking, developed at the end of the eighteenth century, presupposes that humans could be divided up into groups, which were called 'races.' It constitutes a real change from seventeenth century conceptions of the physical body as a sign of difference. For example, in Shakespeare's tragedy Othello's black skin is a symbol, not a cause, of his nature. The black skin signifies that Othello is a muslim, an infidel. With the advent of racialist thinking physical features are taken to be evidence of moral character. They are so conceived because they are understood to cause it.

In the nineteenth century racialist thinking attained its full development. It provided an account that takes individuals who share morphological characteristics, like a black skin, to have similar psychological and moral traits. Furthermore, it stated that these similarities could be fully explained by the presence of physical traits. Racialist thinking, thus, developed a biological concept of race. The rise of the biological sciences, especially evolutionary biology, initially provided the tools for refining this concept. In particular, the development of the regulative techniques typical of bio-power, within the background of racialist thinking, gave to skin color a new significance. This combination has had dreadful consequences, since it has contributed to the creation of racism. In the United States black women were particularly affected. In the context of a racist society, the concern with managing life, and with population control, lead to the perceived need for the regulation of the sexuality of black women. In the twentieth century the regulative effort has taken the form of widespread involuntary sterilization.[7]

Although bio-power has relied on the biological concept of race, the deployment of this notion has not made it real. It has, however, changed cultural practices so that many people treat race as a biological notion. In this way bio-power has contributed to the creation of a social construct: the biological notion of race. Nevertheless, as Anthony Appiah has shown, biological race is a fiction. There is no significant correlation between the moral and biological features of human beings belonging to the same race. Thus, there is no property that has the explanatory power traditionally attributed to biological race (1996: 71). Further, even if one claims that race merely amounts to classification by skin color and other gross morphological features, and carries no moral or psychological connotations, one would still fail to provide a biological notion of race. The classification, thus devised, could be said to individuate races; however, since this classification is of no use to biological scientific practice, it cannot be said to latch onto some biological reality (1996: 74).

In this case disciplinary and bio-power have come together to make biological talk of race possible. Yet, it turns out that this discourse is mistaken. Hence, in some cases, new forms of power, which make a difference to cultural and scientific practice, do not constitute new scientific knowledge. In other cases, as I have argued, power constitutes knowledge. These examples, I have claimed, suffice to show that modern science often is technoscience which cannot be isolated from politics.

Although Foucault has asserted that modern power is not all bad, but merely always dangerous, it is hard not to see his portrait of our world, insofar as it may still be characterized by modern forms of power, as dystopian. Rouse's application of Foucauldian theory gives the same impression. It would be a mistake to draw completely negative conclusions from these accounts. For example, biotechnologies have helped some women. The account I have provided above should not lead to a total rejection of science. Rather, it should engender an healthy skepticism about the power of science to ameliorate our world.

Scientific rationality can be both a source of domination and of liberation. This is a claim endorsed by Rosi Braidotti in her critique of Foucault's notion of bio-power (1994: 108). Braidotti uses Donna Haraway's metaphor of the cyborg to argue that the era of bio-power is about to end. In these years we are witnessing the rise of information technology. The normalizing power which Foucault has analyzed is being replaced by a form of power which relies on connections and networking (1994: 103).

Foucauldian docile bodies have been substituted by a new form of subjectivity which is, like the cyborg, a body/machine hybrid. This approach provides a whole new way of conceiving rationality and other cognitive practices as well as the subject of knowledge. I shall discuss these two themes in chapters 9 and 10.

Further Reading

The application of Foucault's account of disciplinary power to science is carefully explained in chapters 4 and 7 of Joseph Rouse's *Knowledge and Power: Toward a Political Philosophy of Science* (1987). Gena Corea's *The Mother Machine: Reproductive Technologies from Artificial Insemination to Artificial Wombs* (1985) provides an insightful but totally negative feminist assessment of biotechnologies. The articles in Michelle Stanworth (ed.), *Reproductive Technologies: Gender, Motherhood, and Medicine* (1987) represent a wider spectrum of feminist perspectives on this issue.

Notes

1 Biotechnology is a striking example of this phenomenon. For instance, in the US, scientists who have commercial ties with the pharmaceutical industry are often appointed to test the drugs produced by this industry. These issues are discussed in chapter 9 of Hubbard and Wald (1997).

2 For a good explanation of Habermas's position see Vogel (1995).

3 It is commonplace to read Foucault as if he were addressing contemporary issues. His books, however, are mostly concerned with historical phenomena. Nevertheless, it is not absurd to apply his analyses to the twentieth century, since Foucault himself is not opposed to using his interpretations of history to understand current situations (1996: 261).

4 He also warned us against reducing his analysis of disciplinary power to the example of the panopticon (1996: 257).

5 These attitudes are manifested in Gena Corea's *The Mother Machine* (1985).

6 My discussion is indebted to Anthony Appiah's 'Race, Culture, Identity' (1996).

7 A detailed account of birth control and racism in the United States can be found in chapter 12 of Angela Davis's *Women, Race & Class* (1983).

9

Reason and Unreason in Feminism

Twentieth century French philosophy has been characterized by what Richard Bernstein (1986) has tendentiously called a 'rage against reason.' Indeed, the debates about reason have been particularly acrimonious, and feminists have not been immune from this tendency.[1]

This phenomenon is not at all surprising since the very nature of philosophy and of feminism is at stake in these discussions. Philosophy is often understood as the discipline concerned with reason's self-understanding. It involves a rational investigation of the limits of reason itself. The fate of reason is to a large extent the fate of philosophy. The demise of the first would spell the end of the second. Furthermore, radical critiques of reason also require transformations in feminist politics. There is no doubt that the Enlightenment's ideals of equality and emancipation have been important to the feminist movement. These are ideals that seem to depend on the hope for the betterment of human society through rational discussions. Thus, some feminists, like Sabina Lovibond (1994), argue that feminism needs to hold on to some notion of reason, and to struggle for the widespread acceptance of the claim that women are as rational as men. Radical critiques of reason, instead, may appear to undermine philosophy itself, and to go against some feminist objectives. Considerations of this sort underlie many feminist defenses of reason.

The questioning of reason, everybody agrees, is a fundamental philosophical activity. Philosophers have always been concerned with understanding the nature of reason. Current debates seem particularly threatening because, sometimes, they doubt the existence of reason itself. The radical rejection of reason, however, is only one among the different positions held by critics of traditional conceptions of this notion. Furthermore, even those philosophers, who appear to endorse a radical position, do not abandon rationality altogether.

There are at least three different kinds of criticism that have been leveled at standards accounts of reason. The first, which has gained widespread acceptance, is mild. It holds that traditional views are too narrow, because they identify reason with one style of reasoning. These critics point out that there are different styles of thinking, each appropriate for different subject matters, which are equally rational. For example, the kind of reasoning required to judge the beauty of a work of art is bound to be different from that required to decide what to do in a concrete situation. Neither style of reasoning bears many similarities to that employed, say, to solve a mathematical equation.

The second kind of criticism of traditional accounts of reason is more radical. This critique is, partly, an extension of the first. Its supporters object to the reduction of rationality to one mode of thinking. However, they also add that the kind of reason, which is privileged in modern society, has very deleterious effects. This dominant style of thinking is instrumental reason; that is, reasoning about the most effective means to achieve predetermined ends. Some critics of instrumental reason believe that this way of thinking is appropriate to some areas of inquiry (Habermas, 1971). For example, they might believe that it is adequately employed in the natural sciences. Others object to its use even in these cases. Instrumental reason is problematic, according to supporters of this second criticism, because it is connected to the impulse for mastery and control. This impulse, it is argued, can lead to violence and domination. Those philosophers, who believe that mastery is sometimes appropriate, accept a limited employment for instrumental thinking. Those who believe instead that control always leads to domination, support a wholesale rejection of this mode of reasoning. Both groups, however, decry the seemingly unstoppable expansion of the range of application of instrumental reason in Western societies. This style of reasoning is commonly employed to deal with other people, to understand the moral dimension of our lives, and so forth. Since this sort of reason is taken to breed violence and marginalization, pessimism about current society is widespread. However, while some believe that it is far too late for any hope of improvement, others disdain what they see as ungrounded fatalism.

There is a third, even more radical, criticism of reason. It differs from the second because it is directed against reason as a whole. Mastery and control, according to this view, pertain to all forms of rationality. Rosi Braidotti (1991) and Elizabeth Grosz (1993) have presented feminist versions of this critique of reason. Their arguments draw on the resources offered by psychoanalysis, and on feminist accounts of the maleness of reason. I discuss Braidotti's position in the first section of this chapter. Although I provide objections against some features of her position, I argue that she is not endorsing irrationalism.

The most innovative contribution of feminism to the critique of reason resides in the examination of the connections between reason and masculinity. There is no doubt that during the last few centuries women, on the whole, have been seen as emotional creatures. Instead, men have been taken to be capable of engaging in scientific reasoning. Historically, therefore, reason has been seen primarily as a masculine trait. Nobody, I believe, would contest these claims. Disagreements quickly emerge, however, when one attempts to interpret these platitudes. Some may argue that there are real differences in reasoning between men and women, and add that these are based on the biological characteristics of the two sexes. This is a position occupied both by some anti-feminists and, perhaps, even by a few feminists. These feminists would argue, however, in favor of a certain contempt for the notion of reason.[2] Most feminists, nevertheless, reject an easy endorsement of unreason over reason. It appears to many that such a value reversal does not address the real issue.

Roughly speaking, feminists have proposed three different solutions to the problem of disentangling reason from masculinity. Some, notably Martha Nussbaum (1994), have argued that this problem should be addressed by means of rational argument. Women should use reason to demonstrate that they are rational. Both the content of the arguments, and the fact that women provide them, will show the mistake of the association of woman with irrationality. Nevertheless, Nussbaum herself believes that modern conceptions of reason are too narrow, because they exclude emotions from the nature of rationality. Several feminists, for example Genevieve Lloyd and Braidotti, think that this approach will not solve the problem. They present several arguments for this claim, which I discuss in the first section of this chapter. In particular, they claim that, given the current situation, asking women to embrace rationality is tantamount to asking them to reject femininity.

The second solution to the problem of reason starts by examining how philosophical accounts of this notion have been based on the exclusion of woman. On the basis of this examination, it proceeds to develop alternative conceptions of reason that can be more inclusive. This approach, which has been pursued by Lloyd, offers the promise for a rational reevaluation of reason within philosophy. Braidotti has called this solution 'reformist.' She believes that it is not sufficiently radical.

The third, radical, solution has been developed by Braidotti and Grosz. These feminist philosophers do not embrace irrationality; instead, they argue that philosophy cannot offer all the conceptual tools that are necessary to critique reason. They also claim that reason cannot ever operate independently of power and desire. For them, rational discourse is inevitably based on exclusions, which must be acknowledged. One should not embrace irrationality; nevertheless, one must be aware that reason is always inflected by desire. Braidotti also seems to believe that this acknowledgment is impossible from within philosophy. Hence, her disagreement with Lloyd partly concerns the future and the utility of philosophy itself.

Feminist critiques of reason have enormous consequences for philosophy and epistemology. They challenge philosophy's self-conception. They argue that the exclusion of women from this discipline has not been accidental. Some feminists also claim that philosophy cannot solve its own problems. Furthermore, these arguments undermine traditional conceptions of the subject of knowledge. They show that this subject is not universal, and that it is not immune from power relations.

Reason and Masculinity

There is substantial agreement among many feminists on the arguments that show that reason is masculine. Differences of opinion seem to emerge when we consider the consequences of such arguments. Thus, some feminists, like Lloyd (1984), believe that new and better conceptions of rationality can be formulated. Others, Braidotti (1991) for example, are more skeptical. These disagreements, I argue, derive from the different accounts of subjectivity proposed by these feminist philosophers. But, first, feminist arguments that traditional conceptions of reason are masculine must be put in their proper context.

The investigation of the limits of reason has a long philosophical history. It is, for example, the task Kant set for himself in the *Critique of Pure Reason*. Contemporary philosophy has further contributed to the humbling of reason's aspirations. The target of recent critiques has been the conception of reason advocated by the Enlightenment. Reason, according to this conception, leads the way to progress, it is a source of empowerment. By means of it individuals will reach the state of maturity. The twentieth century has witnessed the failure of the promises offered by that movement. There have been different accounts of what has caused this failure. Some, especially Jürgen Habermas, have argued that the problem lies with the employment of instrumental reason in areas for which it is not suited. Ethics and politics constitute his prime examples. Others diagnose a deeper problem. Thus, Michel Foucault, following Nietzsche, believes that any notion of reason which pretends to be unconnected with power is hopelessly misconceived. For him the problem, therefore, goes well beyond the expansion of instrumental reason. Rather we must come to terms with the fact that reason is intrinsically connected with power.

For those feminists who find current ideals of reason problematic, the trouble with reason is not just a matter of the overreaching of instrumental reason. Rather, the problem lies in the complicity of theories of reason with a fantasy of escaping our embodied condition (Lovibond, 1989: 12). They suggest that taking seriously our corporeality involves a dramatic change to our ideals of reason. In particular they claim that reason, as traditionally explained, is male.

Feminists are not the only critics of the current ideal of reason who believe it to be still dependent on Cartesian mind–body dualism. This criticism is justified, but it might be easily dismissed unless its import is made clearer. The contemporary supporters of mainstream ideals of reason do not believe that the mind is made of a different substance from the body. Their commitment to science makes this belief impossible. To hold that minds are radically different from bodies would prevent the scientific study of our cognitive abilities. Thus, when feminist argue that contemporary views of reason are still wedded to Cartesian dualisms they do not literally claim that their opponents believe that minds are made of ghostly stuff. Rather, they claim that dominant views do not consider properly the implications of the fact that we – our minds, our reason – are embodied. Once again, it must be made clear what this criticism amounts to. Dominant views of the mind do not see it as separate from the brain; they take the mind to be embodied in this sense. But this misses the point of feminist criticism.

There are, I believe, several conceptually distinct points feminists make when they claim that dominant conceptions take reason to be disembodied. They all involve the attribution to reason of features opposed to those traditionally associated with the body. First, reason would be unchangeable, immune to history. The body, instead, belongs to the realm of change. Of course, this criticism applies only to some philosophical accounts of reason and not to others. Hegel, for example, developed a notion of reason which is essentially historical. Nevertheless, this is still a fair criticism of dominant conceptions in analytic philosophy. Secondly, while bodies are sexed, reason is conceived as being indifferent to sexual difference. This claim also is not applicable to every traditional conception of reason. Furthermore, it seems equally inadequate to argue that reason is sexually differentiated. Rather, one may want to claim that, although sexual differences do not determine the features of the mind, they are not totally irrelevant either. Once the mind is seen as multilayered rather than unitary, it is possible to conceive new connections between the mind and the sexed nature of bodies. This is a difficult issue which I explore in this section. An excessive separation of mind from body is also at the root of the traditional failure to see that reason cannot be independent of emotions, and of other cognitive capacities which are closely connected to bodily functions. This is a distinctively modern attitude toward reason, since Greek philosophers tended to see these capacities as being part of reason rather than outside it.

Therefore, when feminists criticize traditional conceptions of reason for their Cartesianism, they have in mind something rather complex. They are opposed to a view of reason as autonomous from history, the body, and other cognitive faculties. Descartes's dualism contributed to the formation of an autonomous notion of reason, but this conception was further developed by Kant, for example. Furthermore, such a conception has survived the demise of the Cartesian belief that the stuff the mind is made of sets it apart from the body.

It is now time to turn to feminist claims that the ideal of disembodied reason is masculine. In the English-speaking world the most detailed argument for the claim that traditional ideals of reason are bound up with masculinity has been presented by Lloyd in her book, *The Man of Reason*, which is a *tour de force* in the history of philosophical conceptions of reason. In it she concludes that 'rationality has been conceived as transcendence of the feminine' (1984: 104). Lloyd does not, however, assume that philosophical norms of rationality have remained unchanged throughout history. On the contrary, she shows how different ideals of rationality have mutated and substituted one another. There is very little these ideals have in common besides their uneasy relation with all that is represented by women. It would be too facile, however, to hold that reason has been simply constituted through an exclusion of women. Although there is some truth in this claim, the nature of this exclusion is complex and historically variable. As Lloyd points out, the exclusion is not a consequence of a male conspiracy (1984: 109). Often, she adds, 'it happened despite the conscious intent of the authors' (1984: 109). Descartes is an example of this phenomenon.

It is not possible to reduce what Lloyd has to say about the maleness of reason to one neat argument. Instead, one must follow her varied historical interpretations. For her the historian of philosophy is a sort of cultural critic, since philosophy is part of culture (1984: 109). It is not 'a timeless rational representation of the real' (1984: 109). Although this starting point distances Lloyd's position from traditional conceptions of the discipline, it allies it to the sort of cultural approach I have been advocating in this book. To see philosophy as part of culture is, among other things, to address the role played by metaphors in philosophical discourse. Michèle Le Doeuff (1989), to whom I shall return in the next section, has discussed the relevance of metaphors to understanding how women have been excluded from philosophy. The maleness of reason investigated by Lloyd also pertains to the metaphorical dimension of philosophy.

Lloyd does not claim that reason is essentially masculine, instead she holds that some conceptions of reason are male. A critique of the maleness of reason is not a critique of any conception of reason but of those which have been developed by past philosophers. Her analyses do not lead necessarily to a rejection of reason. Similarly, they do not give support to the view that there are distinctively female criteria of justified belief (1984: ix). As a first approximation one could say that Lloyd is not concerned with reason itself but with the metaphors surrounding this ideal. She is also not concerned with real women and their reasoning abilities, but with the ways in which 'woman' has been used as a symbol for the other of reason. Nevertheless this characterization of Lloyd's discussion is only partly correct. She is not saying that the maleness of reason has no consequence for real women, nor does she believe that reason itself can just be salvaged intact from its metaphorical associations.

Lloyd traces the history of the ideal of reason from Plato to Hegel. I shall not attempt to summarize in a few pages her detailed interpretations. Instead, I shall try to individuate three different modalities of the relationship between reason and what is symbolized by woman. All of them support the claim that reason has been understood as transcendence from the feminine, but they present different views of what must be transcended and of what transcendence amounts to.

The first account presents woman as symbolizing what is less rational than the male ideal. Woman is not outside reason, but is represented by the lower functions of this faculty. In his early dialogues Plato conceives of

rational knowledge as involving transcendence of matter, which is represented as feminine (1984: 4). Transcendence involves going beyond matter
and the material body, and leaving them behind. In his later writings Plato
modifies his account. Reason becomes a divided faculty, it includes lower
instinctual parts which are in conflict with the higher cognitive parts.
Instincts and passions, associated with matter, are thus a lesser part of
reason. They do not stand outside it (1984: 7). Woman, because of its
connection with matter, is taken to be rational, but not as much as man.
Nevertheless, this account still construes rationality as a matter of transcending femininity, since the ideal human is the person in whom the higher
functions of reason have supremacy over the lower parts. The ideal person
has transcended femaleness, although what is associated with the feminine
is not completely left behind. Instead, it is properly dominated by the male
features of reason (1984: 26).

The second account of reason presents woman as symbolizing what
stands outside reason. Since Francis Bacon, rational knowledge has been
conceived as a matter of power and mastery (1984: 10). This conception
comes to replace the earlier view, endorsed by Plato and Aristotle, that
knowledge is contemplation of objects. As Bacon puts it, knowledge
requires domination over Nature and matter, both of which are conceived
as feminine. Once again rationality involves domination over woman. But
in this second account the knower, conceived as male, dominates the
object of knowledge conceived as female. In the earlier Platonic account
some parts of reason must dominate other parts to make contemplative
knowledge possible. In the context of this Baconian conception of knowledge Cartesian philosophy makes it possible to conceive woman as other
than reason.

Descartes reintroduces unity within the faculty of reason (1984: 41). The
Cartesian method is a way of reasoning which is taken to be appropriate to
intellectual reflection on every subject matter. This is consonant with
seventeenth century conceptions of reason as an achievement, a skill to be
learned. One may say that before Descartes reason encompassed the whole
of human thought, while after him it becomes associated with one very
specific way of thinking, namely the ordered mode of abstract thinking.[3]
Passion and instincts are conceived as irrational – outside reason – rather
than a part of it. Furthermore, since reason is now restricted to one way of
thinking, there can be styles of thought which are irrational. It thus
becomes possible to claim that there can be more than one kind of
intellectual character. Before one could only distinguish between more and
less accomplished examples of individual rationality.

Descartes himself thought that both men and women shared reason. Thus his intentions were egalitarian. His views were, for this reason, appropriated by women philosophers to argue that women were not less rational than men.[4] Ironically, Cartesian philosophy made it possible to see women as irrational. Since Descartes advocated a complete separation of the rational mind from the body, woman, who was already associated with matter, comes to be associated with what is outside reason. This Cartesian conception of reason involves transcending the feminine insofar as it involves excluding the influence of the body on the mind.

The third account of reason also conceives of reason as transcending the feminine, but sees the latter as representing a kind of intellectual character which complements rationality. Rousseau is one of the first philosophers to claim that the ideal character for a woman is different from what is ideal for a man. Men should aspire to become good citizens, while women should be good private persons (1984: 77). Women should restrict themselves to the private sphere, and leave the public domain to men. Rousseau reaches this view partly because of his conception of the history of the human race. At the beginning there was an Arcadian state of nature; civilization marks a fall of the human race. Nevertheless, by means of reason human beings can achieve a new and superior state of oneness with nature (1984: 58). This achievement is ultimately masculine. Women for Rousseau never left the state of nature and, therefore, cannot engage in the progress toward nature.

Hegel's account of reason also confines women to the private sphere of the family. For Hegel, reason is a matter of achieving self-consciousness. This can be accomplished only in the public sphere where consciousness confronts other consciousnesses. Women are thus excluded from the process of becoming a subject which requires the development of self-consciousness (1984: 92). Hegel's account of reason as self-consciousness does not just exclude women from achieving the status of the subject, it also implies that the process of becoming self-conscious requires transcending the private sphere of nature and of the family, symbolized by woman. Hegel's conception of transcendence, however, does not involve rejection or exclusion. On the contrary, each stage of consciousness constitutes a fuller realization of earlier stages which find their rationale in the more mature stage. Hence, if the feminine must be transcended, then woman is to be understood 'as being what she truly is only by virtue of what lies beyond her' (1984: 73).

This third conception of how reason is constituted as transcendence of the feminine should be credited with the insight that this process is also one that constitutes femininity (1984: 106). In other words femininity has been constructed as that which is excluded by reason. There is no brute fact of femininity which precedes its constitution as what is opposed to reason (1984: 104). The history of reason is 'not a simple exclusion of women, but a constitution of femininity through that exclusion' (1984: 106).

The first model of reason sees woman as less rational, the second identifies her with a disvalued irrationality, the third takes her as the symbol of what complements rationality. All of these conceptions have unacceptable consequences for real women. The first conceives them as deficient males, the second encourages them to abandon femininity to embrace a 'male' reason, and the third sees them as a kind of being who should not pursue reason, whose real nature however can be understood only by considering what they are not. Women are in these three models understood by their relation to a norm which is male.

Given Lloyd's account of the history of reason, it would be rather simplistic for feminists to claim that the notion of reason is fine as it stands. One cannot just claim that women are rational. Unless reason itself is conceived differently, such a claim would merely amount to encouraging women to shed femininity. Of course, it is politically important to say that women's rational abilities do not necessarily differ from men's (1984: 104). But it is not enough to stop there, since such a claim would be interpreted as saying that women have masculine features. The opposite position, however, is also fraught with difficulties. It is important to highlight feminist alternatives to traditional rationality. However, if one stops there, 'any emphasis on a supposedly distinctive style of thought . . . is liable to be caught up in a deeper, older structure of male norms and female complementation' (1984: 105).

It is necessary to bring into clearer focus what Lloyd means by claiming that reason is male in order to assess several criticisms raised against her views by more 'radical' and more 'conservative' feminists. This clarification of her position will also help to assess its political and philosophical consequences. I have already explained that when Lloyd is talking about reason she is not commenting on the reasoning abilities of men or women. But, and this has often been misunderstood, she is not talking about gender identity either. She does not hold that reason has those features which pertain to the character traits of constructed masculinity (Lloyd, 1993: 71). Instead, Lloyd intends to capture the symbolic or metaphorical content of the concept of reason. She is saying that reason as a concept has a metaphorical dimension. It is the symbolism that accompanies the notion of reason which is male. In other words, the loose grouping of metaphors that have accreted on the concept of reason are metaphors of maleness. Maleness here is also taken as a symbol. Commenting on her earlier work, Lloyd claims: 'The Man of Reason was centrally concerned with male and female as symbolic content (metaphors); it was concerned with the literary dimensions of philosophical texts' (1993: 71).

More analytically-minded commentators on Lloyd's work seem to fail to grasp the metaphorical dimensions she studies.[5] Analytic philosophers still like to think of themselves as having nothing to do with metaphorical talk. However, philosophers, even those who belong to the analytic tradition, use metaphors all the time. Lloyd believes that we cannot simply shed the metaphors and be left with a philosophical theory that can be studied for its own merits. Metaphors in philosophical texts do philosophical work (Alcoff, 1995/6: 72). They function to make claims plausible, to give a flavor of obviousness to a given way of looking at things. Metaphors, like hypotheses, guide our investigations about what needs to be explained in a theory, and what can be taken for granted. They are not merely colorful embellishments of philosophical writing. Furthermore, the distinction between literal speech and metaphors is not always clear cut. Many expressions, such as 'the neck of the bottle,' which we now take literally, are stale metaphors. It is therefore impossible to just decant a pure theory without the metaphors which have encroached upon it. I shall look in more detail at the role of metaphors in philosophy in the second section of this chapter.

Ultimately the lesson to be learned from Lloyd's detailed cultural analysis of the history of reason is that this concept has a metaphorical import which concerns the symbolism of sexual difference. Lloyd thinks that the concept of reason might necessarily involve metaphors, but she holds that they do not have to be metaphors of maleness. Furthermore, she believes that the metaphors associated with reason do not have to relate at all to sexual difference (1993: 76).[6] It is because she believes that the connections between reason and male/female symbolism are only contingent that Lloyd holds that the view that reason has no sex might embody a hope for the future (1984: 107).

This latter point is, in my opinion, one powerful source of disagreement among feminists who believe that there is something seriously wrong with traditional conceptions of reason. These feminists have been categorized by Braidotti into two groups: the reformists, which include Lloyd, and the radicals with whom Braidotti joins forces. As Linda Alcoff points out, the opposition between these two camps is not as stark as some critics have argued (1995/6: 67). Nevertheless, there are some differences. I would like to mention two of them, which I believe to be the most important. Firstly, Lloyd believes that we can hope to construct accounts of reason which are free of the symbolism of sexual difference. For Braidotti, the radical position is 'opposed to the reformists' belief in the possibility of cleansing the rational of its sexist biases, the theoreticians of difference argue that rationality is the mode of thinking of an idealized form of masculinity' (1991: 212). Instead, Braidotti's radicals attempt to 'empower the female subject' by realizing the conditions for the creation of an alternative feminine symbolic. This is, for example, the position elaborated by Luce Irigaray, one of Braidotti's radicals, which I discussed in the second section of chapter 2. Reason, according to this view, is compromised, and cannot be redeemed. This position, however, does not recommend that we embrace irrationality. Instead, it proposes that we develop another way of thinking, of advancing arguments and criticism. This alternative would acknowledge the 'bodily roots of the thinking process' (1991: 8). It would require a deconstruction of the modern rational subject (1991: 8).

The second related source of disagreement between radicals and reformists concerns the future of philosophy. Lloyd, for example, believes that a transformed discipline of philosophy can help to conceive new and better ideals of rationality. This belief, for Braidotti, characterizes the reformist position. Reformists, she says, hold that 'the excesses of philosophical Reason can be tempered and siphoned off within the field of philosophy itself' (1991: 182). Radicals deny it. This disagreement between reformist and radicals, however, could be taken to be verbal. Lloyd, like Braidotti, believes that we need a cultural critique of reason. Braidotti thinks that such a critique requires that we move partly outside philosophy. Lloyd, instead, argues that it can be conducted in philosophy, once our conception of this discipline has been transformed. So they agree that philosophy as it stands cannot provide the necessary tools of criticism. They also agree that cultural criticism is required. If we ignore for a moment their different positions with regard to psychoanalysis, it would seem that their views are substantially similar. They differ only about which kind of inquiry they are willing to label philosophical.

I believe this assessment of their views about the future of philosophy to be basically correct. It must be supplemented, however, with an awareness of the politics of naming. Lloyd's choice to preserve the name 'philosophy' for a transformed discipline has political consequences. For example, it indicates a willingness to work from within the mainstream to bring about change. The radicals have made different political choices, and adopt other political strategies. They abandon philosophy because they believe that engagements with mainstream philosophical thinking distract feminist intellectuals from dealing with more urgent tasks. Thus, as Braidotti claims, 'the relation between the heterogeneous and complex field that is feminist theory and the "dominant" discourse of philosophy can only be political' (1991: 9). Braidotti, in my opinion, occupies a moderately radical position. She does not believe feminist theory needs to reclaim philosophy. Nevertheless, she does not reject this discipline altogether. I cannot even begin to address this political issue faced by feminist thinkers trained in philosophy here, since it would require another book. I shall, instead, express my very personal opinion in the concluding remarks for this chapter.

I have claimed that the first disagreement between reformists and radicals concerns the relation between reason and sexual difference. Radicals believe that the connection is essential to reason itself, while reformists think that it can be severed. Psychoanalytic conceptions of the subject play a fundamental role in these discussions. According to Braidotti, 'reformists live theoretically in a pre-modern universe, where the subject, although he or she may be made complex and seen as multiple, still coincides with his or her wilful conscious self' (1991: 200). In other words, reformists ignore the lesson taught by psychoanalysis. They still rely on the Cartesian presupposition that the subject coincides with consciousness.

Braidotti and Grosz argue, instead, that psychoanalysis has shattered this presupposition because it has shown that the unconscious plays an important role in the human psyche. It would seem relatively easy to remain unmoved by this discovery. Even if unconscious motives and desires play an important role in our choices, and actions, reason, one may claim, is also relevant. Psychoanalysis could teach us that the conscious self is rarely in control, it might even show that rationality is not as central to our lives as we thought it was. Nevertheless, one may say, psychoanalysis does not warrant a total overhaul of current conceptions of rationality. This reply would be far too simplistic. An account of human subjectivity that divides it into watertight compartments cannot be satisfactory. Psychologically desires and reasons are not disconnected, they are both involved in our choices. A theory which attempts to separate the two would be empirically mistaken. So understood, psychoanalysis raises the problem of the psychological inadequacy of conceiving reason to be autonomous from desires. This interpretation, however, would not move us beyond the issues presented by other critics of a disembodied reason. It would merely be another voice in the chorus of the critics of the autonomy of reason.

Braidotti and Grosz, however, believe that psychoanalysis generates a crisis of rationality. It does not lead only to a rejection of reason's autonomy from desires and emotions, it makes it hard to see how rationality itself can be salvaged. This is, indeed, a radical claim. In my opinion this position is best understood as a crisis about epistemic legitimation and authority. Psychoanalysis would show that standard accounts of justification must be rejected. There are several advantages to framing Braidotti's discussion, for example, in this manner. Firstly, it shows how the debate is not dependent on a rather old-fashioned notion of reason as a distinct cognitive faculty. Secondly, it helps to understand why for Braidotti this crisis is central to epistemology itself.

The modern episteme, which I have discussed in several chapters of this book, takes knowledge to be a matter of representations. The grounds which justify these representations are found within the subject. That is, the processes by means of which the subject forms representations provide at least sometime a justification for them. The challenge offered by psychoanalysis has been to show that we are not the sort of subjects who can provide these grounds. Firstly, the unconscious desires which are among the causes of our representations cannot be seen as reasons that justify them. Thus, whenever these desires are at the root of our beliefs, the beliefs cannot be warranted. Secondly, it is usually assumed that subjects have conscious access to the grounds or reasons for their representations. But this psychoanalysis denies; it claims, instead, that beliefs are often grounded on unconscious desires. Finally, the traditional account of justification presupposes that it is up to us to decide what to believe.[7] However, if psychoanalytic theory is right the notion of a masterful self is merely an illusion.

Furthermore, psychoanalysis seems to threaten the notion of agency, since it appears to undermine the legitimacy of intentional explanations. Often, we explain the actions of individuals in terms of their conscious belief and desires. We take their behavior to flow from their intentions; we assume that they are in control. These explanations, therefore, presuppose exactly the kind of masterful subject that psychoanalysis has shown to be an illusion. But, if intentional explanations are ruled out, the very notion of agency is undermined. The behavior of individuals would never be the result of their decisions, they would, therefore, not be responsible for their own actions. In a word, they would not be agents. Agency, however, is not something that feminists can reject light-heartedly, since it is not clear how politics, including feminist politics, could survive without it.

Braidotti is acutely aware of this problem. She is rather skeptical about declarations that the notion of the subject is in crisis, which are voiced at the same time as feminism emerges as a political force (1994: 97). Nevertheless, she believes that this 'crisis' offers to feminist philosophy the opportunity to provide new conceptions of the subject that are more adequate for women (1994: 97). She attempts to resolve the tension between political and psychoanalytic notions of the subject by distinguishing between two levels. The first concerns subjectivity, while the second is about identity. For her, 'the feminist project encompasses both the level of subjectivity in the sense of historical agency, and political and social entitlement, and the level of identity that is linked to consciousness, desire, and the politics of the personal; it covers both the conscious and the unconscious levels' (1994: 163). Thus, Braidotti seems to locate agency at the level of political engagement. It is at this level that with the acquisition of subjectivity one gains 'entitlements to certain practices' (1994: 99). The level of identity, instead, concerns the subject as studied by psychoanalysis. At this level the subject is constituted 'through a process of identification with culturally available positions' (1994: 162). These identifications are mainly unconscious. It is at this level that unconscious desires play a central role in the formation of the subject. Braidotti attempts to find ways of connecting these two levels. Nevertheless, the way in which she draws this distinction illustrates that, while she wants to preserve the notion of agency, she believes that psychoanalysis undermines it.

I don't agree. Psychoanalysis encourages us to adopt non-intentional interpretations of many psychological phenomena. Some of them (slips of the tongue, for example) never seemed suited to explanations in terms of intentions. Others may have appeared intentional. Psychoanalysis, however, does not undermine the very notion of intention. It does not show that explanations of actions in terms of conscious beliefs and desires are always mistaken. Instead, psychoanalysis undermines intrinsic intentionality. That is, it rejects a Cartesian picture of conscious beliefs and desires. According to this view, the meanings of beliefs and desires can simply be read off by the subject who has them. Conscious mental states would have self-presenting meanings which do not require interpretation. But if psychoanalysis is right, many of our conscious beliefs and desires find their roots in unconscious endorsements of cultural symbols. The meanings of our psychological states reflect these origins. The contents of consciousness need interpretation, they are not immediately available to the subject. Thus, the conscious subject is not masterful, it does not entirely control its beliefs and desires. It cannot bring them about at will, and it cannot simply bestow their meanings upon them. Nevertheless, it still makes sense to explain intentionally some of the actions of this subject. What subjects do is, at times, made intelligible by giving their beliefs and desires as the reasons for their action. Subjects can, thus, be conceived as agents because their behavior at least sometimes flows from their intentions.

This answer to the problem about intentionality raised by psychoanalysis also offers a solution to the crisis of legitimation. The meanings of psychological states, such as beliefs, I have claimed, are not self-presenting. Instead, they always require interpretation. Naomi Scheman's view that beliefs are socially constituted, which I discussed in chapter 2, provides the required interpretative account. We attribute psychological states with a semantic content to individuals who engage in actions. The significance of both actions and beliefs is constituted by the social practices in which individuals engage. In chapter 1 I argued that practices are ways of doing things which embody standards of appropriateness or norms. Agents participate in these practices when they, perhaps implicitly, acknowledge these norms. Furthermore, I have shown in chapter 8 that social practices, including those concerning knowledge and justification, are never immune from power relations.

Reason, I would like to argue, should not be seen as a psychological faculty which each individual possesses in isolation from a community of agents. Although it is individuals who are rational, this is a feature they possess in virtue of their memberships to communities. Rationality should be understood in terms of communal practices. It is embodied in the standards of argument, dialogue, and questioning implicit in practice. The practices themselves can be brought into question. One may argue that the standards of reasoning implicit in them are mistaken. Feminist critiques of reason engage in this activity. They bring about changes in our practices in more than one way. Firstly, they provide a rational critique of reason. They rely on some aspects of current epistemic practices to demonstrate the contradictions present in other aspects of this practice. This is the kind of internal criticism preferred by reformist feminist thinkers. Secondly, they engage in political activity to bring about changes in power relations and sociocultural practices concerning gender and the body. These political interventions, if successful, can modify the standards of reasoning implicit in epistemic practices. This is the kind of external critique of reason preferred by radicals.

An example may help to clarify how political activism can function as an external critique of reason. Political interventions can change the significance attributed to many linguistic and non-linguistic actions. For instance, a claim that was once read as a joke acquires now the significance of sexual harassment. The offender's defense that he was only jesting will not sound convincing. The meaning of his actions and claims is not determined by psychological states over whose meanings he has absolute control. What his claims and beliefs mean is not something that he can understand simply by introspection. Suppose that a woman listening to the so-called joke is offended, feels threatened or uncomfortable. Before the vocabulary of sexual harassment was introduced, she could not invoke her reaction to justify the claim that the so-called joke was unacceptable. Once feminist politics has unearthed the true significance of the offensive remark, the epistemic relevance of referring to one's feeling to justify the claim that the 'joke' was offensive can be recognized. The harasser might not be willing to listen, but it is now possible to recast this unwillingness as self-serving irrationality. Feminist political interventions on these topic have changed the standards of reasoning by giving epistemic legitimacy to claims that could not otherwise be justified.

Thus, I take the lesson to be learned from psychoanalysis to be twofold. Firstly, the subject should not be seen as masterful; the individual cannot bestow meanings on her psychological states. The significance of meanings and desires cannot simply be read off by the subject who has them. Secondly, rationality and justification cannot be found within the subject. Instead, we must understand them in terms of practices. Once we do this, we will be able to see that belief in a conception of reason which is immune from power is a dangerous illusion. Although Braidotti does not talk about practices, I think she subscribes to these conclusions. In particular, it would be a mistake to believe that she endorses irrationality. On the contrary, she attempts to find ways for women 'to elaborate a truth which is not removed from the body' (1991: 8).

I return now to the issue of sexual difference. Firstly, Braidotti's claim that reformist feminists rely on a modern conception of the conscious self might be true, but it is not an essential feature of reformism. In particular, it does not seem correct to read Lloyd's in this manner. Nevertheless, Lloyd and Braidotti adopt different views on subjectivity, and this difference explains why for Lloyd feminists should strive to undermine the association of reason with any metaphor concerning sexual difference. Talking about Irigaray, one of Braidotti's radicals, and her account of symbolic woman, Lloyd asks:

> In claiming it as a new conceptualization of both reason and the feminine are feminists perpetuating the link between sexual difference and symbolization of reason that is the heart of the problem? Does this Irigarayan mode of criticizing the maleness of reason perpetuate a

symbolic use of sexual difference that we would do better to part company with altogether? (1993: 74)

For Lloyd feminist epistemologists should attempt to find new conceptions of reason which do not make use of metaphors of sexual difference. Braidotti, and other radicals, attempt instead to find a feminine symbolic. In order to understand what motivates this disagreement, however, it is first necessary to point out the similarities in their positions. Both Braidotti and Lloyd reject the once popular stark dualism of sex as biological and of gender as social. This dualism supports a conception of gender as free floating with no connection to bodily differences. Lloyd argues that this account of gender tends to give rise to an erasure of femaleness under a 'human' male norm. Seeing gender as an arbitrary and infinitely malleable social construction encourages a politics of equality based on the disappearance of distinctions of gender, which too often merely recapitulate the equation of masculinity with humanity (1989: 15). Similarly Braidotti criticizes gender theorists for their social reductivism (1994: 153). At the same time Braidotti and Lloyd agree that any account of the subject should take seriously the fact that as human beings we are embodied beings – without thereby naturalizing sexual stereotypes.

What is needed is an account of gender which relates it to sexed bodies. For this purpose the notion of the body must be brought into focus. Lloyd wants to resist two opposite views of the body. The first takes it to be 'natural' and irrelevant to the cultural symbolism surrounding gender, the second sees the body itself as a product of symbolic social construction (1989: 19). The first view understands the body as a biological entity whose features are completely independent of cultural interpretations. The second assimilates the body to language. It takes the body itself to be a representation. The attempt to find a third way of understanding what it means to be embodied is also shared by Braidotti.

Lloyd adopts a Spinozistic model. The body is seen as endowed with powers and pleasures. The mind is not separated from it. Rather the mind is understood as awareness of the body, and as elaborating an understanding of its powers and pleasures. This account of the individual is anti-Cartesian not just because it rejects a mind–body split, but also because it takes the mind to be multifaceted rather than unitary and simple. Since Lloyd follows Spinoza in seeing the mind as complex, she can say that the view that reason has no sex might embody a possibility for the future. Bodies are sexed, therefore some of their powers and pleasures will be sexually differentiated. It is to some extent appropriate to speak of male and female minds, since minds enact the powers and pleasures of the body. Bodies, however, are complex and minds reflect this fact. Some powers and pleasures will be the same in male and female bodies. Minds too 'can be alike in some respects, different in others' (1989: 21).

If the mind is an awareness of body, the subject's self-understanding cannot be floating free of bodily differences. At the same time, however, our own understanding of the body cannot simply take it as natural. Social factors can impose limitations on the body's pleasures and powers. They can do so by affecting the body directly, or by affecting the awareness of it in the mind. Social images or metaphors of sexual difference play a role in the mind's understanding of the body. Either way 'our bodies, *as they figure in our self-consciousness*, are always already socially constructed' [my italics] (1989: 20).

There is much in Lloyd's account of the subject that Braidotti would approve of. Nevertheless, the starting points of Braidotti's investigations are different and these are reflected in her conclusions. Braidotti emphasizes the challenge raised by psychoanalysis and post-structuralism to the traditional conception of the subject as a self-reflecting conscious self. Psychoanalysis disrupts the view of the subject as coincident with the rational self by analyzing the importance of desire in the constitution of subjectivity. Post-structuralism rejects the view that the subject precedes language. An individual can acquire a sense of self only through the incorporation of some of the meanings and representations made available by language.

Symbolic man and woman are some of these meanings which can be employed in the construction of subjectivity. They are metaphors that delineate what sort of speaking positions, what sort of subjectivities are currently available. Symbols play for Braidotti a fundamental role in the structuring of subjectivity. Following Irigaray, Braidotti believes that the current symbolic of the universal subject disguises the fact that the cultural images of the subject are male. The so-called sexless subject is not sexless at all, given the association of woman with sex.

Several factors are at the root of Braidotti's apparent rejection of Lloyd's claim that we should fight against the connections between metaphors of reason and sexual difference. The first is Braidotti's account of the embodied subject. For her, to take seriously the fact of embodiment, and the reality of bodily differences that flow from it, is to view reason as emerging from the desires of the sensuous body. Reason is therefore grounded on unreason, on desires which belong to the realm of the unconscious. Feminist psychoanalytic accounts of desire and the subject, for example Irigaray's, encourage a metaphysics that takes sexual difference to reverberate through every single aspects of our lives. The second factor is Braidotti's insistence that we cannot step outside the current cultural framework. Under the present circumstances, it is necessary to affirm sexual difference across the board. This latter disagreement with Lloyd can be interpreted as a matter of political strategy. Finally, I am inclined to believe that Braidotti, with all her insistence on the multilayered character of the subject, still derives the inevitability of sexual difference in regard to reason from the mere fact that we are essentially embodied. She seems to assume that since bodies are sexually differentiated, this difference must imply that an embodied reason is also sexed.

In her more recent work, Braidotti has explored the possibility of a genderless reason. This utopian conception, she holds, would require a new understanding of the body which does not make sexual difference its focus. For Braidotti, Donna Haraway's figure of the 'cyborg' offers this understanding. The cyborg 'is a creature in a postgender world' (Haraway, 1990: 192). It is partly organic and partly machine. Haraway uses the cyborg as a myth, a metaphor. It is a literary device to facilitate thinking about subjectivity in a new manner. The cyborg is not exactly a human being. It does not belong to our biological species. The unconscious and sexual difference do not play a role in understanding this creature. Similarly, traditional views of humanity do not apply. The cyborg cannot be understood either in terms of sexually specific ideals or in terms of the male, but supposedly universal, human norm. Nevertheless, the cyborg is a person. It is an agent.

Braidotti finds the metaphor of the cyborg useful for political analysis. The cyborg offers a non-humanistic view of the kind of agent required by politics (1994: 170). However, she claims that this figure does not help when we are concerned with the individual who constitutes herself by means of unconscious identifications. The notion of the cyborg 'announces a world "beyond gender,"' but it does not explain how that world can be reached from our 'gender-polarized system' (1994: 170). Furthermore, I would like to add, this distinction between identity, located at the personal level, and subjectivity, located at the political level, is similar to liberal distinctions between the private and the public spheres. The public has always been the domain of men, while women have often been identified with the private. Braidotti does not endorse this separation of roles, and she attempts to find ways of connecting the two levels (1994: 170). Nevertheless, her distinction is always in danger of being assimilated by traditional views, since it accepts that the political agent might become genderless, while the gendered individual is limited to the personal sphere.

On these issues Lloyd's Spinozistic conception of the relations between reason and the body appears more convincing. Nevertheless, one must remember Braidotti's claim that reason is never immune from power. Thus, we must be careful that when trying to realize a genderless reason we do not permit the opposition between reason and corporeality to be reinscribed through the identity-marker of race (Alcoff, 1995/6: 75). Feminist struggles with reason would have been in vain if the association between reason and whiteness were to be preserved.

Reason and the Philosophical Imaginary

I have said that, for Lloyd, philosophical metaphors of the ideal of reason construct femininity as what must be transcended. These metaphorical elaborations have real consequences for women. Furthermore, since philosophy conceives of itself as the queen of rational thought, it has also been based on the exclusion of the feminine. These processes of exclusion have been carefully analyzed by Le Doeuff. My interpretation of her account of the relations between women and philosophy does not always follow her text. Nevertheless, I think that what I say might meet with her approval. This discussion of Le Doeuff's analyses allows us to reconsider whether feminists should abandon philosophy to its own devices or whether they should try to change it.

Philosophers have been prone to making some very stupid comments when they explicitly addressed the topic of women. It would be easy to see these comments merely as an expression of misogynist attitudes. There is no doubt that misogyny is rife in philosophy. Nevertheless, these comments can also be read as symptomatic of an attitude, and an anxiety which is specific to philosophy itself. This interpretation is pursued by Le Doeuff, who believes that 'when philosophy discusses women, women are not the real subject' (1991: 13). 'Woman' is instead a metaphor, an image by means of which philosophy tries to keep at bay its own problems. The first problem for philosophy is its inability to cope with incompleteness; it aims to explain everything. It cannot accept that some things might exceed its limits (1989: 127). Le Doeuff suggests that the philosophical obsession with completeness might be a consequence of the fact that the impulse to philosophize stems from a lack (1989: 111). It finds its beginning in a disappointment with one's teachers, from whom one had hoped to learn true knowledge. Instead, one is made aware of one's own lack of experience, and the inability of the other (the teacher) to fill the gap (1989: 107). The impulse to philosophize is the impulse to think for oneself.

The sense of inadequacy that comes with the desire to do philosophy needs to be subdued. The traditional response to this anxiety has been to build by oneself systems of thought that attempted to explain everything. This is indeed a fragile strategy, which needs to be propped up all the time. What philosophy cannot explain, it must declare unphilosophical. Since philosophy is identified with rational propositional thought, it must relegate to images and metaphors what it cannot cope with. There is a level of the imaginary in philosophy which is specific to it. This is what Le Doeuff calls 'the philosophical imaginary.' These images do not just function to hide the incompleteness philosophy cannot accept, they also set 'the conditions of what can be constructed as rationality' within philosophy (1991: 23). Rationality is understood in terms of what it must exclude.

There is another dimension to the dream of achieving completeness. Philosophy might seem a worthwhile activity only if the dream is fulfilled. The philosopher, thus, sets for himself an impossible task; he sets himself up for a failure which renovates his own sense of inadequacy. The sense that philosophy is still worth doing is preserved by claiming that some are incapable of doing it. The image of 'woman' is used for this purpose. It is, Le Doeuff claims, 'the desire to assert the extreme worth of philosophy [which] gives rise to philosophers' sexist utterances' (1991: 26). When philosophers talk about women, the real topic is the value of philosophy. Hence,

> by affirming that 'woman' is incapable of philosophical thought and that it is no task for her, philosophers strengthen and reassure themselves with the idea that philosophy can do something and has a task, no need to state exactly what. The exclusion of someone maintains the structure, even if the structure is empty. (1991: 25)

The exclusion of women from philosophy, however, does not only take the simple form of prohibition. It is often more subtle, and it affects even those women who seem to have been allowed access to the discipline.

It might seem that the exclusion of women from philosophy is a doubly trivial problem. First, philosophy has excluded nearly everybody but a privileged white, male, upper middle-class elite. Secondly, it would seem that, in the context of the very many exclusions women have to endure, claiming access to an academic discipline should come very near the bottom of any feminist priority list. Le Doeuff is aware that a concern with women's status in philosophy seems to be something that only a few privileged women can share. Nevertheless, she argues that this should be an important concern for feminists.

There is something special about the exclusion of women from philosophy. It takes a different form from other exclusions, and it plays a different role for the discipline. Metaphorically woman symbolizes the incompleteness and indeterminacy that philosophy wants to keep at bay. Therefore, 'woman' has a special place in the philosophical imaginary. Furthermore, the philosophical ideal of rationality has been constructed out of these exclusions. On these matters Le Doeuff's position is not dissimilar to Lloyd's.

Le Doeuff also provides an account of the exclusion of real (middle-class, white) women from philosophy. The subtle form this exclusion takes is exemplified by the lives of past women philosophers. Hipparchia and de Beauvoir, for example, had love relationships with their male philosopher teacher. These women have not had access to philosophy, but to the philosophy of particular men. Both men and women are seduced to philosophy by means of an influential teacher (1989: 106). In the case of men, however, the love component is sublimated and turned into a desire for the discipline. In this way, men are capable of experiencing the lack which gives rise to the need to philosophize. Women, however, cannot achieve sublimation. The teacher, who has captured their desire, responds to it. He needs the adulation. In this manner, women are excluded from the experience of inadequacy from which philosophy stems.

This, I suppose, could be an argument for having more women teach philosophy in academic institutions. Le Doeuff suggests as much (1989: 120). There are, however, some dubious assumptions in this argument. It presupposes that knowledge requires the repression of erotic love, which is a Freudian conception of knowledge. Le Doeuff's employment of Freudian psychoanalysis to understand women of the past appears misplaced. In particular, it does not seem to apply to the Hellenic woman philosopher Hipparchia. The ideal relation between teacher and pupil in ancient Greece was understood in erotic terms. Plato argued that the way toward the love of wisdom (philosophy) was via the erotic love for one's male teacher. This form of love had to be transcended, but it was not repressed or sublimated. The Freudian model can be applied to Hipparchia only if one assumes that psychoanalysis embodies timeless truths about human psychology. I think this assumption is unwarranted.

Nevertheless, suppose Le Doeuff is right to say that there is something special about the exclusion of women, as opposed to other groups, from philosophy. Suppose she is also right that the exclusion from philosophy is different from the other kinds of exclusions women have had to endure. One may still ask: why should feminists care? The answer, according to Le Doeuff, is that feminism and philosophy are essentially linked to each other. Every feminist is a philosopher. A feminist is a woman who 'does not leave others to think for her' (1991: 29). The desire to judge for oneself is what is shared by the feminist and philosophical attitude. Philosophy, then, should matter to feminists. It embodies a tradition of thought which, despite its sexism, gets its inspiration from a desire that animates feminism.

There is a difference, however, between thinking for oneself and relying only on one's own thoughts. The desire for completeness of philosophy is generated by the need to think alone. It is this notion of autonomy in thinking that gives rise to the individualism I have criticized in chapter 2. There is no doubt, however, that the philosophical attitude also embodies the desire to think for oneself. This is a desire that can be satisfied in collaboration. When the philosopher realizes that he does not have to do everything by himself, perhaps, the obsession with systems which purport to explain everything will subside. Such a change of attitude will make it possible to admit within philosophy that some things can not be known. It will not be necessary to suppress what is undetermined by means of images and metaphors. Philosophy, as the exercise of rational thought, will continue; but it will be less obsessed with a conception of rationality that privileges abstract thinking over other forms of rational cognition.

Granted, one may say. But still, why bother to change from within a discipline that has been particularly hostile to women? Because it can be done. Not everybody is interested, and rightly so. There are many ways and traditions for feminist thought to develop. But, for those of us for whom the philosophical 'exercise of thought is sometimes a very joyful . . . activity' (1991: 8), there is no choice. And although, as Le Doeuff says, it may sound naive, the desire to philosophize can impose itself upon us. And, if we stay in the discipline, we do not want to repeat old views about female difference and its complementary role to male reason. The best way forward is a rational and political critique of old philosophical views, including those concerned with ideals of rationality.

Further Reading

Genevieve Lloyd's *The Man of Reason: 'Male' and 'Female' in Western Philosophy* (1984) provides the best historical account of the metaphorical associations between reason and maleness. Linda Alcoff's 'Is the Feminist Critique of Reason Rational?' (1995/6) offers an excellent overview of feminist critiques of reason. The exclusion of women from philosophy is examined by Michèle Le Doeuff 's 'Long Hair, Short Ideas' in *The Philosophical Imaginary* (1989).

Notes

1   Martha Nussbaum's (1994) review of some recent feminist work on reason is a good example of the sort of tone employed, at times, in these debates.
2   McMillan (1982) is a good example.
3   Descartes himself often used 'thinking' to encompass much more than methodical reason. But he also used 'thinking' as that which is restricted to this mode of reasoning. These shifts are indicative of the Cartesian attempt to model all our cognitive abilities on abstract thinking. In this respect Margaret Atherton's (1993) criticism of Lloyd is off the mark.
4   For a discussion of these interpretations, see Atherton (1993).
5   An example is offered by Atherton (1993).
6   Thus, although Christine Battersby's remark that romantics associated woman with rationality might be an objection to the view that reason has always been understood in terms of metaphors of maleness, it confirms the point that somehow all the metaphors concerning reason have involved sexual difference (1989: 113).
7   Conscious access to the grounds of belief is required by internalist epistemologies. The deontological conception of justification presupposes that beliefs are under our voluntary control. I have mentioned these features of traditional epistemology in chapter 1.

10

Feminism and Postmodernism

What is postmodernism? The more the term is used the less clear it becomes. It is, therefore, not easy to explain its complex relations to feminism. There seems to be a battle within Anglo-American feminism with regard to its stance toward postmodernism. Some feminists, like Seyla Benhabib or Sabina Lovibond, are vehemently opposed; others, for example Jane Flax and Susan Hekman, have articulated a qualified acceptance. But often what is rejected or partly accepted is not the same. Debates, internal to feminism, about postmodernism reveal different conceptions of this position. It is, therefore, difficult to provide a fair description of these views.

In this chapter I focus my discussion on North American feminists who have expressed in their work some sympathy for postmodernist views. I also consider only those aspects of postmodernism which, in my opinion, raise important questions about knowledge and epistemology. The reason motivating the latter choice should be apparent, since this book is concerned with theories of knowledge. The first decision stems from my belief that postmodernism is a North American creation. I cannot fully justify this claim here; but I can provide some reasons for it. Jacques Lacan, Luce Irigaray, Julia Kristeva, Jacques Derrida, and Michel Foucault, among others, never used, to my knowledge, the term 'postmodernism' to characterize their views. Furthermore, their positions on many issues are incompatible. For example, Foucault's views on the subject are opposed to Lacan's statements on this topic. Postmodernism is a *bricolage* of some of their opinions, which has been assembled in the United States. Jean-François Lyotard, a French philosopher, has written about the postmodern condition; that is, the situation encountered by those who live in postmodernity. But he has not taken his philosophical views to constitute a new theory called 'postmodernism.' As a theoretical position about the self, language, knowledge, truth, and power, postmodernism has been developed in the United States.

These comments are not intended to be derogatory. Firstly, feminists who have endorsed postmodernism recognize the differences in opinion among the philosophers whose views they discuss. For example, Hekman acknowledges the differences between Derrida and Foucault, while claiming that it is 'nevertheless possible to define common themes among them' (1990: 8). Secondly, postmodernists themselves have talked about bricolage in approving terms.

Since postmodernism means different things to different people, it is hard to explain the content of this position. It is easier to capture its mood. Postmodernism is a negative, skeptical view. For some it is also the embodiment of a hope for the new. Mainly, however, it is a rejection of the old ways. The preferred target is the project of the Enlightenment. I have already presented in chapter 7 an outline of this project. One could, perhaps, summarize it in a slogan: it is the promise that the autonomous use of reason will make us free. This catchy motto, however, is rather unfair. It attempts to summarize in a few words what has been a very varied tradition. It is a tradition whose track record is, without any doubts, checkered. Its promoters, who supported the emancipation of Man, forgot all women and non-European people.

There is also no doubt that this forgetting was no mere oversight. Nevertheless, as I shall argue, it remains an open question whether the project of the Enlightenment should be jettisoned altogether. This is a pressing question, above all, for the feminist movement, which initially understood itself as a movement for the emancipation of women. Hence if feminism is to reject the ideals of the Enlightenment, it must in some sense also abandon those ideals which animated the early history of the feminist movement itself. The debates about postmodernism within feminism can be read as disputes about whether feminism should break with its own past.

Of course, the history of feminism has also been checkered. The feminist movement has, for a long time, ignored differences among women. Rather, it has functioned as the movement of white middle-class women. Nevertheless, it would be a mistake to ignore or minimize the achievements of that movement. Furthermore, postmodernism is, in my opinion, not very useful when one attempts to develop a new political alternative. Here lies the political problem for feminists who want to take seriously some of the claims made by postmodernism. As an approach postmodernism is a sort of skeptical quietism. It attempts to capture the mood of the times. It expresses a quite widespread loss of faith in big ideals, and theories. Perhaps as a diagnosis it is correct. That does not mean that resigned acceptance is the right attitude to take in this situation.

In this chapter I focus on the two issues that characterize the debate within feminism about postmodernism and knowledge. The first concerns the normative dimension of knowledge. The second concerns the subject of knowledge. Postmodern thinkers often claim that traditional epistemology must be debunked, and that nothing which is in any respect similar to it should take its place. They make this claim at a time when epistemology is a flourishing area of study in feminist theory. In this chapter I argue in favor of several claims made by postmodern feminists on the issues of knowledge and subjectivity. I also claim that many of the conclusions they appear to draw from these claims are unwarranted, and should be rejected.

Epistemology: Rejection or Transformation?

Postmodernism is a philosophy of endings. It proclaims the end of philosophy, metaphysics, epistemology, and of other old time favorites. The end of the second millennium of the christian era is in sight. Postmodernism is the expression of the sense of exhaustion which characterizes these times. There is no univocal postmodern position. Rather, postmodernism is the attempt to come to terms with the current situation. The starting point of reflection is nearly always the West. Attention is concentrated on the state of liberal democracies in advanced capitalist societies. It is argued that the ideals which sustained the development of these nations have come to grief. The values of reason, progress, and human rights endorsed by the Enlightenment have shown their dark side. The West exemplifies the disasters brought about by modernity.

The idea that the Western world is fast moving toward decadence, exhaustion, and horror is not new. It was expressed in prophetic tones by Nietzsche nearly a hundred years ago. The label 'postmodernist' has been applied to those philosophers who have developed further Nietzsche's pessimistic views about European culture. Hence, thinkers who have very little in common have been grouped under this term.

The starting points of many discussions about postmodernism are two alleged old illusions: the belief in a masterful, self-conscious, and universal subject; and the belief that justification or reason has no connection with power or force. Once these two illusions are unmasked, innocence is lost.

I discussed the first illusion in chapter 9, and the second in chapter 8. In both cases I have argued in favor of loss of innocence. In this chapter I am primarily concerned with the conclusions one can warrantedly draw from these claims. I argue that one must resist the view that rationality is always rationalization, and that the subject is completely dominated by forces external to her conscious grasp. The claim that reason is never completely innocent of power and desires for mastery is different from the assertion that reason is merely a mask for domination. Further, the rejection of a subject who is always self-conscious and in control does not entail that subjects have no autonomy.

It is not clear whether any feminist postmodernist asserts the nihilistic conclusions I want to resist. However, Flax and Hekman make several ambiguous claims that can be reasonably interpreted in this manner. In what follows I analyze their positions, and disentangle the different meanings that can be attributed to their claims. I discuss their definitions of postmodernism, and of epistemology, and assess their views about the theory of knowledge as an evaluative enterprise.

For Hekman, postmodernism challenges the tradition of the Enlightenment: it 'question[s] the foundationalism and absolutism of modernism' (1990: 1); it rejects 'the fundamental dichotomies of Enlightenment thought, dichotomies such as rational/irrational and subject/object' (1990: 2). These ideas are not entirely new. For example, in chapter 1 I have shown that Heidegger, who cannot really be classified as a postmodernist, developed an epistemology that does not presuppose a stark opposition between subject and object. I mention this point because supporters of postmodernism tend to present their views as if they were a novelty. When they do so, they betray their modernism. In literature and in the fine arts modernism has been characterized as the rebellion against tradition, as the search for the shock of the new. In this regard, postmodernism is all too modern.

The relation between epistemology and postmodernism is, according to Hekman, rather problematic. Postmodern thinkers do not engage in epistemology as defined by the Enlightenment. Hekman also claims that 'a postmodern approach to feminist issues entails the attempt to formulate not an "epistemology" in the sense of a replacement of the Enlightenment conception, but, rather, an explanation of the discursive processes by which human beings gain understanding of their common world' (1990: 9). Therefore, according to Hekman, postmodern reflection on knowledge does not attempt to serve the same purposes as traditional epistemology. Postmodern theories of knowledge are not simply different from those advanced by Enlightenment thinkers, they have different objectives. They do not try to replace traditional epistemological views.

In this book I have defined epistemology as a theory of knowledge that has a normative character. Epistemology presupposes that there is a difference between what we merely take to be knowledge, and real knowledge. I want to examine whether Hekman's postmodern theory of knowledge acknowledges this difference. Her account is, in essence, Foucauldian. She takes the study of knowledge to be the study of discursive formations. For Foucault, discursive formations are systems of rules governing the relations among statements, and between claims and practical activities. For example, the biological sciences, which I have discussed in chapter 8, are a kind of discourse structured by a discursive formation. This formation includes rules about how to make experiments which regulate the practical activities of biologists. It also exhibits rules concerning the relations between experimental results and claims. These rules are intended to prescribe which conclusions a scientist can draw from her experiments. Finally, discursive formations contain rules of inference, that tell us which claims are entailed by any specific claim. The theory of knowledge, according to Hekman, studies these systems of rules. In particular, it analyses 'the kind of power/knowledge nexus that characterizes' each discursive formation (1990: 19). These analyses would show that discourses 'create subjects, objects, and regimens of power and truth' (1990: 19). They demonstrate that 'all knowledge is contextual and historical' (1990: 153).

Hekman, like Foucault, is concerned with an examination of the relations between power and knowledge. The dependence of modern laboratory science on disciplinary power, which I discussed in chapter 8, would constitute an example of these relations. I have argued that laboratory science yields knowledge only in contexts shaped by power relations, which are then exported to the world outside the laboratory. Scientific knowledge, I have claimed, is socially constituted. It is, as Hekman says, contextual and historical. These claims, however, do not settle the epistemological question. They do not show whether Hekman acknowledges the distinction between knowledge and what we merely take to be knowledge. In chapter 8 I argued that novel power relations sometimes constitute knowledge as in the case, say, of high-response crops. I have also claimed that sometimes these relations only give rise to statements that purport to be knowledge when they are not. I have presented the biological study of race as an example of this phenomenon. Knowledge of hybrid plant varieties and presumed knowledge of biological race are both dangerous. Both truth and error sometimes have bad political consequences. They must, however, be distinguished. One resists biological theories about race by, among other things, arguing that they are mistaken. Resistance to the introduction of hybrid crops in non-Western agriculture takes a different form. One must argue that these crops produce high yields only under conditions which would spell the end of many local practices that, for political reasons, we want to preserve. These distinctions are fundamental when we try to articulate the forms that oppositions to dominant views should take.

Hekman's study of human practices for the production of knowledge, and of their relations to power, constitutes an epistemology only if it helps to make these distinctions. I would argue that Hekman is deeply ambiguous on this point. Firstly, there is no doubt that Hekman does not intend to abolish evaluative distinctions. She claims with Gadamer that one can reject epistemological absolutism without believing that any interpretation is as good as any other (1990: 15). She also argues that Foucault's views offer a critique of oppressive claims to knowledge (1990: 183). Therefore, Hekman wishes to make a distinction between legitimate and illegitimate claims. It remains to be seen, however, whether her study of knowledge supports this distinction.

Hekman claims that postmodern discursive theories of knowledge describe knowledge and its acquisition (1990: 1). For her, we must be concerned with historical investigations of knowledge that are genealogical (1990: 183). In other words, Hekman believes that we must describe the history of our epistemic practices, and we must unearth the fields of power that make these practices possible. However, she also seems to believe that the theory of knowledge must not attempt to go beyond these descriptions. Instead, I would like to argue that they constitute only part of epistemology, which is also concerned with an evaluation of these practices.

Hekman points out that her theory of knowledge does not rule out the possibility of resistance. She claims that 'postmodernism's discourse theory of knowledge presents an understanding of language as fluid and multiple. . . . The gaps, silences and ambiguities of discourses provide the possibility for resistance . . . Within these silences and gaps new discourses can be formulated that challenge the dominant discourse' (1990: 189–90). For example, Foucault provides the means for 'the creation of a discourse that does not constitute women as inferior' (1990: 21). The critics of postmodernism, however, have never disputed these claims. They do not argue that postmodernism prohibits talking about issues in new ways; rather, they claim that it gives us no reason to believe that these alternatives are better than what they try to supplant. The dispute is not about whether postmodernism offers the means to resist dominant discourses, but whether it can show resistance to be legitimate.

Hekman has claimed that some interpretations are better than others. Thus, she must hold that we can evaluate interpretations. It should be possible to provide reasons why in a given case resistance to dominant discourses is to be preferred to compliance. On this issue, Hekman's analysis is deeply unsatisfactory. She believes that dominant discourses should always be opposed. This belief would be correct if 'dominant' meant oppressive. Hekman instead thinks that since 'power [is] everywhere, [it] must be opposed everywhere' (1990: 186). Thus, for her, power is always bad. Hekman mistakenly attributes this view to Foucault who, instead, claimed that power is always dangerous, it is not necessarily bad. For him, oppressive forms of power must be resisted. Resistance, if successful, would bring about new power relations that are supposed to be less oppressive. But, Foucault reminds us, we must be aware that power is dangerous; thus, we must be alert to the fact that resistance might have generated new forms of oppression.

Hekman also displays a high degree of political naiveté when she claims that, for Foucault, 'in all cases . . . the specific instance of oppression will generate a specific resistance to that oppression. The oppression produces the resistance, no other grounding is required' (1990: 185). There is no automatic connection between oppression and resistance, and Foucault never claimed that there was. Rather, he insisted that no form of oppression can be so successful so that to make resistance absolutely impossible. Hekman's remark suggests that she thinks that real resistance to oppression emerges spontaneously. It is likely that Hekman would resist this interpretation of her position. Nevertheless, I think that Hekman fails to notice that in order to resist oppressive power relations one must be able to explain why they are oppressive, and to find out how they can be subverted. The first explanation requires that we differentiate between different forms of power. Since the knowledge produced by the oppressed also generates power, we must be able to distinguish between it and the sort of power relations which must be opposed. This is why Foucault never said that power is always bad. Furthermore, oppression does not, on its own, produce resistance. The struggle against subjugation requires evaluative judgment. One must distinguish between different forms of oppression. For example, the fight against racism requires many diverse approaches. Appiah's work to demonstrate that biological theories of race are false is a part of that struggle. The attempt to preserve farming communities in Africa, instead, will not involve disputing biological

theories about hybrid crop varieties. Resisters will point out, however, that
these theories are an example of local knowledge. They will argue that the
price one must pay to export these theories to the African environment is
morally and political unacceptable. The fight against oppression, thus,
requires that we make epistemological distinctions between knowledge and
what people mistakenly believe is knowledge. At the same time, one must
recognize the contextual and socially constructed character of all knowledge. Thus, as Hekman claims, resistance must be tailor-made, it must be
specific to the form of oppression it opposes. We do not need grand
theories about all kinds of oppression to understand one form of subjugation. However, it is precisely because there is no recipe for liberation that
epistemic evaluation is of fundamental importance. Each time one must
judge whether a field of power relations is oppressive, one must evaluate
whether one is fighting against false theories.

These questions must always be addressed. They rely on epistemic
distinctions which cannot be avoided. A theory of knowledge that employs
the insights offered by Foucault has to provide answers to them. Hence,
postmodern and Enlightenment epistemology must have something in
common. They must both provide the tools one can use to judge whether
claims that are presented as knowledge are warranted. Postmodernists reject
foundationalist accounts of warrant, they also refuse to provide universal
recipes that can be applied in every case. But, they must provide contextual
accounts of justification. Otherwise, their position would become identical
to the caricatures some of their critics supply.

Hekman avoids answering these questions. She does not explicitly state
that they are illegitimate, but she does not address them. Instead, she does
not appear to see what they are. If power were always bad, and oppression
always generated resistance, these questions would not even arise. But
power is dangerous, not necessarily bad; while resistance is always possible,
never automatic. These questions, therefore, are vital. Hekman's confusion
on these issues is most evident when she address the dualism between
rationality and irrationality.

Postmodernism, according to Hekman, challenges the rational/irrational
dichotomy (1990: 2). It must first be said that the dualism of rational and
irrational has never been understood, properly speaking, as a dichotomy.
For example, blind and sighted do not constitute a dichotomy because
some things – trees, for instance – are neither blind nor have sight.
Similarly, according to the tradition Hekman opposes, some things, like
stones, are neither rational nor irrational.

The Enlightenment tradition distinguishes rational from irrational, it assumes that rationality can exist without irrationality, and values rationality over irrationality. For Hekman, postmodernists argue that this dualism should be dissolved (1990: 5) or displaced (1997: 17). She also explains that to displace an opposition does not involve erasing the categories employed by the dualism thus displaced (1990: 26). Thus Hekman does not wish to abolish the distinction between irrational and rational. She is also particularly critical of any attempt to reverse the value judgment implicit in this dualism, while preserving its nature (1990: 41). Hence, Hekman does not value irrationality over rationality. She must, therefore, be rejecting the Enlightenment belief that rationality can exist without irrationality. There are at least two ways to interpret the claim made by the Enlightenment tradition, and two corresponding interpretations for its denial. Firstly, it could mean that an individual might attain full rationality. Such a person would have no unconscious desires, no unjustified anxieties. After Freud, this empirical claim about human psychology would not find many supporters. Secondly, the claim, made by Enlightenment thinkers, might mean that rationality does not require or presuppose in any way irrationality in order to exist. It is this latter claim, I believe, that Hekman thinks is undermined by postmodernist arguments.

Her discussion of Gadamer's views illustrates this point. For Gadamer all understanding is rooted in tradition and prejudice or prejudgment (1990: 14). Rational agreements and disagreements presuppose prejudgments, and could not exist without them. In order to have a rational conversation individuals must share an enormously large number of unargued assumptions. The vast majority of these assumptions will seem trivial. For example, we assume that our conversants do not believe that everything they experience is a fiction of their imagination. Some assumptions will be shared only by members of one culture. We assume people will understand references to news items, TV programs, or popular entertainment. These assumptions are usually left unspoken, but without them, agreement or disagreement could not exist. This observation, however, does not support the view that rationality requires irrationality, and could not exist without it. Hekman, I am inclined to believe, thinks it does. I attribute this view to her, because I cannot see any other way of reading her claims about the displacement of the irrational/rational dualism that would support her view that Gadamer provides such a displacement.

The bedrock of unspoken agreement that makes rational conversation possible is not irrational. For Gadamer some of these unspoken assumptions are legitimate, and some are not (1990: 15). Those that are legitimate must be rational, the others might be false or wrong. Hence, Gadamer has not shown that in every case rational conversation presupposes some irrational assumptions. Gadamer, instead, has shown that explicit rational agreement and disagreement presuppose implicit, but equally rational, agreement. Alternatively, if we decide to say that a claim is rational only if we have provided reasons for it, the bedrock of agreement is neither rational nor irrational. It is, however, something which can be subjected to rational evaluation.

Gadamer, therefore, has not displaced a dualism. Instead, he has provided a definition of rationality that, like its Enlightenment counterpart, does not require the existence of irrationality. There is nothing particularly postmodernist about Gadamer's position; Wittgenstein, for example, made the same point. However, since Hekman thinks that Gadamer has shown that there is a germ of irrationality in rationality, she believes that she has found a way to avoid the epistemic issues I have raised above. However, even if postmodern theorists reject foundationalist, non-contextual accounts of justification and reason, they still owe us explanations of contextual, socially constituted forms of rationality and warrant. They must also show how rational statements differ from irrational claims which present themselves as rational. Hence, Hekman is deeply, and I would add, dangerously mistaken when she claims that 'if we assume, as the postmoderns do, that knowledge is not in need of absolute foundations, then the charge of nihilism, like that of relativism, becomes irrelevant' (1990: 153). I have argued that, on the contrary, these issues become especially pressing. Hekman dismisses them by claiming that postmodern knowledge is neither absolute nor relative (1990: 134). This claim is inconsistent with her views about displacing dualisms. For her, a dualism is displaced when the categories that constitute it are not erased. And yet, this is precisely what she does when she avoids dealing with pertinent objections.

For these reasons, among others, Hekman's portrait of feminist epistemology is deeply unfair. She often depicts it as 'an epistemology that privileges the feminine as opposed to one that privileges the masculine' (1990: 9). I do not deny that some feminists have held this position. Hekman, however, seems to think that whoever is concerned with questions of warrant and justification must subscribe to it. I have argued, instead, that those North American postmodernists, who think that they can avoid these questions, are deeply mistaken.

Similar problems are raised by Jane Flax's view that in epistemology we must shift 'the discussion away from the relations between knowledge and truth to those between knowledge, desire, fantasy, and power of various kinds' (1993: 143). I interpret this claim to mean that the theory of knowledge should not be concerned with normative notions, like justification, but with psychoanalytic and social factors, such as unconscious desires and power relations. I believe this view to be mistaken (and politically dangerous) for the same reasons I have given to support my disagreement with Hekman. In what follows I discuss Flax's account of postmodernism, and her position about knowledge. I analyse her views because they embody a negative attitude toward feminist epistemology. Some of her criticisms, I believe, are important and should be taken into account; others, I argue, should be rejected.

I have derived my characterization of postmodernism as a philosophy of endings from Flax's description of this position. She provides an overview of postmodernism by means of three theses: the death of Man, the death of History, and the death of Metaphysics (1991: 32–7). Flax describes under each thesis a variety of positions of differing strengths. Some of these positions are acceptable to most feminists, others have been taken to be incompatible with feminist aims. However, all of them undermine the traditional conception of epistemology and the Cartesian conception of the self.

When Flax talks about the 'death of Man' she is referring to the concept of the subject explored by Foucault in *The Order of Things* (1970). Man – the subject – is the individual capable of finding in himself the grounds for justification. The subject is the autonomous knower who does not rely on others to acquire knowledge. Appeals to his own reason are sufficient to justify his claims. Flax holds that postmodern theory has shown that this transcendental conception of the subject is fictitious; this conception is a social artefact. In its place, postmodernist thinkers propose a view of the subject as 'decentered.' According to this position, the individual's 'attempts to impose a fictive or narrative order . . . on [her] experience . . . is preconstituted and undermined' by forces that are beyond her control: the unconscious, power, and language (1991: 32). Therefore, subjective experience is always fractured or fragmented since external forces undermine the subject's disposition for order. Furthermore, these forces preconstitute the limited order that can be imposed on subjective experience. Postmodernists thus conclude that 'the subject is merely another position in language' (1991: 32). Once this thinning out of the notion of the subject has been accepted, according to Flax, it becomes impossible to subscribe to old epistemological conceptions. Instead, one must come to terms with the fact that there is 'no moment of autonomy, no pure reason or constituting consciousness with independent, nonlinguistic, or nonhistorical access to the Real or Being of the World' (1991: 33).

Postmodernists, in Flax's account, reject an old fashioned conception of the subject and put in its place a new one. Critics, in particular Benhabib (1995), carefully articulate conceptual distinctions about the different positions which one may occupy on these issues. Benhabib points out that there can be two versions of the thesis that Man is dead. A weaker version 'would situate the subject in the context of various social, linguistic and discursive practices' (1995: 20). The character of subjectivity, therefore, would be unintelligible outside the context of the cultures within which it is formed. The stronger version of this thesis would claim that subjectivity is determined by power, language, and the unconscious. This stronger version, according to Benhabib, entails 'the dissolution of the subject,' and along with it 'disappear of course concepts of intentionality, accountability, self-reflexivity, and autonomy' (1995: 20). In other words, although people often explain what they do in terms of their conscious choices, if this thesis is true, they are always deluded. The correct explanations of human actions would always make reference only to factors over which the person has no control. Benhabib observes that this second version of the death of Man denies agency, since it takes individuals to be determined by social circumstances. Therefore, Benhabib concludes, this stronger version is not compatible with the political aims of feminism (1995: 20). I pursue this discussion about subjectivity in the next section.

The 'death of History' is the second thesis which for Flax characterizes postmodernist theories. This thesis has several aspects. Firstly, it involves a rejection of a conception of history in terms of inevitable progress toward perfection in human society (1991: 33). This aspect of the thesis is relatively uncontroversial. Few would nowadays believe that the history of humanity has been marked by steady improvement. Second, the thesis also explicates the reasons for taking history to be always progressive. Belief in progress functioned as a justificatory strategy. It could legitimize the present as the culmination of human development up to that point in time. It could also be used to justify change, when some group claimed that the forces of history were on its side. Communism is the clearest example of an ideology that has employed both of these strategies. This use of history as a justificatory narrative encourages a linear account of human history. This narrative presupposes that there is a predetermined state of human perfection, a given goal toward which history is moving. It thus tends to explain all historical events in terms of the same causes, which move history along toward its destiny (Flax, 1991: 33).

On this point feminists are quite united. This traditional account of history as progress is an illusion. It is also dangerous because it can be employed by one group to claim that their interests coincide in the long run with the interests of humanity as a whole. Their dominance, this group may say, is a necessary step in the course of history toward perfection. This view of history has been and can be used to justify violence and oppression. The belief in progress, typical of Enlightenment thought, has a dark side. It can breed domination. Some of the critics of the traditional conception of history, however, do not only reject the notion of progress it embeds, they also object to some of its more general features. They have, for example, argued against any historical account that aims to be global. As Benhabib has pointed out, these two objections are conceptually distinct (1995: 23). One may still provide large scale historical accounts without endorsing the traditional approach which sees history as a matter of progress. In particular, given the long history and pervasiveness of sexism, it does not seem possible to understand it without trying to understand global and long-term phenomena (Fraser and Nicholson, 1990: 34). Thus, feminism seems to require global historical accounts, it cannot be restricted to local explanations.

The 'death of History' thesis also raises another pressing issue for feminists. It concerns the role played by social historical accounts independently of whether they are local or global. Traditional historical narratives had justificatory aims. Flax takes the lesson imparted by postmodernism to be that justificatory accounts must be abandoned. What takes their place is a genealogy with no normative dimension (1993: 143). For Flax the problem lies with the attempt to pass judgment on the validity of claims made within a culture or a practice. Each culture or practice will have its criteria about what is right and what is wrong, what is justified and what is not. There is no appeal outside these criteria (1993: 138). Theories might make them explicit, might explain their genesis. What they cannot do, however, is evaluate them. Or more precisely, any theoretical attempt at validation is an excuse for an imposition of one's own criteria. It is a matter of interests and force, not of reason. Flax reaches this conclusion because she believes that 'there is no way to test whether one story is closer to the truth than another because there is no transcendental standpoint or mind unencumbered by its own language and stories' (1993: 139). Thus, Flax seems to relinquish the normative dimension of criticism.

In my opinion this conclusion is unwarranted. Firstly, traditional historical narratives offered a special kind of justification. Since they explained history in terms of progress, they legitimated every facet of history. Anything that happened was seen as a necessary step toward the betterment of human society. These narratives, therefore, could be employed by dominant groups to justify their dominance as a good thing. This use of history to legitimize the victory of the powerful, however, is dependent on the optimistic notion of progress. It does not follow that any attempt to justify the actions of an individual or a group is always a mask for the imposition of force. Instead, evaluation is required to explain why the victors might not have been right. Second, the stark opposition between transcendental justificatory theories and merely descriptive projects is a false antithesis. We do not have to acquiesce in the criteria adopted by our culture: what the majority says is right is not necessarily so. However, we cannot claim direct and privileged access to notions of rightness and justification which would inhabit Platonic heavens. The search for this middle ground animates much feminist reflection on these issues. Usually, the middle ground is given the name of situated criticism. I shall return to this issue after I have discussed the third thesis which for Flax is characteristic of postmodernism.

This thesis is the 'death of metaphysics.' The label is misleading, since this thesis amounts to a rejection of all the main features of modern philosophy. It goes beyond a repudiation of metaphysics. Modern philosophy is centered on epistemology. Further, the theory of knowledge is seen as a first philosophy. In the first chapter I have distinguished two interpretations of this notion, and Flax attacks both of them. She rejects the view that it is possible to find out from the armchair features which always pertain to real knowledge, and distinguish it from what is merely pretended knowledge (1991: 35). She also objects to the view that takes the theory of knowledge itself to bestow legitimacy to all other knowledge (1991: 34). Foundationalism, the view that all knowledge is based on foundations, is another feature of modern epistemology which Flax rejects. She claims that 'there are no immediate or indubitable features of mental life. Sense data, ideas, intentions are already preconstituted' (1991: 35). There are no mental states which could count as knowledge independently of other bits of knowledge.

The rejection of indubitable foundations for all knowledge also entails the demise of a Cartesian conception of the mind as transparent to the knower. Instead, Flax holds that 'what we call the mind or reason is only an effect of discourse' (1991: 35). As a consequence, 'the categories or concepts by and through which we structure experience are themselves historically and culturally variable' (1991: 35). Flax's view about the mind, however, is not the only alternative open to those who wish to reject the Cartesian conception. In particular, as I have already argued in chapter 9, reason could be socially constituted without being an effect of discourses. I suspect that Flax's position is motivated by her rejection of epistemology as an evaluative enterprise.

Flax outlines the metaphysics presupposed by modern epistemological theories. It is the view that reality is composed of things which exist in themselves independently of the knower. Further, knowledge is a mirroring relation between the mind and reality (1991: 34). Flax and postmodernist thinkers are not alone in rejecting this view of the world and of our cognitive relationships to it. At least since Kant, many philosophers have criticized modern epistemology and metaphysics, and attempted to provide alternatives to them. For example, Hegel rejected foundationalism, and also argued that knowledge must be socially situated. Heidegger argued that the world is primarily a world of human involvements, rather than of things in themselves. He also rejected the view that knowing is a matter of mirroring reality. More recently, Quine has argued against any conception of epistemology as first philosophy. Feminist epistemologists have further elaborated these critiques, and provided alternative views about justification, reality, and the mind.

The novelty introduced by the kind of postmodernism endorsed by Flax seems to be a belief that philosophy has nothing to contribute to the study of knowledge. Rorty has explicitly advocated this view (1979: 176), but it is also a consequence of Flax's claim that 'philosophy is necessarily a fictive, nonrepresentational activity' (1991: 37). For her,

> as a product of the human mind, philosophy has no special relation to Truth or the Real. The philosopher merely creates stories about these concepts and about his own activities. His stories are no more true than any other. There is no way to test whether one story is closer to the truth than another because there is no transcendental standpoint or mind unenmeshed in its own story. (1991: 37)

Since philosophical theories of knowledge are intended to provide guidelines for the evaluation of beliefs and claims so as to find out whether they are legitimate, if there is no way of making such distinctions, these theories are worthless. But, the price to pay for holding this postmodernist view seems to be unbridled relativism. Such a position, I have already argued, is politically dangerous. It is also likely to be self-refuting since it entails its own fictional status.

It must be noted, however, that it is not always clear whether Flax actually holds these beliefs. It certainly seems premature to conclude that any view is as good as any other because there are no things in themselves (the Real) and no transcendental subjects, as Flax seems to do in the passage cited above. One cannot dismiss out of hand the many attempts to provide culturally situated criteria for evaluation. Perhaps then, Flax only intends to claim that beliefs cannot be evaluated for their truth, but they can be evaluated for other features. For example, we might be able to judge them for their legitimacy, we might be able to discriminate which views are more adequate.

Flax herself does not refrain from talking about evaluation, adequacy, and legitimacy. Hence she does not appear to endorse relativism. For example, she holds that 'the legitimacy or authority of a knowledge claim arises out of and depends upon a set of linguistic practices and communicative interactions' (1991: 38). Flax must hold that some claims, but not others, are legitimate. Thus, one could interpret her seemingly relativist claims to deny the existence of a universal recipe for evaluation, while allowing contextual accounts of justification. This reading of her position is confirmed by Flax's claim that

> philosophy may be able to describe how understanding is possible in particular contexts; it cannot create a universalizing theory of knowledge (an epistemology) that can ground and account for all knowledge or test all truth claims because these are necessarily context dependent. Pragmatics, knowing how we understand one another and the different ways we do so, should replace epistemology. (1991: 38)

There is no universal theory of justification, because justification is always context dependent. Within a particular context, furthermore, evaluation should be understood in terms of know how, rather than, for example, following explicitly formulated rules or methods.[1] Flax's views thus seem to be very similar to the Heideggerian position I have advocated in this book.

This position encourages us to see all knowledge as practical knowledge. In particular, theoretical knowledge is taken to be a matter of knowing how to make and defend assertions. There are no absolute criteria of justification; rather, a vast background of social practices contributes in each case to the legitimacy of our beliefs. In a given context a defense of a particular claim will count as gaining an entitlement to it; within a different background what may seem to be the same defense could nevertheless fail. For example, imagine a society where women are presumed to be unreliable witnesses. In that society if I were to defend a claim on the basis of my observations, I would fail to gain entitlement to it. My defense is not granted any legitimacy, even if it should be. In cases such as this one the best course of action might be a political effort to change the social cultural practice that casts women in the role of unreliable observers. Were such a political struggle to succeed, claims made by women would acquire a different significance. The epistemic practices adopted by that society would have undergone some change. Thus, although the best way to modify the epistemic standards implicit in the practices of a community might not require that one engages in rational conversation about these standards with one's opponents, nevertheless it involves an acknowledgment that what society takes to be right might after all be wrong.

On this point the Heideggerian position I have endorsed differs from Flax's postmodernism. The standards of evaluation invoked by Flax are those which are already implicit in current practice. For this reason she believes that the role of philosophy is limited to a description of the sort of understanding which is licensed by current practices. Flax recognizes the importance of giving reasons why one view is better than another (1991: 42). But she holds that what can count as a reason is determined by current practices. Thus, Flax claims that each discourse has implicit rules for meaningfulness and truth. For her, 'the rules of a discourse enable us to make certain sorts of statements and to make truth claims. The same rules force us to remain within the system and to make only those statements that conform to these rules' (1993: 138). Of course, Flax recognizes the existence of several discourses which, she believes, are often mutually incommensurable. Speakers might be conversant with more than one discourse, and switch between them in their conversations. Nevertheless, what makes conflict resolution possible is prior agreement on rules to which we are forced to conform (1993: 138). I presume that Flax, despite these claims, would not exclude innovation altogether. However, she must believe that any change in the rules is arbitrary and cannot be justified. Ultimately, for Flax we cannot ever rationally judge current standards to be mistaken. I believe we can. This is not to say that we can occupy an absolute standpoint; it simply means that we can endorse changes in current practices. When we do so, we undertake commitments to gain entitlement to our claim. We can discharge our commitments in many ways. We can highlight internal contradictions in current standards, or we can give other reasons in favor of our proposal. We can also engage in political action which will bring about those changes in cultural practices that are necessary for our reasons to be seen as reasons.

Flax's view, instead, opens the door for widespread relativism. In her account there is no conceptual space for the distinction between real and merely presumed knowledge. Her position permits the distinction between claims licensed by current rules, and claims that are not authorized by these rules. It entails, however, that current rules cannot be epistemically evaluated. Thus Flax's view makes it impossible to say that society is wrong, and be right about this claim. One can criticize current practice, and, depending on one's political leverage, one may also succeed in achieving widespread acceptance of one's views. But, this is merely a pragmatic issue of power with no epistemic dimension. For this reason, Flax enjoins feminists to admit that 'what we really want is power in the world, not an innocent truth' (1992: 144). This conclusion is not only profoundly mistaken, it is also extremely dangerous for feminist politics. Flax's epistemological nihilism, like Hekman's, ultimately amounts (despite their protestations) to an endorsement of a status quo which cannot be rationally evaluated.

For these reasons Flax's utterly negative assessment of feminist epistemology is unwarranted. I do not think that those feminist epistemologists whose views I have discussed in this book believe in innocent truth. They are aware that all knowledge is dangerous; they do not separate epistemology from politics. Flax is mistaken to attribute to Harding the belief that 'the success of the feminist projects of creating effective analyses of gender and of ending gender-based domination' depends exclusively on developing epistemological theories (1993: 142). Harding is not unaware that political struggles are also necessary. *Pace* Flax, Harding does not confuse the need for justification with the need for power (1993: 144). Rather, Flax commits this error when she suggests that sometimes disagreements can be settled by the use of force alone (1993: 138). This might be true, but it leaves open the question whether the victors are right. To believe, as Flax does, that there is no answer to this further question is to accept the beliefs of the powerful. Enlightenment narratives of progress legitimized the viewpoint of the victorious by saying that their dominance was in the interest of all. Flax's postmodernism achieves the same result by refusing to engage in rational evaluation of the standards imposed by dominant groups. Flax leaves us with a struggle to build 'discourses which privilege some of those who have previously lacked power (at the necessary expense of others)' (1992: 143). Fascists, creationists, and fringe extreme right-wing groups presumably are also entitled to develop their own counter-discourses. And if they win, they will have been right. I presume Flax would reject this conclusion, and yet her view leaves her with no alternatives.

Flax also criticizes feminist epistemologists because they wish to find 'ways to increase the general sum of human emancipation' (1993: 143). I, for one, plead guilty to this charge. In my opinion Flax and other sceptics have never provided any convincing reasons why this wish could not be fulfilled. We might not be able to achieve a perfect society, but it does not seem impossible to bring about a better one. Above all, however, I believe that having this wish makes one a better human being. Abandoning this hope, on the other hand, diminishes us since it encourages either political inaction or the narrow pursuit of the interests of our own group.

Despite my overall negative assessment of the views elaborated by Hekman and Flax, there is much that is valuable in their positions. Knowledge, as they claim, is always contextual and never immune from power relations. Further, a philosophical account of knowledge, as Flax states, should start from the practical knowledge manifested in our engagements in cultural and epistemological practices. Finally, as Flax points out, sometimes political action rather than philosophical discussion might be the best way to achieve entitlement to one's claims. But, in any case, it is never purely a question of power.

Knowledge and the Subject

Foucault suggested that, when studying knowledge, we should not take the subject as our starting point (1988: 10). I believe that it is rather unhelpful to characterize Foucault as a postmodernist. Nevertheless, it is fair to say that one of the distinguishing features of North American postmodernism is the refusal to take theories about subjectivity to be crucial to reflection about knowledge. Further, these postmodernist thinkers rely on Foucault's views to support this stance.

This approach appears to pit postmodernism against several feminist philosophical accounts of knowledge. Lorraine Code, for example, believes that feminist epistemology takes the question of the subject to be central to the study of knowledge (1992: 138). Also, for Kathleen Lennon and Margaret Whitford, the contribution of feminism to epistemology has been to reveal that subjectivity has an inevitable effect on knowledge. Furthermore, it shows that the subject, who is reflected in knowledge, is masculine.

[Feminist critiques of the Enlightenment] implicate the subject in the production of knowledge. It is argued that it is not simply due to bad practice that masculine subjects have allowed their subjectivity to imprint on their product. Such imprinting of subjectivity is inevitable.

> Knowledge bears the marks of its producer. Given this, feminists were
> concerned to ensure that female subjectivity should also be allowed to
> make its mark on knowledge-production. (1994: 2)

So interpreted, feminist epistemology starts its enquiry from the subject.
It examines traditional accounts of knowledge so as to make explicit the
understanding of subjectivity which they presuppose. For example, traditional theories of knowledge usually assume that the subject is a spectator
who knows because he has representations of the surrounding environment. Feminist epistemologists join forces with other critics of the tradition
in their rejection of this account of subjectivity. The specific contribution
made by feminists to the dismantling of the traditional subject consists in
revealing its masculinity. They show that the subject's alleged universality
is a pretense. The male has been implicitly taken as the standard for the
human. At the same time, feminist epistemologists claim that subjectivity
always influences knowledge. Hence, they attempt to provide theories of
knowledge that are compatible with a female subject.

This approach has been extensively criticized by feminist postmodernist
philosophers. For example, Hekman rejects the attempt, made by many
feminist theorists, 'to reconstitute the subject along anti-Enlightenment
lines while at the same time repudiating the postmodern alternative of
decentering the subject; [these theorists] want to carve out a space between
the Cartesian subject and the postmodernist "death of man"' (1990: 80).
But, Hekman holds, there is no such space in between. Hence, these
feminist theories of subjectivity unwittingly reproduce a Cartesian account
(1990: 81). They remain caught in the Enlightenment assumption that a
socially constituted subject would be passive, unable to resist political
oppression, and incapable of acquiring knowledge (1990: 81). Instead,
Hekman holds that such a subject is not wholly determined by external
forces. Therefore the postmodern account of subjectivity does not entail
political inactivity. For Hekman, the lesson to be drawn from Foucault is
that 'we must reject the philosophy of the subject because subjectivity
entails subjectivation' (1990: 81). Consequently, she holds that any epistemology grounded on the subject will have oppressive consequences. In
particular Hekman endorses the view, which she attributes to Irigaray, that
any such epistemology 'is inherently phallocratic' (1990: 82).

Feminists who reject postmodern accounts of subjectivity are often
motivated by political reasons. These feminists are not necessarily concerned with epistemology; instead, they believe that a fairly robust notion

of subjectivity is essential to feminist politics. These sentiments are, for example, voiced by Christine Di Stefano when she claims that:

> the postmodernist project, if seriously adopted by feminists, would make any semblance of a feminist politics impossible. To the extent that feminist politics is bound up with a specific constituency or subject, namely, women, the postmodernist prohibition against subject-centered inquiry and theory undermines the legitimacy of a broad-based organized movement dedicated to articulating and implementing the goals of such a constituency. (1990: 76)

For Di Stefano feminist politics requires robust opposition to oppression, and the elaboration of substantial alternatives to the current situation. She believes that only a politics of shared identity could achieve these aims. The fractured identities and decentered subjectivities endorsed by postmodernists could, in Di Stefano's opinion, at most support 'local and negative solidarity' (1990: 76). Political alliances of this kind would have a transient nature. For this reason Di Stefano doubts whether a postmodern politics of opposition would 'capable of sustaining itself through time' (1990: 76). Similar concerns are also expressed by Hartsock when she remarks that it would seem hardly a coincidence that exactly at the time when women are gaining access to the position of the subject, the latter is being discredited (1987: 196).

In this political context the debate about subjectivity internal to feminism is usually understood in terms of the opposition between political identity and solidarity. More precisely, the disagreement concerns whether we need shared identities to ground or solidify political solidarity. Di Stefano believes that solidarity without shared identity will often result in an alliance which is too fragile to support sustained political activity. Postmodern feminists, instead, reject any attempt to base solidarity on the subject. They hold that solidarity is 'groundless.'[2] Although this is a debate about politics rather than epistemology, I believe it can serve to illuminate the corresponding disagreements in the theory of knowledge. Both disputes, in my opinion, attempt to deal with similar problems concerning norms.

Politics requires that we identify oppressive power relations as oppressive. We try to understand how people are treated, and we often judge that they ought not to be treated in that way. If we are right about these judgments, we have probably discerned a form of oppression. Resistance will involve becoming clear about how people ought to be treated instead. That is, one tries to formulate more just alternatives to the current situation. Epistemology also involves evaluative judgments. Individuals claim to have knowledge of many things, and sometimes we wonder whether we ought to believe them. Some scientists, for example, claim to have discovered the biological cause of homosexuality. Their claims, however, can count as knowledge only if they are entitled to them. Otherwise, these scientists will think they have knowledge of the cause of homosexuality when they do not. Both epistemology and politics trade with 'oughts.' That is, both enterprises have a normative or evaluative dimension.

Kant claimed that to be a person is to be subject to norms. What distinguishes rational creatures from other entities is their sensitivity to oughts. This feature differentiates persons from objects, and non rational animals. Other kinds of entities are only constrained by causal laws, while persons are also constrained by norms. For example, we take ourselves to be subject to morality, and the law. It is not physically impossible for us to act immorally or to go against the law. However, when we do so, we will usually provide reasons for our behavior. For instance, we might claim that a given law is unjust, and that we feel no obligation to comply to it. In this case, we invoke moral norms to undermine the legitimacy of a law. In all of these cases we acknowledge norms and their power to constrain our behavior.

A presupposition of ordinary use of normative discourse, political and epistemological, is that mistakes are always possible. One could sincerely believe that one ought to be treated in a given manner, and yet be mistaken about it. Society as a whole could also be wrong about these matters. Similarly, one could sincerely believe that one knows something when one is not entitled to the corresponding claim. Also, other people might take that individual to be entitled to her claim, and yet be wrong about it. Neither individuals nor communities can claim infallibility about norms. Instead, mistakes are always possible.

Kant and other Enlightenment thinkers drew a metaphysical conclusion from these considerations about fallibility. They held that how people ought to be treated depends on who they are. They concluded that since we can always be wrong about norms, it must be the case that we can be wrong about who we are. They took this conclusion to show that we must have a supernatural metaphysical nature, a deep essence, since the latter is precisely the sort of thing about which individuals, and even the whole of society, can be wrong. Moral and political norms would be, thus, grounded on this essence. For this reason, philosophers have often provided theories of human nature before developing their accounts of morality and politics.

Epistemology has suffered from a similar pull toward a metaphysical framework. Since persons are sensitive to the norms of reasoning, even though they might be wrong about what these norms are, they must have a special metaphysical nature which allows them to grasp these norms. Thus, the Enlightenment thought assumed that a metaphysical account of subjectivity or personhood was a necessary prerequisite for any theory about how we ought to think, and how we ought to be treated by others, and treat them in turn.

Post-Enlightenment thinkers, including postmodernists, deny the existence of deep metaphysical identities. They point out that the postulation of a human essence amounts to a fiction, which also has pernicious consequences. Any metaphysical theory of human nature will consider features pertaining only to one group of human beings as defining of humanity. In this way the characteristics of Western, middle-class, white heterosexual men have been understood to pertain to true human nature. Individuals belonging to this restricted group are thus taken to embody the human norm. It is implied that all human beings ought to be like them.

It is generally assumed, broadly speaking, that there only two options available to those who reject metaphysical identities. One might claim that identities are socially constituted, or one might reject them altogether. These options, often, are not taken to be incompatible. For example, when Flax and Hekman talk about decentered subjectivity, they implicitly recognize the existence of socially constituted identities. At the same time, however, they claim that identities of this kind cannot be used in identity politics. Thus, they believe that there are no identities in the sense required by this form of political engagement. One must deconstruct identities so as to display the cultural norms that constitute them, rather than attempt to develop a politics based on them. Other feminists disagree. Like Di Stefano, these feminists believe that identities are a necessary component of oppositional politics. However, they do not take these identities to be deep metaphysical essences. For them also, identities are socially constituted.

This whole debate is predicated on my opinion on a mistaken assumption which post-Enlightenment thinkers, postmodernists and non, share with their Enlightenment precursors.[3] They all assume that to claim an identity for yourself is to describe some of your features. Supporters of the Enlightenment thought assumed that one would be describing a metaphysical essence. The others assume that one describes one's social role, or psychological makeup, or a combination of both. Instead, I argue that identity claims are endorsements, they are not descriptions. An example might help to clarify what I mean.

Suppose you are a parent. This is one of your identities. When you claim yourself to be a parent, you are saying that you have undertaken commitments and responsibilities toward your children. Parenthood is not just a matter of having offspring, it carries obligations. Identifying as a parent is a matter of accepting those obligations, while at the same time claiming that others ought to facilitate your attempt to fulfill the responsibilities associated with parenthood. When this help is not forthcoming, as is often the case with working mothers, we are dealing with a potential case of oppression. Thus, when somebody takes being a parent as a matter of identity one endorses a set of commitments for oneself, and also makes a claim on others that they should recognize those commitments. However, one might not endorse the obligations that are currently associated with a given parental identity. For example, many feminist mothers reject several of the norms currently associated with motherhood. They believe that society is wrong about how mothers ought to behave. For these feminists, being a parent is a matter of identity since they accept obligations toward their children, but their endorsement of motherhood is an attempt to change its current understanding. An identity claim of this kind does not describe a biological fact, a psychological state or a social role. It is an endorsement of a range of attitudes and behaviors to which one takes oneself and others to be committed. These attitudes and behaviors might be different from those society expects from individuals who occupy the social role currently associated with that identity. Thus, claiming an identity for oneself is a political act of endorsement which is not based on any metaphysics. There are, of course, connections between identities and social, and sometimes perhaps even biological, facts about the person who has the identity. Somebody who has no relation whatsoever to any child could not be a parent. Nevertheless, these facts to do not constitute the identity.

This non-descriptivist account of identity claims explains how each one of us, and even the whole of society, can be wrong about norms without invoking deep metaphysical natures. According to this view, there are no natural (cultural, social, biological) or supernatural (metaphysical) facts that make normative claims, such as claims about identity, true. Rather, an endorsement of a range of commitments and entitlements is correct whenever one has those entitlements and commitments. And this is a substantive political and moral issue which cannot be settled by sociology, psychology or metaphysics.

Thus, I am inclined to agree with postmodernist thinkers such as Hekman that we should not try to ground normative politics on some descriptive account of subjectivity. It is not possible to base norms on metaphysical nature because there is no human essence. It would be a mistake to ground norms on identities understood as social roles, because it would grant infallibility to society. If having a given identity is a matter of occupying a social role, assuming that identity must be a matter of taking on that social role. One cannot reject the current social role associated, for example, with motherhood, and say that one identifies as a mother, if being a mother is just a matter of being the kind of person who occupies that social role. Any social-descriptive account of political identities is ultimately committed to conservatism.

However, I also agree with Di Stefano that oppositional politics often requires shared identities. Di Stefano claims that political activity which is not sustained by a sense of shared identity could not develop substantial alternatives to the current situation, and could not be maintained over time. If, as I have being claiming, identity is a matter of endorsing a range of behavior and attitudes for oneself and others, one can see how identities supply what Di Stefano requires for political activity. First, identities provide continuity. As a matter of endorsements, they involve commitments that project into the future. If I claim to be gay as a matter of identity I commit myself to the preservation of my sexual inclination. I do not merely predict that it will not change in the future, but I assume a stance that makes such a change something I would have to justify to myself. Second, identities can provide substantial political alternatives. This is an immediate consequence of taking identity claims to be endorsements. So understood, identity claims are political acts. Oppositional identity politics involves identity judgments that have a revisionary character. A feminist mother who takes being a mother as a matter of identity will not, by doing so, endorse the standards currently associated with motherhood. Her identity endorsement will commit her to attitudes that are at a variance with those that are normal in society. There will, of course, be some overlap since it is hard to see otherwise how the new identity could still concern motherhood.

In conclusion, the alternative non-descriptive account of identity I have proposed finds me in substantial agreement with postmodernist thinkers who deny that politics can be based on pre-existing identities. On the other hand, my account also explains why critics of postmodernism are correct to believe that political identities are often necessary to political struggle. Identity formation is, in my view, a political act which emerges when engaging in political activity, and which can foster the development of such an activity. This is claim which critics of postmodernism have been making for sometime. Unfortunately, however, they have also attempted to explain identity in descriptive terms. Thus, for example, Linda Alcoff takes identity as a political notion but proceeds to define it in terms of social role when she claims that 'the very identity of women is constituted by women's [social] position' (1997: 349). All such attempts, I have claimed, are doomed to failure. This is not to say, however, as some postmodernists seem to assert, that identities are the effects of power struggles and relations. To make such a claim amounts to providing yet another descriptive account of identity. In this case, the social facts which putatively constitute the identity come into being only after political activity, but identity is still seen as a matter of social role. In my view, there are identities, and they are socially constituted. This should be taken to mean that some identity claims are correct (or true), and that what makes them correct has a social character. However, these correctness conditions have nothing to do with facts, they concern entitlements to a variety of social behaviors and attitudes corresponding to the endorsements made in identity judgments.

A similar non-descriptive account of subjectivity helps to dispel some of the tensions between feminist epistemology and postmodernist rejections of the philosophy of the subject. I shall argue with postmodernist philosophers like Hekman and Flax that epistemology should not begin with a metaphysical subject. Nevertheless, I also argue along with Code that the study of subjectivity is an important component of epistemology. Firstly, I will provide a summary of the reasons which have led epistemologists to ground their theory of knowledge on a metaphysical subject. My summary will be brief since most of these reasons will be familiar to the reader of earlier chapters. Secondly, I will show how many feminist theories of knowledge still rely on metaphysics, and argue that this is a mistake. Thirdly, I employ the Heideggerian alternative which I have presented in this book to argue that an epistemology which is not grounded on a metaphysical notion of the subject can recognize the importance of subjectivity for contemporary theories of knowledge.

The view that the study of knowledge must start with an account of the subject predates the Enlightenment period. For example, it features centrally in the epistemologies developed in the early modern period by Descartes and Locke. I have already argued, following Foucault, that this characteristic of traditional epistemology must be traced to a concern with representations. Knowledge is thus understood as a matter of having adequate representations, whose adequacy is secured. Epistemology, therefore, must begin with a theory of the subject who is capable of having representations, and spell out the conditions under which these representations are legitimate. With the emergence of the concept of evidence at the end of the early modern period, the issue of the legitimacy of representations acquires its more contemporary form. Knowledge requires justification, one must have reasons for one's representations. This conception of knowledge undergoes yet another transformation in the hands of Kant. For him, only a subject who is sensitive to norms could be able to form representations.

The epistemic subject, for Kant, inhabits the space of reasons. This claim, in my opinion, captures a powerful intuition. An example might help to make this point clearer. An individual, who could not see any of the immediate consequences of her claims, could not really be said to understand her own words. Similarly, for Kant representations are not just isolated pictures or sentence-like structures in the mind. Some entity could contain items of this sort, but if it cannot treat them as rationally related to each other, we would be inclined to think that these items are not representations for that creature. Rather, they would be merely meaningless objects. Thus, for Kant, rational individuals alone are capable of representations, and consequently of knowledge. Kant, however, also believed that only a transcendental subject could have these characteristics. Thus, he postulated the existence of a deep metaphysical nature for human beings.

Fallibilism about norms motivated this move, as it did in the case of morality and politics. Individuals often engage in faulty reasoning. They are sometimes wrong about what follows from their opinions, and about what counts as a reason for them. Hence, psychology, which studies how individuals think, cannot settle issues about reason; it does not tell us how we ought to think. The problem is not solved by looking to society, since we might have all acquired bad ways of thinking from each other. Thus, no empirical study can adequately explain the nature of epistemic reason. Kant, however, went beyond this negative claim. He believed that, since the rational subject cannot be identified with the empirical subject, there must be another (metaphysical) entity it can be identified with. He was led to this conclusion because he also believed that knowledge is a matter of representations. Representations must be 'in' a subject. There must be an entity that has them. Since Kant had already excluded empirical entities, he resorted to postulating the existence of a metaphysical subject.

Thus Kant inaugurated what Foucault has called the modern episteme, and what Habermas has subsequently called the 'philosophy of the subject' (1987: 294). In a nutshell, this view encourages us to begin thinking about knowledge in terms of subjects who know and objects that are known;

representations are meant to bridge the gap between the two. This basic structure is preserved after Kant by more positivist philosophers. They reject, however, Kantian transcendental subjects and opt for worldly empirical ones. Contemporary supporters of naturalized epistemology are the heirs of this positivist turn. For them epistemology becomes a chapter of empirical science which might include sociology as well as psychology. They believe that the epistemic subject can be studied scientifically.

Hekman's complaint that a philosophy of the subject involves subjectivation is particularly suited to these recent developments in epistemology. A theory of knowledge that begins with the study of the subject will make that subject an object of knowledge. But naturalized epistemologists also assume that the study of this subject must be conducted scientifically. Thus, the objectifying attitude typical of the natural sciences is turned toward the subject. In this manner, people come to be understood as causal mechanisms, like any other physical object. They are treated as if they were things devoid of meaning or purpose.

It would a mistake, however, to assume that any study of the subject must involve objectification. Some forms of knowledge do not objectify what is known. For example, we do not oppress our friends simply by trying to get to know them. Furthermore, objectification is not merely the result of using science to study subjects. This link is best seen in the context of examples. Consider, for instance, relations between doctors and patients. Far too often women, when they visit a doctor's surgery, are told, after a cursory glance, that there is nothing organically wrong with them. In many cases the doctor resorts to the neutral language of science to dismiss patients' complaints. The mantle of scientific authority is thus used to avoid engaging with the person who is seeking help. Often this results in oppressive power relations, where doctors' detachment gives them undue power over their patients. In these cases, however, the problem does not seem to lie with the use of science to know human beings, but with a traditional conception of the sort of psychological makeup which, allegedly, best suits scientists. Thus, it would seem, once we understand that scientific objectivity does not require emotional neutrality, we can avoid the objectification of human beings by science.

Up to a point, this conclusion is correct. Nevertheless, it is not readily applicable to epistemology. While it seems entirely appropriate to employ science to know the human body which, after all, is a biological entity, this approach might be unacceptable when applied to persons as subjects who have knowledge. Although persons are, in my opinion, their bodies, we cannot tell the whole story about them by describing their biology. In particular, when we think about knowing subjects we think about individuals who are capable of justifying at least some of their opinions. To believe that reason and justification can be explained scientifically is to believe that they can be explained in terms of cause and effect. This is the approach pursued by naturalized epistemologists. To see why this view leads to an objectifying conception of the person, consider that this position encourages us to see ourselves merely as complex mechanisms.

Given the history of epistemologies which based themselves on accounts of the subject, one is led to wonder why feminists have preserved a central role for the study of subjectivity in the theory of knowledge. I believe that they have been motivated by a variety of considerations, two of which I will discuss here. The first concerns false theories, sexist science, and androcentric assumptions. The second is deeply linked to the issue of political identity I analyzed above.

Early feminist discussions about science and knowledge aimed to show how often theories and claims reflected hidden masculine biases. They demonstrated how the experiences of women were ignored and their lives distorted. The examples of sexist science I presented in chapter 3 illustrate this point. Since numerous theories reveal themselves to be biased when reconsidered from a more inclusive viewpoint, it would seem appropriate to adopt a methodological precept which requires that we start from women's lives and perspectives. This is the approach adopted, for example, by Harding, who believes that research should begin by looking at the lives of marginal groups (1991: 124). This recommendation is entirely sound: it offers a way to address widespread masculine bias whose existence in the natural and social sciences has been sufficiently documented.

Feminists who endorse this methodology are not necessarily offering an epistemology that is based on a female subject. Rather, they are making claims about evidence. They hold that the lives and experiences of people in marginal positions should be considered as evidentially relevant to theories about society, the human body, biology, and so forth. This point is obvious, and yet, as I have shown in chapter 3, it is consistently ignored. Some of the claims made by standpoint feminist epistemologists such as Hartsock and Rose can also be understood in these terms. They do not claim that women's experiences are infallible, they do not take them as epistemological foundations in the traditional sense. Rather, they believe that women's experiences are epistemically important and that any theory that ignores them is likely to be biased.

Early standpoint theorists also insisted on the centrality of experiential knowledge in the project of developing a new understanding of social reality. This focus on experience might have been too exclusive. There are, often, different routes to knowledge. For example, one might learn about the lives of working mothers by being one, by living that life. However, one can also learn about them by listening to working mothers, studying economics and law. Furthermore, people often internalize oppression. In these cases, their experiences will not be very reliable. Thus we will not want to rely on the closeted homosexual to tell us the last word on gay lives. Early standpoint theorists were never so naive as to believe that the oppressed always experience their oppression as oppression. This observation, however, warrants the adoption of Harding's modified version of the methodological precept of standpoint epistemology. We must always consider the lives of marginal groups, and we will try to know these lives in a variety of ways. Experiential knowledge figures centrally in this program, but it is not the sole approach one pursues.

The features of standpoint epistemology I have described so far are absolutely neutral with regard to the epistemology of the subject. They do not entail any claim about whether epistemic norms must be understood in terms of metaphysical or empirical subjectivity. Rather, standpoint epistemology proposes new epistemic norms about which kind of evidence is relevant to which type of theory. It also claims that women should be granted more cognitive authority than they were previously taken to have. Thus standpoint epistemology uncovers contradictions in current epistemic practices. It shows that these practices do not license some entitlements that should be granted, and license others that should be revoked. For example, women's experiences are not given the epistemic status they deserve, and sexist theories are mistakenly taken to be knowledge. These features of standpoint epistemology concern which norms we should adopt, they are not speculations about the grounding of these norms in the subject. Thus, standpoint epistemology might not contravene postmodernist rejections of an epistemology of the subject.

Nevertheless, there is a tension even between these features of standpoint epistemology and some tendencies in postmodern thought. This tension concerns the issue of experiential depth. With the exception of Lacan, recent French philosophers like Derrida have, in general, avoided discussing the experiential aspects of subjectivity. This attitude might be a result of a turning away from any account of the self provided in the vocabulary of authenticity. These philosophers reject the view that buried within us there is an authentic (metaphysical) self awaiting to be discovered. However, since most recent feminist accounts of experience do not rely on this notion of authenticity, I do not believe this issue gives rise to an incompatibility between feminist epistemology and postmodernism.

Standpoint theorists also take subjectivity to be crucial to knowledge for political reasons. Women had been for centuries the object of speculations made by men, their own voices had rarely been heard. This silence is and has been both a source and the result of oppression. Feminist epistemologists, therefore, insist on the importance of a social transformation that would make it possible for women to become the producers of knowledge. They have analyzed the political conditions that impede this transformation, and provided social and psychological accounts of the development of character traits in women which makes it hard for us to place ourselves as knowers in contemporary society.

Further, feminist epistemologists have claimed that knowledge can never be separated from politics. They have argued that politically informed research is epistemically superior to work that is allegedly value-neutral. I have reviewed some of these arguments in chapter 3, and argued that several of them are extremely convincing. These arguments indicate that, as things stands, it matters epistemically whose knowledge we are talking about. For example, when we consider a sociological theory or a medical hypothesis we may want to know whether its proponents have listened to women's voices. We do not want to know this simply because we might uncover oppressive power relations, but also because we know that a refusal to listen to these voices is good evidence for the claim that the resulting theory is probably biased.

These features of feminist epistemology are also quite consonant with the claims made by postmodernists. They also believe that knowledge is always political, and are aware of the political importance of making it possible for marginalized groups to develop a voice. Thus postmodernist claims that feminist epistemology is an epistemology of the subject might appear unwarranted. This is not the case. Although, as I have been trying to show, most of the important claims made by feminist epistemologists can be presented in a way that does not implicate a grounding in the subject, several have in fact developed their theories in this direction. Standpoint epistemology provides a good example of this phenomenon.

Early standpoint theorists, such as Hartsock and Rose, supplemented their Marxist position on privileged standpoints with a psychoanalytic account of the psychological development of women in current society. Although it may seem that this supplement was intended to show that women have enough in common to attribute a standpoint to them, this interpretation contradicts other aspects of standpoint theory. For example, Hartsock claimed that a standpoint is an achievement, it is a feminist standpoint (1983: 285). Thus, it is not reserved for women. Furthermore, one does not achieve the standpoint merely by being raised as a woman.

The role played by psychoanalytic theory in standpoint theory was dual. First, it broadened the scope of standpoints. Marxist theory only warranted the claim that the oppressed have a distinct, and epistemically privileged, viewpoint on matters concerning their oppression. The psychoanalytic account provides a description of a distinct kind of personality. If true, this account warrants the claim that women have a different approach to knowledge on all subject matters. Second, psychoanalysis is also presumed to give us some indication about what sort of character would best suit a knower. This ideal knower would have many of the features currently associated with femininity.

I have already argued in chapter 6 that standpoint epistemology becomes much less plausible when its scope is broadened by means of psychoanalysis. I see no reason to believe that one sort of personality is best suited for pursuing knowledge in every field. I find it even less likely that one perspective might be the best one to take in every inquiry. I now want to add that the inclusion of a psychoanalytic dimension to standpoint theory transforms it into an epistemology of the subject. As in the case of naturalized epistemology, the question about which epistemic norms we ought to adopt is recouched in terms of what an ideal subject would believe. Thus, the study of knowledge becomes focused on the study of the features of the epistemic subject. Further, since standpoint resorts to psychoanalysis, it adopts causal accounts of subjectivity. It reduces norms to causes because it provides a descriptivist study of the empirical subject. This problem, however, is not limited to versions of standpoint theory that use psychoanalysis. For example, I have shown in chapter 7 that Harding's epistemological theory also falls in the same trap.

Thus, Hekman's and Flax's complaints that many feminists develop epistemologies of the subject are warranted. Further, their belief that this approach can have negative political consequences is also plausible. However, as I have tried to show, most of what feminist epistemology has to offer can be preserved when one abandons causal and metaphysical accounts of the subject. A theory of knowledge can be sensitive to epistemic differences, real or presumed, made by the social locations occupied by individuals without grounding itself on a notion of the subject.

There is, I believe, a good explanation of why many feminist theorists in the early 1980s adopted epistemologies of the subject. This explanation is provided by descriptivist conceptions of identity politics. These feminists believed that knowledge is always political, and held that feminist politics requires identity politics. However, they also thought that identity claims are descriptive, and thus assumed there must be entities they describe. Thus these feminists grounded politics on empirical subjects. Consequently they were drawn to make a similar move in epistemology, which like politics is primarily concerned with norms.

In conclusion, feminist epistemology does not need to be grounded in the subject, and it is better pursued without this. The Heideggerian framework I have presented in this book offers a way in which this can be done. It is a way that confirms and justifies several of the claims made by those feminist epistemologists whose views I have presented in this book. The contribution made by feminist theories of knowledge to philosophy, sociology, and cultural studies has been invaluable. They have shown that epistemic norms can only be evaluated and understood in the context of their social and cultural background. These theories have also demonstrated that epistemic and political judgments cannot be neatly separated. I do believe that feminist epistemology still has much to offer; for this reason, among others, I reject postmodern quietism and skepticism.

Further Reading

Susan Hekman's *Gender and Knowledge: Elements of a Postmodern Feminism* (1990) and Jane Flax's 'The End of Innocence' (1993) provide good introductions to postmodern views about knowledge. Flax explores the relations between feminism and postmodernism in *Thinking Fragments: Psychoanalysis, Feminism, & Postmodernism in the Contemporary West* (1991). For a sympathetic but critical account see chapter 7 of Harding's *Whose Science? Whose Knowlege?* (1991).

Notes

1 Flax is not consistent on this point. Her claim that understanding is a matter of knowing how, should rule out any account of it in terms of following explicit rules. Flax, however, adopts the vocabulary of rules elsewhere, without suggesting that this talk should be taken less than literally. I have ignored this problem in the text, and presented her account in terms of rules.
2 For a feminist defense of groundless solidarity see Diane Elam (1994). Rorty has developed a different account of the groundlessness of solidarity in (1989).
3 I have discussed these issues in Tanesini (1994) and Tanesini and Lance (1998).

References

Addelson, Kathryn Pyne. (1983) 'The Man of Professional Wisdom' in Sandra Harding and Merrill B. Hintikka (eds), *Discovering Reality: Feminist Perspectives in Epistemology, Metaphysics, Methodology and Philosophy of Science*, Dordrecht: D. Reidel, pp. 165–86.

Addelson, Kathryn Pyne. (1990) 'Why Philosophers Should Become Sociologists (and Vice Versa)' in Becker and McCall (eds), *Symbolic Interaction and Cultural Studies*, Chicago: The University of Chicago Press, pp. 119–47.

Addelson, Kathryn Pyne. (1993) 'Knower/Doers and Their Moral Problems' in Linda Alcoff and Elizabeth Potter (eds), *Feminist Epistemologies*, New York: Routledge, pp. 265–94.

Addelson, Kathryn Pyne and Potter, Elizabeth. (1991) 'Making Knowledge' in Joan E. Hartman and Ellen Messer-Davidow (eds), *(En)Gendering Knowledge*, Knoxville: The University of Tennessee Press, pp. 259–77.

Alcoff, Linda Martín. (1992) 'Continental Epistemology' in Jonathan Dancy and Ernst Sosa (eds), *A Companion to Epistemology*, Oxford: Blackwell, pp. 76–81.

Alcoff, Linda Martín. (1995/6) 'Is the Feminist Critique of Reason Rational?', *Philosophic Exchange*, 26: 59–79.

Alcoff, Linda Martín. (1996) *Real Knowing*, Ithaca: Cornell University Press.

Alcoff, Linda Martín. (1997) 'Cultural Feminism Versus Post-Structuralism: The Identity Crisis in Feminist Theory' in Linda Nicholson (ed.), *The Second Wave: A Reader in Feminist Theory*, New York and London: Routledge, pp. 330–55.

Alcoff, Linda Martín and Potter, Elizabeth. (1993) 'Introduction: When Feminisms Intersect Epistemology' in Alcoff and Potter (eds), *Feminist Epistemologies*, New York: Routledge, pp. 1–14.

Alston, William P. (1989) *Epistemic Justification: Essays in the Theory of Knowledge*, Ithaca: Cornell University Press.

Alston, William P. (1994) 'Belief-forming Practices and the Social' in Frederick F. Schmitt (ed.), *Socializing Epistemology: The Social Dimension of Knowledge*, Lanham: Rowman & Littlefield, pp. 29–51.

Antony, Louise M. (1993) 'Quine as Feminist: The Radical Import of Naturalized Epistemology' in Louise M. Antony and Charlotte Witt (eds), *A Mind of One's Own: Feminist Essays on Reason and Objectivity*, Boulder: Westview Press, pp. 185–225.

Antony, Louise M. (1995) 'Is Psychological Individualism a Piece of Ideology?', *Hypatia*, 10 (3): 157–74.

Appiah, K. Anthony. (1996) 'Race, Culture, Identity: Misunderstood Connections' in K. Anthony Appiah and Amy Gutman, *Color Conscious: The Political Morality of Race*, Princeton: Princeton University Press, pp. 30–105.

Atherton, Margaret. (1993) 'Cartesian Reason and Gendered Reason' in Louise M. Antony and Charlotte Witt (eds), *A Mind of One's Own: Feminist Essays on Reason and Objectivity*, Boulder: Westview Press, pp. 19–34.

Barnes, Barry. (1977) *Interests and the Growth of Knowledge*, London: Routledge.

Bar On, Bat-Ami. (1993) 'Marginality and Epistemic Privilege' in Linda Alcoff and Elizabeth Potter (eds), *Feminist Epistemologies*, NewYork: Routledge, pp. 83–100.

Battersby, Christine. (1989) *Gender and Genius. Towards a Feminist Aesthetics*, London: The Women's Press.

Benhabib, Seyla. (1995) 'Feminism and Postmodernism' in Seyla Benhabib, Judith Butler, Drucilla Cornell, and Linda Nicholson (eds), *Feminist Contentions: A Philosophical Exchange*, New York and London: Routledge, pp. 17–34.

Benjamin, Jessica. (1988) *The Bonds of Love: Psychoanalysis, Feminism, and the Problem of Domination*, New York: Pantheon Books.

Bernstein, Richard J. (1983) *Beyond Objectivism and Relativism: Science, Hermeneutics, and Praxis*, Oxford: Blackwell.

Bernstein, Richard J. (1986) 'The Rage Against Reason', *Philosophy and Literature*, 10 (2): 186–210.

Biology and Gender Study Group. (1988) 'The Importance of Feminist Critique for Contemporary Cell Biology', *Hypatia*, 3 (1): 61–76.

Bleier, Ruth. (1984) *Science and Gender: A Critique of Biology and Its Theories on Women*, New York: Pergamon Press.

Bleier, Ruth. (1986) 'Sex Differences Research: Science or Belief?' in Ruth Bleier (ed.), *Feminist Approaches to Science*, New York: Pergamon Press, pp. 147–64.

Bordo, Susan. (1987) *The Flight to Objectivity, Essays on Cartesianism and Culture*, Albany: SUNY Press.

Bordo, Susan. (1990) 'Feminism, Postmodernism, and Gender-Scepticism' in Linda J. Nicholson (ed.), *Feminism/Postmodernism*, New York and London: Routledge, pp. 133–56.

Boyd, Richard. (1991) 'Confirmation, Semantics, and the Interpretation of Scientific Theories' in Richard Boyd, Philip Gasper, and J. D. Trout (eds), *The Philosophy of Science*, Cambridge: The MIT Press, pp. 3–35.

Braidotti, Rosi. (1991) *Patterns of Dissonance: A Study of Women in Contemporary Philosophy*, transl. by Elizabeth Guild, New York: Routledge.

Braidotti, Rosi. (1994) *Nomadic Subjects. Embodiment and Sexual Difference in Contemporary Feminist Theory*, New York: Columbia University Press.

Brandom, Robert. (1983) 'Heidegger's Categories in Being and Time', *The Monist*, 66: 387–409.

Brandom, Robert. (1994) *Making It Explicit. Reasoning, Representing, and Discoursive Commitment*, Cambridge and London: Harvard University Press.

Brennan, Teresa. (1989) 'Introduction' in Teresa Brennan (ed.), *Between Feminism and Psychoanalysis*, London: Routledge, pp. 1–23.

Campbell, Richmond. (1994) 'The Virtues of Feminist Empiricism', *Hypatia*, 9 (1): 89–115.

Chodorow, Nancy. (1978) *The Reproduction of Mothering: Psychoanalysis and the Sociology of Gender*, Berkeley: University of California Press.

Code, Lorraine. (1991) *What Can She Know? Feminist Theory and the Construction of Knowledge*, Ithaca: Cornell University Press.

Code, Lorraine. (1992) 'Feminist Epistemology' in Jonathan Dancy and Ernst Sosa (eds), *A Companion to Epistemology*, Oxford: Blackwell, pp. 138–142.

Code, Lorraine. (1995) *Rhetorical Spaces: Essays on Gendered Locations*, New York and London: Routledge.

Code, Lorraine. (1996) 'What is Natural About Epistemology Naturalized?', *American Philosophical Quarterly*, 33 (1): 1–22.

Collins, Patricia Hill. (1991) *Black Feminist Thought: Knowledge, Consciousness, and the Politics of Empowerment*, New York and London: Routledge.

Corea, Gena. (1985) *The Mother Machine: Reproductive Technologies from Artificial Insemination to Artificial Wombs*, New York: Harper & Row.

Crasnow, Sharon L. (1993) 'Can Science Be Objective? Longino's Science as Social Knowledge', *Hypathia*, 8 (3): 194–201.

Dalmiya, Vrinda and Alcoff, Linda. (1993) 'Are "Old Wives' Tales" Justified?' in Linda Alcoff and Elizabeth Potter (eds), *Feminist Epistemologies*, NewYork: Routledge, pp. 217–244.

Dancy, Jonathan. (1985) *An Introduction to Contemporary Epistemology*, Oxford: Blackwell.

Davis, Angela Y. (1983) *Women, Race & Class*, New York: Vintage Books.

de Beauvoir, Simone. (1988) *The Second Sex*, transl. and ed. H. M. Parshley, London: Picador.

Descartes, René. (1980) *Discourse on Method and Meditations on First Philosophy*, transl. Donald A. Cress, Indianapolis: Hackett.

Di Stefano, Christine. (1990) 'Dilemmas of Difference: Feminism, Modernity, and Postmodernism' in Linda J. Nicholson (ed.), *Feminism/Postmodernism*, New York and London: Routledge, pp. 63–82.

Duran, Jane. (1991) *Toward a Feminist Epistemology*, Savage: Rowman & Littlefield Publishers.

Elam, Diane. (1994) *Feminism and Deconstruction: Ms. en Abyme*, London and New York: Routledge.

Fausto-Sterling, Anne. (1992) *Myths of Gender: Biological Theories about Women and Men*, 2nd ed., New York: Basic Books.

Fee, Elizabeth. (1983) 'Women's Nature and Scientific Objectivity' in Marian

Lowe and Ruth Hubbard (eds), *Woman's Nature: Rationalizations of Inequality*, New York: Pergamon Press, pp. 9–27.

Flax, Jane. (1991) *Thinking Fragments: Psychoanalysis, Feminism, & Postmodernism in the Contemporary West*, Berkeley: University of California Press.

Flax, Jane. (1993) 'The End of Innocence' in Jane Flax, *Disputed Subjects: Essays on Psychoanalysis, Politics and Philosophy*, New York and London: Routledge, pp. 131–47.

Foucault, Michel. (1970) *The Order of Things: An Archeology of the Human Sciences*, London: Routledge.

Foucault, Michel. (1978) *The History of Sexuality I: An Introduction*, transl. Robert Hurley, New York: Pantheon Books.

Foucault, Michel. (1979) *Discipline and Punish*, transl. Alan Sheridan, New York: Vintage Books.

Foucault, Michel. (1980) *Power/Knowledge: Selected Interviews & Other Writings 1972–1977*, ed. Colin Gordon and transl. Colin Gordon, Leo Marshall, John Mepham, Kate Soper, New York: Pantheon Books.

Foucault, Michel. (1988) 'The Ethic of Care for the Self as a Practice of Freedom' in James Bernauer and David Rasmussen (eds), *The Final Foucault*, Cambridge, Mass.: MIT Press, pp. 1–20.

Foucault, Michel. (1996) *Foucault Live (Collected Interviews, 1961–1984)*, ed. Sylvère Lotringer, transl. Lysa Hochroth and John Johnston, New York: Semiotext(e).

Fraser, Nancy. (1989) *Unruly Practices: Power, Discourse and Gender in Contemporary Social Theory*, Cambridge: Polity Press.

Fraser, Nancy and Nicholson, Linda J. (1990) 'Social Criticism without Philosophy: An Encounter between Feminism and Postmodernism' in Linda J. Nicholson (ed.), *Feminism/Postmodernism*, New York and London: Routledge, pp. 19–38.

Fuller, Steve. (1993) *Philosophy of Science and its Discontents*, 2nd ed., New York and London: The Guilford Press.

Gemes, Ken. (n.d.) 'Epistemological vs Causal Explanations in Quine', unp. man.

Ginzberg, Ruth. (1987) 'Uncovering Gynocentric Science', *Hypatia*, 2 (3): 89–105.

Glymour, Clark. (1980) *Theories and Evidence*, Princeton: Princeton University Press.

Goldman, Alvin. (1985) 'What is Justified Belief?' in Hilary Kornblith (ed.), *Naturalizing Epistemology*, Cambridge: MIT Press, pp. 91–113.

Goldman, Alvin. (1986) *Epistemology and Cognition*, Cambridge: Harvard University Press.

Grant, Judith. (1987) 'I Feel Therefore I Am: A Critique of Female Experience as the Basis for a Feminist Epistemology', *Women and Politics*, 7 (3): 99–114.

Griffiths, Morwenna. (1995) *Feminisms and the Self: The Web of Identity*, London and New York: Routledge.

Grimshaw, Jean. (1986) *Feminist Philosophers: Women's Perspectives on Philosophical Traditions*, Brighton: Wheatsheaf Books.

Grosz, Elizabeth. (1993) 'Bodies and Knowledges: Feminism and the Crisis of Reason' in Linda Alcoff and Elizabeth Potter (eds), *Feminist Epistemologies*, NewYork: Routledge, pp. 187–215.

Habermas, Jürgen. (1971) *Knowledge and Human Interests*, transl. Jeremy J. Shapiro, Boston: Beacon Press.

Habermas, Jürgen. (1987) *The Philosophical Discourse of Modernity, Twelve Lectures*, transl. by Frederick G. Lawrence, Cambridge: MIT Press.

Hacking, Ian. (1975) *The Emergence of Probability*, Cambridge: Cambridge University Press.

Hacking, Ian. (1983) *Representing and Intervening: Introductory Topics in the Philosophy of Natural Science*, Cambridge: Cambridge University Press.

Hacking, Ian. (1990) 'Making Up People' in Edward Stein (ed.), *Forms of Desire: Sexual Orientation and the Social Constructionist Controversy*, New York and London: Garland Publishing, pp. 69–88.

Hacking, Ian. (1992) 'The Self-Vindication of the Laboratory Sciences' in Andrew Pickering (ed.), *Science as Practice and Culture*, Chicago and London: The University of Chicago Press, pp. 29–64.

Haraway, Donna. (1988) 'Situated Knowledges: The Science Question in Feminism and the Privilege of Partial Perspective', *Feminist Studies*, 14 (3): 575–99.

Haraway, Donna. (1989) *Primate Visions. Gender, Race, and Nature in the World of Modern Science*, New York and London: Routledge.

Haraway, Donna. (1990) 'A Manifesto for Cyborgs: Science, Technology, and Socialist Feminism in the 1980s', in Linda J. Nicholson (ed.), *Feminism/Postmodernism*, New York and London: Routledge, pp. 190–233.

Haraway, Donna. (1992) 'The Promises of Monsters: A Regenerative Politics for Inappropriate/d Others' in Grossberg, Nelson, and Treichler (eds), *Cultural Studies*, New York: Routledge, pp. 295–337.

Harding, Sandra. (1986) *The Science Question in Feminism*, Ithaca: Cornell University Press.

Harding, Sandra. (1991) *Whose Science? Whose Knowledge?*, Ithaca: Cornell University Press.

Harding, Sandra. (1993) 'Rethinking Standpoint Epistemology: What Is "Strong Objectivity"?' in Linda Alcoff and Elizabeth Potter (eds), *Feminist Epistemologies*, NewYork: Routledge, pp. 49–82.

Hardwig, John. (1985) 'Epistemic Dependence', *Journal of Philosophy*, 82 (7): 335–49.

Hardwig, John. (1991) 'The Role of Trust in Knowledge', *Journal of Philosophy*, 88 (12): 693–708.

Hartmann, Heidi. (1981) 'The Family as the Locus of Gender, Class, and Political Struggle: The Example of Housework', *Signs: Journal of Women in Culture and Society*, 6 (3): 366–94.

Hartsock, Nancy. (1983) 'The Feminist Standpoint: Developing the Ground for a Specifically Feminist Historical Materialism', in Sandra Harding and Merrill B. Hintikka (eds), *Discovering Reality: Feminist Perspectives in Epistemology, Metaphysics, Methodology and Philosophy of Science*, Dordrecht: D. Reidel, pp. 283–310.

Hartsock, Nancy. (1987) 'Rethinking Modernism: Minority vs. Majority Theories', *Cultural Critique*, 7: 187–206.

Haslanger, Sally. (1993) 'On Being Objective and Being Objectified' in Louise M. Antony and Charlotte Witt (eds), *A Mind of One's Own: Feminist Essays on Reason and Objectivity*, Boulder: Westview Press, pp. 85–125.

Haugeland, John. (1982) 'Heidegger on Being a Person', *Noûs*, 16: 15–26.

Heidegger, Martin. (1962) *Being and Time*, transl. John Macquarrie and Edward Robinson, New York: Harper & Row.

Hekman, Susan J. (1990) *Gender and Knowledge: Elements of a Postmodern Feminism*, Cambridge: Polity Press.

Heldke, Lisa M. and Kellert, Stephen H. (1995) 'Objectivity as Responsibility', *Metaphilosophy*, 26 (4): 360–78.

Hempel, Carl Gustav. (1965) *Aspects of Scientific Explanation*, New York: The Free Press.

hooks, bell. (1984) *Feminist Theory: From Margin to Center*, Boston: South End Press.

hooks, bell. (1990) *Yearning: Race, Gender, and Cultural Politics*, Boston: South End Press.

Horkheimer, Max and Adorno, Theodor W. (1991) *Dialectic of Enlightenment*, transl. John Cumming, New York: Continuum.

Hubbard, Ruth and Wald, Elijah. (1997) *Exploding the Gene Myth: How Genetic Information Is Produced and Manipulated by Scientists, Physicians, Employers, Insurance Companies, Educators, and Law Enforcers*, with a new afterword, Boston: Beacon Press.

Hull, David. (1988) *Science as a Process*, Chicago and London: University of Chicago Press.

Irigaray, Luce. (1979) 'Etabilir un généalogie de femmes', *Maintenant XII, 28 mai*.

Irigaray, Luce. (1985) *Speculum of the Other Woman*, transl. Gillian C. Gill, Ithaca: Cornell University Press.

Irigaray, Luce. (1987) 'Is the Subject of Science Sexed?' transl. Carol Mastrangelo Bové, *Hypatia*, 2 (3): 65–87.

Irigaray, Luce. (1993) *An Ethics of Sexual Difference*, transl. Carolyn Burke and Gillian C. Gill, London: The Athlone Press.

Jaggar, Alison M. (1983) *Feminist Politics and Human Nature*, Totowa: Rowman & Allanheld Publishers.

Jaggar, Alison M. (198?) 'Love and Knowledge: Emotion in Feminist Epistemology', *Inquiry*, 32: 151–176.

Kant, Immanuel. (1965) *Critique of Pure Reason*, transl. Norman Kemp Smith, New York: St. Martin's Press.

Kant, Immanuel. (1986) 'What is Enlightenment?', transl. Lewis White Beck, in *Philosophical Writings*, ed. Ernst Behler with a foreword by René Wellek, New York: Continuum, pp. 263–9.

Kaplan, Mark. (1991) 'Epistemology on Holiday', *Journal of Philosophy*, 88 (3): 132–54.

Keller, Evelyn Fox. (1985) *Reflections on Gender and Science*, New Haven: Yale University Press.

Kitcher, Philip. (1990) 'The Division of Cognitive Labor', *Journal of Philosophy*, 87: 5–22.

Kitcher, Philip. (1994) 'Contrasting Conceptions of Social Epistemology' in Frederick Schmitt (ed.), *Socializing Epistemology*, Lanham: Rowman & Littlefield, pp. 111–34.

Kornblith, Hilary. (1994) 'A Conservative Approach to Social Epistemology' in Frederick Schmitt (ed.), *Socializing Epistemology*, Lanham: Rowman & Littlefield, pp. 93–110.

Kuhn, Thomas. (1970) *The Structure of Scientific Revolutions*, 2nd ed., enlarged, Chicago: The University of Chicago Press.

Latour, Bruno and Woolgar, Steve. (1979) *Laboratory Life: The Social Construction of Scientific Facts*, London: Sage.

Laudan, Larry. (1977) *Progress and Its Problems*, Berkeley: University of California Press.

Lazreg, Marnia. (1994) 'Women's Experience and Feminist Epistemology. A critical neo-rationalist approach' in Kathleen Lennon and Margaret Whitford (eds), *Knowing the Difference: Feminist Perspectives in Epistemology*, London and New York: Routledge, pp. 45–62.

Le Doeuff, Michèle. (1989) *The Philosophical Imaginary*, transl. Colin Gordon, London: The Athlone Press.

Le Doeuff, Michèle. (1991) *Hipparchia's Choice: An Essay concerning Women, Philosophy, etc.*, transl. Trista Selous, Oxford: Blackwell.

Lennon, Kathleen and Whitford, Margaret. (1994) 'Introduction' in Kathleen Lennon and Margaret Whitford (eds), *Knowing the Difference: Feminist Perspectives in Epistemology*, London and New York: Routledge, pp. 1–14.

LeVay, Simon. (1996) *Queer Science: The Use and Abuse of Research into Homosexuality*, Cambridge: MIT Press.

Lloyd, Elisabeth A. (1995) 'Objectivity and the Double Standard for Feminist Epistemologies', *Synthese*, 104: 351–81.

Lloyd, Genevieve. (1984) *The Man of Reason: 'Male' and 'Female' in Western Philosophy*, Minneapolis: University of Minnesota Press.

Lloyd, Genevieve. (1989) 'Woman as Other: Sex, Gender and Subjectivity', *Australian Feminist Studies*, 10: 13–22.

Lloyd, Genevieve. (1993) 'Maleness, Metaphor, and the "Crisis" of Reason' in Louise M. Antony and Charlotte Witt (eds), *A Mind of One's Own: Feminist Essays on Reason and Objectivity*, Boulder: Westview Press, pp. 69–83.

Locke, John. (1975) *An Essay concerning Human Understanding*, edited with an introduction, critical apparatus and glossary by Peter H. Nidditch, Oxford: Clarendon Press.

Longino, Helen H. (1990) *Science as Social Knowledge: Values and Objectivity in Scientific Inquiry*, Princeton: Princeton University Press.

Longino, Helen H. (1990a) 'Feminism and Philosophy of Science', *Journal of Social Philosophy*, 21: 150–9.

Longino, Helen H. (1993) 'Subjects, Power, and Knowledge: Description and Prescription in Feminist Philosophies of Science' in Linda Alcoff and Elizabeth Potter (eds), *Feminist Epistemologies*, New York: Routledge, 101–20.

Lovibond, Sabina. (1989) 'Feminism and Postmodernism', *New Left Review*, 178 (Nov./Dec.): 5–28.

Lovibond, Sabina. (1994) 'Feminism and the "Crisis of Rationality"', *New Left Review*, 207 (Sept./Oct.): 72–86.

Lyotard, Jean-François. (1984) *The Postmodern Condition: A Report on Knowledge*, transl. Geoff Bennington and Brian Massumi, Minneapolis: University of Minnesota Press.

MacKinnon, Catharine A. (1987) 'Feminism, Marxism, Method, and the State: Toward Feminist Jurisprudence' in Sandra Harding (ed.), *Feminism and Methodology*, Bloomington: Indiana University Press and Milton Keynes: Open University Press, pp. 135–56.

Mangena, Oshadi. (1994) 'Against Fragmentation. The Need for Holism' in Kathleen Lennon & Margaret Whitford (eds), *Knowing the Difference: Feminist Perspectives in Epistemology*, London and New York: Routledge, pp. 275–82.

McMillan, Carol. (1982) *Women, Reason and Nature: Some Philosophical Problems with Feminism*, Princeton: Princeton University Press.

Merchant, Carolyn. (1980) *The Death of Nature: Women, Ecology, and the Scientific Revolution*, San Francisco: Harpers & Row.

Millman, Marcia and Kanter, Rosabeth Moss. (eds) (1975) *Another Voice: Feminist Perspectives on Social Life and Social Science*, New York: Anchor Books.

Mills, Charles. (1988) 'Alternative Epistemologies', *Social Theory and Practice*, 14: 237–63.

Mitroff, Ian. (1974) 'Norms and Counter-Norms in a Select Group of the Apollo Moon Scientists: A Case Study of the Ambivalence of Scientists', *American Sociological Review*, 39: 579–95.

Moi, Toril. (1989) 'Patriarchal Thought and the Drive for Knowledge' in Teresa Brennan (ed.), *Between Feminism and Psychoanalysis*, London: Routledge, pp. 189–205.

Moi, Toril. (1994) *Simone de Beauvoir: The Making of An Intellectual Woman*, Oxford and Cambridge: Blackwell.

Mulkay, Michael. (1990) *The Sociology of Science*, Bloomington: Indiana University Press.

Nagel, Ernest. (1961) *The Structure of Science*, New York: The Free Press.

Nagel, Thomas. (1986) *The View from Nowhere*, New York and Oxford: Oxford University Press.

Nelson, Lynn Hankinson. (1990) *Who Knows: From Quine to a Feminist Empiricism*, Philadelphia: Temple University Press.

Nelson, Lynn Hankinson. (1993) 'Epistemological Communities' in Linda Alcoff and Elizabeth Potter (eds), *Feminist Epistemologies*, New York: Routledge, 121–59.

Nelson, Lynn Hankinson. (1993a) 'A Question of Evidence', *Hypatia*, 8 (2): 172–89.

Nelson, Lynn Hankinson. (1995) 'A Feminist Naturalized Philosophy of Science', *Synthese*, 104: 399–421.

Nelson, Jack and Nelson, Lynn Hankinson. (1994) 'No Rush to Judgment', *The Monist*, 77 (4): 486–508.

Nietzsche, Friedrich. (1968) *The Will to Power*, transl. Walter Kaufmann and R. J. Hollingdale, ed. Walter Kaufmann, New York: Vintage Books.

Nussbaum, Martha. (1994) 'Feminists and Philosophy', *New York Review of Books*, Oct. 20, pp. 59–63.

Okruhlik, Kathleen. (1992) 'Birth of a New Physics or Death of Nature?' in E. D. Harvey and K. Okruhlik (eds), *Women and Reason*, Ann Arbor: University of Michigan Press, pp. 63–76.

Petchesky, Rosalind Pollack. (1987) 'Foetal Images: the Power of Visual Culture in the Politics of Reproduction' in Michelle Stanworth (ed.), *Reproductive Technologies: Gender, Motherhood, and Medicine*, Minneapolis: University of Minnesota Press, pp. 57–80.

Pickering, Andrew. (1992) 'From Science as Knowledge to Science as Practice' in Andrew Pickering (ed.), *Science as Practice and Culture*, Chicago and London: University of Chicago Press, pp. 1–26.

Potter, Elizabeth. (1988) 'Modeling the Gender Politics in Science', *Hypatia*, 3 (1): 19–33.

Potter, Elizabeth. (1993) 'Gender and Epistemic Negotiation' in Linda Alcoff and Elizabeth Potter (eds), *Feminist Epistemologies*, New York: Routledge, pp. 161–86.

Potter, Elizabeth. (1994) 'Locke's Epistemology and Women's Struggles' in Bat-Ami Bar On (ed.), *Modern Engendering. Critical Feminist Readings in Modern Western Philosophy*, Albany: SUNY, pp. 27–50.

Potter, Elizabeth. (1995) 'Good Science and Good Philosophy of Science', *Synthese*, 104: 423–39.

Putnam, Hilary. (1994) 'Sense, Nonsense, and the Senses: An Inquiry into the Powers of the Human Mind', *Journal of Philosophy*, 91 (9): 445–517.

Quine, W. V. O. (1961) 'Two Dogmas of Empiricism' in *From a Logical Point of View: Nine Logico-Philosophical Essays*, 2nd ed. rev., Cambridge, Mass.: Harvard University Press, pp. 20–46.

Quine, W. V. O. (1969) 'Epistemology Naturalized' in *Ontological Relativity and Other Essays*, New York: Columbia University Press, pp. 69–96.

Quine, W. V. O. (1990) 'Three Indeterminacies' in Robert B. Barrett and Roger F. Gibson (eds), *Perspectives on Quine*, Oxford: Blackwell, pp. 1–16.

Reinharz, Shulamit. (1983) 'Experiential Analysis: A Contribution to Feminist Research' in Gloria Bowles and Renate Duelli Klein (eds), *Theories of Women's Studies*, Boston: Routledge, pp. 162–91.

Rorty, Richard. (1979) *Philosophy and the Mirror of Nature*, Princeton: Princeton University Press.

Rorty, Richard. (1989) *Contingency, Irony, and Solidarity*, Cambridge: Cambridge University Press.

Rose, Hilary. (1983) 'Hand, Brain, and Heart: A Feminist Epistemology for the Natural Sciences', *Signs: Journal of Women in Culture and Society*, 9 (1): 73–90.

Rose, Hilary. (1986) 'Women's Work: Women's Knowledge' in Juliet Mitchell and Ann Oakley (eds), *What is Feminism?*, Oxford: Blackwell, pp. 161–83.

Rose, Hilary. (1994) *Love, Power and Knowledge. Towards a Feminist Transformation of the Sciences*, Cambridge: Polity Press.

Rose, Hilary and Rose, Steven. (1976) 'The Problematic Inheritance: Marx and Engels on the Natural Sciences' in Hilary Rose and Steven Rose (eds), *The Political Economy of Science: Ideology of/in the Natural Sciences*, London: Macmillan, pp. 1–13.

Rouse, Joseph. (1987) *Knowledge and Power: Toward a Political Philosophy of Science*, Ithaca and London: Cornell University Press.

Rouse, Joseph. (1996) *Engaging Science: How to Understand Its Practices Philosophically*, Ithaca and London: Cornell University Press.

Scheman, Naomi. (1983) 'Individualism and the Objects of Psychology' in Sandra Harding and Merrill B. Hintikka (eds), *Discovering Reality: Feminist Perspectives in Epistemology, Metaphysics, Methodology and Philosophy of Science*, Dordrecht: D. Reidel, pp. 225–44.

Scheman, Naomi. (1987) 'Othello's Doubt/Desdemona's Death: The Engendering of Scepticism' in Judith Genova (ed.), *Power, Gender, Values*, Edmonton: Academic Printing & Publishing, pp. 113–33.

Scheman, Naomi. (1996) 'Reply to Louise Antony', *Hypatia*, 11 (3): 150–3.

Schmitt, Frederick F. (1987) 'Justification, Sociality, and Autonomy', *Synthese*, 73: 43–87.

Schmitt, Frederick F. (1994) 'Socializing Epistemology: An Introduction through Two Sample Issues' in Frederick F. Schmitt (ed.), *Socializing Epistemology: The Social Dimension of Knowledge*, Lanham: Rowman & Littlefield, pp. 1–27.

Schor, Naomi. (1994) 'This Essentialism Which is Not One: Coming to Grips with Irigaray' in Naomi Schor and Elizabeth Weed (eds), *The Essential Difference*, Bloomington: Indiana University Press, pp. 40–62.

Scott, Joan W. (1992) 'Experience' in Judith Butler and Joan W. Scott (eds), *Feminists Theorize the Political*, New York and London: Routledge, pp. 22–40.

Sellars, Wilfrid. (1997) *Empiricism and the Philosophy of Mind*, with an introduction by Richard Rorty and a study guide by Robert Brandom, Cambridge, Mass.: Harvard University Press.

Sen, Amartya. (1993) 'Positional Objectivity', *Philosophy and Public Affairs*, 22 (2): 126–45.

Smith, Dorothy. (1988) *The Everyday World as Problematic: A Feminist Sociology*, Boston: Northeastern University Press.

Soble, Alan. (1994) 'Gender, Objectivity, and Realism', *The Monist*, 77 (4): 509–30.

Solomon, Miriam. (1994) 'Social Empiricism', *Noûs*, 28 (3): 325–43.

Solomon, Miriam. (1994a) 'A More Social Epistemology' in Frederick Schmitt (ed.), *Socializing Epistemology*, Lanham: Rowman & Littlefield, pp. 217–33.

Spelman, Elizabeth V. (1990) *Inessential Woman: Problems of Exclusion in Feminist Thought*, London: The Women's Press.

Spivak, Gayatri Chakravorty. (1994) 'In a Word. Interview' in Naomi Schor and Elizabeth Weed (eds), *The Essential Difference*, Bloomington: Indiana University Press, pp. 151–84.

Stanworth, Michelle. (1987) 'Reproductive Technologies and the Deconstruction of Motherhood' in Michelle Stanworth (ed.), *Reproductive Technologies: Gender, Motherhood, and Medicine*, Minneapolis: University of Minnesota Press, pp. 10–35.

Stanworth, Michelle (ed.) (1987a) *Reproductive Technologies: Gender, Motherhood, and Medicine*, Minneapolis: University of Minnesota Press.

Stout, Jeffrey. (1981) *The Flight from Authority. Religion, Morality, and the Quest for Autonomy*, Notre Dame and London: University of Notre Dame Press.

Tanesini, Alessandra. (1994) 'Whose Language?' in Kathleen Lennon and Margaret Whitford (eds), *Knowing the Difference: Feminist Perspectives in Epistemology*, London and New York: Routledge, pp. 203–16.

Tanesini, Alessandra and Lance, Mark. (1998) 'Identity Judgments: Is Heterosexuality Heterosexist?', unp. man.

Taylor, Charles. (1987) 'Overcoming Epistemology' in K. Baynes, J. Bohaman and T. McCarthy (eds), *After Philosophy: End or Transformation?*, Cambridge, Mass.: MIT Press, pp. 464–88.

Tong, Rosemarie. (1992) *Feminist Thought: A Comprehensive Introduction*, London: Routledge.

Traweek, Sharon. (1992) 'Border Crossings: Narrative Strategies in Science Studies and among Physicists in Tsukuba Science City, Japan' in Andrew Pickering (ed.), *Science as Practice and Culture*, Chicago and London: University of Chicago Press, pp. 429–61.

Tuana, Nancy. (1992) 'The Radical Future of Feminist Empiricism', *Hypatia*, 7 (1): 100–14.

van Fraassen, Bas. (1980) *The Scientific Image*, Oxford: Clarendon Press.

Vogel, Steven. (1995) 'New Science, New Nature. The Habermas–Marcuse Debate Revisited' in Andrew Feenberg and Alastaur Hannay (eds), *Technology and the Politics of Knowledge*, Bloomington: Indiana University Press, pp. 23–42.

Webb, Mark Owen. (1993) 'Why I Know As Much As You: A Reply to Hardwig', *Journal of Philosophy*, 90 (5): 260–70.

Weir, Allison. (1996) *Sacrificial Logics. Feminist Theory and the Critique of Identity*, New York and London: Routledge.

Whitford, Margaret. (1991) *Luce Irigaray: Philosophy in the Feminine*, London: Routledge.

Williams, Bernard. (1985) *Ethics and the Limits of Philosophy*, Cambridge, Mass.: Harvard University Press.

Woolgar, Steve. (1988) *Science: The Very Idea*, London: Tavistock.

Woolgar, Steve (ed.). (1988a) *Knowledge and Reflexivity: New Frontiers in the Sociology of Knowledge*, London: Sage.

Index

Addelson, Kathryn Pyne, 23, 64n, 115, 132–4
Adorno, Theodor, 21
agency
    attributed to objects, 166, 177
    and postmodernism, 248
    and psychoanalysis, 225–7, 240
    see also identity
Alcoff, Linda, 4, 5, 34, 36n, 113n, 157n, 222, 232, 236, 262
Alston, William, 35n, 64n
Antony, Louise, 34n, 35n, 43, 46, 51, 86, 115, 122
Appiah, K. Anthony, 210, 211n, 243
Aristotle, 78, 219
artefacts
    and science, 181–3, 200
    and social constitution, 182
artifactualism, 184
Atherton, Margaret, 236n
autonomy
    as dynamic, 167–9
    and epistemology, 17–18, 39, 41, 44–5, 235
    and psychological development, 54–6, 167–8
    as static, 54–6, 167–9
    see also individualism

Bacon, Francis, 219
Barnes, Barry, 30, 129, 136
Bar On, Bat-Ami, 144–5, 149, 157, 157n
Bath school, 37n, 136n
Battersby, Christine, 158n, 236n
Benhabib, Seyla, 237, 248–9
Benjamin, Jessica, 64n
Bernstein, Richard, 54, 57, 113n, 212
bias
    good and bad, 86, 88, 89, 93n
    as inevitable, 43, 86
    as present in science, 66–7, 70–2, 72–5
    as undesirable, 42, 79, 140, 157n, 174, 265, 267
    see also scientific method
biological theories
    of homosexuality, 72–5
    of human fertilization, 67, 78, 91
    of race, 209–10
    of sex-related cognitive differences, 70–2, 75
Biology and Gender Study Group, 78, 91
Bleier, Ruth, 71, 74, 85
Bloor, David, 30, 129
body, 57, 59, 60, 140–1, 198, 204–7, 209, 211, 216–17, 223, 227, 228, 229–30, 231

see also embodiment, mind–body
  dualism
Bordo, Susan, 32, 36, 37n, 57–9, 145,
  169–70
Boyd, Richard, 37n, 76
Boyle, Robert, 79–81, 83, 112n
Braidotti, Rosi, 205–6, 208, 210,
  213–15, 222–6, 228–32
Brandom, Robert, 35n, 185n
Brennan, Teresa, 59

Campbell, Richmond, 111, 111n, 112n,
  113n
Chisholm, Roderick, 36n
Chodorow, Nancy, 64n
Code, Lorraine, 16–17, 21, 34, 35n, 36n,
  41, 44, 45, 58, 63, 63n, 93n, 116,
  117–21, 171, 179–80, 255, 262
Collins, Harry, 37n
Collins, Patricia Hill, 152–5, 157, 159n
confirmation, 25, 32, 67–9, 76
  and background assumptions, 99–100
  and intersubjective criticism, 100
  theories of, 76–7, 84, 85–7, 98–100,
    101–2, 107, 108, 112n
  see also evidence, scientific method
context of discovery, 25, 39, 46, 76, 77,
  85, 88, 93n, 96, 97, 109, 114
context of justification, 25, 39, 76–7, 85,
  92, 93n, 96, 97, 100, 109, 114
Corea, Gena, 211, 211n
Crasnow, Sharon, 112n
cyborg, 210–11, 231

Dalmiya, Vrinda, 113n, 157n
Dancy, Jonathan, 34
Davis, Angela, 211n
de Beauvoir, Simone, 165, 185n, 234
Derrida, Jacques, 237–8, 266
Descartes, René, 8, 10, 17, 20, 35n,
  40–3, 46, 57–8, 64n, 77, 144, 217,
  218–20, 236n, 262
disciplinary power *see* power
discursive formation, 241
Di Stefano, Christine, 257, 259, 261
Duran, Jane, 111n, 115, 122

Edinburgh school, 30–1, 136n
  see also Strong Program
Elam, Diane, 269n
embodiment, 147, 216–17, 229–30
emotions, 4, 29, 44, 51, 54–6, 141, 144,
  158n, 168, 180, 214, 217, 264
empiricism
  as contextual, 97–8, 98–101
  defined, 25
  and feminism, 25, 27, 92, 93n,
    95–111, 112n, 113n, 158n
  as naturalized, 97–8, 101–9, 130, 136n
  traditional versions of, 41–2, 76, 77,
    112n
enlightenment, 170, 212, 238, 255, 256,
  258–9, 262
  project of, 44, 186, 187, 190–1, 249,
    254
  and reason, 187, 190–1, 215–16,
    238–9, 240–1, 244–6
episteme
  classical, 10, 177
  modern, 11, 174, 177–8, 190, 225,
    263
epistemic authority, 6–7, 8, 9, 11, 14–16,
  31, 33, 41, 42, 61, 69, 83, 92,
  132–3, 149, 204–6, 225, 252, 264,
  266
epistemic practices *see* practices
epistemology
  in analytic philosophy, 4, 16, 17, 18,
    19–20, 21, 24, 35n, 36n, 42, 45,
    251
  in continental philosophy, 4, 18–19,
    20–1, 251
  as descriptive, 132–6
  as first philosophy, 6–7, 11
  as historically situated, 40, 128
  and individualism *see* individualism
  naturalized *see* naturalized
    epistemology
  'negative' theories of, 5, 29–30, 247,
    251, 254
  as normative, 95, 131, 250
  not as first philosophy, 103, 121, 124,
    126, 128, 134, 136n, 250, 251

and standpoint *see* standpoint
    epistemology
see also empiricism, fallibilism,
    foundationalism, justification
essentialism
    critiques of, 58, 81, 144–7, 258–9,
        261
Evans, Ruth, 185
evidence, 27, 29, 30, 41, 49, 69, 84–5,
    91–2, 131, 135, 158n, 263
    and empiricism, 25, 42, 84, 97,
        98–110, 112n, 122–7
    and feminist values, 75–6, 78, 84,
        86–7, 97, 128, 173, 175
experience
    and critiques of foundationalism, 8, 98,
        100, 104, 250
    and empiricism, 25, 26, 43, 76–7,
        99–100, 102–5, 121, 125–7
    and non-inferential, non-foundational
        knowledge, 8, 16, 35n, 91, 98,
        159n, 183
    as not infallible, 150, 155–6, 265
    and sensory stimulations, 102, 125–7
    and standpoint, 47, 138, 140–2,
        143–7, 148–9, 150–1, 154–6,
        157n, 158n, 265–6

fallibilism, 20, 148–9, 263
Fausto-Sterling, Anne, 70–1, 73–5, 92
Fee, Elizabeth, 36, 81, 84
Flax, Jane, 5, 30, 237, 240, 246–55, 259,
    262, 268, 269, 269n
Fodor, Jerry, 35n
Foucault, Michel, 2, 9–11, 19, 41, 72,
    154, 159, 174, 177, 188, 189–201,
    203–8, 210–11, 211n, 216, 237,
    238, 241, 242–4, 247, 255–6,
    262–3
foundationalism, 10, 131
    critiques of, 9, 35n, 98, 104, 111n,
        148–9, 240, 244, 246, 250, 251
    defined, 7–8
Fraser, Nancy, 189, 193, 195, 197, 198,
    249
Frege, Gottlob, 34n
Fuller, Steve, 23, 34, 36n, 83

Gadamer, Hans-Georg, 242, 245–6
Gemes, Ken, 136n
gender
    as analytical category, 145–6
    and psychoanalysis, 54–7, 57, 59,
        59–61
    and sex, 57, 147
see also identity
Ginzberg, Ruth, 35n
Glymour, Clark, 112n
Goldman, Alvin, 64n, 127
Grant, Judith, 158n
Griffiths, Morwenna, 155, 157
Grimshaw, Jean, 51, 169
Grosz, Elizabeth, 213, 215, 224

Habermas, Jürgen, 19, 188, 189–94, 196,
    211n, 213, 216, 263
Hacking, Ian, 36n, 40, 41, 87, 93n, 189
Haraway, Donna, 32, 33, 34, 37n,
    160–1, 166, 171–2, 176–7, 180–4,
    210, 231
Harding, Sandra, 23, 25, 27, 29, 31, 36n,
    37n, 69, 85–8, 92, 93, 93n, 95–7,
    100, 101, 109, 111, 111n, 115,
    129–32, 134, 136, 137n, 145, 148,
    150–2, 154, 157, 158n, 159n, 171,
    172, 174–9, 184, 185n, 188, 190–1,
    254, 265, 266, 268, 269
Hardwig, John, 49–50, 53, 64n, 94n
Hartmann, Heidi, 157
Hartsock, Nancy, 18, 140–5, 147–9,
    152, 157, 158n, 159n, 257, 265,
    267–8
Haslanger, Sally, 36n
Haugeland, John, 35n
Hegel, G. W. F., 8, 18, 20, 35n, 116,
    165–6, 185, 217, 218, 220, 251
Heidegger, Martin, 11–12, 15–16, 28,
    35n, 110, 164–5, 185, 240, 251,
    252–3, 262, 269
Hekman, Susan, 170–1, 237–8, 240–7,
    254, 255–6, 259, 260, 262, 264,
    268–9
Heldke, Lisa, 185n
Hempel, Carl, 76–7, 85, 93, 96, 98–9,
    109

Hesse, Mary, 99
historical rationalism, 27, 36
holism, 102–3, 108
hooks, bell, 149, 154
Horkheimer, Max, 21
Hubbard, Ruth, 74, 208, 211
Hull, David, 48, 89
Hume, David, 10, 41, 64n

identity, 35n, 146, 155, 158n, 226, 231, 257, 260–1
    descriptive accounts of, 256–9, 261
    non-descriptive accounts of, 259–60
incommensurability see theories
indirect realism, 10, 162–3, 185n
individualism, 16, 21, 38, 39–45, 46–48, 49, 64n, 118, 122, 129
    and autonomy, 17–18, 39, 41, 44–5, 235, 247
    and psychoanalysis, 53–4, 56
    in science, 89, 95, 97, 100, 109
    see also psychological states
instrumentalism, 27, 36
intentionality, 11, 225–7, 248
    see also psychological states
Irigaray, Luce, 36n, 37n, 59–63, 65n, 171, 172, 223, 228, 230, 237, 256

Jaggar, Alison, 41–4, 63, 83, 157, 168
Justification, 6, 8, 19–20, 35n, 48, 188, 218, 225
    causal theories of, 88, 106, 114–15, 117–19, 121–7, 129–31, 134, 137n, 176–9, 191, 193
    deontological conception of, 45, 46, 225
    and externalism, 45–6
    internalist constraints on, 45, 46, 64n, 225, 236n
    and practices, 15–16, 19, 117, 227–8, 244, 246, 250, 252–4
    see also confirmation, epistemology, evidence, fallibilism, foundationalism, individualism, naturalized epistemology, practices, reliabilism, scientific method

Kant, Immanuel, 4, 7, 10–11, 18, 43, 44–6, 111n, 116, 178, 190, 215, 217, 251, 258, 263–4
Kanter, Rosabeth, 111n
Kaplan, Mark, 20
Keller, Evelyn Fox, 18, 32, 35n, 36n, 37n, 44, 54–9, 63, 64n, 166–70, 177, 179, 184, 185n
Kellert, Stephen, 185n
Kitcher, Philip, 46–9, 94n
knowledge
    as normative, 3, 134, 194, 242
    as not inferential, 8–9, 15–16, 91
    as partial, 20, 88, 152–3, 156
    as perspectival, 18, 101, 138–43, 150–7, 176–7
    as practical, 11–13, 15–16, 90, 110, 188–9
    and social influences, 16, 21, 38, 39, 59
    as socially constituted, 1, 12–16, 48, 52, 90–2, 119, 134–6, 189, 199–201, 241
    as socially situated, 16–18, 33, 35n, 40, 42, 114, 129, 152–3, 166, 172, 176, 183, 250, 251
    and subject/object separation, 15, 165, 172, 192, 264
    as view from nowhere, 161–3
    see also, epistemology, power, representationalism, science
Kornblith, Hilary, 115, 117, 122
Kristeva, Julia, 237
Kuhn, Thomas, 24–7, 30, 36n, 98, 108, 112n

laboratory
    and fields of power, 189, 199–204
    science, 188–9, 199, 201, 203–4, 208, 241
Lacan, Jacques, 37n, 59–60, 237, 266
Lance, Mark, 269n
Latour, Bruno, 31, 36n
Laudan, Larry, 29, 36n
Lazreg, Marnia, 158n
Le Doeuff, Michèle, 65n, 232–5, 236
Lennon, Kathleen, 255

LeVay, Simon, 72–5, 93n
Lloyd, Genevieve, 144, 170, 185n, 214–15, 217–18, 221–3, 228–32, 234, 236n
Locke, John, 10, 17, 18, 40–1, 43, 64n, 77, 98, 104, 162, 165, 262
logical positivism, 4, 25, 27, 42, 76, 102, 108, 109
Longino, Helen, 2, 23, 26, 29, 82, 84, 86–7, 90, 92, 93n, 97–101, 107–110, 111, 111n, 112n, 128, 159n, 171–5
Lovibond, Sabina, 116, 212, 216, 237
Lycan, William, 35n
Lyotard, Jean-François, 7, 11, 19, 34n, 123, 136n, 237

MacKinnon, Catharine, 166
Mangena, Oshadi, 155–7
Marx, Karl, 18, 20, 28, 36n, 139–40, 142, 144, 145, 147, 152, 154, 157n, 158n, 159n, 267, 268
matter
    as female, 60, 79–80, 220
McClintock, Barbara, 4, 158n
McMillan, Carol, 236n
Merchant, Carolyn, 36n, 79, 81
metaphor
    and philosophy see philosophical imaginary
    and reason, 218, 221–2, 228–30, 232, 236n
    and science, 57, 67, 78–9
    and vision, 161, 166, 183–4
Millman, Marcia, 111n
Mills, Charles, 34
mind–body dualism
    critiques of, 216–17, 220, 229–30
    defined, 10
Mitroff, Ian, 92
Moi, Toril, 49, 169, 171, 185n
Mulkay, Michael, 36n

Nagel, Ernest, 76–7, 85, 93n, 96, 98, 99, 109
Nagel, Thomas, 163, 165
natural

and cultural, 116
and supernatural, 116
    see also naturalism
naturalism
    and analytic philosophy, 45–6, 114–15, 116–17
    and feminism, 116, 117–19
    see also naturalized epistemology
naturalized epistemology, 45–8, 85, 88–9, 114–15, 121–9, 130–2, 132–5, 191, 193, 264, 268
    see also empiricism, justification (causal theories of), naturalism, reliabilism
Nelson, Lynn Hankinson, 2, 35n, 36n, 49–50, 53, 64n, 76, 85, 88, 90, 93n, 94, 97–8, 101–10, 111, 111n, 112n, 115–16, 122–8, 130, 131, 134, 136, 136n
Nicholson, Linda, 249
Nietzsche, Friedrich, 11, 216, 239
nihilism, 246, 254
Nussbaum, Martha, 214, 236n

object relations theory see psychoanalysis
objectification, 2, 56, 156, 161, 165–9, 171, 183–4, 191–2, 196, 264
objectivism, 29, 36n, 55, 58, 174, 190
objectivity
    as dynamic, 55, 167–9
    and emotional detachment, 18, 29, 42, 53, 56, 167, 170, 175, 214
    as inclusive of perspectives, 101, 157, 172–3
    as stronger notion, 151, 174–9
    and value-neutrality, 29, 42, 44, 77, 161, 163–5, 175
    see also objectification, objectivism
observations
    and background assumptions, 29, 84, 86, 99
    as theory-laden, 98–9, 101, 104, 108, 111n
Okruhlik, Kathleen, 84, 93n
oppression, 140, 141, 144–6, 149,

151–4, 157n, 169, 208, 243–4, 249, 256–7, 266–8
see also objectification

patriarchy, 18, 140, 143, 157n, 158n
Petchesky, Rosalind Pollack, 206, 208
philosophical imaginary, 232–4
philosophy
    and exclusion of women, 234–5
Pickering, Andrew, 34, 36, 37n, 136
Plato, 79, 116, 196, 218–19, 234, 250
positivism, 25, 42, 152, 178, 264
posits, 102–3, 104
postmodernism
    characterized, 237–8, 239
    and 'death of history', 248–9
    and 'death of man', 247–8
    and 'death of metaphysics', 249–250
    and epistemology, 5, 29–30, 95, 170, 189, 240–7, 250–5
    and identity, 256–61
    and the subject, 239, 247, 262
    see also subject, subjectivity
post-structuralism, 4, 19, 148, 170–1, 230
Potter, Elizabeth, 4, 5, 23, 32, 37n, 64n, 80–3, 93n, 112n, 115, 119–21
power
    as bio-power, 188, 190, 196, 197, 204–6, 207, 208, 209–10
    as disciplinary power, 196–9
    and knowledge, 2, 11, 117, 174, 178, 186–9, 194–6, 199–210, 216
practical mastery, 12, 15, 166
practices
    defined, 13, 181
    descriptivist view of, 249–50, 252–4
    discursive, 113–15, 164–5
    epistemic, 14–16, 17, 90–2, 116–17, 119, 134–6, 160, 164–5, 178, 181–2, 227–8, 263
    of giving and asking for reasons, 14–16, 52–3, 164
    as socially instituted, 12–15
    and social significance, 13–15, 23, 33
    see also social constitution
probability, 40–1, 92, 135

psychoanalysis
    and the imaginary, 59–63, 65n
    Lacanian, 59–61
    object relations, 54–6, 58–9, 143, 166–9
    and reason, 61–4, 224–5, 226
    and the symbolic, 59–63
psychological states
    and psychoanalysis, 224, 225, 226–8
    and psychological individualism, 50–2
    as requiring interpretation, 226–8
    and social constitution, 51–2
    see also intentionality
Putnam, Hilary, 185n

Qualities
    primary and secondary, 162–3
quietism, 24, 33, 69, 188, 239, 269
Quine, W. V. O., 7, 34, 36n, 45, 47, 69, 84, 87, 98, 101–3, 109, 111, 111n, 112n, 115, 117, 121–3, 125–7, 126n, 129–36, 251

race, 146–8, 152–3, 209–10
    see also racialism, racism
racialism, 209–10
racism, 63, 67, 209
    see also biological theories
rationality
    and communities, 89–90, 94n
    in science, 23–6, 29, 30, 69, 90, 120, 190, 210
    see also science, scientific method
reality
    as mind-independent, 43, 162–4, 165, 178
    and social constitution, 164–5, 178
    see also social constitution, world
reason
    as autonomous, 41, 43–4
    in crisis, 212, 225
    as desublimated, 116–19
    as instrumental, 21, 90, 128, 191–3, 196, 213–14, 216
    and irrationality, 244–6
    and masculinity, 2, 144, 170, 214–15, 215–21

and metaphors of sexual difference, 2,
214, 221–2, 228, 236n
radical critiques of, 212, 213–14, 215,
223–5
reformist critiques of, 213, 223, 224
as socially constituted, 227–8
as subject-centered, 192–3
as transcending femininity, 217, 219
see also embodiment, enlightenment,
mind–body dualism, psychoanalysis
Reinharz, Shulamit, 158n
reliabilism, 46–8, 64n, 127
and standpoint, 47, 53, 58, 88–9, 143,
150, 167
see also naturalized epistemology
representationalism, 1, 9–11, 17–19, 21,
32, 41, 43, 48, 50, 162–3, 165, 172,
174, 177, 180–1, 183, 188, 225
representations, 9–11, 15, 19, 35n,
37n, 42, 43, 152, 160–1, 178–9,
180, 182, 184, 185n, 190–2, 256,
262–4
resistance, 243–4
and marginality, 154
Rorty, Richard, 5, 9, 251, 269n
Rose, Hilary, 36n, 66, 140–1, 143–4,
157n, 158n, 265–7
Rose, Steven, 36n
Rouse, Joseph, 2, 24, 27, 33, 34, 36n,
37n, 110, 181, 183, 196–7,
199–200, 202, 204, 210–11
Rousseau, Jean-Jacques, 220

Scheman, Naomi, 50–3, 64n, 227
Schmitt, Frederick, 35n, 63n
Schor, Naomi, 65n
science
and arationality assumption, 29
arguments against internalism, 82–92
as autonomous, 23, 68, 76, 83
bad and as usual, 82
bad and good, 30–1, 66, 68, 69, 80–2
cultural studies of, 32–3
as culture, 180
and externalism, 23, 68, 69
and internalism, 23–4, 26–7, 68–9,
79, 87–9, 95, 96, 109

scientific communities
as subjects of knowledge, 49–50, 104,
105, 106
and vested interests, 31, 100, 132, 174,
208, 211n
scientific method
as hypothetical-deductive, 76–8, 85,
93n, 96, 98–9, 109
as unable to screen bias, 78, 84–6, 96
scientific realism, 27, 36n, 112n
scientism, 104, 115, 117, 118, 120, 121,
122, 128, 130, 131, 134
Scott, Joan, 148–9, 150
Sellars, Wilfrid, 35n, 111n, 112n, 159n
Sen, Amartya, 185n
sexual orientation, 72–5, 261
empirical, 191, 268–9
and epistemically significant, 16–17
philosophy of, 192, 194, 255–6,
262–4, 265–9
as speaking position, 60–1, 170–1,
230, 248
transcendental, 191
see also biological theories, mind–body
dualism
situated knowledge see knowledge
skepticism, 10, 64n, 145, 238–9, 255,
269
Smith, Dorothy, 140–5, 147, 149, 152,
155, 158n
Soble, Alan, 64n
social constitution
and social construction, 178, 182
of tools and objects, 12–13, 15, 35n,
90, 164–5
social constructivism, 27, 31, 36n, 177–8
sociology of knowledge, 22, 23, 24, 26,
29, 30–1, 32, 35n, 69, 87, 89,
124–5, 130–1, 176
see also Bath school, Edinburgh school,
Strong Program
Solomon, Miriam, 89
Spelman, Elizabeth, 64n, 146
Spivak, Gayatri, Chakravorty, 148
standpoint epistemology
and epistemic privilege, 138–9, 140–4
and marginality, 141, 152, 154

Marxian version of, 139–40
and 'outsider-within', 152
and partial perspectives, 152–4
as underestimating differences among
  women, 145, 150
see also experience, reliabilism,
  resistance
Stanworth, Michelle, 206, 211
Stout, Jeffrey, 42, 63n
Strong Program, 30–1, 37n, 129–31, 136
Subject
  Cartesian, 43, 54, 57, 170–1, 224,
    226, 250, 256
  as decentered, 247, 257, 259
  and masculinity, 56–7
  as master-narrative, 123, 136n
  philosophy of, 23–30
  psychosociology of, 54–7
  and scientific communities, 89–90,
    94n, 173
  as a social activity, 100, 104–5
  and symmetry hypothesis, 30, 87, 176
  theory-dominant accounts of, 110
  as value-laden, 29, 84–6, 91, 97, 99,
    100, 106, 127
  what makes it good, 77, 87, 89, 114,
    175–6
  see also confirmation, context of
    discovery, context of justification,
    empiricism, evidence, historical
    rationalism, indirect realism,
    instrumentalism, knowledge,
    scientific method, scientific realism,
    social constructivism, technoscience
subjectivity, 18, 35n, 42–3, 54, 56, 58,
  59–61, 77, 155–6, 160, 165–6,

170, 179–80, 191, 226, 228, 230–1,
  248, 255–7, 259, 262, 265–8

Taylor, Charles, 35n
technology
  and reproduction, 197, 204–8
technoscience, 201–3, 210
theories
  as artefacts, 102
  as incommensurable, 30, 98, 108
  as underdetermined, 69, 80, 84, 87,
    98, 99, 101, 106
Tong, Rosemarie, 157n
Traweek, Sharon, 32–3, 37, 113n
truth
  analytic and synthetic, 101, 109
  and knowledge, 27, 28, 62, 153, 163,
    173, 195, 199, 241, 246, 249,
    252–3, 254
  as regimens, 204–6, 241
Tuana, Nancy, 136n

van Fraassen, Bas, 36n
Vogel, Steven, 211n

Wald, Elijah, 208, 211n
warrant *see* justification
Webb, Mark, 48
Weir, Allison, 185n
Whitford, Margaret, 61, 65, 255
Williams, Bernard, 163, 165, 170
Wittgenstein, Ludwig, 116, 246
Woolgar, Steve, 182–3
world
  as present-at-hand, 164–5
  as ready-to-hand, 164–5
  see also practices, reality

Printed in the United States
32209LVS00012B/73-81